MW01062273

THE MIDNIGHT KINGDOM

ALSO BY JARED YATES SEXTON

American Rule

The Man They Wanted Me to Be

The People Are Going to Rise Like the Waters Upon Your Shore

THE MIDNIGHT KINGDOM

A HISTORY OF POWER, PARANOIA, AND THE COMING CRISIS

JARED YATES SEXTON

DUTTON

DUTTON

An imprint of Penguin Random House LLC
penguinrandomhouse.com

LIBRARY OF CONGRESS CATALOGING-IN-PUBLICATION DATA

Names: Sexton, Jared Yates, author.
Title: The midnight kingdom: the rise of the West and the corruption of the globe / Jared Yates Sexton.
Other titles: Rise of thc West and the corruption of the globe
Description: [New York]: Dutton, [2023] | Includes bibliographical references and index.
Identifiers: LCCN 2022019093 | ISBN 9780593185230 (hardcover) |
ISBN 9780593185247 (ebook) Subjects: LCSH: Civilization, Western—History. |
Group identity—Political aspects—Western countries.
Classification: LCC CB245 .S448 2023 | DDC 909/.09821—dc23/eng/20220920
LC record available at https://lccn.loc.gov/2022019093

Printed in the United States of America

1st Printing

BOOK DESIGN BY KRISTIN DEL ROSARIO

For Lois Burk

- CONTENTS -

PROLOGUE: The World Needs Ditch Diggers 1

CHAPTER ONE: By This, Conquer 13

CHAPTER TWO: The Great Chain of Being 36

CHAPTER THREE: The Empire of Man over Inferior Creatures 59

CHAPTER FOUR: To Begin the World over Again 83

CHAPTER FIVE: A Man Is but a Machine for Creating Value 115

CHAPTER SIX: A Veneer over Savagery 149

CHAPTER SEVEN: Lightning from the Dark Cloud of Man 182

CHAPTER EIGHT: The Machine 209

CHAPTER NINE: Flying Ever Closer to the Sun 245

CHAPTER TEN: Almost Midnight 272

EPILOGUE: Digging out of the End of the World 299

Acknowledgments 303

Notes 305

Index 355

THE MIDNIGHT KINGDOM

- **PROLOGUE** -

The World Needs Ditch Diggers

My earliest memories are of the apocalypse. As a child I would sit on my grandmother's knee as she read scripture from the Holy Bible and bellowed end-times prophecy. While my friends were told fairy tales and legends of heroes and faraway magical places, my stories revolved around fire, ash, blood, and tribulation, great clashes of angels and beasts and the armies of man, all of it culminating in the final battle between God and the Devil for the fate of the world.

This war dominated every aspect of life.

Our preachers spent more time on the Book of Revelation than on any other part of the gospel, pounding the pulpit as they prepared us for the blast of trumpets announcing Armageddon. Satan's minions, they warned, stalked the Earth, some as murderous demons waiting to pounce on susceptible Christians straying from the flock. Others donned disguises. They were our friends at school. They infiltrated our families, our communities, our culture, even our government, their lies punctuating our days and poisoning the airwaves. To let our guard down would be tantamount to spiritual suicide.

Grandma took the preachers at their word. On Sunday mornings in the 1980s she grabbed the remote control and expertly switched between the many apocalyptic televangelists she loved and the news, where scenes from what she believed was prophecy unfolding played out in striking detail. The center of evil in the world, she had been assured by those same preachers and a bevy of politicians, rested in Moscow; it wasn't even debatable whether the Kremlin was in league with Satan. The Soviet Union was the kingdom of the Antichrist, she believed. A place of abomination and heresy and terrors.

Like many others, Grandma had faith the United States was God's champion in that war. She had played her part in the 1940s by rolling up her sleeves and working in the factories while men like my grandfather fought fascism thousands of miles away. Good had prevailed and would prevail again, thanks to the hard work and sacrifice of people like our family, who sweated on the factory floor, labored in limestone quarries, poisoned their lungs in the depths of the mine shaft, and generally gifted their bodies and fates to the fight. In their own small way, they were martyrs in a religious crusade.

Back then, the world was still strange and baffling to me. All I knew was that it seemed like there were many different lives to live, and some, like my loved ones, seemed destined to toil and suffer. In some of her brief sojourns away from Revelation, Grandma talked about how someday the meek would inherit the Earth, occasionally stopping to reflect on our lots in life and granting the suffering an air of righteous responsibility, reasoning, with a distinct note of pride, "The world needs ditch diggers."

In school it was more of the same. American history was laundered, our books full of smiling cartoonish Native Americans happily handing over the continent and tales extolling the unique virtues of our nation. Sometimes, during emergency drills, as we ducked and covered and lined up in the halls on our knees and buried our heads against the concrete, teachers would talk about disasters sent by God and the Devil, tornados and falling bombs, all while reminding us how lucky we were to be born Christians in the Lord's chosen nation.

Growing up in the eighties, I was pumped full of endless propaganda exalting American strength and the splendors of capitalism. My town and my family, with all of their struggles and blemishes, served as proof positive that God was working through the United States. And then, as the new decade arrived, and as the Evil Empire fell, something changed. Our people were laid off. Our factories closed, their windows boarded up; the buildings that had given us a livelihood were left to rust and rot. Stores dotting our modest Main Street shuttered. It was as if God had suddenly cast his judgment and found us lacking.

Grandma kept stacks of tablets scribbled over with her notes in light, looping cursive, one hand furiously flipping the thin pages of her King James Bible in search of answers while the other guided a pencil. As things changed, she turned more and more to stories of demonic possession and the secret world of magic and miracles. She was frantic to find something in the printed word that gave her direction and knowledge, and as conditions declined, new books appeared detailing the New World Order that explained how God's chosen nation had been betrayed by its own in service of Satan's evil plans. Grandma devoured these books in a manic flourish before foisting them upon everyone around her.

In her search for clues, Grandma cross-referenced the New World Order idea with the Book of Revelation and believed she had found her answers. We were living in the end-times, that much was certain, and surely the evil spirits in the Devil's employ had managed to find some wayward sinners in the United States to do his bidding. The plan was to destroy the Kingdom of God from the inside out, leaving it vulnerable to attacks and domination, all of it culminating in a one-world government lorded over by the Antichrist himself. A literal hell on Earth.

Grandma continued buying these books, many hawked by the same televangelists on the TV who were now preaching about the insidious plot between calls for donations. Her bookshelves were swollen with them, the table next to her favorite chair piled high with tabloids from the grocery store checkout detailing an invisible world where monsters walked among us and a secret machinery whirred just under the surface of the material realm.

She died still believing this conspiracy theory, still desperate to understand why her life had played out as it had. She needed a story to explain it, to make sense of why she had suffered so terribly in the Great Depression, why she had lost friends and family in battles fought in lands she would never see, and why, having won the peace and then war with Satan's empire, the heavenly kingdom promised to her by preachers and televangelists had failed to materialize.

As a child, I lived and breathed this poisoned reality. The framework of a world filled with magic and monsters was fascinating and granted life a sheen that sparked my imagination. Through the mythology, I crafted for myself a complicated narrative of how the world worked, creating a story for myself in which I was a warrior in a much, much larger war, my every decision, my every thought, another theater in an ongoing battle. It served a purpose but was exhausting and maddening.

When I would reach my limit or find a snag in the rationality, I asked questions. Of Grandma. Of my teachers. Of my pastors. Of anyone who would listen. The mythology was fine, I could use it and live within it, but there were always things that needed clearing up. Contradictions. Limitations. I wanted to know why the world functioned the way that it did. And when the people answering my questions attempted to explain it, the best they could often offer was to say, "Because that's the way that it is."

Much of life revolves around this concept. We are born into a world that preceded us, with laws and culture and customs and expectations that stretch well into the past. We learn these things through our elders, through our education, and through trial and error as we walk through a life haunted by ghosts. The stories we tell attempt to save order from chaos, most often allowing us to rationalize our own decisions and fates within the larger framework.

The story of my grandma and my people is tragically common. We live in a moment lousy with conspiracy theories and misinformation because the stories we have been told are losing their gravity and require updates and new explanations. The narrative is getting stranger by the day, with events adding twists and turns, inconsistencies and contradictions, leading to weirder and more convoluted stories.

Over the past few years I've watched family members and my community be radicalized in ways that mirrored what happened with my grandma, but with insidiously modern twists. As some joked about the obviousness of Donald Trump's lies and the ridiculous nature of QAnon, I witnessed people I love swallow those ideas whole. There was a strangeness to it, a surreal quality, like watching someone trapped in quicksand sink into oblivion and being unable to save them.

I harbor intense anger toward the charlatans who peddle these alternate realities tailor-made to prey upon the worst instincts and religious upbringing of their targets. The politicians. The conspiracy theorists. The televangelists who bilked Grandma out of what little money she had. Writing this book, I continually returned to my family and neighbors sitting in their pews on Sundays, still aching from their backbreaking labor, tired and anguished, unable to rest because they were kept terrified of sinister forces, and my anger continued to grow.

It was in 2015 that I first realized this affliction that troubled my family had become a pressing, existential threat. I was halfheartedly covering the presidential campaign and reporting from rallies, trying to gain some sense of what was to come and generally anticipating a rather lackluster, boring affair. But then it became obvious to me that something sinister was brewing among the developing MAGA movement. My conversations in the crowds at Donald Trump's rallies were almost exclusively about the conspiracies and evil plots my family held as sacrosanct. And, in believing these stories, the rallygoers were convinced not only that the betrayal was real but that it was high time somebody did something about it.

There was a general dismissal of the growing danger. Media members and politicians were largely affluent and privileged and out of touch with what was happening on the ground in other parts of the country. When they looked at Trump, they saw a lark, a passing, boorish fad that could boost ratings and drive donations but would eventually burn itself out and give way to something else. They lacked an understanding of religion as possessing the elements I grew up surrounded by, including conspiracy theories and the type of repugnant white nationalism percolating on the political scene. Even as some of us sounded the alarm regarding authoritarian trends fueled by these ideas, it was more or less regarded as hysterical hairpulling.

Years later, in August of 2017 and following Trump's election, the Unite the Right rally in Charlottesville, Virginia, reverberated through the culture like a thunderclap. Scenes of white nationalists marching with torches and chanting anti-Semitic, fascistic phrases gave way to bloodshed. There wasn't much use denying that something was very, very wrong in the body politic and that we were heading toward something, even if we remained unsure what it was.

As this radical Right made itself known, its leaders, its figureheads, and even Trump himself continually referenced a battle over history. The basis of the movement, they claimed, was the preservation of Western civilization, the protection of a long heritage of culture, principles, and philosophy that had created the modern world and raised humankind to unprecedented heights. Progressive voices calling for a reckoning with that history, for reform and the tumbling of statues representing the troubling past, were framed as enemies hell-bent on ruining everything, agents of chaos and evil dead set on destroying America with the help and backing of shadowy elements within and outside the country.

This is, unfortunately, part of an ongoing cycle throughout history. The powerful have continually used this exact same formulation—the outside threat partnering with internal traitors and taking advantage of populations through manipulations and lies—to protect themselves, particularly to protect the white, patriarchal establishment, which relies on these conspiracy theories as a means of diverting populist anger to their enemies and opponents. It is the same song and dance that has inspired wars, genocides, and coups.

In all of this, the fervor with which the Right reacts to any challenging of their chosen history is telling. Every aspect of that mythology, from its chronicling to its depictions, is guarded fiercely and violently. The entire structure, which they claim serves as the rock-ribbed foundation of the world itself, is actually a flimsy edifice, a house of cards that could collapse with the slightest challenge.

As I peeled back the layers of domestic history in my book *American Rule,* I discovered the conventional story of America was a series of lies obscuring manipulation. Strangely enough, this project drew more ire from the Right than my reporting years earlier from those Trump rallies. The backlash was commensurate with the myriad attacks on works that sought a more accurate and honest assessment of America, setting off a reactionary struggle over how the story should be told and who should tell it. Current efforts to destroy public education, vilify accurate histories, and infiltrate local elections speak to this. The anger and fear are palpable. And this propagandized history of America positions the nation as the centerpiece of a larger history of Western civilization, a structure these same people continually trumpet as being under attack and requiring extreme measures to protect.

To understand where this came from, what it meant, and what it might lead to, I wanted to find my way back to the beginnings of so-called Western civilization and answer some of the questions I had been asking since I was a child.

Where did these laws that served and protected the wealthy and powerful come from?

How did society come to function like this?

When and where did these seemingly intractable conflicts of race and class and sex originate?

Why had my family labored for generations without reward?

And how had we arrived at this bizarre moment rife with so much absurdity, contradiction, and danger?

I started with the same King James Bible my grandma relied on, scanning the same stories she turned to decades ago, stopping at times to admire the notes she'd made on the backs of hymnals and scraps of paper. And then, leaping forward from the prophecies that caused her so many sleepless nights and drove my loved ones to radicalizing propaganda, I traced the history through the centuries, discovering how these stories and their weaponization were used to protect the powerful and subjugate the rest of us.

The religious dedication to the preservation of the story of not only the United States but all of "Western civilization"—the supposed narrative of how the modern world came to be—is the means by which power shields and hides itself. The conspiracy theories that afflict people like my family, people willing to die and kill for those ideas, serve as a buttressing of that system. This stream of lies is designed to hide the origins of their material lives, consecrate their suffering, and co-opt them as guardians of their own inequality.

This crisis we are now facing, in which authoritarians and authoritarian movements are gaining power around the world, is many years in the making and these stories are preparing the people I love for insidious solutions, including the destruction of democracy, widespread violence, worsening exploitation, and a final battle between forces that, at first blush, might resemble the armies of good and evil described in Grandma's old, dog-eared Bible.

But they are far from supernatural and are all too real.

My journey through the past in search of answers, and in trying to understand this mythical "Western civilization," begins with the merging of power and Christianity in Rome. The Christian faith, with its monotheistic focus, missionary impulse, reliance on divinely revealed knowledge, and twin, interlocking elements of martyrdom and the utility of power, all of it protected by apocalyptic narrative, was a world-altering development; the decline of the mythology of Rome's exceptionalism turned Christianity from a persecuted sect to the defining ideology and worldview of the Western world.

Following Rome's fall, much of the power in the region resided in centralized Christianity, where religious leaders defined orthodoxy and enforced discipline through subservient monarchs reliant on the endorsement of the church and the teachings of priests who emphasized fealty and terror. In managing this system, internal tensions were redirected at enemies outside through crusades and sanctified wars that gobbled up territory and material resources, all while peasants were continually assured their suffering might be rewarded in the afterlife should they remain faithful and loyal.

A struggle would emerge between the secular nobility and the church. When the affluent educated themselves in universities in order to carry out administrative functions, they discovered that much of the information they had been fed was fraudulent and reckoned the mythologies could be used to grow their own influence and wealth. Empires grew as exploration enabled colonization—the subjugation of Indigenous people around the world through enslavement and genocide—and tales of white supremacy and future heavenly utopias rationalized the rampant violence.

A new system of accumulation emerged, giving rise to concentrated wealth that ultimately undermined the feudal system and the sovereignty of kings. Capitalism developed as a means of laundering the treasures extracted by oppression, and with it emerged a system of liberalism intended to move beyond the grasp and violent divisions of religion and prioritize the wishes of an aristocratic class of white men championing their own liberty and freedom while trafficking enslaved people and suppressing supposed lesser elements, including people of color, Indigenous cultures, women, the poor, and vulnerable populations.

The battle between this liberal order and conservative forces obsessed with rolling back history and reestablishing "natural" hierarchies has dominated history ever since. Wielding the remaining elements of cultural Christianity, including its prophecies of hidden machinations and fear of persecution, conservatives have continually attempted to destroy liberalism, taking advantage of opportunities to crack down on individual liberties and reassert control lost in liberalization, all while liberalism prioritizes private property and the fates of wealthy white men behind the veneer of progress and equality.

This capitalist structuring has continually run aground, causing financial meltdowns, monopolistic conditions, vast inequality, genocides, and wars on massive scales. In times of crisis, like the one we are living through now, conservative reactionaries have attempted to reverse time and reaffirm authority, often through propaganda, conspiracy theories, attacks on education and culture, and bloodletting made holy through the lens of established religious mythology.

History reveals itself in these cycles, and we are witnessing it play out again with recognizable patterns. As capitalism overheats and convulses, the wealthy turn to violent force to protect themselves from populist uprisings. The elements of religious mythology, with all its paranoias and revealed knowledge, are used to radicalize and prepare.

Once more, we are in the midst of a gathering crisis that stands ready to explode.

The story that is most commonly told about the United States, how it won its freedom through revolution before rising as the great hope of the world, is itself a religious mythology. It presents a story of a superpower that fights for good and for justice, for the rights of humanity and everything sacred in the world, while obscuring the blood and suffering and injustices that made it so. Eight decades past the fall of the Third Reich, thirty years beyond the end of the Cold War, and now, still navigating the fallout from September 11, America's mythology of exceptionalism is weakening as it comes to the precipice of something new, the edge of something we can sense if not see clearly.

Because they were taught America was God's chosen champion in the battle between Good and Evil, my family believed this uncharted territory was the apocalypse. A final showdown marked by great suffering and hardship that would birth the Kingdom of God on Earth. They had been prepared for years for its arrival, convinced they were soldiers in a righteous army that would stand down the forces of wickedness in preparation for deliverance. They would be betrayed by the Devil's minions, tortured by his cruelties, and tested by the conditions of the world, but if they swallowed their fear, accepted their lot, and fought with every available fiber of their being, they would be rewarded with paradise.

The power of America has rested largely on its sway over reality itself. Following the world wars, it grasped control of the capitalist order and the mantle of the foremost benevolent superpower. By wielding the mythologies of Western civilization and white supremacy, a disinfected story of progress and achievement that omits or rationalizes the brutality, and the Christian narrative, the wealthy and powerful have entrenched themselves as the protagonists in this ongoing drama and the protectors of everything won and accomplished.

Ties between these extremists and white nationalists are anything but coincidental. Under the surface of the glistening façade is pure, unvarnished white patriarchal supremacy. The wealth and laws and traditions encompassed by the phrase "Western civilization," itself an imaginary construction, are nothing but sanitized expressions of entrenched hierarchy. Time and again, when the systems are challenged, whether through collective action or political and socioeconomic changes, entrenched power turns to these extremists to reinforce discipline and attack their enemies.

As economic inequality, undeniable racism, and climate change worsen, the authoritarian nature of the system becomes more apparent and less hidden. The powerful would much rather hide behind the veneer of respectability and tolerance and progress while continuing to accumulate wealth and rinsing the blood from their dollars, but the truth is coming into full and horrific focus.

After being told history had stopped and that the present status quo might last forever, we are awakening with a start to realize we are living in an epochal moment. As we will see, history is filled with these times, where the past order has exhausted itself and is already unwittingly pregnant with its successor. Those who recognize these moments for what they are define the future, and right now, as much of society languishes in the delusion that things are fine or that the current crises will simply pass, individuals and organizations dedicated to rolling back progress and re-forming draconian systems are busily planning and working to shape what will come.

One such person is a Russian neofascist philosopher named Aleksandr Dugin, who wields substantial influence on both his country's leaders and reactionary revolutionaries around the world. He is the type of figure I would've imagined as a child synthesizing my apocalyptic teachings with tales of horror from Russia. Dugin grasps that we are perched on the edge of an abyss. In his lectures and books, he has laid out his vision for what should come to pass, a return to oppressive traditions and the destruction of the modern world.

To Dugin, we are inhabitants of a midnight kingdom, subjects of an empire and a secular world nearing its conclusion. His diagnoses and solutions are emblematic of generations' worth of esoteric tinkering, conspiracy peddling, racist and anti-Semitic worldviews, and the intentional weaponizing of faith and fear in the pursuit of power and profit. Dugin and others like him, including Steve Bannon and a great many politicians, provocateurs, and traffickers of white nationalism and illiberal reactionary forces, see an opening presenting itself in which humanity might be ushered back into the dark of unilateral and unquestionable authority.

Though many would like to believe Donald Trump's electoral defeat in 2020 represented a "return to normal," Trump's victory was a symptom of a larger disease. The forces that led to his ascent in the first place are consolidating power and gaining momentum by the day. This reality is disturbing, but we can no longer afford to live in delusion or put off this absolute reckoning with these truths.

To understand fully what we face, what lies in the shadows just beyond our vision, what it could be and, more importantly, what it *should* be, we must first go back and understand how all of this began. We must work our way through the mists of time and reconstruct how these systems and meanings we inherited came to pass, separate truth from propaganda, and grasp for ourselves how this clock ticking ever closer to midnight was set into motion.

- CHAPTER ONE -

By This, Conquer

The Great Fire of Rome erupted in July of 64 AD, and grew until it consumed everything in its path. Beginning in the merchant district around the Circus Maximus, for six days it raged, racing from one end of the city to another and back again, laying waste to homes, businesses, and temples before it was momentarily snuffed out. Then it reignited and terrorized the Romans for three more days.

People fled as best they could, many escaping the city to the countryside, carrying their belongings, dragging the injured to safety, while some, demoralized and hopeless from having watched their lives burst into flame, surrendered themselves to the fire. When the blaze relented, more than half of Rome was left in ruins. Dazed survivors wandered the streets, sifting through the ash and collecting the dead in the shadows of "charred vestiges of buildings."[1]

It must have felt like the end of the world for a people who believed themselves the pinnacle of human civilization. In becoming an empire, Rome had cultivated the belief that it was the chosen city of the gods, a superior people guided by providence and destined for glory, but even before the fire, that concept had begun to flicker, as for nearly a century Rome had been ruled by the Julio-Claudian dynasty, a series of rulers more and more inept and vicious with each passing generation.

Now, reigning over an empire of dust, there was the mad emperor Nero.

Born Lucius Domitius Ahenobarbus, Emperor Nero was only sixteen when he ascended to the throne in 54 AD. His wickedness was legendary. As emperor, he would reportedly escape his palace in "a cap or a wig, and ramble about the streets in sport," hunting commoners he could harass, trick, needlessly rob, or murder in cold blood.[2] At public events he reveled in watching his subjects savage one another, instigating bloody and murderous battles by tossing the crowd scraps of food and tokens of wealth.[3] Paranoid, Nero had his opponents, their children, and even his own wife and mother murdered.

This madness defined the late Julio-Claudian dynasty, the initial rulers of the Roman Empire, and set a disastrous tone. Unburdened by the fetters of representative government and held as living gods, the early emperors of Rome engaged in unrestrained brutality. Life in Rome was characterized by wild, extravagant, homicidal passion plays among the elite and an existence of "broken teeth" and repression for common people.[4]

There is no doubt the culture and lineage that birthed Nero was corruptive. Emperor Caligula, Nero's uncle, was consumed by "innate depravity" and infamous for his madness.[5] A megalomaniac, he embraced his given role as a living deity at the top of the religious pantheon and declared war on the other gods. Described as "perverse" and a "lover of malice," he terrorized Rome and its people.[6] While he was "dining or carousing" he would have prisoners tortured and maimed nearby so he could revel in their suffering.[7] In 41 AD, after a reign of terror, he was "hacked to pieces" by his own Praetorian Guard following a play with a mock crucifixion.[8] He was so despised his body was "half burnt" and, in lieu of a proper burial, "had some dirt hastily thrown upon it."[9]

Nero carried on Caligula's despotic legacy and was so distrusted that in the aftermath of the Great Fire rumors spread that he had started the fire himself and planned to destroy Rome so that he could claim "the glory of founding a new city, one that was to be named after him." An apocryphal legend gained traction that as Rome burned, Nero, a self-styled actor and performer, donned a costume and "appeared on his private stage and sung about the destruction of Troy," basking in the attention of a crowd and the warm glow of the nearby flames.[10]

Before the embers had even cooled, Nero surveyed the ruins and planned the construction of his "Golden House," a massive, decadent palace that would cover a large swath of Rome and stand in testament to his greatness. Suspicion grew that he had personally sacrificed the lives and livelihoods of the people in order to clear the way for his narcissistic project, stirring an environment of distrust and anger similar to the mood when his uncle Caligula had been assassinated and dismembered. To cover his tracks and quell the people, Nero would need to find a vulnerable population upon whom he could lay the blame for the colossal tragedy and mete out violent retribution.

"To dispel the gossip," Nero turned to a small cult known as the Christians and "inflicted the most exotic punishments."[11] Under Nero's command, members of the cult were "covered with hides of wild beasts" and "torn to pieces by dogs," while others were crucified and "burned to provide lighting at night."[12]

Nero's choice to persecute the Christians was predicated on their position in Roman society. Considered a fringe group obsessed with "perverse and unruly superstition," the Christians of first-century Rome were outliers and regarded as fanatics and a destabilizing force in the tenuous community.[13] With their religion outlawed, Christians worshipped in secret, prompting outrageous rumors of twisted rituals involving the sacrificing of babies and wild orgies. Romans imagined Christians in catacombs and shadowy spaces, drinking the blood of children "with thirsty lips" before reveling "in the shameless dark with unspeakable lust."[14]

Rumors aside, the Christians were seen as disruptive and "a class of persons quite unfit for the intercourse of social life."[15] As an empire, Rome had sustained societal peace via an intentional blending of cultures that valued pluralism and diversity within its borders. This mixing was best exemplified, and made possible by, the process of religious syncretism, or the merging of religions. As Rome grew in size and scope, uniting disparate peoples and cultures, their religious mythologies were wed as well, their gods and stories intertwining to form a new, cohesive mythology for all people to live within.

With each military victory, the Romans welcomed their new citizens into the empire and initiated their gods into the bustling pantheon of deities, where they cohabitated peacefully. To expedite cultural absorption, the Romans even constructed altars to "the unknown gods" to come as their territory expanded.[16] When the Christian cult first made its way to Rome, its members were greeted with the news that their god and messiah were more than welcome and that one of the altars for an unknown deity was theirs to claim.

The system of syncretism and cultural pluralism was reliant on polytheism, or the worship of multiple gods. In Rome, there was scant competition between the many cults, and a citizen could be a member of an assortment of belief systems, picking and choosing their gods depending on the day, engaging in rituals and mysteries and a plethora of public festivals. The only requirement was that the Roman participate in the "state-sponsored emperor worship," or the imperial cult, and use their sacrifices and prayers with their other gods to bolster Rome's fortunes.[17]

Christians had no problem lobbying their god for Rome. Like other Romans, they believed it was the empire "which keeps at bay the great violence which hangs over the universe and even the end of the world."[18] Much like the Greeks before them, Christians saw themselves as members of a greater civilization constantly troubled by the evil threat of so-called barbarians—an "emotional, cruel, dangerous, polygamous, and incestuous" people, some of whom reportedly practiced "human sacrifice"—who lived just beyond the borders of the empire.[19]

The term *barbarian* itself was a creation meant to denote a person outside of "civilization," or rather someone unprotected by the laws and privileges afforded a citizen. As defined by Professor Rick Altman, it was a means of "distinguishing inclusion from exclusion." This separation determined everything from who deserved protection and resources to who could be killed without repercussions. In this way, the powerful could alter the perception of reality, including and excluding based on their needs, and either bringing peoples into the fold when terms and expectations were met or excluding them as punishment.

Christian prayers were laced with appeals to maintain the Roman order, but as a fervently monotheistic religion, Christianity made no room for the worship of the emperor as a living deity. This refusal by Christians to commit to emperor worship made them pariahs and easy targets for Nero's retribution. Their perceived fanaticism raised suspicion that they might engage in terroristic behavior and set fire to the city in the name of their isolated god. But it is also likely that Christians were not alone in their martyrdom and suffering at the hands of the mad emperor. Some believe it is very possible another cult was punished for the Great Fire alongside the Christians: the cult of Isis.

A "goddess of immense magical power," Isis arrived in Rome from Egypt, where she was held as one of the principal deities.[20] The parallels between the cult of Isis and Christianity are extraordinary and speak to the evolution of religion from a mythology of how the natural world operated to promises of a supernatural world that overlaid our own. Through Isis and Christ, followers were "resurrected" and could achieve "salvation" through "baptism."[21] Like Christianity, the cult of Isis spread by evangelical missionary work orchestrated by a priest class actively seeking to convert believers. It is very likely that the cult of Isis was one of Christianity's main rivals for religious influence in the ancient world.

Nero's punishments—clothing the martyrs in hides and burning them alive—hints at the possibility the persecution was specifically a ridicule of Isis, as that faith featured adherents who idolized animals and included fire as an integral part of their rituals. It is near impossible to know for sure, however, because the historical record is incomplete and information about the cult of Isis and many other religions of ancient Rome was eradicated by Christians after they came to power centuries later. Over time, the cult of Isis was all but destroyed, the goddess Isis herself absorbed into the Christian mythology as an influence on the construction of the Virgin Mary, the mother of the Christian messiah, Jesus Christ.

The story of how Christianity overtook other faiths and evolved from a persecuted cult on the fringes of society into the official religion of Rome, and eventually the mythology through which the modern world was formed, is the story of how systems of domination are constructed, solidified, and weaponized.

It is the story of geneses and apocalypses.

Only four years after the fire, Nero's reign collapsed into paranoia and bloodshed. Having wreaked havoc on Rome, the emperor realized even his staunchest allies had abandoned him. He believed that around every corner lurked assassins readying to dispatch him, as had been his uncle Caligula's fate. Desperate, Nero fled Rome in disguise and escaped to a villa, where he dug his own grave and prepared to meet his fate. In June of 68 AD, Nero believed he heard the "swift-heel'd steeds" of his would-be assassins and either committed suicide by plunging a dagger into his throat or ordered one of his last remaining companions to do it for him.[22] The mad emperor died as his blood soaked the dirt.

But Nero was so despised and infamous that his demise was only the beginning of his story. After his escape and death, rumors spread that he had faked his death and was amassing troops for an all-out assault on Rome. There were tales of court "astrologers" who had warned the emperor he would be "deserted by all the world" but would find power in "the East" and "the kingdom of Jerusalem."[23] Still others believed Nero's malevolence was stronger than mortality and that evil itself would resurrect him from the grave.

Called the Nero Redivivus legend, this story was so powerful that several "counterfeit Neros" appeared with claims to his legacy.[24] These imposters emerged from the far borders of the empire and hypnotized populations with stories of resurrection. They looked like Nero, performed like Nero, and in one case a false Nero roused enough of a following that it nearly escalated to the point of war. But the Nero Redivivus legend wasn't purely a Roman or civic legend. Among persecuted Christians, there were prophecies he would return as well, "making himself equal to God" before a final battle where the Christian god would "prove him naught."[25] One such telling of this story has been immortalized in the Book of Revelation in the Christian Bible and has had unbelievable repercussions on human civilization for millennia.

Prepared by an unknown author who has come to be called "John of Patmos," the Book of Revelation was composed as a letter to the Christian churches of Asia Minor near the turn of the second century. The letter seems to be an address on Christian persecution under the rule of Emperor Domitian, who demanded his subjects refer to him as "master" and "god," and served as a warning against Christians succumbing to the imperial cult. It swims with lush and apocalyptic imagery, painting a portrait of a final battle between good and evil.[26] That climax is teeming with memorable characters and moments, including the Four Horsemen of the Apocalypse, the Whore of Babylon, horrid beasts and monsters, plagues and celestial judgments, and the final victory of God over his eternal antagonist Satan, resulting in the Devil being hurled into a "bottomless pit" for a thousand years before rising again and being "cast into a lake of fire burning with brimstone" for the rest of time.[27] In the aftermath, John of Patmos promised, devout and loyal Christians would be rewarded with "a new heaven and a new earth."[28]

Due to the persecution of Christianity and the dangers of openly criticizing Rome, Revelation is coded, and its intentions are unclear as to whether it is a prophecy for a future event or a metaphor-laden account of contemporary occurrences. What seems clear is that Nero plays an integral role as a blasphemous "beast" who rises from the sea, wounded "by a sword" and yet resurrected, with an identifying number of "six hundred threescore and six," the number "666," which, in Hebraic gematria, was understood to represent the deposed emperor.[29]

Three centuries after Nero's death, early Christian scholars like Augustine of Hippo believed that Nero possibly represented the legendary "Antichrist," or Satan's profane answer to the messiah Jesus, saying many Christians believed he would rise from the dead and be "restored to his Kingdom."[30] Similar legends held that "Beliar, a great angel," would "descend . . . in the form of a man, a lawless king, the slayer of his mother."[31] St. Victorinus wrote that Nero was the Antichrist and that God would send him as a punishment "worthy" of the worst unbelievers, "namely the Jews and those who persecute Christ."[32]

Apocalypticism was a carryover from the Jewish tradition that came to define the Christian faith and perpetuated its consolidation of power. As had been the case with the writings of the Old Testament, Christian apocalyptic narratives arose from "a situation of crisis" and served as a means to spur action and propagate faith.[33] Primarily a "minority phenomenon," these apocalypse narratives highlight the actions of the majority and warn that the current "course leads to perdition."[34] The stories are predictably similar and feature a "present age" under the control of Satan and ripe for the rise of an Antichrist while a renewal of faith promises a "glorified" future.[35]

The Christian and Jewish faiths differed on the question of the presence and influence of embodied evil in the scope and trajectory of the world. While Jewish thought tended to view Satan as "a symbol of the tendency to evil within humanity," the Christians believed they were engaged in an active and dire war against the literal personification of evil.[36] This battle defined Christian mythology and was a worldview based on "transcendent reality" divorced from empirical evidence and based on "visions" and faith.[37]

This mindset drew a violent line between Christianity and its "pagan" contemporaries. Polytheistic religions were defined, as noted by

Walter Burkert, by their "absence of religious demarcation and conscious group identity," while the burgeoning monotheistic mythology depended upon them.[38] Pagan gods in a syncretic system helped in the formulation of an open, pluralist society. Monotheistic Christianity, with its apocalyptic mission, considered anything besides a homogenous society ordered by its own tenets and beliefs as evil and a direct path to Satan conquering the world.

It would have been one thing had the monotheism of Christianity simply precluded believers from worshipping other deities, but the god of the Jewish and Christian faiths was a "jealous god" who demanded followers "not bow down" to other gods and ordered them to "overthrow them, and quite break down their images."[39] The Bible is filled with such commandments, orders to "destroy their altars, break their images, and cut down their groves: For thou shalt worship no other god; for the Lord . . . *is* a jealous God."[40]

Monotheistic Christianity thrived on the act of demonization, which not only set its own faith apart and above its competitors but painted them as engaged in an evil scheme on behalf of Satan and hastening the end of the world. If pagans and polytheists were allowed to carry on unabated, it would mean certain disaster and the triumph of supernatural evil. In this way, Christians cast themselves as the ultimate arbiters of right and wrong, a responsibility that found them "beset by perceived enemies both outside and within."[41]

Using invented concepts like supernatural forces and the looming consequence of an eternity spent in punishment in hell, Christians manufactured a mythology entitling them to dominion over society, while anyone who refused to join them would necessarily be dispatched for the good of the world. To this end, the Bible promised a cosmic reckoning at the end of time wherein God, as judge, would "separate" the faithful from the wicked, reward the good with an immortal kingdom, and order the disbelievers "into everlasting fire."[42]

Over the centuries, as Rome suffered one setback after another and the imperial cult lost its grip over the realities of its people, the

Christian doctrine and system of hierarchies gradually replaced the decaying order and draped its worldview over the flagging Roman myth. That Christianity won out over rivals like the cult of Isis can be explained by how its worldview aligned more with Roman values and how it girded traditional hierarchies.

Roman society was extremely stratified, relying on a strict divide between *humiliores,* the common people, and *honestiores,* the privileged who enjoyed wealth and status.[43] These existences were similarly composed of in-groups and out-groups and constituted wholly separate spheres. Common people were mostly frozen in their station and subject to cruelties and humiliations, while the elite were respected and protected from punishments unbecoming their status. It was necessary, in order to protect this hierarchy and social order, to shift from a mythology where the most powerful were deemed superior by the gods to one where those holding "divine truth" and the favor of a monotheistic god enjoyed a "natural" advantage.

In another instance of Christian principles supporting deeply ingrained Roman values, the Christian faith was stringently patriarchal. In the creation myth of the Garden of Eden, after the first woman, Eve, ruins paradise and damns humanity to an existence of pain and suffering, the mother of the human race is told that her husband, Adam, and all subsequent men "shall rule over thee," setting a tone for patriarchal domination based in theological law.[44] While the cult of Isis held that women were equal to men, Rome had been founded on the principle that women were "expected to conform themselves entirely to the temper of their husbands" and to exist as "necessary and inseparable possessions."[45]

The cult of Isis and Christianity were similar, but their distinctions determined much of the fate of history as Christianity's tenets converged with Rome's economic and political interests. While the cult of Isis stressed a symbiotic relationship between humanity, animals, and the environment, Christians believed they had been given unquestionable authority over nature, having been told by their god they had "dominion over the fish of the sea, and over the fowl of the air, and over the cattle, and over all the earth," which allowed humanity to plunder resources and bend nature to its will.[46] And while the cult of Isis "did not allow room for any quarrel between science and religion, any prudery about sex," or "discrimination and segregation," Christianity relentlessly warred against knowledge as an assault on God, shamed individual expression, and provided the theological framework for the intentional oppression of vulnerable peoples.[47]

Several features of Christian monotheism made it especially potent as a replacement mythology for the imperial cult of Rome as the mythology lost its luster and appeal. The creation of in-groups and out-groups inspired by divine intention, with a system of supernatural rewards and punishments to entice fealty and stave off disruptions, meant that Rome's fragile order could be revitalized. The existence of divine truth that lay beyond the realm of the senses meant objective reality could be discarded by possessors of heavenly revelation. This "revealed truth," wielded by supposed prophets of the Christian god, was more authoritative than "deceitful evidence," which was treated as "seduction" on behalf of "false gods" like Satan and his demonic horde.[48]

This invention created a manipulatable weapon in the form of revelation. Individuals claiming godly inspiration or a direct channel to the creator of the universe could wield unquestionable power in the name of a holy mission, legitimizing great acts of persecution, all of it in the higher service of defeating evil before it destroyed human civilization.

The Roman Empire fell on hard times in the third century. A destabilizing series of crises hit, including a pandemic that left the cities strewn with carcasses; climate change that ravaged agriculture and drew so-called barbarians, or more accurately refugees, to the edge of the territory; and rampant political instability and infighting. With this chaos, the influence of the imperial myth, that Rome and its leaders were divinely endowed, lost much of its remaining sheen.

As Christians gained in power, many began blaming them for the decline. The philosopher Porphyry, part of a consortium of polytheistic leaders who recognized the growing danger of Christianity, laid responsibility directly on the cult, blaming their insistence on monotheism for the gods' disfavor, saying the deities who had protected Rome were "no longer dwellers among" the Romans and that "no one has seen any succor for the people while Jesus is being honored."[49]

From their beginnings worshipping in the shadows and being suspected of unfathomable cruelties, Christians had become fixtures in Roman society by the third century. Members of the faith served in the government and military and held positions of authority. That would change as the fourth century began and Emperor Diocletian, spurred by his assistant emperor Galerius, carried out widespread and systematic persecution. Diocletianic persecution was vicious. Beginning with an edict to "tear down the churches to the foundations, and to destroy the sacred Scriptures by fire," Diocletian wanted Christians "degraded" and "deprived of their liberty."[50] They were barred from public life, intimidated, and subject to brutal torture and executions. Christians were "tormented with the rack and excruciating scrapings," some "suffering decapitations, some the torments of the flame," the violence so extensive and exhausting that Diocletian's executioners were often "wearied with slaughter" and their weapons so well used they grew "blunted."[51]

In this way, Diocletian believed he might spur a renaissance in Roman culture by reestablishing polytheistic and imperial worship and destroying the "exclusivity" and "novelty" of the Christian faith.[52]

Instead, Diocletian made the Christians martyrs.

Over centuries of persecution, Christians cultivated a sense of nobility in suffering. In fact, their faith, founded on the suffering and persecution of their messiah, Jesus Christ, was predicated on the concept of martyrdom. Though stories of Christian persecution are often exaggerated for effect and political purposes, as early as the second century, Christians were described by their own leaders as possessing a "pathological yearning for martyrdom" that would "glorify Him who suffered" so that they might experience salvation.[53] The push by Christians to martyr themselves and offer their lives so that they might be gifted holy favor was so intense that a Roman official, wary of granting fervent Christians the deaths they so deeply desired and demanded, exclaimed, "You wretches, if you want to die, you have cliffs to leap from and ropes to hang from."[54]

By seeking martyrdom and continually telling a story of persecution, Christians were able to portray themselves as holders of an unconquerable divine truth so potent and so undeniable that even the leaders of the Roman Empire were desperate to snuff it out. By pursuing their religion in the face of discrimination, Christians grew in moral stature.

Though Galerius had played a crucial role as an enforcer of Diocletianic persecution, he changed his stance on Christianity during his time as emperor. As he lay dying, Galerius passed the Edict of Serdica, granting Christianity the status of *religio licita,* which had previously been granted to the Jewish people. The decree cited the "great numbers" who "still persist in their opinions" as reason to end the abuse, requesting that they "offend not against good order" and that they "pray to their God for our welfare."[55]

Whether the Christians honored the request to appeal to God on behalf of Rome or not, the empire continued to languish. Because Rome had left its republic behind in favor of totalitarian rule, succession became a point of contention, and the state was racked with internal fighting and civil war. It wasn't until 312 AD that Rome was again reunited under the reign of a single emperor named Constantine.

Constantine met his rival Maxentius on October 28 for the Battle of the Milvian Bridge, which would determine who would become the sole leader of Rome. Constantine's forces prevailed and Maxentius drowned in the Tiber River. His corpse was recovered and his head "torn from his body" to be used as a trophy by Constantine's triumphant army as they entered Rome before being "mounted on a pike" and subjected to public scorn and continual disfigurement.[56] Constantine took his seat as the emperor of Rome and attempted to reunite the empire.

The story of how Constantine managed to wrest control from Maxentius has been the subject of intense scrutiny and debate ever since. Seizing on Constantine's eventual conversion to Christianity and his shows of support for the faith, Christians have propagated the legend that on the eve of the Battle of the Milvian Bridge, Constantine saw "a vision in the skies of a cross inscribed with the words, 'By this, conquer,'" and that "the following night Christ had appeared to him in a dream bearing the same sign."[57] In this telling, Constantine ordered his men to adorn their shields with the likeness of the Christian cross and fashioned his own standard glorifying God.

Though Constantine was exceedingly more tolerant of Christians than his predecessors before his own conversion to the faith, he had been historically polytheistic, with a public preference for the sun god Sol Invictus, symbols for which adorned many of the emperor's seals and monies. Contradictory reports held that Constantine claimed to have received a vision from the solar god Apollo, not Jesus, offering "laurel wreaths" and promises of "victory."[58]

In early 313 AD, Constantine released the Edict of Milan, a declaration that stated a belief that "Christians and all men" should have "the freedom to follow religion, whichever one each one chose, so that whatever sort of divinity there is in heavenly regions may be gracious and propitious to us and to all who live under our government."[59] Instantaneously, the emperor became the object of love and fealty from Christians around the empire and was lauded as being divinely inspired. Legends grew that he had even retrieved the very cross that Jesus Christ had died upon and used the nails driven into his flesh as "bridle-bits and a helmet" so that they might protect him in his godly crusades.[60]

Like kings and prophets of the Bible, Constantine was transformed into a divine agent with whom God had chosen to share his sovereignty. Suddenly, the merging of power with the cult of Christianity revealed a new function and feature of the form. When relegated to the minority within a society, Christians could rely on their martyrdom as proof of conviction and apocalypticism as a means of undermining the majority.

When aligned with the state, Christians could look to their leaders as divine agents, backed by the will of God and nearly as infallible, incontestable, and holy as Christ himself.

Though Constantine would only convert at the end of his life, the empire used Christianity and its potent mythology to replace the dwindling imperial cult. Faith in Rome and its emperors had all but vanished in the crises of the third century, and monotheistic religion made for a heady substitution. By combining the empire with a religion that held itself above all others and featured a system of rewards and consequences that transcended earthly matters, Constantine was able to briefly reunite the empire.

But Christianity was far from done dividing the world between the holy and the wicked. A battle over the very nature of the faith raged between rival sects and called into question whether Christianity was actually monotheistic or secretly polytheistic. The Arian sect believed that "God alone" was divine, and in contrast to Jesus Christ was "without beginning, unbegotten, and eternal," meaning the Father and the Son were separate entities.[61] This nod toward a division between God and Christ posed a unique problem for early Christians who recognized the potential of monotheism and its particular strengths in regard to winning converts and establishing authority.

To solve the problem, Constantine met with Christian leaders at the First Council of Nicaea in 325 AD. Upon arriving, Constantine found himself surrounded by Christians who had suffered unbelievable agonies at the hands of prior emperors, men who had been tortured and imprisoned in official persecutions. According to Christian legends, the emperor redeemed himself and the state of Rome by lowering himself to the station of these men, seeking their forgiveness, and, in one case, kissing "the empty eye sockets of a blind old man whose eyes had been gouged out by imperial torturers."[62] Inside, Constantine presided over a council that ruled on church division, establishing an orthodox faith that considered God, Christ, and the Holy Spirit as inseparable, and creating a new in-group and out-group between the "true believers" of the Christian faith, as outlined by official doctrine and backed by Roman power, and heretics straying from orthodoxy. This determined that "divine truth" and "prophecy," so integral to the claim of authority, remained the possession of a chosen few and prevented adversarial prophets from challenging the establishment.

As much as the Christians believed Constantine to be divine, he was of course still mortal. In 337 AD he fell deathly ill and traveled for treatment to Helenopolis. There, he sought out Bishop Eusebius of Nicomedia, engaged in a hurried Christian education, "laid aside his purple" royal attire for a simple white baptismal robe, and was washed of his sins.[63] Following his death, Eusebius of Nicomedia supposedly discovered a hidden "will" authored by the late emperor, revealing that he had been "poisoned" and demanding that "his murderers be punished."[64] The list of murderers, conveniently, included all of Constantine's possible heirs save for his three sons, who were favored by the church, legitimizing a murderous purge of their rivals.

The church quickly used its mythology to immortalize Constantine and create, in Rome, a new Christian empire. Chief among the propagandists was Eusebius of Caesarea, the originator of much of the church's official history. To cleanse the history of Rome's persecutions and embrace the empire, Eusebius positioned the persecution as "God's rebuke to the Christians for dissensions within the church," laying the blame for centuries of suffering at the feet of the newly minted heretics and creating a need to continue limiting their influence.[65] The evil visited upon Christians by Rome was surely the result of these betrayals, but also the work of Satan, the "evil-loving demon," who had worked in concert with past wicked emperors, "impious tyrants," and "profane rulers."[66]

Constantine's legacy was necessary to cement the relationship between Christians desiring power and the empire that had largely conquered Europe. In this effort, Eusebius lionized the emperor, calling him "God's servant," comparing him to Jesus Christ and Moses, and likening his rise to the creation of the universe by God himself, describing it as "a light" in "the dense and impenetrable darkness."[67] He praised his support of Christianity and emphasized his achievements, all while ignoring damning evidence of impiety, such as Constantine's poisoning of his son Crispus and murdering his wife Fausta by imprisoning her in a hot bath.

Those cruelties were buried in favor of retelling the myth of the Milvian Bridge, where the battle with Maxentius, whom Eusebius now framed as an Antichrist engaged in "sorcery" and dissecting pregnant women and babies "for magic purposes," was now likened to the apocalyptic showdown between good and evil in the Book of Revelation.[68] Eusebius made it clear that neither Sol Invictus nor Apollo had revealed himself to Constantine but that "Christ of God appeared to him" following a vision of "a cross of light . . . bearing the inscription CONQUER BY THIS."[69] In this new mythology, written for the church and adopted as orthodoxy, Constantine grew into a "heavenly messenger of God . . . distinguished by piety and godly fear."[70]

A direct relationship between the church and the empire had been established, both in the public sphere and in the church's own mythology. Rome and its emperors became divine agents, earning their sovereignty through God and his supposed will by fighting the battle between divine good and supernatural evil. But Christianity's seizing of the reins of power was only the beginning, as the existence of other religions and challengers to Christian dominance meant the church was still under attack by evil forces as long as there remained a single nonbeliever.

Constantine's embrace of Christianity brought it into the fold of Roman social life but did not establish it as the state religion of the empire. His decrees made it clear other faiths should "be made welcome" and that it was "one thing voluntarily to undertake the conflict of immortality, another to compel others to do so from fear of punishment."[71] In the emperor's view, Christians had picked the right faith, but there was still room for a variety of faiths and mythologies to exist within the borders of the empire.

That would change.

After Constantine's death and the conspiratorial purge, his sons split responsibilities and the empire was divided once more. His son Constans took a hard-line stance in 341 AD regarding religious tolerance, declaring, "Let the superstition cease, let the insanity of sacrifices be abolished."[72] Thus began a path to Christianity as the state religion of Rome, made official in 380 AD with the Edict of Thessalonica, which painted nonbelievers of the Christian faith as "foolish madmen" and "branded" them "with the ignominious name of heretics."[73]

Though often hidden, the persecution that resulted from Christianity gaining power in Rome was horrific, widespread, and undeniably vicious. It was made possible by the Christian belief in divine truth and divine agents, as well as the apocalyptic mindset that posited every event in the natural world was a result of the supernatural battle between good and evil. Christians had long believed polytheistic worshippers had been duped by satanic manipulation, their gods and goddesses serving as traps to lure people astray, their devotees "helpless victims of demonic delusion."[74] The pagan temples in Rome represented "centers of demonic activity," and to let them stand would not only imperil their safety but serve as an affront to their god.[75]

To remedy this, mobs of roving Christians would "attack temples with sticks and stones and bars of iron" before engaging in the "stripping of roofs, demolition of walls, the tearing down of statues and the overthrow of the altars," all while the priests and adherents watched in silence lest they be torn to shreds.[76] When the Christian horde had wrecked the temple and helped themselves to any of the treasures, they moved on to the next target.

This persecution wasn't reserved for polytheists. As soon as Christians gained a foothold, they turned on their Jewish brethren, calling them "diseases of the soul," unclean, and possessed of "shamelessness."[77] Their synagogues were compared to pagan temples "where worship of demons was practiced."[78] In a harrowing turn of events, the Christians, who had been accused of child sacrifice and blood rituals in their early days, leveled the accusations against the Jews, claiming they had "polluted themselves with blood" and trafficking rumors of child abuse, saying Jews "had seized a Christian boy . . . [and] bound him to a cross" and "scourged the child until he died under their hands."[79]

By "means of torture," pagans, Jews, and even Christians outside the established state orthodoxy were converted to the religion.[80] In some cases, religious leaders "wrenched open the mouths of recusants and physically compelled them to receive communion."[81] Church elders called for the "dying limbs of idolatry" to be lopped off and for the world to be rid of nonbelievers.[82]

The widespread persecution was addressed by Bishop Augustine of Hippo, who minted what would come to be known as the concept of "righteous persecution," or justified oppressive, tyrannical behavior. Because Christians held divine truth and faced an omnipresent threat from Satan, they were vindicated in assaulting, murdering, and stealing from their neighbors and rivals. In fact, Augustine posited that persecution by Christians was meant to deliver the persecuted "from their ruinous madness" and help them "recover their right minds."[83] In this twisted worldview, a distinction was drawn between "unrighteous persecution," which was anything done by "the impious" against "the church," and, in contrast, righteous persecution, "which the Church of Christ inflicts upon the impious" in "the spirit of love."[84]

Augustine's reasoning was based on the concept that society was sick because it had not come to embrace Christianity in totality. He likened disbelievers to a delirious patient who needed to be "restrained, like the fever-stricken, with the shackles" of Christianity and urged followers engaging in persecution against non-Christians to treat them like disobedient children "struck in love, not in hatred."[85]

Under this logic, Christians were justified in committing any atrocity, be it the physical and violent compelling of nonbelievers to convert, the razing and looting of temples, or the torture and murder of heretics. Tragically, they took the persecution they had suffered as an oppressed cult and turned it on the rest of the world, enabled by the full force of the Roman Empire. In the words of a Christian monk called to task by authorities for an all-out assault on and looting of a temple, there was "no crime for those who have Christ."[86]

The Christians attacked any remnants of so-called pagan culture, an invention by the Christians themselves, including the bastions of knowledge that had constituted the pinnacle of human achievement. The Christian impulse to destroy any traces of secular scholarship was rooted deep in the faith, stemming from the origin story of the Garden of Eden, in which Adam and Eve infamously betrayed God's command not to eat from the Tree of Knowledge. To rectify this ancient mistake, Christians lashed out at any and all works representing "barbarous and atheistic arrogance" and were ordered to avoid "strange and diabolical" texts, including the vast stores of amassed knowledge in the sciences.[87] They attacked libraries, burning books and smashing all traces of progress in the name of their lord. Philosophers and scientists were "tortured, burned alive and beheaded" or else driven underground and hunted as heretics.[88] Histories detailing pre-Christian Roman civilization were erased. The destruction of art was, as journalist and historian Catherine Nixey puts it, "on a scale never before seen in human history."[89]

The Roman Empire had embraced Christianity as a means to stave off its decline, but in doing so it had given authority to a fanatical cult that sought to use the authority of the empire to establish dominion over humanity. As a result, Christians raged against their fellow citizens, legitimizing their wanton destruction as self-preservation, and were actively annihilating civilization itself.

In 380, Emperor Theodosius made Christianity the state religion and looked the other way as Christians looted temples and terrorized the pagans. In 390 AD, however, he oversaw the senseless killing of thousands in putting down a revolt in Thessalonica, a crime met with nearly universal scorn, including within the Christian church; luminary

Bishop Ambrose of Milan refused to give the emperor communion until he repented for his sins. The confrontation between the head of the Roman state and the church highlighted a shift that had occurred in post-Constantine Rome. The imperial cult that had held sway over society had been completely supplanted, as the authority of emperors was now granted by God on high and the supreme emperor was a divine agent in a religious hierarchy. Eventually, Theodosius relented and engaged in public penance for his crimes, appearing at Ambrose's cathedral sans his imperial robes.

Later, after Theodosius had died in 395 AD, Ambrose presided over his funeral with the emperor's ten-year-old son, Honorius, at his side. In contrast to their earlier public bout and in spite of his butchery, Ambrose insisted that Theodosius had been incredibly holy and that his repentance had involved the fallen emperor weeping openly in the church, where he "prayed for pardon with groans and with tears."[90] The performance had a purpose. The succession was endangered by Honorius's young age, and Ambrose wanted to ensure the church maintained the control it had gained under his father's rule. Ambrose praised Theodosius as having been favored by God and helped by miracles. Over and over again, the bishop appealed to the mourners to see Theodosius in his son while firmly placing Christianity as the driving force of society.

Ambrose succeeded in securing the succession, and Honorius became the emperor of the Western Roman Empire and ruled with the assistance of the general Stilicho. Under Stilicho's leadership, Rome experienced a tense but somewhat stable stalemate with tribes outside the border until the young Honorius was duped by a minister named Olympius, who convinced Honorius that Stilicho's loyalties belonged to the barbarians and that a larger conspiracy was afoot that might end the emperor's reign. Over time, Stilicho was undermined, those around him were massacred, and eventually the general himself was executed. With Stilicho dead, Roman troops began exterminating the families of the barbarians who served in the Roman military machine, inspiring tens of thousands of troops to defect to the armies of Alaric I, leader of the Visigoths.

In August of 410 AD, Alaric and his army laid siege to Rome. During the siege, desperate Romans begged for the reinstatement of pagan rituals, laying blame for the siege on the "wrath of the gods" for "the abandonment of the old religion."[91] Even Pope Innocent I, the head of the Catholic Church, begged for the rituals to be held, joining other Romans who hoped pagan gods might produce "sacred thunder" to drive the Goths away.[92]

After three days, the Goths were let into the city and allowed to freely loot and pillage. Having taken what they needed, they simply left the capital of ancient civilization and went on their way.

The event was apocalyptic. The spell and mythology that had protected Rome and placed it as the center of human civilization were broken. St. Jerome, assisting fleeing refugees, saw the dazed Romans absconding from the fallen city and filling churches and shelters. He recognized that Rome had collapsed and marveled that those who had engaged in the "careless security of wealth" had been "reduced to such extremities as to need shelter, food, and clothing."[93]

Emperor of a crumbling kingdom, Honorius sent word to the far reaches of the empire, letting his subjects know they were on their own.

The fall of the Roman Empire was a novel problem for the Christians. Their own mythology had contended that God himself had chosen the empire and its emperors as his vessels for carrying out his divine plan and as the embodiment of good in the supernatural battle against evil. How then could it have possibly faltered?

Augustine of Hippo was ready to provide the type of innovative reasoning that might explain away the contradiction. Augustine provided a theodicy that took the focus away from the failures of divine agents and placed it squarely on humans who needed to be redeemed, reformed, and ultimately restrained by the word of God.

In the wake of the collapse, Augustine authored his book *The City of God,* which investigated original sin as the cause of all the world's ills, including the current crisis. It was necessary, according to Augustine, to give God thanks for having "seen fit to grant such extended and long-continued dominion to the Roman Empire" while understanding that human sin and continued denial of God were responsible for the fall.[94] Rome's failure was further proof to Christians that a war was raging between good and evil and that even the triumph of Christianity within the Roman Empire didn't mean that war had been won.

Augustine thus reduced the Roman Empire to a stepping-stone for Christianity, which survived its fall. To ensure eternal salvation and the victory of good over evil, Christians would need to destroy the earthly remnants of arrogant human civilization and purge humanity of its evil. In that pursuit, Christians continued the annihilation of temples and libraries, and murdered the remaining pagans, nonbelievers, and public intellectuals, including the legendary scientist Hypatia, who, in 415 AD, after the burning of the Library of Alexandria, was "inhumanly butchered," her body "paraded through the streets" before being "burned in mockery of pagan sacrifice."[95]

Later attempts to purge humankind would lead to wholesale murder on a much grander scale. At the turn of the seventh century, a bishop in Carrhae-Harran was ordered to convert citizens for the good of God, a task he was able to complete with a few nonbelievers, leaving him to deal with resisters by having them "carved up" and "suspending their limbs in the main street of the town."[96]

Civilization itself was unraveling. With the divine mission of the Christians and the murderous lengths to which they were willing to go in order to realize ultimate power, and with the Roman Empire and its accomplishments, in both conquests and human knowledge, vanishing into the haze of history, humanity was plunged deep into the dark.

- CHAPTER TWO -

The Great Chain of Being

As Rome fell to the so-called barbarians, the Western world underwent violent spasms. The empire had been a unifying gravity, at least in how the powerful viewed the rest of the world, and served as a center of civilization, innovation, and technology. To fill the vacuum, the Christian church continued to seek the "purification" of humanity while disparate tribes clashed in the wilderness and sought to construct their own viable kingdoms and destinies.

In the eighth century a new leader emerged in the form of Charlemagne, king of the Franks, a devout Christian who used his position to protect the church while prosecuting pagans. Rallying his men for "glory—heroic and heavenly," Charlemagne conquered vast swaths of Europe, forcing nonbelievers to either convert or die.[1] Chief among his victims were the Saxons, a competing Germanic tribe.

In Charlemagne's initial attacks, he sought to crush the polytheistic faith of the Saxon people, targeting a holy object called the Irminsul. A massive wooden pillar nestled in sacred wilderness, the Irminsul was considered by the Saxons to be the "tree of the universe," or the very foundation that supported their world and the heavenly realm of their gods.[2] Charlemagne recognized its importance to the Saxons and ordered it destroyed. Carrying out a blatant act of religious terrorism, he had the object hacked to pieces as its dispirited devotees looked on. The Franks "carried away the gold and silver" and continued their persecution of the Saxon people as the splinters of their icon were scattered to the winds.[3] To spur them to "renounce the worship of devils," Charlemagne used Christianity to position his new subjects in a world at his command under threat of capital punishment.[4]

Charlemagne sought to enmesh Saxons in a reality determined by the tenets of Christianity and enforced by the point of the sword. His laws detailed a structured Christian society the Saxons were required to live within, including baptism, a mandatory "tithe of their property and labor to the churches and priests," the cessation of sacrifices to their gods and sacred burial rites, and an obligation to respect and obey their "lord king" and "lord or lady" within the designed political and economic system, all under threat of state-sanctioned death.[5] In October of 782, in an event that would come to be known as the Massacre of Verden, under "the authority of the Lord King," 4,500 Saxons who refused Christianity and resisted Charlemagne were beheaded in a single day.[6] Following the massacre, the Franks "marched twice through the land, burning and slaughtering."[7]

For a church in desperate need of an ally, Charlemagne was truly a godsend. The might of the Roman Empire had provided the Catholic Church with a means to compel subservience, but as the empire collapsed, the principal religion of the moment lost much of its secular dominance. The situation worsened in the seventh century as Islam percolated in the Middle East, rallying devotees in a new faith that shared the Christian figures of Abraham, Noah, David, and even Jesus Christ, incorporating them into a new organizing worldview that troubled the established borders of the Western world.

Perhaps no one understood this dilemma better than Pope Leo III, a pontiff who immediately sought alliance with Charlemagne by delivering him the keys of the confession of St. Peter. Recognizing the advantages of affixing his authority to the church, Charlemagne welcomed the entreaties by sending "many generations of loot and tribute" he had accumulated by means of conquering to bolster the church's coffers, buy unremitting favor, and make possible the continued growth of the church, as well as the authority of the new pope.[8]

Leo III had rivals, however, in the form of loyalists to his predecessor. In 799, as the pope was engaged in a procession, a group of men attacked him, "tearing out his eyes and cutting out his tongue" before dragging him to a nearby monastery and leaving him "half-dead and drenched in blood in front of the altar."[9] Though the assault was intended to either dispose of Leo III or strip him of power, it set in motion a chain of events that would give rise to a new post–Roman Empire order.

Shaken and injured, Leo III sought protection from Charlemagne, who provided bodyguards and traveled to Rome to preside over a council with his detractors. Carrying the sacred gospels and swearing an oath "in the name of the Trinity that he was innocent of all that was alleged against him," Leo III was cleared by the Frankish king of any wrongdoing and his opponents summarily dispatched.[10] Two days later, as Charlemagne attended Christmas mass, he bent down at the feet of the pope in prayer and devotion and was crowned the new Roman emperor.

Though accounts differ as to whether Charlemagne expected the coronation or if Leo III surprised him with the honor, it is clear that in that moment the pope created a new authority within his position to bestow the legacy and tradition of Rome, making the church the curator of the lost empire. In the past, Rome had been a fixed place, a territory with discernible boundaries and distinctions, but now it existed as an institution that could be helmed by the very Germanic people who had once comprised the "barbarian" threat. The Franks, represented by Charlemagne, had been considered coarse and unrefined, the focus of Rome and the church's "civilizing" efforts, but now, with Leo III's act, they were lauded as the protectors of civilization.

Leo III made use of the malleability of identification, the same creation of in-groups and out-groups that had allowed Christianity as a novel monotheistic religion to thrive as Rome struggled to maintain its luster. Similarly, warlords and kings among the disparate tribes in the Middle Ages created binding cultures and traditions to fashion coalitions that could conquer others outside their fictional parameters. Though each tribe was, as historian Herwig Wolfram defined them, a "polyethnic medley," the consolidation of peoples into so-called ethnic tribes was "an open process" that allowed newly minted alliances to be lashed together with loosely defined histories and self-styled narratives.[11] In the case of the Franks and the burgeoning Carolingian dynasty that was spawned from Charlemagne's rule, these narratives actively changed and were rewritten to bind the tribe with the church and Rome to reinforce the coronation of Charlemagne, a process historian Rosamond McKitterick calls "constructing the past."[12]

These stories of peoples came to determine, much like the tradition of *humiliores* and *honestiores* in stratified Roman culture, who belonged to the chosen in-group and, in turn, who deserved resources and protection and who was subject to eradication. Whereas Rome and its internal systems had once been the uniting factor, the church and its possession of the Roman legacy became the yoke that held together the world of the early Middle Ages.

This was predictable, as the Christian church's violent assault on knowledge, both its artifacts and its professors, ensured a largely illiterate society ignorant of the past and the workings of the natural world. The church itself held a monopoly on the surviving texts, and learned individuals were primarily priests and members of monasteries who painstakingly copied the writings and teachings of the faith. What little information was bestowed upon the world taught the citizenry to obey its religious leaders without question and to believe that as "the City of Heaven is but one and undivided" in its perfection, then "therefore its likeness on earth should display undivided unity, too," meaning subservience to the will of the church was not only necessary but divinely mandated.[13]

Society, defined by the church and enforced by the rule of kings, took on a violent stratification between the chosen elite and the great majority of oppressed peoples. Churches were built throughout the land as a means of organization and discipline and to host sermons stressing the necessity of humiliation and the great plan of the Christian God to create an unwavering hierarchy. Fashioned after the Greeks' reckoning with forms of life, which saw figures like Aristotle wrestle with the different "classes" of beings, from the lowliest forms to "man . . . the only animal capable of reasoning," the church enforced a strict caste system that descended from the perfection of God all the way down to the lowliest of peasants.[14]

The church's intellectuals contributed to this tradition, starting with St. Augustine, who reasoned that "if all things were equal, all things would not be."[15] Later, Thomas Aquinas would liken the hierarchy to a colony of bees, where "there is one king bee and in the whole universe there is One God, Maker and Ruler of all things," and a class of workers below who served the noble whims of both in carrying out the ordained needs.[16] This constituted what would come to be called the Great Chain of Being, an ordered hierarchy beginning with God, traveling down through his subservient angels, then reaching the kingdom of man, presided over by the church and then a monarch, his assembled nobles, and finally, beneath them all and subject to their commands, the great unwashed masses destined to carry out the wishes of those born above them.

This philosophy, conveniently conducive to the continued accumulation of wealth by the church and nobility, laid the groundwork for a new society and order. Around Europe, communities were forged under the watchful eye of the church and king, each with a nobility who oversaw day-to-day operations, their loyal knights serving as law enforcement, and a church that continually reinforced the doctrine of subservience. This feudal state saw peasantry locked to land and damned to miserable lives defined by unremitting toil, terrifying superstition, and the constant threat of both state-sanctioned violence and eternal damnation.

The feudal system worked according to the laws of the Great Chain of Being, conformed to the wishes of a church looking to keep populations ignorant and dependent, and created a power base by which kings could establish legitimacy and stability, all the while accumulating wealth and resources by which the two bodies could pursue their common goals. Churches were assured tithes and fealty and offered, in return, the sanction of the divine right of kings.

As a result of this partnership, Christian apocalyptic mythology embraced the rise of secular kings, writing them into the divination that would come to be called the Last Emperor prophecy. In this new narrative, the coming apocalyptic battle between the forces of good and evil would be led by an earthly monarch, a divine agent who represented the resurrected Roman Empire much in the way Christ had embodied the triumph of God over death itself. This Last Emperor would "lay waste to all the islands and cities of the pagans, destroy all their temples with their idols, and summon all of the pagans to baptism, erecting the cross of Christ in every temple," reestablishing the Roman Empire as the vehicle for the Christian victory over evil.[17]

Though Charlemagne was crowned Roman emperor by Leo III, the resulting Carolingian dynasty, which laid the framework for society as we have come to know it, proved relatively fleeting. Competing groups would grow in influence as their monarchs, overseeing their own exploitative systems, vied over what king and what kingdom might come to embody the foretold Last Emperor and lead humanity into its apocalyptic destiny and, as one prophet had predicted, a battle against "the children of the desert," who waited just beyond the eastern borders of the lost empire.[18]

On November 27, 1095, Pope Urban II delivered a fiery address at the Council of Clermont that would change the world. Appealing to the faith's apocalyptic tradition, its fear of persecution, and the specter of looming supernatural evil, he called upon Christians to unite against "the people of Persia, an accursed and foreign race, enemies of God," who had "invaded the lands of . . . Christians and devastated them."[19] Urban II told the congregation that Christians in the East and in Jerusalem, the holy city, had been enslaved and that churches had been destroyed or converted into mosques, women and children murdered and molested, the men maimed, tortured, and slain in unthinkable fashion. "Whose duty is it to avenge this and recover that land if not yours?" he asked of the men of Europe, reminding them of the tradition of Charlemagne.[20]

When Urban II concluded, the audience erupted into shouts of "*Deus vult! Deus vult!*" ("God wills it! God wills it!").[21] They would leave Clermont and deliver sermons to their own congregations: The pope had received a divine call for a crusade against the Muslim people, and any believer willing to make the violent pilgrimage, secure the churches of the East, and take back Jerusalem would not only keep the plundered riches but also be guaranteed forgiveness of their sins and entrance into heaven.

The call to crusade was a solution to the myriad problems plaguing the church, including the ever-widening division between the East and the West, a rivalry that festered as the papacy demanded supreme authority and theological disagreements led to mutual excommunications. Urban II meant for the call to arms to assist Christians in the East in their battle with the Turks to be a gesture of goodwill in possible reconciliation between the church's two factions.

Since the Carolingian dynasty had devolved into chaos and infighting, the continent had been consumed with frenzied violence between rival nobles. It had grown so unpredictable and vicious that peasants and clergy alike were suffering, the latter drawing the most concern from the church as feuding lords had taken to stealing "the possessions of the holy church . . . by force."[22] Initially, the church had attempted to establish what came to be called the "Peace of God" movement, which served as a revival of sorts, including the display of holy relics, sermons on the virtues of armistice, and a religious decree establishing days of rest where "no one may commit murder, arson, robbery or assault, no one may injure another with a sword, club or any kind of weapon," but the violence could not be contained.[23]

In a precedent that would set the stage for countless wars and atrocities to come, the Crusades eased internal frictions in Western society by redirecting energy outward and coalescing warring factions into a united force. If the men of Europe were so intent on butchery, then so be it, but they could turn to a common enemy, an Other, and act in violent concert. As one contemporary urged the men, "You waged unauthorized war, killing one another . . . we now propose combats to you that bring praiseworthy martyrdom."[24] Urban II was speaking directly to men "who formerly misspent their time conducting private feuds against the faithful."[25] Warring groups could shed their contrasting markers and adopt a new identity based on shared narratives and common goals, becoming one European race and "soldiers of Christ."[26]

By drawing in warring parties under the same Christian banner, Urban II consolidated the church's authority over secular matters and temporarily solved the issue of internal tensions as well as paved the way for economic expansion. As the infighting had been predicated on a lack of resources, including wealth and land, the Crusades were intended to resolve the scarcity at the heart of the division, as Urban II described in his call to arms:

> Your land is shut in on all sides by the sea and mountains, and is too thickly populated. There is not much wealth here, and the soil scarcely yields enough to support you. On this account you kill and devour each other, and carry on war and mutually destroy each other. Let your hatred and quarrels cease, your civil wars come to an end, and all your dissensions stop. Set out on the road to the holy sepulcher, take the land from that wicked people, and make it your own. That land which, as the Scripture says, is flowing with milk and honey.[27]

War and genocide were cloaked in divine revelation. The horrors painted by Urban II were imagined, as was the depiction of Muslims as savages and monsters. It is telling that the Crusades were largely carried out by Europeans who lived far from Muslim societies; those who shared borders with Muslim countries found them agreeable and advanced, their cities "teeming with scholars."[28] Unencumbered by the anti-intellectual biases of Christianity, the Muslim world was awash with innovative mathematics, cutting-edge science and medicine, and a flourishing system of intellectuals and artists. As the Crusaders breached their borders, the Muslims actually regarded *them* as barbarians and "mere beasts possessing no other virtues but courage and fighting."[29]

The story Urban II told spurred a passion and energy that surprised even the pope himself. Around the continent, men, women, and children let loose simmering rage that had been largely kept at bay, particularly in regard to the scattered Jewish populations. Because of a Christian sanction against the practice of moneylending, Jews had served as a workaround as the economy of Europe matured, creating a system wherein a vulnerable population simultaneously accumulated wealth and antipathy. The rise of Christian zealotry, coupled with the faith's vilification of the Jewish people, led to a series of attacks and massacres wherein roving bands of Crusaders decided to "first avenge the Crucified upon His enemies living here among us" before "[setting] off to fight against the Turks."[30]

Like the Crusades, these atrocities were a combination of religious fervor and economic opportunism. While Christian leaders declared the Jews "of all races God's greatest enemy," they were also an isolated community who could be attacked with impunity and their wealth pilfered.[31] Crusaders traveling eastward came across Jewish communities and committed mass murder, eyewitnesses testifying they slaughtered them "without mercy," including men, women, and "children of whatever age and sex."[32] Their goods were distributed, and hefty sums were extorted from survivors in exchange for their lives. The violence was so horrific that towns full of Jews chose to commit mass suicide rather than be subject to the whims of approaching hordes. Entire communities in the German Rhineland were destroyed, and a legacy of murderous anti-Semitism was set in motion.

The brutality continued as Crusaders crossed into Muslim territory and slayed noncombatants, assaulted women, and "cut into pieces some of their babies, impaled others on wooden spits and roasted them over a fire."[33] They rampaged for years until they reached Jerusalem in June of 1099. Following a grueling siege, they breached the defenses and flooded into the city, where they carried out a swift and violent ethnic cleansing. Muslims and Jews alike were killed. "Piles of heads, hands and feet lay in the houses and streets," and Crusaders "seized infants by the soles of their feet from their mothers' laps or cracked and dashed them against walls or broke their necks."[34] Crusaders coated in blood and viscera helped themselves to "vast treasures of gold and silver . . . [and] stores of grain, wine, and oil" and laid claim to households while their prior owners and families bled out on the floor.[35]

When the deed was finished, the Crusaders cleaned themselves and rededicated the holy places in the city, while the few survivors were forced to labor and made to gather the corpses and scrub the gore from the streets and buildings. The casualties were so vast that the piles of bodies stood "as big as houses."[36] Once all evidence of the massacre was disposed of, the first action of the Crusaders was to hold a market to sell plundered goods and profit off the spoils.

The success of the Crusades, in both territorial acquisition and the galvanizing of energy, established an era of papal dominance, firmly placing the church ahead of temporal bodies. This invested in the papacy what Pope Innocent III would call "a fullness of power" and created the possibility of a world unified in the faith of Christianity. In this reality, the "priests of Christ" would be considered, in former pope Gregory VII's words, "the fathers and masters of kings and princes and of all the faithful," a fulfillment of an arrangement he claimed Constantine, "lord of all the kings and princes of nearly the whole world, plainly understood."[37]

To bolster this understanding, the church, still holding a monopoly over knowledge in its domain, relied on a series of malicious forgeries that cemented its control over history and life as it was experienced by kings and peasants alike. Monarchs, their nobles, and their advisors were still largely illiterate and unprepared to wrestle with the church over such matters, leaving them obedient and in a system where, as Innocent III declared, "the empire derives its origin and its final authority from the papacy" and "the emperor is raised to his position by the pope who blesses him, crowns him, and invests him with the empire."[38]

Building off the initial Crusade, the church continued to call the disparate peoples to action under the banner of Christ, assembling armies and resources at the beck and call of the pope. They focused on expanding Christendom and fortifying church interests at the borders, but also on bringing to heel factions of so-called heretical Christians who strayed from orthodoxy, including the Cathars in southern France. Calling for an internal crusade, the church ordered the faithful to "meet the forerunners of [the] Antichrist and strike down the ministers of the Old Serpent."[39] Seeing an opportunity to expand its own influence, the French crown joined in this task and partnered with the church to kill tens of thousands of Cathars guilty of no crime beyond violating monotheistic decrees.

For two decades, this internal conflict, the Albigensian Crusade, saw countless atrocities. In hunting insurgents nestled among communities of non-Cathars, Crusaders slayed people indiscriminately. One abbot ordered, "Kill them. The Lord knows who are his own."[40] The nastiness of the struggle motivated innovative cruelty and strategic torture, including one incident at the fortress of Cabaret where a commander navigated a castle siege by waging psychological war. After kidnapping a hundred men from a neighboring town, he "gouged out their eyes, and cut off their noses and lips," leaving "a single man with a single eye" to guide the survivors back to their fortress.[41]

The threat of an internal enemy and dangerous autonomous thought inspired the Inquisition, a program by the church to root out surviving heretics, project authority across the continent, and either cure sinful independence or intimidate it into silence. This operation built off the Albigensian Crusade, which saw Crusaders execute and burn Cathars "with joy in their hearts" and created a system by which further punishments and coercions could be carried out on the populace at large.[42] Agents from the church were dispatched far and wide to establish investigations into the population's behaviors and encouraged people to turn on their neighbors, families, and friends, offering to split the discovered heretic's possessions with the informants.

Beginning with Pope Innocent IV's *Ad extirpanda* decree, the church authorized inquisitors to "force all captured heretics to confess and accuse their accomplices by torture," rationalizing the mercilessness by saying, "These heretics are true thieves, murderers of souls, and robbers of the sacraments of God."[43] Sanctioned strategies included starvation to "subdue unwilling witnesses," the usage of the same rack that had been inflicted on Christians by Roman authorities and "dislocated the joints of the wrists and ankles," and eventually the punishment of burning, wherein the heretic would be coated in "grease, fat, or some other combustible substance" before being set aflame.[44]

The church was shockingly organized in its operation of the Inquisition. Copious notes and records were necessary to keep track of the investigations and punishments within the populace, in terms of both who was executed and who survived but carried their penalties with them. To threaten others into submission, many of the people found guilty by the inquisitors were forced to display categorizing symbols, much like the Jewish population, which had to wear markers that kept them separate from the population at large. To run afoul of the church and state could lead to death, but even escaping execution did not mean the individual would not suffer economic and societal retribution. To maintain status meant conforming to all expectations.

This cruel business constituted not just the emergence of administrative law enforcement in the medieval world but the birth of a new bureaucratic system that relied on distributed authority and specialized knowledge. The church had maintained control based on its monopoly over reading, writing, and history, but the operation of its widespread and exhaustive system of oppression meant this monopoly was not long for the world. The state and its aristocratic class would begin to accumulate knowledge and wrest power away for themselves.

On Christmas Eve of 1294, Cardinal Benedetto Caetani was elected by the papal conclave and adopted the name Boniface VIII. He succeeded Celestine V, who had so despised the position that he had resigned in order to return to his previous life, but Boniface VIII quickly made use of his newfound authority and had his predecessor imprisoned in order to prevent any challenges to his supremacy.

Whereas Celestine V had been a quiet and humble leader, Boniface VIII was prone to violent outbursts and reveled in the luxury of the office. Born a noble, he enjoyed the trappings of wealth and forwarded a precursor of the prosperity gospel, decreeing, "He who is healthy, rich, and fortunate has Paradise on Earth."[45] He established a jubilee at the turn of the fourteenth century that offered a "full and copious pardon" for the sins of any believer making the pilgrimage to Rome, ensuring a spike in visitors and donations that would keep the church's treasuries well stocked.[46] In political matters, he reaffirmed the church's authority over the kingdoms of men, regularly intervening in disputes and wars.

This brashness led to Boniface VIII's downfall and would serve to realign the dynamic between church and state for generations to come.

As had been the case two centuries before, when Urban II innovated the Crusades to dispel internal tensions, the church's dominance was threatened by temporal hostilities. England and France, with their perpetual skirmishes, had begun levying taxes on the church and clergy to raise funds for warring. Boniface VIII was quick to condemn the taxes, reminding the kingdoms of the Great Chain of Being and that all authority sprang from God and his church.

Boniface VIII met his match in the form of Philip IV of France, a headstrong monarch whose stubbornness earned him the moniker *le roi de fer,* or "the Iron King." Philip IV sent the pope a strong rebuke and actively denied Rome its resources. In response, Boniface VIII delivered a scolding message that God, and by proxy the church, had the power "to pluck down, destroy, scatter, rebuild, and plant," a reiteration of past missives stating that while the faith was immortal, kingdoms could be replaced.[47] Upon reading this lecture, the king had the message "burned in his presence" and announced his defiance with "the sound of the trumpet through the streets of Paris."[48]

Distraught, Boniface VIII overplayed his hand and released what would come to be known as the *Unam sanctam* on November 18, 1302. This papal bull argued for the reinstitution of papal dominance over all worldly affairs, declaring, "Every human creature is subject to the Roman pontiff," a hierarchy "altogether necessary to salvation."[49] Philip IV predictably rejected this interpretation, asking French nobles "whether the kingdom was to stand immediately under God, or to be subject to the pope."[50]

This insolence inspired Boniface VIII to excommunicate Philip IV, who then leveled over two dozen charges against the pope, including heresy and the wrongful death of Celestine V. Boniface VIII was largely unfazed until September 7, 1303, when two thousand mercenaries under Philip IV's orders arrived at the papal residence in Anagni shouting, "Death to Pope Boniface! Long live the king of France!"[51] Faced with approaching soldiers, Boniface VIII ignored calls to resign his post, likening himself to Christ in saying he had been "betrayed like Jesus" before cladding himself in the cloak of St. Peter and donning the crown of Constantine. He was beaten bloody, but his life was spared. The army held him captive for three days before releasing him. He died a month later; a contemporary, remarking on his rise and fall, and by proxy the trajectory of the power of the church, said, "He entered like a fox, reigned like a lion, and went out like a dog."[52]

Philip IV seized the papacy and relocated the seat of Christianity to Avignon, France, setting the stage for seven consecutive French popes serving the whims of the court, beginning with Clement V, who, as a "gesture of goodwill," reversed Boniface VIII's decree of papal sovereignty.[53] Ever dogged, Philip IV continued his war against his deposed rival, seeking a posthumous trial and an exhumation of the dead pope's bones "so that they could be burned."[54] To broker a peace and settle matters, Clement V "acquitted Philip" of all wrongdoing and, for good measure, "praised his zeal."[55]

The triumph of Philip IV over papal dominance was a turning point in history and a radical reorganization in the hierarchy of the Great Chain of Being. The supremacy of the church had been built upon a narrative that all authority sprouted from the institution, a story that relied on a monopoly on knowledge since the fall of Rome. The church had kept information under lock and key for generations, but the growth of kingdoms necessitated transfer of knowledge on a wider scale.

With society growing more complicated and institutions exercising more authority, a bureaucracy bloomed that required a new managerial class. To fill these needs, universities sprouted across Europe and educated the nobility to prepare them for operation of the nascent systems. While receiving their educations, the nobility began to realize the church had been misleading them for ages in regard to history, tradition, politics, and the rule of law. This realization led to the split of church and state, separating secular matters and what John of Salisbury would come to call "the invisible things of God."[56]

The redistribution of knowledge was a tectonic shift. Now kingdoms and their presiding nobility were able to sort through records on their own and discern truth from fiction, including the myriad documents forged by the church to further enrich itself and "despoil all kings and princes of the West."[57] Philosophically, rebuttals of gospel-based arguments for church dominance were penned, including the groundbreaking work of Marsilius of Padua, who argued the state was the "perfect self-sufficing community" and that the church had overstepped its bounds, using the Bible itself as proof that "Christ did not claim temporal power in this life."[58]

Similarly, Philip IV was able to assert independence from the church by way of a council of lawyers who had received quality educations in the history of papal maneuvering. This laid the foundation for a reshuffling the church was ill prepared to stave off. The vision of a world unified under the banner of the cross, subject to the whims and direction of the pope, and herded by the veiled authority of information monopolies had given way to a new order of national identities armed with the weapon of knowledge.

This realignment saw challenges to Christian mythology as well as the jurisdiction of the church. Whereas heretics had been murdered, tortured, and burned at the turn of the century, a prevailing distrust of the pope now engulfed the popular imagination. A new idea of an *antichristus mysticus,* or the Antichrist as a false prophet, emerged, and critics of figures like Boniface VIII began to fear "a false pope who would attack the evangelical way of life."[59] Orders like the Franciscans were highly and vocally critical of Boniface VIII's extravagance and arrogance, labeling him the Antichrist and chastising him as "an open destroyer."[60] Another Franciscan accused the pope of representing the "Abomination of Desolation standing in the holy place," or the despoiling of the holy church.[61]

Among the new class of learned individuals was a movement furthering the case for the prioritization of the state over the church. Dante Alighieri, the Italian writer best known for penning *The Divine Comedy,* called Boniface VIII a "devouring whirlpool, ever engulfing, but restoring nothing," and argued that "the Church is not the cause of the power of Europe, and therefore not of its authority either."[62] Enlightened by his education and obsessed with loosening the control of the corrupt church, Dante penned *The Inferno,* an epic poem that engaged in its own construction of history, tying the legitimacy of his culture to the legacy of the Greeks and Romans while restructuring the hierarchy to include the mythology of Christianity within the purview of the state. To this end, Dante's infamous trek to the deepest recesses of hell, guided by the Roman poet Virgil, finds the realm swimming with former popes.

Whereas the church had long maintained that the wickedness of man was responsible for the fall of Rome and subsequent suffering, critics informed by history charged that the church itself had failed the people. Faith in the institution waned. Obvious corruption and lust for power seemed to soak every action, every sermon, every prophecy and decree. "The root of this blasphemy, which hath turned the church upside down," charged English priest and philosopher John Wycliffe, "is found in this, that the clergy, shrinking from the poverty of Christ, entangle themselves thus with the world."[63]

Wycliffe tried to remedy this problem by translating the Holy Bible from Latin into the developing language of English, an act of heresy for which his work was condemned and burned in totality, and it was "decreed that his bones be exhumed and cast out of consecrated ground."[64] Though Wycliffe was denounced and his work destroyed, the church was unable to stem the tide of secular opposition. No longer would the pope and Catholic Church be the center of the world. Developing nation-states would determine the ebb and flow of history.

With the church sufficiently silenced, the English and French were able to have their all-out conflict, this iteration taking the form of the Hundred Years' War, which raged off and on from 1337 to 1453. The issue was whether France would remain independent or whether the English crown would assert sovereignty over its neighbor. The grueling nature of the fighting would not just change the idea of warfare but invigorate a sense of identity that took the tribalism of the migration period after the collapse of Rome and captured it in a larger, national sense. The hatred and antagonism felt between the two parties inspired—much like the identification of Romanness emanated from opposition to "barbarian" threats—a cohesion among their peoples that led to shared narratives of purpose, uniting and inspiring historical myths, and competing claims of divine purpose. The power of the pope had been curbed, but the authority of divine mandate remained potent.

While the English called on "God to defend our right" and ordered troops to "advance banners, in the name of God," the French bolstered their cause with contending religious purpose. Foremost in the French imagination was Joan of Arc, a young woman who claimed she received visions from God beginning at the age of thirteen. As a teenager, Joan reportedly witnessed "dazzling light," a "radiance" that sprung from angelic figures who reported to her a message from the almighty creator, who wished "to deliver the people of France."[65] Word that God harbored "pity for the kingdom of France" was delivered by Michael the Archangel, heaven's general in the supernatural battle against Satan, reframing the struggle against England as nothing short of an apocalyptic holy war.[66]

Joan's visions were celebrated as proof that France's battle against England was favored by God. It represented a continuation of the Bible that extended beyond the pages of the gospels and through the legacy of Rome, and authored a new story in which France itself was the chosen nation of the universe. Her revelations changed the conflict from a tug-of-war over temporal power to a religious struggle to determine whom God preferred. Eventually Joan would be captured and burned alive by the English, wearing a placard reading, "Heretic relapser, apostate, idolater," and her execution would become yet another religious skirmish between the English and French.[67] While England's King Henry VI assured his nobles that "the wretched woman" saw the flames and "plainly confessed the spirits that she often claimed had appeared to her were evil, lying spirits," the French account tells of a martyr using her last seconds of life as the blaze consumed her to cry out, "Yes my voices were from God, my voices have not deceived me."[68]

In the end, France prevailed in the war and preserved its independence, but the incessant fighting and suffering took a toll. The dueling monarchies ceded power in pursuit of funds and resources to further their claims while a small window for revolution and upheaval opened.

And a plague unlike any seen before or after, a sweeping apocalypse that left countries littered with corpses, would change literally everything.

Called "the most terrible of all the terrors," the Black Death raced across Europe through the middle of the fourteenth century, killing as many as twenty-five million on the continent and two hundred million people worldwide.[69] The bubonic plague was carried by fleas infesting rats and crisscrossed the continent via the shipping and commercial routes of the developing economy. Sufferers were racked with chills, fever, and intense pain, their bodies ravaged and gangrenous. Entire populations were destroyed, contemporaries writing of such widespread death that each morning found corpses laid in "the doors of the houses," the tragedy becoming so common that "no further account was taken of a dying man than is today taken of the merest cattle."[70]

With bodies decaying in the streets, filling mass graves, and swelling the rivers, it felt as if the final judgment of God had been handed down, as if the Four Horsemen of the Apocalypse had been loosed and Pestilence ravaged the land. Explanations varied as to who or what was responsible, ranging from the corrupted church to an earthquake in Italy rumored to have released toxic vapors from the bowels of the Earth. To appease an angry God and perhaps win some semblance of salvation, hordes of frenzied penitents wandered the countryside "barefoot in sackcloth, sprinkled with ashes, weeping, praying, tearing their hair, carrying candles, relics, sometimes with ropes around their necks or beating themselves with whips."[71] These mobs descended upon the cities and villages of the time, holding impromptu sermons that preached the time of tribulation was at hand and targeting heretics and so-called enemies of God.

Once more, as had been the case in the Crusades, Jewish populations suffered the brunt of the violence as "a general rumor spread . . .

that this epidemic came from the Jews, and that the Jews had cast great poisons in the wells and springs throughout the world, in order to sow the plague and to poison Christendom."[72] As Jewish populations were largely considered separate from the societies within which they resided, their presence during a time of crisis and developing nationalism gave way to rumors of an "international conspiracy" with "an alliance of enemies without and enemies within."[73] With the growing sense that nations were embraced and championed by God, the only explanation for widespread suffering would be a concentrated effort by internal traitors in league with Satan in his ongoing war with heaven.

Jews were continually vilified as evil and inhuman. Libel spread that they "thirsted for human blood" and carried out satanic rituals in which children were heartlessly tortured before being "fixed to a cross in mockery of the Lord's passion" and sacrificed.[74] These baseless rumors, which echoed the stories told of early Christians operating in the catacombs, fueled widespread discrimination and the murder of Jews, including incidents during the plague where "evidence" proved the pestilence was their doing. In one instance, on St. Valentine's Day 1349, Jewish families were rounded up in Strasbourg, Germany, taken to the cemetery, and burned alive on a wooden platform. A witness reported that "everything that was owed to the Jews was cancelled, and the Jews had to surrender all pledges and notes that they had taken for debts."[75] Once more, their wealth was stolen and redistributed "among the workingmen proportionately."

The enormous toll of the plague would change the economic and political structure of Europe. With declining populations, workers found themselves in newfound territory as their labor became in high demand. This meant they could charge more for their services and leverage employers against one another to drive up wages and secure better treatment. This new alignment upset the Great Chain of Being and its inherent top-down system of labor relations, prompting the powerful to decry workers' turning to "evil courses" and lamenting that their behaviors were unholy and amounted to the wicked nations of "Gog and Magog" having "returned from hell."[76]

The kingdoms of Europe attempted to rein in laborers by passing laws requiring peasants to continue operating under the oppressive limits of feudalism that favored the nobility, but with their knights, the wealthy's law-enforcement apparatus, busy with the Hundred Years' War, these laws were largely ignored. Peasants left their estates and relocated to the growing cities of Europe, where the church and nobility exercised less sway, and were able to climb in status and rank. Trade, advancements in technology, education, and a budding middle class of artisans and merchants presented a new challenge to the past order.

This nascent grouping created in the peasants a "consciousness of their own interests."[77] Removed from constant church propaganda and the threat of noble enforcement, the people were able to educate themselves and converse about their status in life, finding in the process that their oppression was cruel and unnecessary. In France, there rose a revolutionary movement that came to be known as the Jacquerie, which believed "it is the lords, and knights, and esquires who have betrayed the Kingdom of France" and that "it would be a good deed to destroy them all."[78] To this end, bands of revolutionaries swept across the kingdom, capturing and murdering every noble, knight, and bureaucrat they could find, inspiring uprisings and attracting recruits before being violently suppressed by noble forces who "flung themselves upon hamlets and villages, putting them to flame and pursuing poor peasants in houses, fields, vineyards and forest to be miserably slaughtered."[79]

While their nobility battled among themselves, the English people joined their French brethren in revolution. In a 1381 event dubbed the Great Rising, the merchant and peasant classes coalesced in opposition to the economic structure of feudalism, calling on the nobility to abolish the institution of serfdom and release workers from unfair and exploitative obligations. The movement was spurred by revolutionaries like Father John Ball, who broke from the church and used the scripture and Christian mythology to undermine inequality, preaching, in a taste of revolutions to come, that "from the beginning all men were created equal by nature, and that servitude had been introduced by the unjust and evil oppression of men, against the will of God."[80]

The Great Rising began with violence in opposition to tax collectors looking to steal wealth from workers to bolster the military exploits of the nobility. Soon it blossomed into widespread rebellion. Countless numbers of peasants and merchants lashed out against the bureaucratic machinery, destroying stores of records detailing debts and obligations, freeing prisoners, organizing strikes, and murdering officials.

They fought their way to London, where they laid siege to the capital, executed the wealthy with reckless abandon, set fire to the luxurious homes and headquarters of the nobility, razed government buildings to the ground, and surrounded the court of King Richard II. As the skyline of London blistered with fire and smoke, the king was forced to meet with the revolutionaries on June 14 in Mile End, where the people's army demanded the abolition of serfdom, blanket immunity for their uprising, and a new economic order that granted autonomy to the people. Richard II relented and "freed and quitted" workers of "bondage."[81] The celebration was short-lived, however, as the ruling class quickly defaulted on their promises as they were "granted under compulsion."[82]

Like the Jacquerie, the revolution came to a bloody end as the powerful suppressed the people and hunted down the responsible parties in order to make an example of them. John Ball, whose words would later inspire both the American and French Revolutions, was "dragged, hanged, and beheaded" before "his dead body was quartered and sent to the four states of the realm" to be displayed as a warning to potential radicals.[83]

Despite these furious remedies, the damage was done and the exploitative system of feudalism had been dealt a mortal blow. The Great Chain of Being would need to be reimagined to include some human dignity and rudimentary rights for even the peasant class. For the hierarchy to survive, the total exploitation of peasant labor needed to be replaced by the utilization of another group of peoples. Again, the alignment of in-groups and out-groups changed, this time dividing the world between the Europeans, a relatively fresh identification, and every other inhabitant of the planet Earth.

Power had shifted since the fall of Rome from the total dominance of the church to the unquestionable sovereignty of kings. Now a fluctuating arrangement grew between the noble class and urban merchants. The new partnership sought to remedy internal frictions: In an echo of the efforts of Pope Urban II, they would redirect energies and violence outward in pursuit of economic growth and hidden by the cloak of a religious crusade. Europe had been sufficiently cultivated and divided, and now it was time to conquer the rest of the world.

- CHAPTER THREE -

The Empire of Man over Inferior Creatures

The Taíno people called their island Ayiti, or "Land of the High Mountains." By the late fifteenth century they enjoyed a complex social and political culture with interlocking systems of tribes; advanced customs, norms, and traditions; and a "vibrant culture" of art and expression.[1] They relied on a sophisticated understanding of science that rivaled that of peoples around the world, particularly in astronomy, and their ability to chart the movement of the stars aided in their navigation as they traversed what has come to be known as the Caribbean.

Undergirding this society was a polytheistic religion known as *cemísm* that focused on co-ruling deities, one male and one female, presiding over a universe with "an inherent tendency toward entropy and disorder."[2] To stave off chaos, the Taíno pursued sustainable relationships with the environment and each other, a desire aided by the dual nature of their gods. Men and women in Ayiti enjoyed relatively equal footing in the political and social structures, and the society was one of mutual cooperation and communal care.

Over four thousand miles away, across the Atlantic Ocean, in a society that functioned more or less as a twisted, dark reflection of the Taíno, the kingdom of Spain was entering a new age with the ascent of King Ferdinand II and Queen Isabella I. Dubbed "the Catholic King and Queen" by Pope Alexander VI, the couple used the faith to oppress their subjects, engaging in wars masked by religious fervor and instituting Inquisitions to surveil, prosecute, and police behavior and thought within their realm.

In March of 1492 they targeted Spain's Jewish population. Describing Jews as a constant threat to Christendom, a state within a state that worked, as the ruling couple believed, to "steal faithful Christians from our holy Catholic faith" and to "subvert them to their own wicked belief and conviction," the couple issued the Alhambra Decree to "prohibit all interaction between the said Jews and Christians and banish them from all our kingdoms."[3] The Jewish people were given four months to either convert to Christianity or else abandon their possessions and property and leave the kingdom in exile. Once more, they were persecuted and scapegoated, their resources taken by force to be used for political purposes cloaked in weaponized faith.

That summer, Italian explorer Christopher Columbus proposed an expedition that might discover a new route to Asia. The Catholic King and Queen were not his first audience: He had already approached Portugal, Genoa, and Venice but had been turned away when their courts determined his calculations were faulty. In Spain, Columbus found a more receptive audience, especially as he touted his expedition as a religious cause that might allow the monarchs to gain profit and power, as well as possibly fund a new crusade to once more liberate the Holy Land and fulfill the long-predicted Last Emperor prophecy of an exalted leader marshaling the forces of good in an apocalyptic final battle.

With their support, Columbus sailed west with the intent of opening up a trade route while promising the "conversion to our holy faith" of India's population.[4] Infamously by mistake, he would reach the continent that would come to be named North America, where he would enslave, terrorize, and massacre the peoples he found there. He believed God had led him to this discovery and "wished to work a miracle" in his voyage.[5] In his later years, looking back on his achievements, Columbus fashioned himself as a new messiah in the mold of Jesus Christ himself and a harbinger of the coming apocalypse, writing, "Of the new heaven and of the new earth . . . [God] made me the messenger and He showed me where to find it."[6]

Columbus's megalomania colored the so-called discovery of the so-called New World from the very beginning. Confronted with the existence of peoples outside the world known to him, Columbus needed to incorporate them into the European frame, and his only means of doing so was to rely on otherworldly concepts of the supernatural, or the realm of religion. Though he had come upon North America by mishap, Columbus immediately proclaimed himself the herald of a new revelation and a new age, and declared the conquering and subjugation of the Natives was necessary to bring about the end of the world and salvation was only possible should Spain "convert the earth and all the islands to the Lord."[7]

The Indigenous peoples received him kindly. His accounts noted the collective nature of their lives, writing, "They refuse nothing that they possess . . . [and] invite any one to share it and display as much love as if they would give their hearts."[8] Witnessing this kindness, Columbus saw only the opportunity for plunder of "incalculable gold."[9] His reports to Spain promised the monarchs "as many slaves as they shall order," considering that the people had "no iron nor steel nor weapons, nor are they fit to use them . . . they are wonderfully timid."[10] All in all, he judged them "fit to be ordered about and made to work."[11]

From 1494 to 1500, Columbus served as governor and overseer of the island that would be renamed Hispaniola; he was as inept and disastrous in this role as he was as a navigator. He ruled the Taíno people as a tyrant, requiring massive tributes of gold or cotton with bodily mutilation as a consequence for failure. The Taíno were forced to labor and thrust into the *encomienda* system, a version of the feudal economy imported from Europe, wherein their work and land were focused for Spanish profit. Columbus was unable to control his men, resulting in widespread anarchy and incalculable cruelties committed by roving militias. So inept was Columbus's leadership that he would be arrested and returned to Spain in chains before the charges of tyranny against him were dropped. He spent the rest of his life attempting to rehabilitate his image and save his legacy, but the damage caused to the Taíno people and the people of the Americas was already done.

This wanton violence and introduction of new diseases led to what would be called "the Great Dying." Before the Europeans came it is estimated there were upwards of sixty million Indigenous people on the continent. Through war, genocide, famine, and disease, roughly 90 percent, or fifty-six million, would perish, a tragedy so massive it actually cooled the climate of the Earth.[12] A native of Yucatán reflected on the development, writing of his people's past, "There was then no sickness; they had no aching bones; they had then no high fever . . . at that time the course of humanity was orderly. The foreigners made it otherwise when they came here."[13] The Europeans, driven by sanctimony, received the suffering and dying masses as a blessing from the heavens, one colonizer exulting, "It appears visibly that God wishes that they yield their place to new peoples."[14]

Those who were not killed by disease or starvation suffered unbelievable cruelties as their civilizations were pushed to the point of destruction. Wishing to escape the misery, thousands upon thousands chose suicide and instead "plunged off cliffs . . . poisoned themselves . . . starved themselves."[15]

The universe, as the Taíno long feared, had descended into chaos.

The "discovery" of the Indigenous people, their land, and their resources constituted a paradigm shift of historic proportions. Like the dichotomous nature of the Roman concepts of "civilization" and "barbarian"—a malleable, constantly changing denotation wielded to conquer and brutalize while also allowing acceptance for populations when politics demanded it—the world was once more divided between an in-group and an out-group. The lens through which all relations would be seen and operated positioned the colonizers as the pinnacle of human achievement and the Indigenous people as "savages" in need of shepherding.

The Indigenous peoples, with their symbiotic, sustainable relationship with the environment, were considered several stages behind in the "natural" evolution of societies and judged for how they contrasted with European nations. This disparity, on one hand, might have been seen as an alternative, especially as the Indigenous people maintained complex societies that enjoyed relative communal, interdependent structures while also refusing a "need" to grow, conquer, and expand, but for Europeans desperate for profit, it was an opening and rationalization for the inhuman measures they would employ.

The spiritual foundation for this new age of pillaging was laid in 1452 by Pope Nicholas V in the papal bull *Dum diversas,* granting Portugal the "full and free power" over "pagans and other infidels and all enemies of Christ," who "might be invaded, conquered, plundered, and subjugated, and their persons reduced to perpetual slavery," their wealth and resources "converted forever to [Portugal's] use and advantage."[16] Building off the Augustinian logic of good persecution in the name of Christ, as well as the Crusades' positioning as legitimized holy war, the stage was set for subjugation.

In 1493, following Columbus's expeditions, Pope Alexander VI issued the *Inter caetera,* which granted the territory of the "New World" to Ferdinand and Isabella and their successors, including "all the islands, and main lands discovered," but noting that the donation was dependent on the Spanish dispatching "upright men . . . to instruct the natives and inhabitants in the Catholic faith."[17]

This gifted the Spanish cover for their crimes as, once more, Christians were tasked with fighting supernatural evil, meaning whatever tactics they used were both appropriate and necessary. The New World meant, within the Christian mythology, a change in apocalyptic narrative, and now the conversion of the Indigenous people—and the accompanying exploitation of their labor, destruction of their cultures, and any resulting woe—was essential to hastening the glorious end of the world.

Operating within the church's command, the Spanish instituted

"The Requirement," a statement that served as a distillation of the Christian mythology, positioned the authority of the pope and church, and named the Catholic monarchs as "subduers of the barbarous nations" and Spain as the chosen empire of God.[18] Natives were forced to exist within it, consider the Spanish their superiors, welcome missionaries to teach them the ways of Christianity and civility, and forfeit their land, resources, and labor. Any attempt to "wickedly and intentionally delay" the implementation, they were cautioned, would lead the Spanish to "make war . . . in all ways and manners" and subject them "to the yoke and obedience of the Church."

Those who refused this ultimatum were considered enemies of Christianity and could be dealt with accordingly. They were beaten, tortured, hunted down in their homes and the countryside, and made examples of. Entering into the agreement was the equivalent of accepting a vassal relationship in the feudal economy and bestowed a "paternal obligation" upon the Spanish, who rationalized the exploitation as a humane, noble endeavor, one practitioner writing, "We give them doctrine, teaching them how to live as men, and they give us silver, gold, or things of value."[19]

Under the guise of "civilizing" and converting the Indigenous people, Spanish forces swarmed the Caribbean and what would come to be known as North and South America, attacking existing civilizations by means of duplicity and outright viciousness, pillaging and raping as they went. In their wake, missionaries meticulously re-created the environment of the Middle Ages in Europe, instructing the people in subordination and humility, systematically deconstructing their cultures while introducing them to a Christian religion tinged with propaganda reinforcing European supremacy. The people were funneled into *reduccións,* or settlements specifically designed to obliterate their traditions, cultures, and identities, and to intentionally disrupt the communal nature of the societies that had existed before colonization.

The Indigenous people of the Caribbean, the Aztecs and Incas of Central and South America, all ensconced in complex, advanced societies, were met with murderous force in any instance where compliance was not total. In some cases they fled to the mountains, created their own societies, welcomed escaping enslaved people, and held their own. There were resistance leaders like Hatuey, who marshaled opposition among the people of Ayiti and Cuba and managed to hold out against the empire's forces for months before being captured and burned alive. Offered the opportunity to be baptized and possibly spend eternity with his oppressors in heaven, Hatuey declined, saying he "preferred to go to Hell."[20]

Witness to the birth pangs of this cruelty was the priest Bartolomé de las Casas, who had come across the ocean to spread the word of God. Once there, however, he observed terrible crimes, including the execution of freedom fighter Hatuey. Disturbed, he returned to Spain to advocate for reform, telling his countrymen that the Natives had "regarded the Spaniards as angels from Heaven" but had suffered dreadfully ever since.[21] In 1542, he penned *The Devastation of the Indies* and described horrific scenes in which Natives were burned alive, tortured, and maimed, and even one dreadful incident where Spanish soldiers had thrown infants into boiling water and screamed, "Boil there, you offspring of the devil."[22]

These efforts by de las Casas found purchase but also earned the criticism of men like Juan Ginés de Sepúlveda, a philosopher in the Spanish court and a fierce proponent of slavery and colonization. Sepúlveda supplied a rationalization of the abuses by saying, "The Spanish have a perfect right to rule these barbarians," likening the Natives' inferiority to the Spanish "as [that of] children to adults, or women to men."[23] He based his position on the reasoning of the Greek philosopher Aristotle and his concept that the world was composed of "natural masters" and "natural slaves," Sepúlveda arguing the Natives were "born to slavery" and their enslavement even "sanctioned in divine law itself."[24]

Despite the exhortations of men like Sepúlveda, de las Casas was at least somewhat successful in capturing the attention of the Spanish monarchy. In 1542 the "New Laws of the Indies for the Good Treatment and

Preservation of the Indians" were handed down to colonizers in the New World. Citing that their mission had always been "the preservation and increase of the Indians, and that they be instructed and taught in matters of our holy Catholic faith," these Spanish reforms sought to outlaw the enslavement of Natives and begin the phasing out of the despotic *encomienda* system.[25]

The *encomenderos* who had built fortunes off the system were outraged, and under the leadership of conquistador Gonzalo Pizarro, the younger half brother of Francisco Pizarro, who had spearheaded the assault on the Incas, they armed themselves in open defiance. They murdered Spanish officials, including the viceroy of Peru, and took territory for themselves. Remarking on the demoralizing turn of events, de las Casas denounced the revolt as "inspired by Lucifer" and criticized the *encomenderos,* writing, "They cannot bring themselves to relinquish the estates and properties they have usurped, or let go their hold on the Indians . . . they are dishonoring God and robbing and destroying the king."[26]

Eventually Pizarro and his conspirators were overcome, but their revolt ultimately succeeded, as word from Spain arrived that the New Laws would be softened, the *encomienda* system would be preserved, and the brutalizing of the Natives would continue largely unabated. Monarchies had come to rely on mercenaries and private operators for their functioning, and the individuals charged with carrying out the business of empire served their homelands and faith insomuch as it coincided with their own interests. This tenuous arrangement ensured the exploitation would continue despite the well-intentioned protestations of people like de las Casas, leading to even more suffering by more organized and concentrated measures.

The Great Dying set off by the Columbian Exchange, as well as developments in European perspectives regarding the fates of Indigenous people, meant someone else would need to supply the labor necessary for the dirty work of empire to continue. That weight, as well as the fate of developing capitalism, would land squarely on the shoulders of enslaved Africans.

In 1510, the Catholic King Ferdinand ordered "the best and strongest available" slaves to be exported to Santo Domingo for use on sugar plantations.[27] Thus began the transatlantic slave trade, which saw anywhere from twelve to twenty million human beings captured, transported, bought and sold, exploited, beaten, raped, and tortured.[28]

The general concept of slavery is as old as civilization itself, and the practice of enslaving human beings for the purpose of labor and profit has been with us since at least the beginning of recorded history. The transatlantic slave trade was novel and insidious in not only how its operation married cruelty and developing knowledge but in how it created the concept of race as a distinction for capitalistic purposes and linked the abuse of a race of people to the economic fate of nations and companies. In the past, anyone might become a slave at any moment, typically if their land was conquered in a war or they happened to worship the wrong god. Now the very notion of who could or should be enslaved meant people of a certain color or origin, by their birth alone, were considered unworthy or undeserving of freedom.

This invention was anchored in religious mythology. Europeans desperate for riches convinced themselves that the people of Africa had been singled out for their lot in life because of the actions of the biblical character Ham. In the Book of Genesis, following the Great Flood, Noah, the savior and redeemer of humankind, got so drunk on his homegrown wine he blacked out naked in his tent. His son Ham was unlucky enough to find him and, in the interest of his father's dignity, covered him up, an act that so enraged Noah he cursed his progeny to be "a servant of servants . . . unto his brethren."[29]

One of the early adopters and promoters of this absurd lie was Portugal's Gomes Eanes de Zurara, who wrote in his work *The Chronicle of the Discovery and Conquest of Guinea* that "because of the curse which, after the Deluge, Noah laid upon his son," the men and women of Africa "should be subject to all the other races of the world."[30] In his history of those people he described them as inhuman, saying, "Without the clearness and the light of the holy faith . . . they lived like beasts."[31]

Armed with this farcical mythology, Europeans viewed the Africans as natural slaves and, considering the nature of the curse, felt that the moral need to educate them or save their souls—long the claimed goal of conquering the Indigenous people of the New World—was unnecessary. To them, Africans were irredeemable, "hideous" creatures.[32] Cannibals unworthy of anything beyond being used for labor. Animals, really, in need of taming and breaking, a classification that moved Africans outside the realm of humanity altogether, such as was witnessed in one trial concerning an incident where over a hundred enslaved people were thrown to their death in the ocean. The question was broached: "What is this claim that human people have been thrown overboard? This is a case of chattels or goods. Blacks are goods and property . . . the same as if horses had been thrown overboard."[33]

As property, these men, women, and children were purchased by Europeans in Africa, where political disarray and civil wars were stoked by colonizers as a means of continuing the supply of free labor, stacked as tightly as possible in the hulls of their ships and forced to withstand a hellish trek across the world. Made to sit in one another's waste, they contracted every imaginable disease, and then often endured being chained for days on end to someone who had died. John Newton, the composer of the hymn "Amazing Grace" and himself a notorious enslaver, described checking the hulls of his ships daily and finding "the living and the dead . . . fastened together." To protect the enslaver's investment, those slaves even suspected of being ill were often removed from the population and tossed over the side of the ship to drown in the uncaring sea.

The enslavement of human beings was an incredibly lucrative and booming industry. Entrepreneurs built business empires off the operation, including the capturing and transportation of slaves, the assessment of their value, their inventorying and marketing, and their psychological conditioning, as well as the study of how to extract the maximum amount of labor before their deaths. The industry was so large and complicated and created so much wealth for the participating nations of Portugal, England, France, the Netherlands, and Spain that it inspired the creation of corporations, or businesses operating internationally with the consent and cooperation of their originating countries.

Corporations became both an extension of the state and states unto themselves, operating the transfer, sale, and management of enslaved peoples, including the branding of men, women, and children with their logos and seals as a means of record keeping. So great was the opportunity for profit that juggernauts like the Dutch East India Company and their rivals the East India Company were granted "full Power to make and declare Peace and War with any [of] the said Heathen Nations" and, with their personal militaries and navies, the ability to declare "Martial Law" for the defense of their property and acquisition of a competitor's property.[34]

Stimulated by the rise of mercantilism, trade, and city-state capitalism, growing emphasis on worldly matters inspired the rebirth of humanism, or the resurrection of the philosophies and worldviews associated with ancient Greece. Among the privileged class, the church's domination of information and literacy gave way to educated spheres of influence, beginning with intellectuals within the clergy and extending into the secular nobility with the proliferation of universities. It is no coincidence that the rationalization of slavery coincided with the reemergence of Aristotle in discourse or that the birth of capitalism corresponded with growing fascination with human affairs.

Considered one of the forebears of the Renaissance, Italian poet Petrarch had lamented in the fourteenth century that in the Middle Ages mankind had been "surrounded by darkness" and promised Europeans, "After the darkness has been dispelled our grandsons will be able to walk back into the pure radiance of the past."[35] That radiance, Petrarch believed, and the rebirth of culture, would be found eventually in the concept of *dignitas,* or human dignity.

Of course, this "dignity" was extremely limited in scope. While wealthy, white, European men pored over libraries of rediscovered texts and pondered whether God had created them or if they had created God, people of color around the world were being either used for labor or subjected to genocidal actions. Europeans' mistreatment of colonized people and the bloody, awful business of trafficking humans and destroying cultures provided the wealth that kept them living in privilege and relative comfort.

While studying the documents of the past and unearthing lost notions of politics, science, and philosophy, learned people began to realize that much of what they considered reality had been a manipulation. Preeminent and revelatory was the work of Plato, whose writings seemed to describe the secret workings of society and provide a blueprint for incredible power. Within Plato's *Republic* was the Allegory of the Cave, in which citizens were "chained foot and neck since childhood" in a cave and existed in a world of shadows that played upon the walls.[36] Unbeknownst to them, the shadows were projections from an outside world beyond their understanding, and as a result, they believed "truth to be the shadows of artificial objects."[37] Beyond the cave was freedom, or at least a truer reality, but Plato was quick to caution that not everyone was prepared to accept truth or reject the game of shadows playing out before them. Instead, chosen and enlightened people—people with the intelligence and strength to survive the shock—should serve as "guardians" for those who would remain in the cave, and use the shadows for their own noble purposes.[38]

This concept of reality within reality, or a division between life in the cave and outside of it, was another instance of the world being divided, in this case the demarcation between the masses of people and the nobility capable of domineering them. One of the first to articulate this was the Italian diplomat Niccolò Machiavelli. In his work, Machiavelli noted that notions of morality and religiosity were merely weapons. To utilize them, Machiavelli instructed, the individual "should seem to be all mercy, faith, integrity, humanity, and religion," all of it shadow puppetry to construct a world to the puppet master's advantage where "everybody sees what you appear to be, few feel what you are, and those few will not dare to oppose themselves to the many."[39]

Also weighing on Machiavelli's mind was Plato's theory of *kyklos,* or that human history and government exist in predictable cycles. Plato had asserted that "all that becomes must fall to decay," that the kingdoms of humankind played out in an expectable and tragic manner, but that if the right man with the right set of gifts might arise, that fate could be averted, or at least delayed.[40] "A true shipmaster," or effective head of state, as Plato wrote, might become a philosopher king versed in "the seasons and climates, the sky, the stars, the winds and everything else" and use their knowledge and talents to serve as "a navigator whether anyone wants it or not."[41]

Machiavelli believed such a philosopher king, armed with ancient knowledge and freed from the illusion of religious and moral obligation, might break the "cycle of history" and, through their maneuverings and mastery, steer their state away from the certain doom of deterioration. The only way, he wrote, was for great men to seize civilizations and "bring them back to their first beginnings."[42]

Among the European intellectuals, there developed an odd worldview that wrestled with the perceived "darkness" and decline of the Middle Ages, a time in which their prized humanist knowledge had been obscured, and what they might do now that it had been rediscovered and they had escaped the metaphorical cave. Lost knowledge, it was believed, could lead to a new era where the world could be shaped and even mastered.

Modern science is rooted in this philosophy and the burgeoning field of utopianism. While colonizers plundered the New World and religious officials rationalized it as preparation for the end-times, focus moved from welcoming the apocalypse to dominating the world and achieving perfection in human society within a life span. Trailblazers like Robert Boyle sought "the Empire of Man over inferior creatures," or the re-creation of the Garden of Eden and Adam's dominion over nature through the mastery of science.[43] Now the fall of man and original sin, which had doomed humankind to suffering, mortality, and a cycle of decline, might be undone through secular pursuits, reestablishing a "Heaven on Earth" without the bloodletting and finality of Armageddon.

Utopianism had previously found purchase in the Middle Ages with legends like that of Prester John, a mythological white, Christian king and messiah figure who supposedly ruled over Muslims in a distant, foreign land. Tales of Prester John's kingdom were popular and omnipresent, promising a paradise just beyond the horizon laden with "precious stones," a "great abundance of bread, wine, meat, and everything necessary for the human body," and a magical fountain where God restored the youth of the faithful.[44]

The story of Prester John was telling. The white, Christian king was supposedly a descendant of the Magi who had visited an infant Jesus Christ and had been so removed from European society as to have avoided the rot and decay of the Middle Ages. Future utopian narratives followed suit, including Thomas More's *Utopia,* which portrayed a paradisiacal society located on an island where Romans and Egyptians had shipwrecked a millennium before and the people had "acquired all the useful arts . . . known to these shipwrecked men."[45] The key to paradise, it seemed, lay in reviving past knowledge and circumventing the damage wrought by the so-called Dark Ages.

Francis Bacon, another father of modern science, laid out his own utopian vision for the future in his work *The New Atlantis,* which resurrected a hypothetical society first used by the Greeks in their discourses and centered his utopia's greatness on the denizens of Atlantis having miraculously received the Bible but having been insulated from the chaos of the last few centuries. Bacon's utopic vision was obsessed with the use of colonization in the New World, urging his fellow British citizens to pursue "empire and greatness" through the "plantation of colonies."[46] In contrast to apocalyptic narratives that sketched out the means by which society would fall, Bacon and other utopians portrayed the possible future should humanity pursue science and greatness at all costs, even the suffering of millions of human beings.

Individuals like Bacon and Boyle, both of whom actively promoted and engaged in colonization—Bacon was one of the key forces in Britain's colonization of the Americas and Boyle served as director of the East India Company—made a case that through science and human exploitation there could be a heaven on Earth. Enslavement and the destruction of cultures in the New World were now a means to an end and necessary should humanity finally, mercifully, realize its potential.

This emphasis on the domination of science over nature and humanity's pursuit of perfection would take even stranger and more sinister turns. Just as Plato had emphasized in *The Republic* that the purposeful and systematic arrangement of marriages was necessary, otherwise "stock will deteriorate," the rediscovery and reinvigoration of his work inspired men like the Italian friar and philosopher Tommaso Campanella to paint their own utopic vision based on genetic manipulation. In *The City of the Sun,* Campanella echoed the themes of More and Bacon, describing a perfect, idealized society where suffering had been erased in favor of a strictly enforced paradise where the "children are bred for the preservation of the species."[47]

This framing of Western civilization as the pinnacle of human achievement placed the dominion of European man at the center of the universe, and science as a means of harnessing the will of God. Nothing could be allowed to delay the march of progress, whether it was the fate of enslaved and oppressed peoples or the destruction of the natural world. Facts and empirical evidence made little difference. Whereas revelatory knowledge had once been the cornerstone of religion, science in the name of "progress" now became a faith all its own and the rewards of its pursuit nothing short of paradise.

Western civilization had become so enraptured with the idea of progress in the pursuit of perfection and profit that religion, or the veneration of a cosmic creator, was giving way to the unabashed worship of power and profit.

On Monday, December 10, 1520, German professor Martin Luther, surrounded by his colleagues, friends, and students, marched to the Elster Gate in Wittenberg, Germany, and approached a roaring fire. In his hand he held a copy of the papal bull *Exsurge Domine,* issued by Pope Leo X, demanding Luther "retract his errors" within a sixty-day time period, lest the church "declare this Martin, his supporters, adherents, accomplices and protectors . . . to be notorious and obstinate heretics."[48] The ultimatum had come from years of tensions between the church and Luther, whose challenges had created fractious discord in Christendom. Faced with excommunication and execution, Luther pitched the order into the flames, remarking, "Because thou hast troubled the Holy One of the Lord, may the eternal fire trouble and devour thee."[49]

The forces set in motion by Luther's posting of his Ninety-Five Theses three years prior had splintered reality once more. The domination of the Catholic Church, originating in the takeover of the Roman Empire, had been dealt a mortal blow from which wars, genocides, and world-shattering events would emerge for centuries. Now an alternative Christianity challenged the status quo—a Christianity that worked in tandem with the emerging nation-states and capitalist system.

Luther's issue with the church was its continued corruption and greed, his critique prompted by the selling of "indulgences," or absolutions of sin for those who could afford them. Calling himself "the very dregs of humanity" and his theses "one grain of dust," Luther petitioned the church to reconsider the practice and the very nature of salvation.[50] The theses were met with scorn and derision, leading Luther to label the church as "the kingdom of sin, death and hell," an abomination so great that even the mythical Antichrist "could think of nothing to add to its wickedness."[51]

That Luther's criticism took hold was made possible by new technology and an irrepressible societal desire to crawl out from under the domination of Catholicism. The invention of the printing press by Luther's fellow German Johannes Gutenberg opened the door for copies of the Bible to be procured by individuals, allowing them to make good on Luther's idea that "we are all consecrated priests through baptism" and that the church's hierarchy and monopoly on knowledge were a means of "human relegation."[52] Additionally, Luther's writing, published in pamphlets and open letters, would comprise 20 percent of all printed materials in Germany over the course of three decades.[53] The rise and spread of Protestantism was a victory of information warfare, a spiritual coup made possible by inescapable materials and appeals.

That upheaval inspired movements and uprisings challenging other entrenched institutions just as Luther had taken on the church. In Germany, radical Protestants like Thomas Müntzer took the power of the Reformation and used it to organize peasants in an attempted overthrow of the cruel, unequal economic system. Müntzer preached that "godless tyrants" had used the gospel for their own purposes, subjecting the people and exploiting them.[54] Gathering the people for revolution, Müntzer warned, "All the world must suffer a big jolt. The game will be such that the ungodly will be thrown off their seats and the downtrodden will rise."[55]

The peasants of Germany organized into armies that overtook the nobles and destroyed the churches that had been used to oppress them. The purpose was to create a fairer, new order inspired by the Reformation and the shaking up of hierarchies. In one of the high-water moments, a document called the Twelve Articles was produced—in 1525, a full two and a half centuries before the Declaration of Independence—that advocated for human liberty, representative government, labor rights, the end of serfdom, communal property, and freedom founded in the teachings of Luther, stating, "Christ has delivered and redeemed us all . . . the lowly as well as the great . . . we should be free and wish to be so."[56]

But the revolutionaries were wrong in thinking Luther believed in wide-scale leveling. For all of his troublemaking, Luther still cherished hierarchies. In response to the Twelve Articles, Luther admonished the upstarts, saying that freedom would make "Christian liberty an utterly carnal thing . . . would make all men equal, and turn the spiritual Kingdom of Christ into a worldly, external kingdom; and that is impossible."[57] However, Luther continued to believe the world required "an inequality of persons" where "some are free, some imprisoned, some lords, some subjects." When the revolutionaries continued to trouble the social order, Luther released his pamphlet *Against the Murderous, Thieving Hordes of Peasants,* calling on nobles to kill the people by any means necessary, as they "act like mad dogs" and "deserved death."[58] With Luther's blessings, the nobility marshaled armies of mercenaries and cruelly put the rebellion down. The leaders were captured, tortured, and killed, the people subject to public execution, of which one contemporary remarked, "Of hangings and beheadings there is no end."[59]

The suppression of the revolt claimed upwards of 130,000 lives.[60]

Like so many revolutionaries before and after, the peasants had made a terrible mistake in believing the new ideology of their time was meant to change everything and not just serve as a reordering of the Great Chain of Being. Though Luther maintained that each individual was their own priest, it did not mean that the individual deserved freedom or was ultimately good. The new faith still maintained that humanity was fallen, and that detestable nature would prove useful for the growing economic system.

Protestantism and capitalism influenced one another in astonishing ways. Salvation, or proof of salvation in the case of Calvinism, became an economic concern. Protestants freed from indulgences and the purview of the church would have to secure their own fates. In the case of Lutheranism, their work and accumulated wealth might denote a secular representation of their religious progress. In Calvinism, which held that salvation was preordained, wealth or financial success seemed to answer the question that Max Weber positioned as the central query of Protestantism in his landmark work *The Protestant Ethic and the Spirit of Capitalism:* "Am I one of the elect?"[61]

The fascination with human wickedness, coinciding with the rise of capitalism, shaped not only the economic direction of the world but its political and social spheres as well. Vocalized by Pierre Nicole, a Jansenist obsessed with the fallen state of humanity, this system was created, organized, and maintained around the idea that the individual was wicked and "covets all sort of Riches, Humours, Pleasures, and Desires" while living in an inherently selfish and debauched world where "each Man is naturally an Enemy to all other Men."[62] Reflecting on this pessimistic belief, and laying the foundation for modern, antagonistic, self-serving capitalism, as well as the continual notion that humanity needed to be protected from itself, Nicole would mourn, "What a Monster we harbor in our Bosoms."[63]

The rupture in Christendom had tragic consequences as political and economic divisions once more intertwined with religious faith, setting in motion terrors like the French Wars of Religion, which raged for decades. Separate conflicts motivated by the split, as well as based on continuing struggles in separate kingdoms, culminated in the Thirty Years' War, which lasted from 1618 to 1648, claimed five million lives, and wiped out an estimated fifth of the population of the Holy Roman Empire.[64] It could in many ways be considered the first world war, as it included Spain, France, England, Russia, Denmark, Poland, Sweden, and the Dutch. Six years in, a German noble lamented, "What God the omnipotent and Lord of all Lords threatened his disobedient people through the prophets had come to pass."[65]

It seemed the end of the world had arrived.

Fighting ceased with the signing of the Peace of Westphalia in 1648, a treaty that sought to bring an end to "Discords and Civil Divisions" and "a long and cruel War."[66] To settle the bloody rift between Catholics and Protestants, the accord prioritized religious freedom, or at least the opportunity for populations to choose faiths. Relatedly, the focus of society moved from the church to the state, freezing borders and making concrete the developing nation-states, and forbidding invasions of territory. Pope Innocent X, desperate to protect his authority, declared the agreement "null and void, invalid, iniquitous, unjust, condemned, rejected, absurd," but his protests proved impotent.[67]

The era of Westphalian sovereignty had emerged, and with it a new environment favoring the economic interest of accumulating capital. As early as 1625, figures like Hugo Grotius, a Dutch philosopher, called for "a common law among nations" that might overcome "a lack of restraint in relation to war, such as even barbarous races should be ashamed of."[68] The international law that blossomed in the era of Westphalian sovereignty was grounded, first and foremost, in the rights of corporations and capitalists, and in establishing the owning of property as the defining characteristic of human civilization. It is notable that as Grotius detailed his plan for international law, he was doing so on behalf of his employer, the Dutch East India Company.

Attempts to stabilize Europe and the developing economic paradigm were successful but often troubled and sometimes aided by surviving divisions and developing philosophies. From the French Wars of Religion an embryonic concept of regicide developed on both sides. The Protestant Huguenots, who had suffered persecution by the state, turned more and more to monarchomachs, or individuals who believed it was sometimes essential to kill kings who had betrayed their people. In their pamphlets and materials they declared that kings in defiance of their people became "private persons whom it is no longer necessary to obey."[69] Soon, both sides of the religious divide would come to accept the murder of kings when they veered from their favor.

Regicide and antimonarchical thinking spread from France to Scotland via the writings and efforts of George Buchanan, who believed tyrants were "justly killed" and that their sovereignty originated not with God but from "the Peoples Power," which was gifted unto the monarch and could just as easily be rescinded.[70] His work, and growing support for parliamentarian limits, created a crisis in mid-seventeenth-century England. Having been taught by his father James I that "kings are not onely GODS Lieutenants upon earth, and sit upon GODS throne, but even by GOD himselfe they are called Gods," Charles I was reticent to surrender authority.[71]

Charles's steadfast defense of royal right, as well as his marriage to a Catholic, led to a civil war beginning in 1642 that pitted the king and the entrenched nobility against Parliament and the ascendant capitalist class. He was arrested in January of 1647 and held until June, when he was taken by members of the New Model Army, a force that had developed over the course of the war and had come to be directed by General Oliver Cromwell. Seizing more and more power, Cromwell eventually made his intentions with Charles clear: "We will cut off his head with the crown upon it."[72]

Having been declared a "tyrant, traitor, murderer, and public enemy to the good people" of England, Charles was led on January 30, 1649, to a night-black scaffold in full view of a large crowd of his subjects. After he told a bishop, "I have a good cause and a gracious God on my side," his head was severed by the blow of an axe and then picked up by an executioner, who held it aloft and proclaimed, "This is the head of a traitor!"[73]

The New Model Army had developed into a radical force in England, many of its members fashioning themselves as revolutionaries forging a new, democratic order. Some worked alongside movements like the Levellers and the Diggers, which sought, respectively, popular sovereignty and something approaching what we would now consider socialist anarchy. With the king dead and the political system in flux, many of the soldiers pushed for massive, substantial reform. *An Agreement of the People,* a revolutionary document that later inspired republican documents in the Age of Revolutions, was put forward to establish a new political system based on liberty and equality and meant to "avoid both the danger of returning into a slavish condition, and the chargeable remedy of another war."[74]

But Cromwell had other plans, and on April 20, 1653, he used the New Model Army to carry out a coup and overthrow Parliament, announcing, "The Lord has done with you! He has chosen other instruments for carrying on His work, that are more worthy. It is the Lord hath taken me by the hand, and set me on to do this thing."[75] Like the men envisioned by Plato and Machiavelli, Cromwell had seized history and was bending it to his will.

In the nearly five years Cromwell ruled as "lord protector," England was a military theocracy, its society dominated by repressive Puritan Protestantism, whose authority was enforced by the New Model Army and its generals. After Cromwell's death, his son Richard became protector for less than a year before the monarchy was restored and Charles II assumed the mantle of his executed father. For his part in the overthrow of the crown, Oliver Cromwell's body would be exhumed, hanged, decapitated, and dumped unceremoniously in a hole.

The Restoration following Oliver Cromwell's domination was short-lived, as remaining tensions, divisions, and paranoia still festered under the surface of British society. Five years into the new era, a plague ravaged London, killing roughly one hundred thousand people; almost immediately, societal suspicions pointed toward Catholic conspirators. A year later, the Great Fire of London destroyed the city, and rumors focused on "a Plot of the Dutch and the French and Papists."[76] Anti-Catholic paranoia in seventeenth-century England reached its zenith around 1678 when serial perjurer Titus Oates fabricated what came to be known as "the Popish Plot," a conspiracy theory that King Charles II had been "marked out for destruction" by the Catholic Church.[77]

Oates's falsehoods surprisingly made their way to the highest ranks of society, including the king and his court, who listened to outlandish stories about a corrosive state within a state. The public was obsessed with the plot, and the story circulated through society as Oates profited off his newfound fame and celebrity. Parliament investigated rumors of this deep state and stunningly declared, "The lords and commons are of opinion, that there hath been and still is, a damnable and hellish plot, contrived and carried on by the popish recusants, for assassinating the king, for subverting the government, and for rooting out and destroying the protestant religion."[78]

These stories dominated the English imagination and inspired baseless rumors of invasions and murderous subterfuge, but, like most grifters, Oates could not help himself. After pointing his finger at the queen and her confidants, he was arrested, publicly humiliated, and cast from his position of influence. But what Oates had tapped into was a deep, deep paranoia that remained from both the schism of Catholicism and Protestantism and the founding suspicious ethos of Christianity.

Just a few years after Oates's fall from grace, James II, who had previously served as Duke of York and leader of the Royal African Company, ascended to the throne, converted to Catholicism, and married Mary of Modena, a devout Catholic. The birth of their son James Francis Edward sparked a crisis as the possibility of a Catholic dynasty terrified a society still obsessed with papal interference. James only made matters worse as he attempted to reestablish the absolute sovereignty of the monarchy.

In June of 1688 a coded letter was sent by a group of seven British nobles to William of Orange in the Netherlands. Claiming "the people are so generally dissatisfied" and "the great part of the nobility and gentry are as much dissatisfied," these men invited William, who was married to James's daughter Mary, to invade England.[79] To prepare for the takeover, mass propaganda campaigns lionized William while spreading lies, rumors, and misinformation about James's loyalties and whether his son was legitimate or a "changeling . . . smuggled into the Queen's bedchambers by Catholic intriguers."[80]

Financed by Dutch capital and supported by the Dutch military, William landed in England on November 5, 1688. By the end of the year, he had assumed control of the kingdom and James had fled for France. As monarchs, William and Mary accepted a new constitutional monarchy that worked alongside Parliament in ruling the land and ushered in a new economic system that began to look a lot like the capitalist order of the Dutch, who had carried out a bloodless invasion and revolution to install one of their own.

In this new era, where the power of monarchs was giving way to capitalists exploiting the people and resources of the world, the British Empire became the dominant force on Earth, and their plundering of other societies, as well as the ramifications of their colonial ambitions and progress centered on domination, would have unintended consequences that would remake civilization in ways unimaginable.

"Western civilization" was picking up speed, and the shadows on the wall were changing shape.

- CHAPTER FOUR -

To Begin the World over Again

For the faithful in Virginia, there were signs 1675 would be a tumultuous year. "A large comet . . . streaming like a horse's tail" illuminated the night sky for a week's time before disappearing over the horizon.[1] That phenomenon was followed by vast "flights of pigeons" and then "swarms of flies" that scuttled "out of spigot holes in the earth" and feasted on leaves and plants before mysteriously vanishing.[2]

Tensions ran hot in the wake of the omens as colonist Nathaniel Bacon stirred a rebellion. The uprising was founded on an obsession with Native tribes on the outskirts of the colonies and a belief that the Indigenous people were planning murderous raids. Though the Native people were sparse in population and engaged in diplomatic relations with the colonies, Bacon and his conspirators in their paranoid fever believed they were in perpetual danger from a threat posed by "so many [yet] none can guess at their number."[3]

Desperate for all-out war, Bacon organized raiding parties in defiance of orders from colonial leadership to stand down. On his way to murder men, women, and children, Bacon left behind a message for those coming to arrest him for mutiny: "I am just now goeing out to seeke a more agreeable destiny than you are pleased to designe me."[4] On September 19, 1676, Bacon captured Jamestown, the first English settlement in America, and "laid the whole town . . . in ashes."[5]

Jamestown had been the center of English colonization in America since the First Virginia Charter of 1606 had given "licence to make habitacion, plantacion, and to deduce a colonie of sondrie" to the Virginia Company of London, a joint-stock operation carrying out colonization for the crown.[6] Like other European efforts to exploit the Native populations, this project was cloaked in a religious crusade, as the colonizers were tasked with seeing to the "propagating of Christian religion to suche people as yet live in darkenesse and miserable ignorance," a charge that "may in tyme bring the infidels and salvages [*sic*] living in those parts to humane civilitie."[7]

Even before Bacon's demolition, life in the Jamestown colony was less than ideal. Though propagandists and stakeholders in the corporate colonization of America promised a veritable Garden of Eden, the original colonists were reduced to eating "vermin" and cannibalism in what has come to be known as "the Starving Time."[8] The colonists' fortunes improved as they stole land from the Native tribes and, to increase production and undermine meddlesome labor disturbances, indentured servants arrived from abroad. In 1619, a ship named *White Lion* delivered "twenty and odd Negroes" to Virginia, beginning a shameful cycle of American slavery.[9]

Bacon's insurrection exposed a fundamental problem. In building his ranks, he had lashed together an unlikely alliance between white planters, indentured servants, and enslaved Black people. To stem future uprisings that bridged the classes, the solution by the ruling class was to permanently divide the white and Black races through identity and the law. In 1705 the Virginia Slave Codes cleaved the communities in two, establishing separate court systems and laws that made ironclad the racial hierarchy.

While Virginia viewed the crisis as requiring the severing of racial solidarity, forces in neighboring Maryland suspected something more sinister. In 1676 an anonymous pamphlet entitled *A Complaint from Heaven with a Hue and Crye* circulated through the province and blamed the disturbance on a Catholic plot "to over terne England with feyer, sword and distractions."[10] This rumor aligned with England's concurrent Popish Plot but refashioned it for the colonies, blaming a "secret Council of priests and natives" aligning "with the help of the French spirits from Canada" and carrying on "a secret correspondence" with the pope.[11]

A year after the Glorious Revolution of 1688, this bred an uprising by a group calling itself "an Association in arms for the defence of the Protestant Religion and for asserting the right of King William and Queen Mary to the Province of Maryland," which took over the capital and deposed its Catholic leaders.[12] In their wake, they established an explicitly Protestant government that outlawed Catholicism entirely and forbade Catholics from practicing their faith or voting under threat of imprisonment and confiscating of their children, all of it in order "to prevent the growth of Popery," a restriction that would last until the forming of the United States of America nearly a century later.[13]

Another spiritual crisis festered to the north in the colony of Massachusetts. Young minister Cotton Mather, the son of politician and president of Harvard College Increase Mather, was warning fellow colonists they lived in the "Evening of the World" and that Satan himself had loosed his demonic hordes in order to war against God and his chosen people.[14] This threat, having been facilitated by "emissaries" of Satan, including "Papists" and "the French," of which "many plots . . . have been strangely discovered," constituted the beginnings of the apocalyptic struggle between good and evil, and the citizens of Massachusetts were caught in the middle.[15]

Since Puritan John Winthrop had christened Massachusetts and its colonization project in 1630 "a city upon a hill" and placed it in the center of God's plans in the New World, the colony and its population lived in certainty they served on the front lines of spiritual war.[16] The threat was simultaneously from within and without, the forces of evil able to seep into the fortifications and past the Puritan defenses, most often finding purchase in the corruptible souls of women and contrarian voices, conveniently allowing the men and spiritual leaders to enforce orthodoxy. From 1692 to 1693, paranoia focused on the evil machinations of Satan, as well as the threats of sinister conspiracies among rivals such as Catholics, Native Americans, and the French, set off a hysteria in Massachusetts in which hundreds of colonists were accused of witchcraft. Thirty were found guilty and nineteen executed.

Like Catholic Inquisitions, these trials represented the merging of ecclesiastical matters with the machinery of government, a nightmarish combination that involved the state in matters of orthodoxy, all while allowing political and personal scores to be settled, agendas to be pushed, and governmental bodies to enforce moral and social discipline upon the populaces under threat of punishment, banishment, torture, or death.

The colonists had carried their paranoia and prejudices with them across the ocean. Many had left to escape religious control, as well as the wars, genocides, and rash of instability that accompanied disparities in faith, and now those same schisms threatened to level the city upon a hill.

In the tradition of the Renaissance and the Scientific Revolution, both concerned with forwarding human progress by emerging from superstition, came the period of the so-called Enlightenment. This was marked by the ascent of philosophers and scientists who believed that through reason and ingenuity humanity could realize its full, utopic potential.

Because knowledge and the church had long been in conflict and resulted in intimidation, censorship, harassment, and even widespread persecution and execution, this pursuit was cast as a rejection, and in some cases the active deconstruction, of religious infrastructure and influence. The transition from revelatory knowledge—truths handed down from on high to prophets, priests, or kings—to empirical knowledge—facts borne out through scientific observation and inquiry—was essential for the shift from feudalism to accumulative capitalism.

It necessitated a new framing of religion replacing the Christian god, a being that regularly intervened in human affairs, with a Supreme Being, or a Creator, who had constructed the universe before setting it in motion to operate based on natural and observable laws. This Deism solidified the concept of progress through science, the need to cultivate societies and economies, and notions of free will, as well as favored liberal democracy over authoritarian and hereditary systems of power.

To philosophers and scientists of the Enlightenment, this Creator was akin to an artisan watchmaker, and the observable universe, with its laws, its predictable and explainable phenomena, was proof of intelligent design. "Throw several pieces of steel together without shape or form; they will never arrange themselves so as to compose a watch," explained David Hume, one of the most influential thinkers of the age.[17] To stroll through nature, glimpse the systems of the natural world and its collection of complex wonders, was to be convinced of something larger than yourself.

In America, Deism and its philosophy, not to mention its society-redefining implications, were best encompassed by Thomas Jefferson, who dedicated a significant portion of his life to erecting a hard and unnegotiable wall between church and state. When not tending to state making, inventing, scientific query, or the enslavement of hundreds of African people, Jefferson spent a good deal of his time scouring the Bible with razor in hand, removing all mentions of the supernatural. Jefferson described Jesus Christ as a man "full of wisdom" and painted him as an early prophet of logic in a superstitious world.[18] To truly understand the "pure principles" of Jesus, Jefferson wrote, it was necessary to strip the "artificial vestments" of miracles and wonders created by priests and religious leaders who used them "as instruments of riches and power."[19]

Religion, at least traditional, revelatory faith, was to Deists and Enlightenment thinkers antiquated and a symptom of humanity's struggling to understand itself and squirming under the weight of naturally occurring and intentionally constructed ignorance. As Paul-Henri Thiry described in *The System of Nature,* the deities that humanity had "trembled under" were "imaginary beings . . . created by himself," constructions attempting to explain systems and laws yet undiscovered and impose order on a chaotic world.[20] These creations had been co-opted by kings and priests who used the concept of revelation to empower and enrich themselves, resulting in endless war.

The focus of the Enlightenment and its philosophers and scientists was to both demystify the natural world and free secular matters, in government and shared society, from the yoke of religious authority. This pursuit meant to both create more liberty for the enlightened—white, wealthy, educated men—and prioritize stability so that scientific progress and the accumulation of wealth could continue free of the disruption of war and spiritual unrest.

It was believed that if religious institutions, with their supernatural paranoia and incessant schisms, could be restrained, science, logic, and progress might usher in the utopias promised during the Scientific Revolution. The end point, as imagined by German philosopher Immanuel Kant, was a cosmopolitan future where all peoples believed themselves connected. There, cultures might blend, influence one another, and result in sustained peace, universal dignity, human rights, widespread representative government, and eventually a moment when all standing armies and military forces might be "entirely abolished."[21]

But the enlightened remained cautious. They remembered the persecutions of the church, and even those with faith that humanity was capable of great reason hedged their bets. With a lack of education and the continued, troubling existence of superstitious thought, the great masses were yet incapable of recognizing, or unwilling to recognize, the shadows on the wall. Plato had sketched a warning from the ancients that, despite the best intentions of the intellectual elite, humans were not rational animals and were so complex that even they failed to understand themselves. Dragging them from the darkness of ignorance was dangerous work.

Enlightenment figures sought one another out through a complex series of correspondence networks, salons wherein they could discuss philosophy and current events, and secret societies like the Freemasons and the Illuminati. These bodies operated beyond the purview of monarchs and priests, allowing radicals to compare notes, trade discoveries, and exist within a Machiavellian environment beyond the public eye. Entrance into these circles was grounded upon established and trusted members vouching for inductees and, in the case of secret societies, an escalating series of trials and ceremonies that revealed more and more profound information as the candidate demonstrated fidelity.

One inductee was Benjamin Franklin, whose entrance into the mysterious world of Freemasonry inspired him to propose in 1731 "a great and extensive project" he called the "United Party for Virtue" or "the Society of the Free and Easy."[22] Mirroring the structure of Freemasonry, this society would grow to encompass the world and form "the virtuous and good men of all nations into a regular body, to be governed by suitable good and wise rules."[23] Kept secret and maintained by endorsement and rituals, these virtuous and good men could watch over the world, ensuring peace and progress, all the while using newspapers, pamphlets, and other media as "means of communicating instruction" in order to educate and prepare the uninitiated and the unenlightened for their eventual removal from the cave.

Franklin's stake in the publishing business, as well as his affinity for personal profit, helped create a phenomenon in eighteenth-century America that would make his liberalizing project possible while solidifying the authority of Christianity in the modernizing world. Despite Franklin's personal qualms about religion—"the way to see by *Faith,*" he wrote, "is to shut the eye of *Reason*"—the potential of popular movements to move newspapers and pamphlets was readily apparent. So when his friend George Whitefield traveled from England to the colonies to spread his increasingly popular ministry, Franklin turned the event into a cultural sensation.[24]

The Pennsylvania Gazette, Franklin's periodical, dedicated extensive coverage to Whitefield's events, reporting in one breathless and dramatized account that "near 20000 hearers" had gathered in "the Presence of God," and the people were so overcome and "under such deep Soul Distress, that by their Cries they almost drown'd" Whitefield's voice.[25] So lavish and relentless was the treatment of Whitefield's colonial tour, and the efforts of other preachers during the so-called Great Awakening, that it became one of the first marketing and consumer trends in America.

Before the Great Awakening phenomenon, there had been, in the words of Jonathan Edwards, one of its chief personalities, "a time of dullness in religion."[26] Edwards had witnessed in his communities a decline of interest in matters of faith, leading to dwindling church attendance and a loss of church authority. The innovation that Whitefield and Edwards brought to bear, enabled and amplified by the burgeoning markets of newspapers and for-profit publishing in the colonies, was a new charismatic gospel where preachers performed for enraptured audiences in captivating spectacles designed to draw massive crowds.

This gospel spurred listeners to take their salvation into their own hands and ensure it with their hard-earned dollars by either purchasing printed tracts or donating to the ministries, all while positioning America and Americans at the center of the spiritual battle between good and evil. Reflecting on the sensation, Edwards reasoned, "The beginning of this great work of God must be near. And there are many things that make it probable that this work will begin in America."[27]

The Great Awakening was a crucial part of the invention of the idea of "the American." The concept that the British colonies constituted a state unto itself, removed from the parent state of England, was forged in both this gathering of converts and the conflict commonly called the French and Indian War. During the war, which raged from 1754 to 1763, Americans coalesced to defend themselves in one of the theaters of the larger Seven Years' War between the British and French. By the time England passed the Stamp Act of 1765, colonists had come to believe they were a unique people charged with an exceptional destiny, an identity that helped an economic clash become a war for independence.

The Stamp Act, which required additional taxes on printed materials, was met with overwhelming derision, primarily among the colonies' merchant class. Economics had moved from feudalism, with its kings and lords, to the budding system of capitalism, wherein personal businesses and international trade meant individuals required as much "freedom" as possible in managing their own affairs. This swing to competition between individuals reflected the growing secularization of science, progress, and especially politics, a change noted by economist Adam Smith when he wrote his study of capitalism entitled *An Inquiry into the Nature and Causes of the Wealth of Nations* (1776), arguing, "What all the violence of the feudal institutions could never have effected, the silent and insensible operation of foreign commerce and manufactures gradually brought about."[28]

Smith admired the coherence of scientific principles and believed the enlightened should seek out similar coherence "in any other system," positing that capitalism, with its free markets and resulting freedoms for the moneyed individual, when partnered with the "invisible hand" that ensured society improved even while the capitalists acted in their own interests, was a scientific principle that would inevitably change the world for the better.[29] If left alone and unhindered by wars, religious squabbles, and disruption, and if monopolistic forces were kept from dominating markets and engaging in financial despotism, Smith and other adherents believed this new system of capitalism would prove a tool of utilitarian joy and freedom, effectively replacing religion as the ordering principle of the world.

In the colonies, where capitalism was thriving and creating significant wealth based on slave labor and plundered resources, some were so angered by British interference that they formed their own secret societies, including the Sons of Liberty, which comprised affluent white men who stood to lose profits to the tax. In their secret meetings, often under the branches of the so-called Liberty Tree, the Sons effectively merged their economic concerns with the apocalypticism of scripture, charging that "monsters in the shape of men" were doing the business of Satan, and that "touching any paper" with the derided official stamp meant that one would "receive the mark of the beast" as forewarned in the Book of Revelation.[30]

The rhetoric that fueled the War of Independence was facilitated by newspapers and books published by the capitalist class. Leading the charge were men like Thomas Paine, whose runaway bestseller *Common Sense* inspired colonists to believe they had the "power to begin the world over again."[31] A fierce critic of the old guard, Paine portrayed the economic and political crisis as a battle between freedom and the "remains of monarchial tyranny."[32] His framing helped give flight to feelings of patriotism and revolutionary fervor but also relied on lingering conspiratorial paranoia from America's past, charging that Britain was a "barbarous and hellish power which hath stirred up the Indians and negroes to destroy" the colonists.[33]

It had not been enough to ground calls for independence in economic tensions between the merchant class and Great Britain, but stoking paranoia of conspiracies and omnipresent threats would move matters along. Anonymous letters were "discovered" and subsequently published that supposedly showed plots by England to "put into the hands of Negroes, the Roman Catholics, the Indians and Canadians" weapons and arms necessary to destroy the colonies.[34]

America's independence was grounded on racist paranoia as elucidated by men like James Iredell, one of the original Supreme Court justices, who believed the "state of hostility with [the colonies'] parent country" was made even more dangerous by the British prompting enslaved people to "cut our throats, and involve men, women and children, in one universal massacre."[35]

White supremacy had long inspired these baseless fears. In 1739, a rumor that Spanish forces had plotted to "stir up an insurrection among the negroes" and a disrupted slave rebellion led to widespread killing and the passing of the Negro Act of 1740.[36] In 1741, a series of fires in Manhattan led to paranoia and rumors that enslaved people had hatched a plan to revolt and help themselves to white women. To remedy the "villainous design of a very extraordinary nature" facilitated by "Spanish emissaries" who had allegedly maneuvered enslaved Black people into serving as willing agents of destruction, some two hundred of them were arrested, more than thirty executed, with at least thirteen burned at the stake.[37]

By the time the American War of Independence was declared, the fearmongering had been cemented as reality for the colonists. In writing the Declaration of Independence, Thomas Jefferson cited in his litany of offenses that King George III of England had "excited domestic insurrection among us and has endeavored to bring on the inhabitants of our frontiers, the merciless Indian savages."[38] On Long Island, as the bells signaled war, the people tailored an effigy of the king with a blackened face "in likeness of the runaway slaves" and stuffed feathers in his crown to resemble the "savages" before lynching him in celebration.[39]

The shadows on the walls of the cave had changed. A new and ambitious generation had gained control over the illusions and was telling a new story. With it, they had transformed an economic disagreement into something resembling a revolution. Having won their independence with the help of a populace primed by white supremacist paranoia and united by a manufactured religious crusade, they would construct a new government, designed to rearrange, once more, the Great Chain of Being.

An aristocratic system robed in democratic representation emerged. The machinery of government was rigged so as to mitigate democratic elements and the ignorance of the masses, locking out enslaved people, the Indigenous, women, and the poor. All of it was undertaken with the express purpose of establishing a new type of nation where the wealthy, the industrious, and the white might guide secular matters free of the disruption of religious tumult and realize the promise of enlightened paradise.

In the summer of 1780, as the war for independence raged in America, Britain was rocked by unrest at home. Sparked by efforts to reduce anti-Catholic sentiment, Protestant associations took to the streets of London and claimed their violence was intended to stave off ruin by foreign conspiracies. The economy was reeling from the war and its associated trade interruptions, so the Protestants were joined by scores of the disaffected, a motley crew described by one witness as a "poor, miserable, ragged rabble . . . ready for any and every mischief."[40]

Before the riots were contained, throngs surged through the city, destroying the homes of the ruling elite and demolishing government offices. One of the targets was Newgate Prison, a symbol of monarchial authority. With what another witness described as "the phrensy of the multitude," rioters razed Newgate.[41] In defiance of the monarch's sovereignty, it was rumored that what remained was scrawled with graffiti declaring the prisoners had been freed under the authority of "King Mob."

The issue facing the growing empire was how to continue serving its own interests while molding its people and conquests through culture and exorcising subversive actors through the use of law. Much like how the church had protected orthodoxy through its Inquisitions, the British had wielded the law as a weapon to turn debtors, radicals, and those wounded by its aristocratic hierarchy into prisoners and exiles, making it possible to lock up anyone deemed threatening or ship them elsewhere for labor, including the American colonies.

To maintain order, the British Empire turned to legal punishment. As economic conditions worsened, and Britain spent more and more of its treasure on wars and colonial projects, its jails swelled with its own citizens, creating a crisis of manageability that saw decommissioned ships transformed into "prison hulks" in order to accommodate the growing ranks of the incarcerated. But finding new and dismal ways to house prisoners wasn't nearly enough. An innovative philosophy of crime and punishment was required.

Legal reform in the eighteenth century hinged on the work of philosophers like Cesare Beccaria and Jeremy Bentham. These men believed that legal systems should not only punish people in order to deter threats or protect property but also shape society and direct it toward progress. Beccaria held that laws sprung from liberty "sacrificed" by people who had grown "weary of living in a continual state of war," and so they had transferred portions of their own sovereignty to the state in exchange for safety.[42] Laws then should be formed to prevent "the despotism of each individual from plunging society into its former chaos."[43]

Bentham is credited as one of the forerunners of utilitarianism, or the philosophy that society and individuals should stimulate the most happiness among the most people by behaving in the most logical manner, a logic he claimed could even be calculated via algorithms. Systems of justice, he argued, were "public instructions" that, when enforced and communicated effectively, served to enlighten citizens and usher them into benevolence over time.[44] Considering this, it was "the business of government . . . to promote the happiness of the society, by punishing and rewarding."[45]

Bentham obsessed over the application and execution of law as a means of perfecting society and came to believe the answer lay in his invention the panopticon, a prison structure where inmates were housed in a circle surrounding a darkened watchtower. In this environment, the most prisoners possible would be observable, and the placement of the watchtower meant the prisoners would never know when their jailer's gaze fell upon them, creating the sensation of perpetual observation. "The more constantly the persons to be inspected are under the eyes of the persons who should inspect them," Bentham reasoned, "the more perfectly will the purpose of the establishment have been attained."[46]

But Bentham's passion for organizing and directing society knew no bounds. His panopticon structure, intended originally for penal matters, could also be handy in other facets of life, whether it was in controlling the criminal and insane or in "training the rising race in the path of education."[47]

While a new means of societal control was being envisioned, the empire needed to continue addressing its crisis while seeking out new territories. As a "remedy for the evils likely to result from the late alarming and numerous increase of felons," Britain plotted the establishment of a penal colony in what would come to be called Australia.[48] Though the plan explicitly cited the prisons being in "so crowded a state" as reason for the project, in true colonial fashion it still claimed to have, at its heart, an intention "to promote the Christian religion among thousands of . . . fellow creatures, who . . . are totally destitute of all rational worship."[49] Those "fellow creatures" were Aboriginal tribes who, upon first contact with British explorers, were described as living "in a tranquility which is not disturbed by the inequality of condition," with British captain James Cook noting, "The earth and sea of their own accord furnish them with all things necessary for life. They covet not magnificent houses."[50] Quickly British colonization descended into "wholesale slaughter" where the British "stole and ill-treated native children, seized upon the young women to subject them to their brutal passions, and wounded or slew complaining husbands and fathers."[51]

For profit, Britain leaned on India, where the East India Company had enjoyed a foothold for over a century. The EIC's personal military, which at times dwarfed the size of British forces, had bested the combined efforts of the French and Native peoples during the Seven Years' War and, to solidify their domination, had passed on ruling openly. Instead, setting the course for future colonizing projects, they relied on regional puppets to lead in their thrall. The EIC regularly installed leaders, created uprisings, and controlled the politics of India to their liking. By 1770 the company's rule and manipulation of agriculture and the economy created a massive crisis that came to be called the Bengal

Famine. The measures of taxation were so cruel that Indians were reduced to terrible actions—many "sold their children to raise money"—but management compounded the problem until upwards of ten million, or a third of the population, perished.[52]

Soon, the EIC's operations had grown so bloated it required a bail-out from the British government in order to remain solvent, setting off a controversy in which reformers like Edmund Burke criticized the corporation as "repugnant" and having grown to "too vast a magnitude for the capacity of any administration whatever to grasp."[53] In its present state, Burke bemoaned, the EIC had become a "mill-stone" that would drag Great Britain "into an unfathomable abyss." Regardless, the company was rescued.

In 1788 the tug-of-war between Parliament and the EIC spilled over into the impeachment of Warren Hastings, who, as governor-general in Bengal, had overseen the great famine, the plundering of India's riches, and the exploitation of its people. Lambasting Hastings, Burke described him as "a heart blackened to the blackest, a heart dyed deep in blackness, a heart gangrened to the core."[54]

The impeachment process took seven long years to play out and saw Hastings acquitted, but by the time he was cleared of the charges, the political environment in Britain had changed completely; even staunch reformers found themselves fully engrossed in defending the old order. For the British Empire to survive, they believed, old hierarchies and inequalities would have to be strengthened, and a system of control that disturbingly resembled Bentham's panopticon would be required.

Edmund Burke had been one of the strongest voices allying with the American cause. To Burke, the push for independence was only natural, as Americans were "descendants of Englishmen" and "devoted to liberty . . . according to English ideas, and on English principles."[55] In fact, the English might even look upon the uprising as a sign of their own achievement, reckoning that their "ancestors have turned a savage wilderness into a glorious empire," and while England had been "civilizing conquests and civilizing settlements," in time America, armed with its "hereditary dignity," would come to do the same.[56]

But the growing unrest in France was much different. Even Burke considered the unfurling revolution a "new and grievous malady," a "contagion" and "pestilence" that needed to be contained at all costs.[57]

Britain was brimming with reformers and radicals, many of them meeting in revolutionary societies the likes of which had influenced the uprisings in both America and France. There were calls for fairer and more representative government, possibly even the establishment of republican politics and the eradication of the monarchy and colonialism. It was a sermon of minister Richard Price that first drew the public ire of Burke and set off a conservative reactionary movement in Britain. Price had sermonized the drastic need for change, lambasting the British elite for their "love of domination; a desire of conquest, and a thirst for grandeur and glory," all of it serving and necessitating "extending territory, and enslaving surrounding countries."

Critics like Mary Wollstonecraft decried "the demon of property" and denounced established systems as having been "settled in the dark days of ignorance, when the minds of men were shackled by the grossest prejudices and most immoral superstition," and proposed a massive restructuring relying on Enlightenment ideals and leaving behind hierarchical notions that continually resulted in inequality.[58]

Even as Burke had fought raucously to reform British economics and politics, he considered these developments destructive and possibly apocalyptic. Though the masses were rallying to cries for democracy and change, Burke thundered back in his 1790 pamphlet *Reflections on the Revolution in France* that "men should frequently be thwarted, their will controlled, and their passions brought into subjection."[59] The political order that maintained tranquility was founded, Burke asserted, on natural hierarchies and the moral bedrock of spiritual faith. In France, and with possible movements in Britain, Burke believed the true purpose of the revolution was not progress or equality but a secret plan by Enlightenment figures obsessed with "the utter abolition under any of its forms, of the Christian religion."[60]

A pair of treatises supporting Burke's claims ushered in the modern age of conspiracy theories. Physicist John Robison published *Proofs of a Conspiracy Against All the Religions and Governments of Europe,* declaring, "Under the specious pretext of enlightening the world by the torch of philosophy . . . AN ASSOCIATION HAS BEEN FORMED for the express purpose of ROOTING OUT ALL THE RELIGIOUS ESTABLISHMENTS AND OVERTURNING ALL THE EXISTING GOVERNMENTS OF EUROPE," and stating that this association, "in time, should govern the world."[61] Joining him was the French priest Augustin Barruel, whose *Memoirs, Illustrating the History of Jacobinism* placed the blame for the French Revolution on a plot between the Freemasons and the Illuminati. The stakes were dire: Barruel warned the grand scheme "must be crushed or society overthrown."[62] If successful, the planners would root out the world's traditions, costing all of the nations' "altars and their thrones, their pontiffs and their kings," leading to the promotion of democracy and universal freedom and a reliance on logic and empiricism, and resulting, ultimately, in "the destruction of the religion of Christ."[63]

Writing to Barruel to express his support, Burke called the book a "wonderful Narrative" supported by what he believed to be thorough research and said it was "admirable in every point of View, political, Religious, and . . . philosophical."[64] Further, Burke confided in Barruel, he had personally been "a Witness" to the conspiracy, having known five of the alleged collaborators, who, in Burke's words, had been "busy in the Plot you have so well described and in the manner and on the Principle which you have so truly presented."

British reaction to the revolution in France is considered by many to be the origin of modern conservatism: a worldview entrenched in the fear that secret forces conspire to annihilate Christianity and the sovereignty of nations, and, with their destruction, topple existing hierarchies. Actions taken to guard against this threat, including legislation, societal pressures, the establishment of internal and external intelligence operations, and the construction of a coordinated police state, were all riddled with paranoia, greed, and apocalyptic fear, inspiring the state, in a bid to protect itself from this supposed contagion, to declare war on the individual.

As with the paranoid mindsets inspired by the Black Death and later the Popish Plot, the British state saw itself as under attack by forces within its borders who operated in the shadows in coordination with external rivals, a secularization of worries over evil beings corrupting the souls of the people. As chaos grew in France, refugees streamed to England, and these "very unwelcome visitors" were considered by authorities possible pawns of forces "desirous of creating confusion," necessitating a new system that would track their movements and activities.[65]

In addressing the revolutionary societies, Britain secretly surveilled meetings, taking note of which groups and individuals had advocated reform or liberalization of the political structure. A report implicated the groups in treacherous activities, including daring to "assert the natural and unalienable rights of man" and "expressing a hope that the hydra of tyranny and imposition may soon fall under the guillotine of truth and reason."[66] To head off this internal threat and the alleged conspiracies, a series of acts banned public meetings of a certain size as they had "of late been made use of to serve the ends of factions and seditious Persons, to the great danger of public peace, and may become the means of producing confusion and calamities in the nation."[67] Further, criticism and calls for abolition of the monarchy were outlawed, making political ideology a punishable offense.

Previously, the British elite had balked at the prospect of a coordinated police force, relying instead on the employment of personal security and groups like the Association for the Prosecution of Felons, which protected "gentlemen of the first rank and property."[68] These moneyed few had seen little reward in paying for widespread policing, but the French Revolution changed their minds and the financing of law enforcement found favor. Under the lead of Prime Minister William Pitt, the prevailing opinion became that it would be "impossible to protect the lives and properties of His Majesty's subjects without the establishment of a police in the hands of a magistracy."[69] Law enforcement was given widespread authority and permission to operate "wherever anti-government activities required assistance."[70]

Much of the responsibility over policing revolutionary forces fell into the hands of a man named John Reeves, who had declared ideological war on radicals and reformers. Reeves believed that the strength of Britain lay in its dedication to firm hierarchies and the British people's responsibility to "conform to subordination, and to respect rank and station."[71]

Reeves was an avowed nationalist and rejected the push for cosmopolitan-style liberal democracy. "I am not a *Citizen of the World,*" he declared, "I am an Englishman—and I thank God for having placed me among a People who, I think, possess more goodness of heart and more good sense than any other in the world."[72]

To protect this good sense, and neutralize British citizens with "mischievous opinions," Reeves formed his own secret society, the Association for Preserving Liberty and Property Against Republicans and Levellers.[73] Out of hand, the association dismissed any liberal reforms, claiming its champions expected the British people "to surrender everything [they] now possess; [their] Religion and [their] Laws . . . and . . . to trust to the formation of something New, upon the principles of Equality, and under the auspices of speculative men, who have conceived ideas of perfection that never yet were known in the World."[74]

In their twin roles as policers and members of the association, Reeves and his fellow reactionaries made use of the law, as well as extralegal measures, to nullify any and all threats. In the light of day, the police used acts of Parliament to prosecute supposed traitors, and by the cover of darkness the association infiltrated revolutionary groups, surveilled them illegally, and used intimidation to silence them. Often, the paramilitary group that operated outside legal measures comprised the same individuals who had taken an oath to uphold the law.

To protect its ruling class and the private property of the wealthy few, Great Britain had transformed into a relatively new entity: a state whose citizens either were under constant scrutiny or feared they were being surveilled, their actions, words, and thoughts policed by formal and informal organs of state power that could arrest or kill them, that were either undercover among them or listening through their keyholes.

Commemorating the anniversary of the storming of the Bastille, French revolutionaries staged a massive national celebration called the Fête de la Fédération in the summer of 1790. In the year that had passed, French society had changed in unimaginable ways, and, stimulated by Enlightenment philosophies, simmering tensions, detestable inequalities, and gathering revolutionary sentiment, the process was only gaining steam.

To mark the moment the revolution had begun, the Champ de Mars was transformed into a massive staging ground accommodating one hundred thousand attendees, replete with a bridge over the Seine, an enormous arch, and a national altar upon which the new faith of the revolution would be consecrated. Military forces paraded, banners flew, and a coerced King Louis XVI and Queen Marie Antoinette attended in a show of cooperation and ceremonial unity.

Officiating was Charles Maurice de Talleyrand-Périgord, a minister and politician who, in his religious capacity, had shocked the system by urging to the National Assembly, in "improving the condition of the whole body" of France, that the "immense resource" that was the property of the Catholic Church be seized and the nation "become the sole and only proprietor of all the clerical land in the kingdom."[75] Free from the bounds of Christian service, Talleyrand delivered a nationalist sermon equating the revival of France to mystical resurrection, imploring attendees to "sing and weep tears of joy, for on this day France has been made anew."[76]

What had made this radically altered scene possible was the gross disparity between the wealthy and the lowest citizens. Peasants had accounted for 80 percent of the French population, and the country was full of visions of poverty, as recounted by the writer Arthur Young, who reported on his visit to France just prior to the outbreak of revolution seeing "many beggars," shoeless citizens, and scenes of utter human "misery."[77]

These conditions had led to not only suffering among the lower class but conspiracy theories that made revolution possible, including the so-called Famine Plot, a rumored "secret game" among French elites to introduce "famine into France" in order to cause "part of the people to perish from hunger."[78] By the time political and economic struggles took hold in the 1780s, the population was primed to strike against forces they believed were withholding resources and plotting their demise.

As the National Assembly asserted its independence from the king in 1789, a "Great Fear" took hold in the countryside. Echoing the fourteenth-century Jacquerie movement, peasants overthrew their feudal masters, the lords and the clergy, creating a crisis where authorities lamented, "Castles are being burned, monasteries destroyed, farms given up to pillage. Taxes, payments to lords, all are destroyed; the law is powerless."[79] The National Assembly reacted by passing the August Decrees, announcing that feudalism was completely abolished and forwarding a new, more equitable system.

These actions were inspired by Enlightenment ideals and allowed room for them to flourish, including the production of the Declaration of the Rights of Man and of the Citizen, authored by Lafayette and Thomas Jefferson. This document was considered the guiding force of the budding revolution, an assertion that "men are born and remain free and equal in rights" and that, contrary to attempts by states to dominate their citizens, the "law is the expression of the general will."[80]

Already, though, there were troubling signs the revolution might not be all that it seemed and that beneath the veneer of progressive reform lurked the machinations of power that had necessitated the uprising in the first place. The contradictions that plagued the American project, also influenced by Jefferson, were ingrained in the French version of "freedom." Like the American system, the proposed design instituted a hierarchy, in this case between "active" and "passive" citizens, granting the vote to men who paid taxes, while enslaved people, servants, and women were considered nonpersons.

For women, it constituted an incredible betrayal. The hard-fought victories of the revolution had been assisted, if not driven, by women who had fought alongside their male counterparts. Mary Wollstonecraft, having emigrated to France to participate, castigated the men for "considering females rather as women than human creatures" and relegating them to "a state of perpetual childhood."[81] Advocating for representation and reform, the revolutionary women of France continued meeting in their own societies and groups until the revolution came to consider them unruly and dangerous, ruling in 1793, "Clubs and popular societies of women, under whatever denomination, are forbidden."[82]

One of the most vocal advocates for equal representation, Marie-Olympe de Gouges, likened the patriarchal oppression to a "tyrannical empire" and called her male counterparts "bizarre, blind, bloated by science and degenerate."[83] Following her execution in November 1793 by guillotine, an obituary cited the reason for her death as "having forgotten the virtues which befit her sex." Her murder would be one of many as ruthless and ambitious men sought to grasp the revolution for themselves and construct a society to their liking.

French revolutionaries believed their new world depended on their ability to dechristianize France and effectively amputate the church from the state. Everyday life was meticulously reconfigured, including the very concept of time. Months changed. The week expanded from seven to ten days. Even the concept of what represented a second was uprooted and changed to what Gilbert Romme described as "the pulse rate of an average-sized healthy man, marching at a military pace."[84] These steps, according to Romme, would free the French from the "credulity and superstitious routine" that had marked "centuries of ignorance" and reduced them to servitude.[85]

Worship of Enlightenment ideals replaced worship of the Christian god, allowing secular replacements like the Cult of Reason to fill the vacuum. An attempt to re-create the rituals of the pagan cults of the pre-Christian Roman Empire, the Cult of Reason promoted the concept of Liberty as a goddess to be venerated and adored and staged grand ceremonies in former churches and temples, including the Notre-Dame cathedral in Paris, where Liberty emerged from a temple of philosophy, carrying forth a "Torch of Truth" and presiding over an "Altar of Reason."[86]

But dedication to reason, freedom, and reform lasted only as long as revolutionary France went untested. The imprisonment of Louis XVI and the royal family, as well as efforts to supplant the monarchy with representative government, drew the ire of the surrounding kingdoms, who formed alliances to head off revolutionary fervor. In April of 1792, France attacked the forces on its borders, leading to the Brunswick Manifesto being delivered on behalf of the opposing allies, threatening "total destruction" should Parisians not return to the "laws of nature" and immediately "submit to the King."[87] A month later, a supposed plot was "discovered for assassinating all good citizens during the night," setting off a frenzy of massacres in the prisons that saw between 1,100 and 1,400 people killed as the radicals declared it "an act of justice . . . after the long series of treasons that have led . . . to the brink of the abyss."[88]

Louis XVI would be stripped of his crown and then decapitated, his executioner holding his severed head "by the hair, dancing at the same time around the scaffold—as people chanted '*Vive la Nation. Vive la République*.'"[89] Louis was one of upwards of forty thousand people to die in the building Reign of Terror and one of more than sixteen thousand to meet their fate at the guillotine.[90] This orgy of violence was a crusade by revolutionaries to, as voiced by its foremost leader, Maximilien Robespierre, "crush both the interior and exterior enemies," and worked, disturbingly and ironically enough, much like the Inquisitions carried out in days past by the church.[91]

As foreign threats troubled the borders and internal political enemies mobilized within, the apparatus of the state was marshaled by Robespierre and his associates to investigate and dispose of traitors and enemies. The orthodoxy imposed by the church in religious matters had become a political and ideological orthodoxy enforced by the state. Similarly, as blasphemy or heresy had once been enough to earn the sinner torture or death at the stake at the hands of the church, the revolutionary government enacted laws against "spreading false news" and "slandering patriotism" that earned the blade of the guillotine.[92]

The similarities between religious eradication and political purging are not accidental. Both fundamentally rely on the concept of revelatory knowledge, in one instance a message from God and the other the spirit or inspiration of revolution. They also both manifest an environment where preemptive violence is considered not only warranted but essential. Possession of the "one true religion" or "one true revolution" meant the possessor was beset on all sides by enemies and conspiracies and was responsible for defending themselves in order to forward the crusade. And both ideologies promised that should the dissenters or enemies be eliminated, should the land be made holy or prepared for revolution, then a perfect utopia awaited in the form of a new heaven or paradise and the perfect nation transformed.

As Robespierre carried himself as a prophet, it should be no surprise his political role transformed rapidly into a religious one. At the apex of his power, in May of 1794, Robespierre delivered a shocking lecture condemning the cults of reason and attacked the secularization of France, thundering, "The only basis of civilized society is morality."[93] In fact, the worship of a "Supreme Being and of the soul" would be a revolutionary act that propelled the nation forward and ensured continued progress.[94] The course of action was clear as he implored, "Let us leave the priests and return to the Divinity."[95]

A motion passed immediately making official the state's belief in "the existence of the Supreme Being and the immortality of the soul."[96] Robespierre fashioned himself the leader of the new Cult of the Supreme Being, a position that transcended politics and made him a nascent pontiff of a blossoming religion. On June 8, less than a month after the cult's founding, the Festival of the Supreme Being was held. The Champ de Mars was again prepared for celebration, this time outfitted with an enormous artificial mountain that Robespierre descended from like a revolutionary Moses. As prophet, he spoke on behalf of the Supreme Being, who charged the revolution with struggling "against all the oppressors of the human race," including kings and priests, and intended France to serve as his champion in annihilating these oppressors and delivering humanity into a new age.[97] To strike a covenant, Robespierre then set fire to an effigy of Atheism, proclaiming, "He has returned to nothing."[98]

The pretentiousness of the event struck Robespierre's rivals as a sign of his growing megalomania, with one attendee remarking, "Look at the bugger. It's not enough for him to be master, he has to be God."[99] Almost immediately the tide turned against him; helping seal his downfall was the rumor of a developing cult led by the mystic Catherine Théot, who reportedly had been gathering converts to a new religion heralding Robespierre as "the Son of the Supreme Being, the Eternal Word, the Redeemer of Mankind, the Messiah foretold by the prophets."[100]

Accused of leading a new religion designed to destroy the revolution and of becoming an enemy of the state, Robespierre was arrested on July 27, 1794. Like the thousands he had condemned to the cold steel of the guillotine, he was decried as a traitor and beheaded, the assembled crowded cheering "as if a great victory had been achieved and the long-sought blessings of the Revolution attained."[101]

Twelve years later, German philosopher Georg Wilhelm Friedrich Hegel looked up from his work and witnessed Napoleon Bonaparte entering the city of Jena on the eve of battle. Stunned, Hegel wrote a friend, marveling, "I saw the Emperor—this world-soul . . . an individual, who, concentrated here at a single point, astride a horse, reaches out over the world and masters it."[102]

Hegel's work demystified traditional religion while injecting mysticism and spirituality into temporal matters. It was Hegel's assertion that history was the process of the human spirit "coming to a consciousness of itself," an ongoing progression wherein humanity would free and perfect itself over time.[103] This progress would be ensured by "world-historical men," or "great men" who "fell in with the needs of the age" and were able to harness the masses, who would feel "the irresistible power of their own inner Spirit thus embodied."[104]

This innovation took the concept of divine agents from the Christian religion, the idea that God chose individuals to carry out his will, and transformed it for the developing secularizing age. There existed a spirit or soul, an intangible, revelatory matter, but it was yanked from the heavens and yoked to the Earth and humanity. Great men chosen by destiny could rise to positions of influence regardless of hereditary legacy and become arbiters of destiny itself.

In climbing through the military ranks, capturing control of France in the waning days of the revolution, conquering vast swaths of the world, and crowning himself supreme emperor, Napoleon was the living embodiment of the theoretical man of destiny. But that mythology was crafted and weaponized by a man well aware of the necessity of dominating reality. Regarding history, Napoleon would later call it "a fable agreed upon," or a story told to explain matters through a lens beneficial to the powerful.[105]

Announcing, "The Revolution is over," Napoleon and his conspirators took advantage of political discord and carried out a coup d'état in 1799.[106] Napoleon explained his hand had been forced by the "deplorable weakness and indecision" of the incompetent government, leading the nation "to search for a man able to save it."[107] In this account, Napoleon portrayed himself as a "liberator, impatiently awaited," who, upon revealing himself, was divined by "the national instinct."[108] True to form, throughout his life, Napoleon would again and again explain his ambitions and actions, all self-serving and self-aggrandizing, as being noble sacrifices to his "destiny."[109]

From the beginning, Napoleon had worked hard to cultivate his image. As a general he obsessed over coverage of his exploits in the French press. Mild criticisms and insufficient praise were met with angry letters railing against "absurdities" and "petty paragraphs . . . which [did France] more harm and [made it] more enemies."[110] Believing that journalists bore him "a grudge," Napoleon commissioned multiple publications to cover his exploits, publish op-eds and poetry that fawned over his victories and glories, and report back to France his ascending greatness so that by the time he usurped power he was already regarded as a potential savior.[111] He exercised complete dominion over the press, flooding it with articles he had written himself and, at the height of his reign, overseeing every piece of printed material in his empire.

In this, Napoleon was not only the great man of Hegel's philosophy but the ideal Machiavellian figure. Through control of the media, Napoleon fostered a cult of personality that colored the opinions of his subjects and constructed an impenetrable veneer that hid his machinations. And, in true Machiavellian tradition, as the man himself had prescribed, religion was one of his primary weapons.

Not long after his coup, Napoleon reestablished the Catholic Church in France with the Concordat of 1801, an agreement "for the good of religion as for the maintenance of internal tranquility."[112] In his own words, Napoleon confessed to having used the faith "as a social means in order to repress anarchy" and "consolidate . . . domination over

Europe," goals that required religion because "the restlessness of man is such that he must have this vague and mysterious element that religion presents to him."[113]

Religion, for Napoleon, was a tool, a weapon that could be used to battle and sue for peace. "By turning Catholic," he boasted, "I ended the war in the Vendée, by becoming a Moslem I established myself in Egypt, by becoming an ultramontane I won over the Italians. If I was governing a people of Jews, I would rebuild the Temple of Solomon."[114] And it was in this vein that Napoleon christened himself the next coming of Charlemagne, combining elements of tradition and nostalgia with developing concepts of sovereignty, by arranging in 1804 an elaborate ceremony wherein he would be crowned emperor. Pope Pius VII attended and gave his blessing, but Napoleon had "given express directions that Pius should not touch" the crown and that authority resided within himself.[115]

Just as he had risen above the pope, Napoleon challenged the Great Chain of Being and established sovereignty based on an individual's apparent mastery over destiny and embodiment of the will of history. In teaching his subjects to respect his authority, Napoleon returned to the means favored by medieval monarchs, a blend of personal mythology mixed with religious indoctrination, while innovating media as a means of propaganda, providing the blueprint for all future authoritarians and despots.

In August of 1791, as a tropical storm seethed off the coast of Haiti, an enslaved man from Senegambia named Dutty Boukman and a priestess named Cécile Fatiman presided over a religious ritual at Bois Caïman that would set off a revolution. Gathered with them were hundreds of representatives from plantations bound by an oath to rebel against the cruel abuses of French planters. A sacrifice was made to commemorate the plan and call upon mystic forces to bless the revolt, while Boukman promised that a god watched over them and "He sees all that white man does."[116] For the plan to be successful, for the enslaved people to free themselves, Boukman told them, they must reject generations of indoctrination and "throw away the image of the god of the whites who thirsts for our tears and listen to the voice of liberty which speaks in the hearts of all of us."

French treatment of the colony of Saint-Domingue had been disgusting and cruel, and all in the effort to produce vast exports of luxury items like sugar, cotton, indigo, and coffee for the wealthy around the world. Planters had relied on incredible brutality to maintain production, and France, which benefited greatly from the colony's resources, had aided them by passing laws and codes making it illegal for enslaved people "to carry any weapon, or large sticks, on pain of whipping," forbidding "slaves belonging to different masters to gather in the day or night," and sanctioning cruel abuses to punish them, including being chained and "beaten with rods or straps."[117]

News of the French Revolution reached the island via merchants, and word of the Declaration of the Rights of Man stimulated hope that changes might follow. Petitioning for equal rights and representation, the Haitians were harshly denied. The colony's rulers refused to make equal a "bastard and degenerate race," and especially the slave class, which they referred to as a "species of orangutan."[118]

With the advent of capitalism and Enlightenment principles, white supremacy was evolving. Early colonial projects had operated under the auspices of efforts to "civilize" and evangelize and had rationalized the enslavement of Africans through the biblical story of the curse of Ham, but racists during the Enlightenment legitimized their ideas through pseudoscience.

The primary debate among white intellectuals was whether whites and people of color had descended from different sources or from Adam and Eve, who were, almost universally among Europeans, considered to have been white themselves. Voltaire, regarded as one of the most significant Enlightenment figures, fell in the former camp, declaring that people of color, including "the Negroes," were "not at all descended from that first man."[119] The very idea that God had created the African people in his own image was considered a joke: "Here is a very pleasant image of the Eternal Being," he wrote sarcastically, "with a flat black nose, with very little intelligence, or none at all." The issue of whether these "brutes" had sprung from the same race as whites was preposterous; to him, the only remaining question was "whether they are descended from the monkeys, or whether the monkeys came from them."[120]

The countervailing opinion, however, was that white and Black people had originated from the same species, but that climate and customs had degenerated people of color and resulted in inferior races. Theorists like Johann Friedrich Blumenbach held that Caucasians—itself a nonsensical and completely arbitrary term—were "the most beautiful race of men" with "the most beautiful form of the skull," while studying people of color and charting what he believed was their deterioration.[121] Georges-Louis Leclerc warned that, if left unchecked, people of color—who, he noted, were "fond of filth"—would "degenerate" and "bastardize the species," but "if properly fed, and unexposed to bad usage, they are contented, joyous and obliging."[122]

Subjugation was not only essential but an ethical, paternal imperative.

It was unthinkable to many white Enlightenment figures that people of color should be treated equally, let alone that they should rise up, displace their oppressors, and attempt self-rule. White supremacy had once relied on the myth of the need to propagate the Christian religion and save the souls of the savages. Now, in the Age of Enlightenment, science and logic offered a new cause: safeguarding the species and an *empirical* need to protect people of color from themselves.

Following the ritual in Bois Caïman, the enslaved people of Saint-Domingue killed their masters and torched their plantations. Fields and homes were set ablaze until "churning clouds of smoke" filled the sky by day and at night they glowed and lent "all objects a livid tint of blood."[123] The planters were aided by their white allies around the world. Calling it "lamentable! to see such a spirit of revolt among the Blacks," George

Washington was so disturbed by events that he sent the modern equivalent of nearly $20 million in aid to help suppress the revolution.[124] Washington assured the French ambassador that the United States would be "well disposed . . . to render every aid in their power . . . to quell 'the alarming insurrection of the negroes.'"[125]

Haitians would be forced to fight off the efforts of the British, the Spanish, and the French, an incomparable feat by a people considered "inferior." Framing a constitution that outlawed slavery and established a legal system that would be "the same for all whether in punishment or in protection," the Haitians eventually petitioned Napoleon to establish relations on equal terms.[126] Napoleon assured them "the sacred principles of liberty and equality will never suffer any change" while confiding in one of his ministers that his goal was to "crush the government of the blacks."[127] In his appraisal, "the black chiefs were ungrateful and rebellious Africans" in desperate need of being "effectually humbled."[128]

French attempts to reassert white supremacy were particularly brutish. Napoleon's primary military leader in Haiti advised, "We must destroy all the mountain Negroes, men and women, sparing only children under twelve years of age," setting off a genocidal fury in which the French attempted to systematically wipe out the population by means of firing squad, lynching, throwing thousands of prisoners in the sea, and, in a disturbing foreshadowing of future white supremacist genocide, gassing them in the hulls of ships.[129]

Once more, with courage and tenacity and talent, the Haitians were able to defeat the forces of white supremacy and maintain their freedom. The victory was only short-lived, however, as the final lesson of the so-called Age of Revolutions was a tragic one. Despite all the rhetoric of freedom, liberty, and inalienable rights, revolution and self-rule had always been strictly intended for white, wealthy men.

Racist conceptions of the world required a hard denial of equality, and so Haiti went largely unrecognized as a state before suffering a humiliating and debilitating setback in July of 1825, when the French returned with warships to force Haitians to accept an agreement to pay for the "misfortunes of the former colonists of Saint-Domingue."[130] The Haitians who had freed themselves through hard-fought revolution were required to pay back planters and investors for destroying the plantations that had served to enslave them, and, as they were still considered property, to purchase their own bodies and freedom from their dethroned masters. This debt crippled the nation and consumed its trade and economy for nearly two centuries.

Consequently, Haitians were forced to borrow the money from the French, the Germans, and eventually the Americans. Their financial hardship was designed, implemented, and enforced by so-called Western civilization and was seen as proof of their inequality, leading to future political and economic crises that saw calls for intervention on behalf of private financial entities holding that debt. In 1914, US Marines would be dispatched to Haiti with a gunboat in order to secure the modern equivalent of $13 million from the government and transfer it directly to National City Bank of New York, now known as Citibank.[131] A year later, explaining it as a "courtesy and kindness," President Woodrow Wilson ordered an invasion and occupation of Haiti to protect business interests in the nation.

In charge of the operation and commanding invading forces was Colonel Littleton Waller, who had been previously court-martialed for war crimes and massacres in the Philippines. A descendant of enslavers, Waller nodded to this legacy in assuring that he "knew the nigger and how to handle him."[132] After having won their independence, held at bay the most powerful nations in the world, and cultivated their own state, Haitians, according to Waller, were still "niggers in spite of the thin varnish of education and refinement . . . down in their hearts they are just the same happy, idle, irresponsible people we know of."

- CHAPTER FIVE -

A Man Is but a Machine for Creating Value

The decree was read from the pulpit of every candlelit church in the land: "Let all Holy Russia condemn Napoleon as the Antichrist."[1] Facing possible defeat at the hands of the French emperor, Czar Alexander I implored his subjects to embrace this "crusade" and war against the seemingly unstoppable, malignant force.

Since the first rumblings in May of 1789, the rulers of Europe had viewed the French Revolution and its resulting chaos as having a "satanic quality."[2] The upheaval of the French monarchy, coupled with societal reform, the confiscation of the private property of the church and the nobility, and the struggles that devolved into the bloody horror of the Reign of Terror, represented the worst nightmares of the entrenched ruling class. The only sufficient explanation was that evil itself had been loosed upon the Earth. Napoleon's march of conquest, in which the sins of the revolution were being sowed across the continent and thrones were being toppled, seemed surely the fulfillment of the prophecies of the Book of Revelation.

Warning Alexander I was a mystic named Barbara von Krüdener who claimed to receive visions from on high. Practicing ancient arts, Krüdener lived as a modern oracle and worked herself into frenzied states of religious fervor, supposedly opening the door for communication from

God. He confirmed for her and the czar that Napoleon was indeed the Antichrist and in league with "the Prince of Darkness."[3]

Adding to the apocalyptic angst was a growing paranoia released by Augustin Barruel, the priest whose 1797 book *Memoirs, Illustrating the History of Jacobinism* had helped popularize the story that the French Revolution had been the secret plan of the Freemasons and Illuminati. Nine years later, fresh off Napoleon's coronation, Barruel claimed he had received a letter in August of 1806 from a man named Jean-Baptiste Simonini. A captain in the Piedmontese army, Simonini lauded Barruel's efforts in exposing the plot but advised that the treachery was much larger in scope than even Barruel suspected. The devilish scheme that cultivated the French Revolution was not just the work of Enlightenment-dedicated secret societies—a "Judaic sect" labored behind the scenes, pulling strings and carrying out a plot to "turn Christians into slaves."[4]

Though Napoleon had decreed that all Jews were "guilty of chicanery unless proven innocent," his reign had seen limited advances in toleration.[5] Debts owed to them were forgiven and their property and businesses seized, but in isolated circumstances Napoleon had made a point of welcoming Jews into his empire, leading suspicious opponents to worry he might inspire them to betray their nations and greet him as a messiah.

The advent of liberal democracy, the tumult of the French Revolution, and the resulting Napoleonic Wars were thus transformed from political developments and struggles into a religious crisis demanding widespread conservative counterrevolution. Threats from within and without dictated a reinforcement of monarchial sovereignty and rejection of Enlightenment ideals. Napoleon's eventual defeat made this new order possible, and in the winter of 1814, representatives from the major European nations met in Vienna to discuss a post-Napoleon world in which the monarchies would be refortified and the contagion of liberalism quarantined.

While the monarchs wrestled with the maneuverings of malevolent forces, an Austrian diplomat named Klemens von Metternich was busy consolidating power. Metternich was not enthralled by spiritual fervor but, like Machiavelli before him, recognized the utility of religion and religion-based monarchial sovereignty in tamping down revolutionary zeal. Looking at Europe, Metternich saw "a vast and dangerous conspiracy" systematically attacking "sound doctrines" with the intent of realizing "the overthrow of everything legally existing."[6] The only option, he believed, was to effectively freeze society and reestablish the regime prior to the Enlightenment.[7]

To "save society from total ruin," Metternich instituted widespread measures limiting the people's rights.[8] He began with the press, what he considered the "greatest and consequently the most urgent evil."[9] Believing newspapers and media served "a party antagonistic to all existing Governments," Metternich worked to constrain them in their ability to reach and communicate information to the populace.[10] Friedrich von Gentz, one of Metternich's most trusted allies, urged "a preventative measure against the abuses of the press," arguing that all publications should either cease or be heavily censored to the point of containing literally nothing of interest until Europeans returned "to God and the truth."[11]

This naturally inspired anger, but the rage only gifted Metternich more leeway to pass further restrictions. In the German states, the 1819 assassination of diplomat August von Kotzebue by a radical student cleared the way for regulation that, by Gentz's own admission, "would be impossible to implement in other circumstances."[12] Metternich seized the opportunity, banning student organizations, further censoring the press, and removing liberal college professors who "by obvious deviation from their duty or by exceeding the limits of their functions, or by abuse of their legitimate influence over the youthful minds, or by propagating harmful doctrines," represented a threat to order.[13] The decrees required "approval of the state officials" for all educational materials and curricula and created investigatory bodies to scrutinize and probe the citizenry.[14]

Metternich's Europe took an incredibly oppressive turn wherein the states established shared intelligence communities and law enforcement that kept a constant eye on their people and, through one action after another, either ensured elections would be more or less rigged or abolished them altogether. Gentz lauded his ally, praising Metternich's "equilibrium" and exhaustively designed system.[15] Calling it "a phenomenon without precedent," this new order that ensured peace between nations and the subservience of their citizens would surely lead to harmony and prosperity for generations to come.

On the American frontier, another apocalypse was playing out. Massive cataclysmic hunts resulted in scenes of senseless carnage, including one hunt in the 1830s by a group of Sioux hunters who had cut down over fifteen hundred bison in a single day for their tongues alone.[16] The prizes were taken to be sold and the carcasses abandoned to bake in the sun, an all-too-familiar sight in an era marked by mounds of "bleached skeletons" strewn across the landscape.[17]

At the beginning of the nineteenth century, tens of millions of bison roamed the American plains. For thousands of years they had served as a cornerstone in the lives of the Natives, and their habits had played a vital role in the natural ecosystem, but soon, after targeted hunting designed to hurt Indigenous populations and ceaseless harvesting for production, only a few hundred would remain.[18] The burgeoning Industrial Revolution required resources and ever-increasing materials, including bison fur and hides for clothes, rugs, and machine belts, and their bones for industrial products and substances. The bison had been reduced to its parts, targeted for maximum profit and utility in the market, and cut down with reckless abandon.

The rapid near extinction was merely one sign that the world had fundamentally changed. The horizon was suddenly dotted with smokestacks belching dark smoke. New markets materialized, bloated with mass quantities of cheap goods. Cities seemingly grew with every single day, the inhabitants stuffed into cramped living quarters and their lives dedicated to gruesome toil as they were assimilated into the swelling ranks of the working class.

By 1848, English economist John Stuart Mill was already concerned. The new system was quickening by the second as frenzied capitalists and industrialists sought to utilize every possible resource. Mill recognized this growth and consumption were unsustainable and would have vast consequences if left unchecked. Environmentally, "unlimited increase" meant a deterioration of the natural world.[19] And if growing inequalities between the classes were not addressed, undoubtedly it would produce a society where "some persons grow richer and others poorer."[20]

The Industrial Revolution triggered a consumer society where goods and luxuries were made quickly and cheaply by combining resources from around the world with exploited labor. It was made possible by the previous eras of colonialism and abuse, building off the established conveyor belts of resource extraction and domestic production, ensuring that the most powerful nations and individuals held sway over the oppressed peoples; guided their mining, agriculture, and labor; and then reaped the benefits in their factories and markets.

Just as early corporations became central to the well-being of the empires that birthed them, the health and interests of these capitalists and businesses came to determine the destiny of the nation. By 1817 British economist David Ricardo had already taken notice of the symbiosis and its costs, observing, "The same cause which may increase the net revenue of the country, may at the same time render the population redundant, and deteriorate the condition of the labourer."[21] Developing technologies had led to expedited production, but workers had become disposable and relatively helpless in their relation to employers. This dynamic was welcomed by a certain class of economists and capitalists. Among them was Andrew Ure, whose examination of British mills produced *The Philosophy of Manufactures* in 1835 and extolled the "great doctrine" of the time that technological development served as a grand tool in teaching workers "docility" and reasserting the rightful order of the "legitimate race" of the elites "over the inferior numbers."[22]

This subordination had consequences. Arriving in the industrialized English city of Manchester in 1842, German economist Friedrich Engels was stunned by what he found. What some praised as progress had already produced "barbarous indifference" among the society at large and a "nameless misery" among the workers.[23] While many British citizens reaped the rewards of the new consumerist society and access to affordable goods, the poor had been "removed from the sight of the happier classes" and isolated in slums.[24] Everywhere Engels looked he saw desolation, disease, and abject despair. "I assert," he wrote in his treatise *The Condition of the Working-Class in England,* "that thousands of industrious and worthy people . . . do find themselves in a condition unworthy of human beings."[25]

For the poor in the Industrial Revolution, life was labor. Free of regulations, capitalists worked their employees for hours upon hours in unsafe conditions. The entire family toiled. Like their fathers and mothers, children were put to work. As secretary of the Treasury and an ardent proponent of industrialization, Alexander Hamilton had presented *Report on the Subject of Manufactures* in 1791, which praised this despicable aspect, arguing the new industry provided "employment of persons who would otherwise be idle," and expressly noted that "women and children are rendered more useful, and the latter more early useful, by manufacturing establishments, than they would otherwise be."[26]

Child labor made use of children's small frames, nimbleness, and disposability. Made to squeeze into cramped spaces, remove jams from machines, and accompany grown men into the depths of mines, children were routinely placed in incredibly dangerous positions. One horrific tale, relayed by a former child laborer, recalled the death of a nine-year-old girl named Mary Richards, caught in a machine in London and "whirled round and round" as her helpless coworkers listened to "the bones of her arms, legs, thighs . . . successively snap asunder, crushed seemingly to atoms," while her blood was "thrown about like water from a twirled mop."[27] Those lucky to have escaped death or dismemberment lived childhoods devoid of whimsy or even basic human decency. Interviews of their ranks found them illiterate, malnourished, subject to abuse and constant suffering.

Defenders like Andrew Ure confessed they found it "delightful" to watch children labor and extolled the benefits of a childhood spent in the factory.[28] After all, the developing system of capitalism and industrialization promised its own utopia, and everybody had a role if the promised future was to be realized. Ure argued that international markets and economic competition had come to replace war as nations "converted their swords and muskets into factory implements" in order to "contend with each other in the bloodless but still formidable strife of trade."[29] In this way, it became an article of faith that capitalism would usher in a new era of world peace.

Adam Smith had alluded to an "invisible hand" in his writings on the markets, but as capitalism evolved, some began to outright evangelize its spiritual components. In his 1825 book *Outlines of Political Economy,* preacher and economist John McVickar declared that capitalism worked in "harmonious alliance with religion" and when left alone carried out God's will.[30] Evidence of divine intent was to be found everywhere, and in observing the workings of industry, it was obvious that, as God's creation and an instrument of his will, "man is but a machine for the creation of value."[31]

Profit, it seemed, was the purpose of life.

With the marriage of capitalism and religion, regulation of the markets was tantamount to heresy. The process of production, accumulation of capital, and growth of economies and markets overshadowed any other concerns, whether it was the well-being of the workers or the dangers of wealth's dominating the public sphere. As with the stories told in the nascent days of colonialism, when slavery and genocide were necessary in order for humanity to reach its heavenly potential, now the exploitation of the labor force, as well as the craven destruction of the natural world, were both essential in the pursuit of progress. The

Industrial Revolution had taken off, full steam ahead, and once more it was the prerogative of the wealthy to conquer in the name of God, profit, and civilization, regardless of the human toll.

On the morning of September 2, 1898, roughly twenty-five thousand British and Egyptian soldiers took the field outside Omdurman in Sudan. To protect their economic interests in the Suez Canal, the British had set off to reconquer the Sudanese and were now face-to-face with a rival force more than twice their number.

One eyewitness recalled, "It was not a battle but an execution."[32]

Armed with superior weaponry, the British side made easy work of the charging dervishes. Journalist Ernest Bennett detailed the "roar of the artillery, the shriek of shells, the crisp volleys of the Lee-Metfords, and the unceasing rat-tat-tat of the deadly Maxims," a cacophony of violence that ensured none of the Sudanese even came within "five hundred yards" of the lines as "the Maxims and rifles rained bullets upon them [and] the murderous sheet of lead mowed them down."[33] When it was all said and done, the opposition was "practically annihilated." Tens of thousands of the Sudanese were either killed or wounded, compared to the British loss of a few dozen.

Developing technologies had gifted the European elites better weapons with which to fight the populations they wished to conquer, as well as the medicines necessary to penetrate deeper into foreign territories. This, coupled with the symbiotic relationship between state and business, meant a new age of intervention and conquering, ensuring that the materials necessary for production and expansion would fall under the control of the states that dominated the world.

No empire of the era made greater use of these innovations than the British. Existing on the edges of the European order, Britain prided itself on being the defining actor on the world stage. Through ceaseless action and aggression, the British Empire grew exponentially in the nineteenth century, motivated by a self-aggrandizing worldview best captured by the words of Henry John Temple, Viscount Palmerston, a twice-elected prime minister, who lionized Britain as "the champion of justice and right" with a dedication to principles both "eternal and perpetual."[34] In Palmerston's and the British's reality, the order of the world had been established by God to divide his people into "separate nations" and "races . . . distinguished by separate languages, habits, manners, dispositions, and characters."[35] At the top of that hierarchy, naturally, were the British, and it was their duty to rule over the "brutes": the people of color of the world.

The hierarchy of the races, backed by the supposed will of God and conveniently in line with the economic interests of the wealthiest few, gifted cover to the dominant states to interfere in the affairs of other nations, particularly if those nations were home to people of color. In China, the British warred in order to support opium merchants, eventually defeating the Chinese and forcing them to both legalize the drug and establish open, preferential markets promising the British freedom to operate "without molestation or restraint."[36] In India, economic interests continued to dominate political affairs. Throughout it all, British military and political bodies ensured that materials necessary to feed the industrial machine flowed without interruption.

This new era of imperialism was best embodied by Cecil Rhodes, a businessman who used the imperial drive to build himself a personal empire in Africa. Rhodes founded the diamond company De Beers in 1888 and grew it into a monopoly that dominated the trade and large swaths of the continent, claiming, all the while, that the "great object" of his pursuits and the reason for his territorial conquests was to "paint the map red for England."[37]

Backed by the forces of empire, Rhodes became the prime minister of the Cape Colony in South Africa, using his position to fortify his economic interests and craft a society to his and his partners' advantage. His regime was explicitly white supremacist and viewed the Black natives as "children . . . just emerging from barbarism" who needed, through his laws and authority, to recognize that "nine-tenths of them will have to spend their lives in daily labour," more than likely in service of his bottom line.[38]

British imperialism in Africa created one conflict after another with natives and competing interests as the empire sought control over more and more territory and resources. Near the turn of the century, the discovery of more precious metals instigated the South African War, between British forces and Dutch colonists known as Boers. A young Winston Churchill traveled to Africa to cover the hostilities before being captured by the Boers and held as a prisoner of war, where he discovered their motivating fear was that the British would proclaim the Black natives "the same as white" and that "the dominant race [was] to be deprived of their superiority."[39] Churchill came to see the disagreement as a "bitter, bloody war tearing the land in twain; dividing brother from brother, friend from friend, and opening a terrible chasm between the two white races."[40]

Eventually, after gaining an advantage in this "white war," the British responded to guerilla tactics with a brutal innovation: the concentration camp. They erected barbed-wire fences and relocated entire families and communities to these structures; the "undesirables" were imprisoned, starved, exposed to rampant disease, and forced to perform slave labor.[41] British reformer Emily Hobhouse traveled to the camps herself to inspect their conditions and was brokenhearted to find long-suffering prisoners with "disease and death . . . stamped upon their faces," including emaciated children starving before her very eyes.[42]

The accumulation of territory and resources for the purpose of expanding markets was an unnegotiable prerogative. All efforts, no matter how grisly, how inhumane, how cruel, were necessary in order for the noble, godly pursuit of wealth and power to be maintained. Technological advancements, partnered with administrative and military energies, weren't just creating new means of profit but escalating the conditions under which the state could dominate the natural world, political conditions, and, ultimately, the individual.

Klemens von Metternich's grand "equilibrium" proved remarkably short-lived as repression naturally bred resentment and stoked the same revolutionary spirits it intended to snuff out. From the beginning of the Concert of Europe, there were spasms of uprising, grassroots protests, and movements focused on breaking the iron grip of the conservative order and founded on individual liberties, economic equality, and nationalism, which the international agreement suppressed. By 1848, conditions were primed for widespread revolution.

Reading the writing on the wall, Metternich resigned as chancellor of Austria in March of 1848 and fled into exile. Before the revolts were put down and a semblance of order restored, uprisings surged in France, the German states, the Austrian Empire, Italy, Denmark, and elsewhere, fueled by nationalistic rejection of empire and a call for the liberalization of Europe. The ruling, monarchial class Metternich had served battled back and crushed the revolutions, engaging in bloody confrontations and rooting out subversives by any means necessary, but in some cases, following brief promises and concessions that would be rescinded, the middle and upper classes were bought off, leaving their allies in the lurch.

In France the specter of yet another revolution and chaos prompted a conservative backlash that harnessed the hesitancy among the landed and rural classes to pay for urban welfare and portrayed itself as the "Party of Order." Thus, capitalism had created a new class conflict that would define the modern era. Whereas the French Revolution in 1789 had been largely a contest between an aristocratic ruling regime and the people, by 1848 a class of individuals with accumulated wealth and capital had emerged with conservative tendencies and at least a tertiary attachment to maintaining the status quo.

In the run-up to the 1848 election of France's first president, a leader materialized who promised to make France great again. Louis-Napoleon

Bonaparte, the nephew of Napoleon Bonaparte, had long chased his uncle's great shadow and actually attempted multiple coups with the goal of reestablishing the past regime. Now Louis promised, "I am not an ambitious man, who dreams of the empire and of war," and assured the public that if elected president he would serve only four years and "leave to my successor . . . the executive powers strengthened, liberty intact, and a real progress accomplished."[43]

Captivated by the allure of a return to the heights of the Napoleonic empire, voters handed Louis an overwhelming victory with nearly three-quarters of the popular vote. Three years later, as his term was coming to an end, Louis predictably betrayed his promise. On the morning of December 2, 1851, Parisians awoke to find their city plastered with notices and declarations from their president warning that France was "a vessel rushing into the abyss" and saying, "The present situation cannot last much longer."[44] Louis-Napoleon cited his rivals and the government as having become "a theater of plots" and claimed he had no choice but to seize absolute authority.[45]

Although the French desired a return to Napoleonic glory, Louis was far from up to the challenge. Considered by contemporaries a man with "immense ambitions and limited faculties," his desire to follow in his uncle's footsteps would doom him and France's lust for empire.[46] This vulnerability was noticed by Otto von Bismarck, a Prussian leader who expertly diagnosed the French emperor as lost in "cherished reminisces."[47] Bismarck's goal was to unify the German states and realize a German Reich, but he knew the fate of such a project would not be decided through diplomacy, negotiation, or uprising but by the "blood and iron" of battle.[48] To forge Germany as an independent, unified state, Bismarck believed war with Louis-Napoleon's France was essential.

Despite his advancing age and the challenge of a formidable foe, Louis-Napoleon could not help but engage Prussian forces in 1870 and demanded to lead his armies in the field as his uncle had decades prior. After being defeated, Louis surrendered himself to Bismarck and was held captive for months before repairing to England in exile. Germany was well on the way to realizing its own state and France was once more cast into chaos.

While the Franco-Prussian War raged, a novel movement took shape in Paris. The collapse of Louis-Napoleon's empire created a vacuum in French society, allowing radicals to gain a foothold. Spurred by militants who had been previously imprisoned for their roles in the Revolution of 1848, they battled the ailing state in the streets and constituted an army of "carpenters, joiners, mechanics, foundry workers, turners, masons" relying on one another to fend off enemies and "improvise all the equipment necessary for war."[49]

After a long-fought battle, the radicals brandished the red flag of socialism and celebrated a momentary victory, declaring on March 18, 1871, "In the name of the people, the Commune is proclaimed."[50] Though it was only a little over two months before the French government broke the Commune and executed its leaders, its brief reign and focus on the interests of the working class signaled to some searching for alternatives to entrenched systems that hope still remained for a future free of economic and political exploitation.

Among them was the German philosopher Karl Marx. Though he recognized the limitations of the Paris Commune, Marx saw it as proof that existing modes of power were already "pregnant" with "the new society" that would inevitably replace them.[51] Marx diagnosed capitalism as a transitory system that would eventually destroy itself through its inherent contradictions before being replaced by socialism and finally a worldwide communism that eradicated the fiction of the nation-state and united the people, thus eliminating war and need forever.

In the capitalist stage, those benefiting from its inequalities portrayed capitalism as naturally occurring and inevitable rather than as a side effect of a designed system. Much like Christianity, with its mythology in which "Adam bit the apple, and thereupon sin fell on the human race," Marx drew a direct line to the myth of capitalist meritocracy, which explained gross, artificial inequality and human suffering by telling a story of two races of people—a "diligent, intelligent, and, above all, frugal elite" with wealth and power and "the other, lazy rascals, spending their substance, and more, in riotous living."[52]

The narrative of history dominating people's minds and imagination was yet another story that served the whims of the affluent. Marx declared with his partner Friedrich Engels, "The history of all hitherto existing society is the history of class struggles," creating a materialistic study of events that focused on how the wealthy had oppressed the masses to enrich themselves.[53] This process created definitive classes, including the bourgeoisie (the middle class) and the proletariat (the working class), and a system that replicated itself around the world by compelling other nations and people, "on pain of extinction, to adopt the bourgeois mode of production" under the banner of "civilization."[54] In this process, however, Marx believed that capitalism had painted itself into a corner. Comparing the bourgeoisie to a sorcerer "no longer able to control the powers of the nether world," Marx believed they had "forged the weapons" that would bring their inevitable demise.[55] Eventually, Marx held, the working peoples would reach a point of class-consciousness and overthrow their oppressors.

The dismal realities of industrialized society, with its human misery and emphasis on rationality, as well as the fallout from Metternich's conservative oppression and developing scientific theories, created a moment of upheaval and change in which several ideologies began to take shape. Reactionary worldviews gained untold numbers of converts, some concerning themselves with the material realities of politics, economics, and science, while others probed more esoteric and mysterious depths.

Beginning with an early rejection of Enlightenment ideals, many followed the path of German philosopher Johann Georg Hamann, who criticized the "purification of reason" and its "failed attempt to make reason independent of all tradition and custom."[56] Hamann's theories on the schism between the Enlightenment's emphasis on reason and its neglect of emotions, sensations, and even nature itself inspired movements of thought and art, like Sturm und Drang in Germany, that embraced the individual, their experiences as well as their heritage.

Relatedly, the Romantic movement that spread throughout the nineteenth century reflected a fear that technology and industrialization had gone too far, that in seeking to conquer nature, humanity had committed a horrific and possibly incurable wrong and reduced the human to a cog in a massive, bloodless machine. In her 1818 book *Frankenstein; or, The Modern Prometheus,* Mary Shelley told the story of a scientist who had meddled with the forces of life and death and confessed, upon realizing the fruits of his labor, "I had desired it with an ardor that exceeded moderation, but now that I had finished, the beauty of the dream vanished, and breathless horror and disgust filled my heart."[57] Similarly, the poet William Blake's work contrasted the idyllic splendor of nature, with its "mountains green" and "pleasant pastures," with the "dark Satanic Mills" that had come to dominate the landscape.[58]

A fear began to permeate that something had been lost in the transition from feudalism to capitalism, from agrarian life to industrial toil. The Enlightenment's methodical divorce of public life from religion and emphasis on science and reason inspired a new search for something beyond the visible world. Pursuits like Spiritualism, a belief in the ability of mediums to communicate with the dead, became fashionable among those looking for explanations of the ugly workings of the physical world and seeking what spiritualist Emma Hardinge Britten called "the shadowy outline of a second world of existence."[59]

This craving for hidden meanings sent people in search of new religions and wisdom that had been supposedly lost for thousands of years. The era prioritized past experiences and esoteric knowledge, the same mythologies spurned by the Enlightenment and labeled as mystification by Marx. A Russian mystic named Helena Blavatsky and called "Madame" by her acolytes studied the origins of a mythical race called "Aryans." She divided the human race into "god-informed men and lower human creatures," as personified in the "Aryan" race and "savages," who were missing the so-called sacred spark.[60] Around these ideas Blavatsky founded the Theosophical Society in New York and earned converts wishing to hear the hidden history of the world and her prophecy for the future. Blavatsky told them that humanity had traveled through multiple cycles and that at the root of history and development raged a life-or-death contest between the races.

The publication of Charles Darwin's *On the Origin of Species* in 1859 troubled the scientific and religious worlds but also gifted momentum to disturbing ideas about race, inequality, and the possibility that science might be harnessed to improve the species. Darwin himself was not immune to this, as he believed it was inevitable that "the civilized races of man will almost certainly exterminate and replace throughout the world the savage races."[61]

In scrutinizing liberal society, Darwin found it problematic that "civilized men . . . build asylums for the imbecile, the maimed, and the sick," that assistance was given to the poor, and doctors were preoccupied with saving "the life of every one to the last moment."[62] Surely, Darwin believed, this restricted the forces of natural selection and was "highly injurious to the race of men," as the "worst animals" continued to breed.[63]

This "breeding" had been a major debate as industrialization and technology created booming populations. Prior to the Industrial Revolution, Thomas Robert Malthus, a British economist, posited that population growth kept humanity from achieving its potential and constructing a heaven on Earth, a theory that gained favor as industrial nations saw their populations wallow in poverty. Rather than advocate social welfare, Malthus and his adherents believed handouts only perpetuated the misery. Solutions were few and far between, but Malthus considered the possibility of a society in which "bad specimens" were prohibited from propagating.[64]

As capitalism was portrayed as the economic expression of natural law, Darwin's theories and widespread inequality coalesced into a philosophy that held poverty was a result of genetic inferiority among the masses; all assistance was therefore detrimental in holding back the forces necessary to improve the human race. Championing a belief in "survival of the fittest," English philosopher Herbert Spencer believed it a "delusion" that "an illworking humanity may be framed into well-working institutions" and posited that their "defective natures" would live on regardless of "whatever social structure they are arranged into."[65]

Following in the footsteps of the visionaries of the Scientific Revolution so many centuries earlier, a belief percolated among the scientific and educated class, armed with Darwin's discovery, that it might be beneficial should elites press their thumbs on the scale and carry out nature's will themselves. Darwin's cousin Francis Galton, himself a leading scientific mind, suggested "supplanting inefficient human stock by better strains" and wondered if "it might not be our duty . . . to further the ends of evolution more rapidly and with less distress than if events were left to their own course."[66]

Debates about which races deserved to continue, which should retreat into oblivion, and what people deserved rights sparked one confrontation after another in the United States of America, where imperialism, industrialization, and calls for reform would combine, explode, and determine the young nation's path.

In securing its independence from Britain and establishing a republic based on Enlightenment ideals, America had largely kicked off the so-called Age of Revolutions in 1776. Colonists had united to deal a staggering blow to England and, in turn, created a government captured by the interests of wealthy, white, property-owning men at the expense of enslaved people, Natives, women, and the poor. The construction of this government had the intended purpose of presenting to the populace the illusion of representation while employing carefully designed measures to maintain control among a limited few.

By 1794, merely six years after the Constitution's ratification, there were already signs the new system would be tested. A tax on distillers led to uprisings in Pennsylvania, where disgruntled citizens rigorously obstructed the business of the state and co-opted past revolutionary rhetoric by erecting "Liberty Poles" adorned with phrases like "Liberty or Death." So pressing was this insurrection that President George Washington raised an army and led it into the field himself to crush the revolt, demanding nothing less than "absolute submission."[67]

Discontent was brewing within the ruling elite. The spoils from the War of Independence had been relegated to a wealthy few and the "freedom" promised had come up short. Aspiring politician and future Republican representative Matthew Lyon lambasted the ruling Federalists as "men who consider the science of government to belong naturally only to a few families, and argue, that their families ought to be obeyed and supported in princely grandure [*sic*]."[68] In assessing the Whiskey Rebellion and a federal call for troops to suppress it, one newspaper charged, "Let stockholders, bank directors, speculators, and revenue officers arrange themselves immediately under the banners of treasury . . . [as] they have already received most of the emoluments of the revolution."[69]

Washington was convinced the new nation faced a tremendous threat from within. In his sixth address to Congress, he warned, "Some of the citizens of the United States have been found capable of an insurrection," and placed a large share of the blame on "certain self-created societies."[70] Writing to John Jay, the first chief justice of the Supreme Court, Washington was even more explicit, citing "self-created societies . . . laboring incessantly to sow the seeds of distrust, jealousy, and of course discontent, thereby hoping to effect some revolution in the government."[71]

The framers of the country had envisioned a state guided by a united ruling class of wealthy white men and operating as a one-party system. Politics, they believed, should be factionless, and a tacit agreement among the aristocracy would lead the way and make the clash of party politics completely unnecessary. Within Washington's first term, however, rivals to the Federalists began coalescing and creating party machinery, Federalists charged, "to unhinge the whole order of government, and introduce confusion, so that union, the constitution, the laws, public order and private right would be all the sport of violence or chance."[72]

Rumors spread through America to the same tune that captivated conservative Europe. Jedidiah Morse, the "Father of American Geography" and a preacher, sermonized that within American society churned "a deep-laid plan" that had, like a virus, infected citizens and made "the unsuspecting American people" the traffickers of its poison.[73] This plot had been enacted by "the dark conspiracies of the *Illuminati* against civil government and Christianity," and, if not discovered and dismantled, would lead to the same chaos and bloodshed as the French Revolution. Timothy Dwight IV, president of Yale College, labeled this threat an "Antichristian empire" aided by "teachers" who, through "impure, loathsome, impudent, pertinacious, proud, deceitful, impious, malicious, and cruel" means, worked to "contend against God, and against his kingdom in this world."[74] This raising of a satanic force in opposition to God, and its political machinations, would certainly lead to the horrors of the Book of Revelation and Christianity being "exterminated."[75]

Supposedly the ringleader of this cabal was none other than Founding Father Thomas Jefferson, who had become the leader of the Democratic-Republican Party and chief rival of Washington's successor John Adams. Jefferson was accused of being "the real Jacobin, the very child of modern illumination, the foe of man, and the enemy of his country," and his developing party of carrying out a "scheme of Illuminatism in America to worm its notaries into all offices of trust, and importance, that the weapon of government upon signal given, may be turned against itself."[76]

Fears that Jefferson would reveal himself as an agent of the Illuminati proved unfounded: His presidency represented a sea change in politics but was far from a betrayal of the country's principles. Jefferson's Southern agrarian background informed his vision for a future in which industrialization was kept across the ocean and America maintained as a land of independent farmers. To seed this vision, Jefferson purchased 530 million acres of land from Napoleon Bonaparte, whose loss of Haiti left him soured on empire in North America. This expanded the nation in one fell swoop and gave America territory west of the Mississippi and the beginnings of access to the rest of the continent.

To carry out Jefferson's dream, however, the problem of Native Americans would have to be solved. Since the days of settler colonialism, the relationship between white colonists and the Indigenous tribes had been fraught, and with the birth of the nation this would only worsen. Jefferson counseled his governors and allies to work to ensnare Natives in debt to the government until "these debts get beyond what the individuals can pay" and they "become willing to lop them off by a cession of lands."[77] Jefferson wrote, "Our settlements will gradually circumscribe and approach the Indians, and they will in time either incorporate with us as citizens of the United States, or remove beyond the Mississippi."[78] In communicating this, Jefferson realized the sensitivity of the subject and his plans, warning it should be kept secret from Natives, saying, "For their interests and their tranquility it is best they should see only the present age of their history."[79]

Under the auspices of protecting and aiding Native Americans, in 1819 the Civilization Fund Act was created to make "provision for the civilization of the Indian tribes" and for the "purpose of providing against further decline and final extinction."[80] This act paid to forcibly remove Native children from their homes and place them in environments where, as had been the case in other colonial projects, their identities would be erased and their homes and beliefs and culture taken from them, all before they were plunged into a reality authored by and in the interests of white culture.

By 1830, this façade of humanitarian aid allowed President Andrew Jackson, obsessed with freeing up Native land for the profit of speculators, to spearhead removal. Jackson duplicitously lamented the Native Americans "surrounded by the whites with their arts of civilization" and worried it would "doom [them] to weakness and decay."[81] To "protect this much injured race," there was no alternative but to force them west, where "the benevolent may endeavor to teach them the arts of civilization."

Jackson, the Democratic Party, and the dominant political actors of the era unleashed what would come to be known as "Manifest Destiny," or the belief that God himself had ordained the white American race to conquer the continent. Anthropologist Lewis Henry Morgan, who spent much of his career studying Native Americans, held that it was the "aggressive" nature of civilization that had led to expansion and the tragedies the tribes endured, blaming "the institutions of the red man," which were "fragile and precarious," in contrast to "civilized man's" drive to "seize" and "grasp" power.[82] Though he claimed to grieve this process, Morgan no less considered it "an absolute necessity."[83]

To make "useful . . . the worthless and troublesome Indian population," reservations were founded to deal with and isolate the refugees.[84] Many children were confiscated and put under the tutelage of men like Richard Henry Pratt, a brigadier general who oversaw boarding schools where the children were indoctrinated, given different names, used as forced labor, abused, and assaulted, and, in several cases, children died only to be tossed into unmarked graves, their families often never learning what had become of them. Pratt's motto was to "kill the Indian . . . and save the man," a process of cultural destruction through military-like processes that might "civilize" the Native.[85] These and other terrible tactics were embraced by John Oberly, commissioner of Indian affairs, who blamed Native American suffering on a culture of "idleness and debauchery" and faulted the communal nature of the Native, saying that before he could advance in civilization "he must be imbued with the exalting egotism of American civilization, so that he will say 'I' instead of 'We,' and 'This is mine,' instead of 'This is ours.'"[86]

The business of displacing the Native Americans had all but been completely achieved as the American experiment spread west and toward the Pacific Ocean, but that expansion would unleash long-simmering divisions. Cultures and economic philosophies were about to clash: The original sin of American slavery, which had made possible the nation's political and economic systems, would finally require an answer once and for all.

American history is largely the story of paranoia. Beginning with the first colonists to arrive on the continent and tracing through the revolutionary era and the adoption of the Constitution, the United States' political path has been determined by fear of conspiracies, whether it was the prospect of the British inspiring Natives and enslaved people to rise up or terror that the Illuminati might spring a trap on the nascent nation.

Following the election of 1800, with its conspiratorial underpinnings, groups like the Know Nothings coalesced in the nineteenth century to combat rumored plots of outside interference in American affairs. The Know Nothings grew in opposition to Irish and German immigrants, whom they believed to be in league with the Democratic Party to steal elections and realize a "foreign potentate over free America."[87]

The Know Nothings believed incredible lies, including the "revelations" of a former nun named Maria Monk who claimed in a runaway bestseller titled *Awful Disclosures* that, in her time in the Catholic Church, she had personally witnessed devilish abuse and violent assaults, including a ritual of killing infants where their "little bodies were then taken into the cellar, thrown into the pit."[88] Rumors like these motivated the group to attack the alleged conspirators and engage in election obstruction.

Another conspiracy theory created a political body called the Anti-Masonic Party, which operated as a reaction against Andrew Jackson, as well as the disappearance and presumed murder in 1826 of William Morgan, a man who sought to publish the Freemasons' secrets. Believing Freemasons controlled society and operated as an organized-crime body, the party gained enough support that multiple members were elected to office before being absorbed by the Whigs.

The American Civil War, which raged from 1861 to 1865, was also birthed from several paranoid fears, primarily the Southern fear that Northern society, including its institutions, schools, organizations, and politicians, was determined to outlaw the practice of slavery. Much of this fear was predicated on a shifting political landscape that saw westward expansion creating new conflicts and debates, including whether new states would be welcomed into the union as free or slave states.

Beginning with the framing of the Constitution, during which the Southern states had held up the process in order to secure slavery as a protected institution and earn representative advantages from those who were enslaved, the South had used the concessions to dominate the political environment. Expansion threatened this stranglehold and brought with it the rise of the Republican Party, which opposed the Southern Democrats and their tactics in a way the Whigs had never dared to.

Southern paranoia stemmed from the institution of slavery itself: a constant fear that those in bondage would rise up against their masters. Past uprisings, including those in the American South and nearby in Haiti, kept Southerners terrified of any sudden change. The Haitian Revolution had proved a lasting terror for enslavers, who referred to it as "the Horrors of Santo Domingo." For years, enslavers remembered going to bed at night, armed with their weapons and "with most sinister thoughts creeping into mind" that the humans they held in vicious bondage might come for them at any moment.[89]

As an enslaver, Thomas Jefferson spent much of his time and energy considering this possibility and had written extensively in correspondence that he believed a day of reckoning for American slavery was inevitable. The time to "proceed peaceably" was running out, and he wrote, "The revolutionary storm now sweeping the world will be upon us."[90]

That revolution was, unlike the famed uprising that secured American independence, organized and eventually won on the efforts of grassroots movements that troubled the political order of the day and brought the issue of slavery to a head. This crusade was helmed by freed and enslaved African Americans, early feminists, and a conglomeration of leftist forces that agitated for a political reckoning several generations in the making, all the while operating with organized defiance in bodies like the Underground Railroad.

Free African Americans fought for the liberation of their enslaved people, helping traffic those escaping bondage, writing books, publishing newspapers, giving lectures, and networking with organizations to bring the issue center stage. David Walker, a Black abolitionist, led the way with his 1829 book *Appeal . . . to the Coloured Citizens of the World* and positioned opposition to slavery as a religious issue, warning that God would "at one day appear fully in behalf of the oppressed."[91] If this counsel was not heeded, Walker promised, "the Lord our God will bring other destructions" upon those oppressors, causing "them to rise up one against another to be split and divided and to oppress each other, and sometimes to open hostilities with sword in hand."[92]

Politically active women served as twin soldiers of both abolitionism and the fight for equal rights. Members of both movements trafficked together, agitating for the United States to make good on its promise of liberty, equality, and freedom, joining to create a solidly unified, grassroots push for change. Part of the genesis of this alliance came in 1840 at the World Anti-Slavery Convention in London, where women were barred from participating despite fervent protest. On their own, early feminists like Lucretia Mott cited the link between African Americans and women, both "degraded by the crushing influences around them."[93] Eventually this would result in the holding of the Seneca Falls Convention in July of 1848, where participants called for equal treatment before the law, a demand echoed by Frederick Douglass, who attended and declared, "We are free to say that in respect to political rights, we hold women to be justly entitled to all we claim for man."[94]

Reactions in the South were apoplectic. Editor Edward Pollard targeted the "great revolutionary element of the North" and laid the blame for these energies on Northern education, in which Pollard claimed teachers were indoctrinating their students into disrespecting institutions and embracing "the agitations of revolution" and "generating 'isms'" like feminism, abolitionism, and socialism.[95] Southern politicians like James Henry Hammond of South Carolina considered the abolitionists and their associations an "infection spread with unparalleled rapidity."[96] Hammond charged that radicals in the North were intentionally splitting the nation in two by lying about the treatment of enslaved people in order to end slavery, the "greatest of all the great blessings which a kind Providence has bestowed."[97]

The rise of the Republican Party made these fears seem all the more plausible. Though members were not necessarily advocating the abolition of slavery, their willingness to oppose its expansion into new territories and brawl with Southern Democrats created a sense that the end was nigh. The political balance present since the adoption of the Constitution, namely the assurance that the South would more or less dominate national politics, had shifted so much that Abraham Lincoln was elected the sixteenth president despite being left off the ballot in all but one of the future Confederate states.

Obsessed with liberal movements in the North and facing a new electoral reality, the South refused to accept this change. "The South will never permit Abraham Lincoln to be inaugurated President of the United States," an editorial appearing in an Atlanta newspaper promised, and any effort to carry out the ceremony would lead to Washington, DC being "crimsoned in human gore" and its streets "paved ten fathoms deep with mangled bodies."[98] A plot was hatched by a secret society calling themselves Knights of the Golden Circle, a white supremacist, Southern paramilitary group that desired to conquer Cuba, Central America, and Mexico in order to create a new slave empire. The group, which included members of the federal government, planned to capture Lincoln in Baltimore while he was on his way to the inauguration, then interrupt the process by overtaking the Capitol and installing outgoing Vice President John Breckinridge as the new president. Tipped off to the plan, Lincoln avoided the kidnapping and swore his oath of office.

The Civil War was not only a political and societal schism but a religious one as well. Abolitionists had long counted in their ranks ministers of conscience, including Henry Ward Beecher, who condemned America as betraying the will of God and, of the nation and slavery, cried, "One or the other must die."[99] In the South, Christian leaders worked to anchor slavery within the doctrines of the faith and legitimize their cause in holy grandeur. South Carolina preacher James Henley Thornwell called slavery "the obligation to labour for another, determined by the Providence of God."[100] In fact, Thornwell preached, "the parties in this conflict are not merely Abolitionists and Slaveholders; they are Atheists, Socialists, Communists, Red Republicans, Jacobins on the one side, and the friends of order and regulated freedom on the other."[101] Jesse Cox of Tennessee took it a step further, labeling the North as the "antichrist, the Beast . . . from the bottomless pits."[102] Preacher J. Jones told the Confederate soldiers it was their duty to fight "the infidel" of the North and engage in "holy war."[103]

Possessed by this idea, the Confederacy conducted its society with the belief that God had chosen them to serve as his champions in an apocalyptic showdown that reflected the warning of the Book of Revelation. Overwhelmed by the forces and technologies of the North, they fell, the people were freed from slavery, and an occupation commenced to ensure a level society would form in the place of the white supremacist regime.

Unfortunately, the festering wounds of the Civil War were ignored, the necessary project of Reconstruction repeatedly interrupted and undermined, and those who were freed betrayed as the modernization of the South and the business of infrastructure required a faster turnaround to the new normal. White supremacy survived through violent, antidemocratic actions in the South and burrowed deep into America's laws, politics, culture, and economics. The nation continued its gross and inhumane inequalities while its infrastructure and economics modernized, laying the foundation for the next stage in civilization.

While America was being dominated by the forces of capitalism, Russia was experiencing convulsions that would put the two states on a collision course that defined much of the twentieth century. This path began in 1825 as Czar Nicholas I succeeded Alexander I, who had played a massive role in the conservative reaction of the post-Napoleon Metternich era. Nicholas I faced an immediate uprising and revolt upon taking the throne, and though he was able to crush this rebellion with overwhelming force, he remained terrified that he was surrounded by conspiracies set in motion by the Illuminati, Freemasons, and Jews.

To counteract this fear, Nicholas I sculpted his reign on the principles of "Orthodoxy, Autocracy, and Nationality," relying on religion, submission to authority, and reverence for Russian character as the bedrocks of his society.[104] To ensure order, constant surveillance and manipulation was carried out by secret police called the Third Section. Meanwhile, politicians like Sergey Uvarov, the minister of education, constructed a system of indoctrination in the nation's schools to combat "a general spread of destructive ideas" that had plagued Europe, relying on professors and teachers "persuaded by one and the same feeling of devotion to throne and fatherland" to "become a worthy tool of the government" and "earn its complete confidence."[105]

This, as well as a string of military failures, fomented a backlash within Russian society. As Russia's self-created myth of strength and dominance crumbled, the cultural stranglehold also gave way. Illusions of might could not survive the obvious humiliation of losing the Crimean War, and Russia was revealed to be a paltry shadow of the mighty power Nicholas I had portrayed it to be. The crashing of mythologies into cold, hard reality inspired disillusionment. Rejecting traditional customs and ideas, the kind that Nicholas I relied on for the bedrock of his authoritarian regime, Russians embraced a skepticism and worldview based on the subjective nature of existence.

The concept had been popularized by the German philosopher Friedrich Nietzsche, who held that the modernization of the world, including liberalism and the establishment of the individual as a force, had revealed the long-hidden truth that religion and tradition were fabrications to maintain order. Nihilism, he forwarded, had been set loose by revelation of "the falsehood and fictitiousness of all Christian interpretations of the world and its history," meaning the individual would have to decide for themselves what morality to abide by, if any at all.[106]

Authoritarians in Russia decried nihilism as a "social disease," a "frustrated religion . . . filled with internal contradictions and nonsense," but as a reaction it allowed alternative philosophies to bloom.[107] For writer Nikolai Chernyshevsky, the loosening of the bonds of tradition meant a possible utopian future in which the working class would come to own the means of production, work joyously, and sing songs of "hearts reborn" and "endless joy."[108] Anarchist Mikhail Bakunin believed "systematic efforts of all governments" maintained the required ignorance and subordination of their people, and, with that in doubt, there was the possibility of a future "free of the religious, legal, social prejudices reigning in the West" and a new world where the people might triumph over the state.[109]

This possibility allowed a revolutionary impulse to possess the moment. Radicals like Sergey Nechayev maintained that "declared or concealed, a relentless and irreconcilable war to the death" raged between the state and the people it oppressed, and from this concept sprung secret societies and organizations dedicated to carrying out this war and overthrowing the regime.[110] This included the group that would come to be known as the People's Will, which held as its guiding principle that "all social forms must rest upon the will of the people themselves" and it was essential to remove "the crushing burden of the existing system" through any means necessary.[111] The chosen tool of the People's Will was terrorism, a strategy designed to disrupt "the fascination with the government's might" among the populace and making the undeclared war between the people and the state an open and recognizable struggle.[112] The People's Will carried out this war against the Russian state and scored its most decisive and consequential blow by assassinating Czar Alexander II on March 13, 1881.

Following the assassination, pogroms broke out in several communities as Russians assaulted Jewish families, ransacked their businesses, and burned their homes. Rather than protect his Jewish citizens, Alexander II's son and successor, Alexander III, told them the reason for their troubles was their "domination" and "exploitation" of the Russian people.[113] Advising him, Minister of the Interior Nikolay Pavlovich Ignatyev supported the assessment, blaming the chaos on "unproductive" Jews who had "captured" the economy.[114]

With the regime's tacit approval, the pogroms raged on. Russians interested in punishing Jews traveled from attack to attack, often bringing with them pictures of their beloved czar that they displayed as they raged and vowed to "defend our motherland from our enemies."[115] In Kyiv, rumors spread that the new czar "had given orders to exterminate the Jews, who had murdered his father."[116] Alexander III would restrict the movement of Jews, steal their property, and hinder their ability to earn a living.

Suspicion that Jewish conspiracies were behind the radical movements grew as men like Jacob Brafman, a former Jew who had converted to Russian Orthodoxy, made a career out of stoking paranoia. Brafman's writings alleged that Jews had created "a state within a state" that worked in secret to undermine the goals and well-being of Russia.[117] By the turn of the century, past fears of Jews betraying Russia for Napoleon had transformed into a new and larger conspiracy theory. In 1905, the mystic Sergei Nilus published what he purported to be a discovered manuscript revealing the Jewish plot in full: *The Protocols of the Elders of Zion*. This document was fabricated and forged, probably by the Russian secret police, but became one of the most influential conspiracy theories in modern history. It supposedly revealed that liberalism, in totality, was a Jewish scheme to undermine the strength of the ruling class and destabilize society. Every war, every revolution, the alleged perpetrators bragged, was "wholly the work of our hands."[118]

Operating from the shadows, Jews had supposedly co-opted newspapers, culture, teachers, and professors "prepared . . . by detailed secret programmes"; the very concepts of liberty, freedom, and equality; and the doctrines of "Darwinism, Marxism, Nietzsche-ism," all to destroy the natural and deserving elite, subvert society, and then, once the moment was right, spring forth a "Super-Government Administration," or a one-world government, "of such colossal dimensions that it cannot fail to subdue all the nations of the world."[119]

The Protocols of the Elders of Zion combined in one document the disparate conspiracy theories that had come to define the conservative, hierarchical worldview and legitimize preemptive violence. With its publication, any aspiring autocrat or opponent of liberalism could either embrace the allegations in full or make reference to them in passing in order to justify whatever cruelty the moment required.

A group called the Black Hundreds emerged to battle these supposed machinations and the Left troubling the regime. These vicious, nationalistic paramilitary groups worked alongside the police and the ruling elite to attack workers, strikers, and protestors as they carried out pogroms against the Jews and brawled with socialists and communists in the streets. Aleksandr Dubrovin, one of the leaders of the group, lectured his followers, "The Holy Russian cause is the extermination of the rebels. You know who they are and where to find them . . . Death to the rebels and the Jews."[120]

Clad in black as they marched by torchlight in search of their enemies, his cohorts took his message to heart, chanting, "Death to the Jews. Death to the Jews."

In June of 1897, Great Britain celebrated Queen Victoria's Diamond Jubilee with massive parades and processions. For days on end, the world's foremost empire reveled in its achievements in a "pageant which for splendor of appearance and especially for splendor of suggestion has never been paralleled in the history of the world."[121] Rudyard Kipling, one of the most lauded writers of the British Empire, composed a work to commemorate the anniversary of a reign that had become synonymous with imperial success. Kipling long peddled the "might, majesty, dominion, and power" of the empire, but the poem he produced was less a triumph than a warning. In it, Kipling spoke of the "far-flung battle-line" of imperialism, the "ancient sacrifice" in striving to civilize the world, and a mission to dominate "lesser breeds without the Law."[122] At the heart of the poem, however, was a caution that the empire's best days might be relegated to the past.

Across the pond, the United States joined in the celebration. *The New York Times* tethered the grandeur of the British Empire to the growing successes of America, boasting, "The achievements of the English-speaking race are our achievements. . . . We are part, and a great part, of the Greater Britain which seems so plainly destined to dominate this planet."[123]

Since the severing of America's direct dependency in 1776, America and Britain's relationship had fluctuated from peace to war, resentment to affection. The nineteenth century, however, with its passions for racial and ethnic ties, drive for empire, and emphasis on cooperation through markets, had created a moment of profound understanding. In fulfilling the quest for Manifest Destiny, Americans embraced the idea of racial struggle to war against the Indigenous tribes and so-called lesser races. In *The New York Herald,* this led to the demand that "all other races . . . must bow and fade" before "the great work of subjugation and conquest to be achieved by the Anglo-Saxon race."[124]

Darwin himself had praised "the wonderful progress of the United States" and "the character of the people," both of which he attributed to the laws of natural selection.[125] The Anglo-Saxon race, he continued, was "highly intellectual, energetic, brave, patriotic and benevolent," a combination of supposedly inherited traits that meant it would "generally prevail over less favored nations."[126] The dominance of the

American project was also explained through the will of God, who favored the Anglo-Saxon race as "the cause of human liberty" and had intended for the "fated aboriginal races . . . to give way to a stronger race."[127] Josiah Strong, a prominent minister and influential national voice, propagated the godliness of imperialism and the divine need for Americans and Anglo-Saxons, as the "noblest races," to conquer the world and subjugate its people in order to carry out the Christian mission.[128]

In 1899, as the United States considered annexing the Philippines following the Spanish-American War, Rudyard Kipling urged them into the fray. The cause of the British Empire in assuming responsibility for civilizing the world, and all of the energies and duties that Kipling had worried over during Victoria's Diamond Jubilee, were at stake as he wrote the poem "The White Man's Burden." Kipling pressed Americans to "take up the White Man's Burden / Send forth the best ye breed" to deal with their "new-caught, sullen peoples / Half-devil and half-child."[129] President William McKinley reportedly agonized over the decision before falling to his knees and begging "for light and guidance from the 'ruler of nations.'"[130] In a message directly from God, McKinley was supposedly instructed "to educate the Filipinos, and uplift and Christianize them."

One of the true believers in American exceptionalism was a senator from Indiana named Albert J. Beveridge, who credited God with having "put in the brain of Jefferson and of Hamilton . . . and of all the imperial intellects of his race—the dream of American extension."[131] God's plan involved the "disappearance of debased civilizations and decaying races," as well as the spread of American markets and, with them, undoubtedly, the flag and American civilization, all of it riding "on the wings of [US] commerce."[132] To accomplish this, Beveridge advocated "Anglo-Saxon solidarity," or "an English-American understanding upon a basis of a division of the world's markets," amounting to "an English-speaking people's league of God."[133]

In England, such an idea had already taken root. Cecil Rhodes, who had used the British Empire and its resources to conquer great swaths of Africa and build his own dominant business, was enamored with his own pieced-together worldview that paired the Darwinist philosophy of race struggle with the need for a massive, ambitious project that might reunite America and Britain. "God," Rhodes claimed, "is manifestly fashioning the English-speaking race as the chosen instrument by which He will bring in a state of society based upon Justice, Liberty, and Peace."[134] By realizing this, Rhodes hoped to make "the Anglo-Saxon race but one Empire."[135] The driving force, he believed, would be the accumulated wealth of white businessmen who had risen to the top of society through capitalism, thus becoming the enactors of God's will. Rhodes saw it as a "secret society" that might leverage "the wealth of the world" to establish a union that dominated all affairs, swore allegiance to the principles of capitalism, and operated based on the supposed values of the white race.[136]

Futurist and science fiction writer H. G. Wells believed the alliance was inevitable and that a "synthetic reconstruction within the bodies of the English-speaking states," as well as the "collapse of the old liberalism," was already under way.[137] Communication technology had linked nation-states, and the triumph of big business had created economic giants that transcended borders and nationalism. In the future, he posited, these corporations, enabled by advanced machinery and lightning-quick communication, would evolve beyond democracy and run the business of world affairs.

Approaching an uncertain future and the dawning of a new century that seemed destined to belong to the white race, Wells wondered, "How will the new republic treat the inferior races? How will it deal with the black? How will it deal with the yellow man? How will it tackle the alleged termite in the civilized woodwork, the Jew?"[138] In finding his answer, Wells reasoned, "The world is a world, not a charitable institution, and I take it they will have to go . . . it is their portion to die out and disappear."[139]

As Wells peered into the future, American John Randolph Dos

Passos argued in his 1903 book *The Anglo-Saxon Century* that in the present moment this alliance was essential if the human race was to avoid destroying itself. The need, he believed, stemmed from the fact that the era of colonization had ended: There were "no more worlds to discover, and territorial absorption by purchase or force of arms is the sole means by which the most powerful nations can add to their possessions."[140] The game of empire building had come to a stalemate, creating a moment of tension that could turn historically tragic as "each nation is armed to the teeth" and the prospect of mobilized, modern warfare had reached the point where, in the case of tensions spilling over and war commencing, the nations involved would "not stop on this side of national solvency and extermination."[141]

- CHAPTER SIX -

A Veneer over Savagery

Fresh off their decisive victory in the Franco-Prussian War, the newly minted state of Germany faced an immediate challenge. Their European rivals had spent centuries building their colonial empires, establishing strategic footholds around the globe, battling and replacing native populations, and constructing a system that fed their coffers and kept the industrial machine humming. Now, desirous of their own empire, the Germans would have to find an entry into the global order.

"Wishing in a spirit of good and mutual accord," Chancellor Otto von Bismarck called the Berlin Conference in 1884 "to regulate the conditions most favourable to the development of trade and civilization in certain regions of Africa."[1] This meeting was Germany's attempt at maintaining a semblance of geopolitical stability while entering the world of colonization. Without so much as hearing from a representative from Africa, the powers planned to share the spoils and fostered a tentative agreement that unleashed a great race to conquer the continent.

Like its competitors, Germany fashioned a national mythology to rationalize its tyranny. The genesis lay in the period precipitating German unification as artists and philosophers dreamed of a unified people and culture. The Sturm und Drang movement had inspired voices like Johann Gottfried Herder to laud the "Fatherland" and claim an individual was nothing without the state, and truly any German without pride in their country had "lost himself."[2] In fact, Herder argued, the "perfect human mind" was that of a soldier steadfast in their loyalty and unquestioning patriotism.[3]

German militaristic identity was far from the only defining characteristic. Philosopher Johann Gottlieb Fichte spoke often of the *Volk,* or masses of people "joined to each other by a multitude of invisible bonds" and "by nature one and an inseparable whole."[4] This mystical association bound the German people to one another and created a shared destiny as they, through this mass, were locked in a cycle of "creating themselves naturally and spiritually out of themselves."

This concept was supported in its infancy by the work of a British-born philosopher named Houston Stewart Chamberlain, who was so enamored of German culture that he emigrated there as the new nation took shape. Chamberlain proclaimed Germans as the "lawful heir" of the Roman Empire and said that, as inheritors of that legacy, they held the responsibility of "the rescuing of agonizing humanity from the clutches of the everlastingly bestial."[5] The struggle to "civilize" the world, Chamberlain believed, was a brutal war between "Aryans" and dangerous people of color and a Jewish conspiracy that had "a large, and in many ways an undoubtedly fatal, influence upon the course of European history."[6]

Germany's national identity emerged from this poisonous collection of racist nonsense, gaining traction as the people were brought under a solitary banner. The concept of a unique destiny, as it had with the other nations, immediately spurred Germany to begin accumulating colonies and resources in order to compete globally. Friedrich Ratzel, a geographer, lent the pursuit a scientific air, cribbing theories from Charles Darwin's concept of evolution in defining a nation as "an organism attached to the land" and that organism as engaged in a natural struggle for survival.[7] In order for the state as a living, breathing creature to persist, Ratzel believed it required Lebensraum, or "living space," into which its inherent culture and peoples could expand.[8]

As the twentieth century approached, these ideas had effectively captured the zeitgeist and made the task of empire building a foregone conclusion. In 1897, foreign minister and future chancellor Bernhard von Bülow declared, "The days when Germans granted one neighbor the earth, the other the sea, and reserved for themselves the sky . . . those days are over." It was time for Germans to "demand our place in the sun."[9]

Like colonial projects before, Germany's entry into colonization was a joint project between the state and wealthy individuals. This partnership would see German colonists settle in South West Africa and raise cattle alongside the native Herero people while businesses helped themselves to the region's supply of diamonds and copper. As German settlers arrived, the Herero were forced onto reservations and their land stolen. In 1904, the Herero retaliated against their colonial invaders, setting off a frenzy of racial genocide.

To handle the uprising, Germany turned to General Lothar von Trotha, who had commanded troops in the state's efforts to crush the Boxer Rebellion in China. Trotha's approach was based strictly in a white supremacist and genocidal mindset. To his commanders, he ordered, "The nation as such should be annihilated . . . the Negro does not respect treaties but only brute force."[10] To the Herero, Trotha delivered a warning: "You have stolen, killed and owe white people . . . You Hereros must now leave this land it belongs to the Germans. If you do not do this I shall remove you with the big gun."[11] German forces ruthlessly sought out the natives and drove them into the nearby desert, where they erected fences and poisoned any available water sources. The results of the first genocide of the twentieth century were horrific. Over 80 percent of the Herero, an estimated sixty-five thousand, were shot, lynched, starved, or worked to the point of death.[12] Any survivors were intended to exist "in a permanent state of forced labour, a kind of slavery."[13]

Survivors were moved into concentration camps patterned after the structures used by the British Empire, where they continued to suffer while being forced to build the railways, homes, and infrastructure necessary for the German empire to continue encroaching on their land. A missionary observing the process grieved as they were worked "until they broke down" and "like cattle . . . were driven to death and like cattle they were buried."[14]

Amid this tragic scene a young scientist named Eugen Fischer traveled to Africa and, with the blessing of leaders, experimented on the natives with the goal of investigating "racial purity." After inflicting torturous, inhumane suffering on the Herero, Fischer came to believe that races that had "assimilated the blood of inferior races . . . paid for this absorption of inferior elements by intellectual, spiritual, and cultural decline."[15] Fischer, through his brutality and disregard for the lives of his victims, discovered what he saw as a "crisis" of white supremacy that would soon shape Germany, its peoples, and the world forever.

On November 9, 1898, several hundred white men huddled in a Wilmington, North Carolina, courthouse. Tensions had been running high for months as a concentrated effort to unseat the town's coalition government and Black elected officials created a firestorm of racist paranoia and organized intimidation. Campaign materials and speeches called on "a proud race, which has never known a master, which has never bent to the yoke of any other race," to "crush the party of Negro domination" by any means necessary.[16] "Before we allow the Negroes to control this state," promised future governor William W. Kitchin, "we will kill enough of them that there will not be enough left to bury them."

The day before, paramilitary and racist mobs had patrolled polling locations and threatened voters, allowing the white supremacists to steal the elections, but those victories weren't enough. If the white race was to maintain a stranglehold on power, more direct action was required. A story in the local paper invited all white men to a meeting, where, squeezed into the cramped room, they listened as the organizers of the white supremacy campaign warned that the very fate of the nation was at stake. Following the Civil War and emancipation, African Americans had rapidly mobilized, winning offices throughout the South. In cities like Wilmington, at the time the largest in North Carolina, Black entrepreneurs had even chiseled out successful businesses and thriving communities. As the white supremacists surveyed the landscape, they were convinced liberal democracy itself was to blame.

Alfred Moore Waddell, a former Confederate soldier and congressman, read to the assembled mob a document titled "The White Declaration of Independence," a manifesto announcing an intention to seize wealth from the Black population and ban them from politics. "Believing that [constitutional] framers did not anticipate the enfranchisement of an ignorant population of African origin," the declaration stated, "we, the undersigned . . . do hereby declare that we will no longer be ruled, and will never again be ruled, by men of African origin."[17]

The next day the men armed themselves, massacred hundreds of African Americans, and destroyed their homes and businesses. The mob grew in bloodlust and size by the minute and soon numbered in the thousands. By the time they were finished, they had entirely taken over Wilmington, expelled the elected leaders by force, and set up a new government in the service of white men.

This white supremacist coup in Wilmington was but one incident in a wave of post–Civil War violence that sought to overturn any semblance of progress or equality for African Americans. Years of reconstruction finally came to an end in 1877 when Republicans seeking to install Rutherford B. Hayes as the nineteenth president of the United States promised to withdraw federal troops and cede the South to white power. Quickly, an apartheid state privileging whites was established.

But the fear gripping the white supremacists in North Carolina was far from exclusive to the South. Throughout the United States, and around the world, white supremacists' anxiety was growing that their domination might be endangered. An Australian politician named Charles H. Pearson contributed to this paranoia in 1893 with the publication of his book *National Life and Character: A Forecast.* Pearson argued that liberalism had so changed the norms of society that it had become "against the fashion of modern humanity" for populations of color to "suffer decrease or oppression," creating an environment where they might increase in size and influence.[18]

Future American president Theodore Roosevelt was so impressed, he penned a letter to Pearson detailing how his colleagues were "excited" by the study and saying that it had "caused so many men to feel that they had to revise their mental estimates of facts."[19] Roosevelt believed that African Americans "as a race and as a mass" were "altogether inferior to the whites" and as president presided over a foreign policy where America effectively controlled countries in its region predominantly inhabited by people of color.[20] Despite this dominance, Roosevelt was still haunted by the specter of what he called "racial suicide," or the possibility that, having conquered the world, the noble races would become stagnant and decay. Chief among these concerns was that the best white citizens might be outbred by lesser individuals and people of color.

Though he championed liberal democracy, Roosevelt saw progress as a double-edged sword: While it improved living conditions, it also motivated people in ways that might injure society and the "race." Social programs and charity, which cared for the poor and downtrodden, ensured their numbers would grow, while tolerance for people of color meant thriving populations.

Animating developing gender struggles was a new battle over modern contraception, which allowed women to choose their own reproductive fates. The prospect sent a bolt of terror through both misogynists and racial paranoids like Roosevelt, who attacked the institution and declared, "The severest of all condemnations should be visited upon willful sterility."[21] Still, Roosevelt claimed he supported feminine independence, as long as women didn't attempt to "substitute" their roles as "the wife, the mother, the sweetheart, the sister," or abandon "their prime duty to the race to leave their seed after them to inherit the earth."[22]

American racial paranoia over population change existed before Roosevelt's presidency and motivated incredibly authoritarian measures in response. In 1873's Comstock Laws, the federal government had passed draconian and repressive measures allowing authorities to censor publications, inspect mail and correspondence, and seek out "every obscene, lewd, or lascivious, and every filthy book, pamphlet, picture, paper, letter, writing, print or other publication of an indecent character," including "offensive" content, pornography, and, notably, information for women seeking birth control or abortion.[23]

The same coalition of African Americans and women that had sparked a progressive revolution again troubled the establishment as America leapt into the twentieth century. White supremacists had all but declared open war on Black citizens as a result, lynching and massacring them, and misogynists did everything possible to slow down a push for gender equality. Building off the organizations that had pressed for abolition, however, white women formed a movement to finally achieve suffrage.

As they did when people of color asserted independence and their rights to self-determination, conservatives characterized the call for reform as a disaster in the making and an affront to divine will. Figures like former president Grover Cleveland spoke against suffrage, arguing that God had made women "loving, long-suffering, self-sacrificing and tender," and that giving them the right to vote would trouble the designs of "a higher intelligence than ours."[24] James Gibbons, the archbishop of Baltimore, concurred, arguing that "to debar women from certain pursuits is not to degrade her" but to merely ensure she continued performing her "special role" assigned by God.[25]

To oppose suffrage, groups like the Man-Suffrage Association littered the nation with screeds characterizing suffragettes as "fanatics" determined to disrupt the laws of nature and sow the destruction of the nation itself.[26] Their pamphlets and booklets warned of a social order overturned and the natural, rightful rule of man terribly undone. "God forbid," they quoted a sermon, "that we should ever see the day that a man, a husband or a father, is to find his will opposed and thwarted at the polls by his daughter or his wife."[27]

The movement would fight on. For decades, women organized and agitated tirelessly against a system obsessed with maintaining privilege for white men alone. At the heart of the fight was a question posed by Susan B. Anthony: "Are women persons?"[28] The movement shined a light on the founding of the United States and its Constitution, both intended, by design, to create a nation helmed and piloted by white, wealthy men ruling over people of color, women, and the poor, all of them either virtually or explicitly reduced to nonpersons. In 1872, Anthony had challenged this notion by voting illegally in Rochester, New York. As she was sentenced for her crime, she denounced a system "made by men, interpreted by men, administered by men, in favor of men, and against women."[29]

In August of 1920, nearly five decades after Anthony's civil disobedience and 133 years after the ratification of the Constitution of the United States of America, the Nineteenth Amendment was ratified and women won the vote. It was the result of unflagging activism and a growing progressive movement in the United States that sought to usher in new, logic-based, informed restructuring. But hidden within the progressive movement, with its emphasis on "logic" and obsession with reorganizing society through science and reason, were long-held prejudices that would continue to trouble humanity and enable the same oppression it sought to reform.

The battle between the North and South was also a clash of civilizations and economic destinies. Industrial forces conquered agrarian society, opening the door for massive, sweeping projects that saw railroads crisscross the continent, telegraph wires connect distant localities, and buildings dot the skylines of major cities. Wealth in the form of tax dollars would be redistributed from the population via the federal government to businesses and capitalists who made this transformation possible, establishing new, ultra-rich classes of citizens and corporations that came to overshadow government and dominate most facets of society.

Despite this domination, concentrated capital continued to seek new means of wringing every last possible bit out of their laborers. Offering his services was engineer Frederick W. Taylor, whose philosophy of scientific management reduced production to an almost automated process that could fit workers into roles like so many cogs in a machine. The discipline relied on statistics, empirical measurements, and a new generation and class of educated managers who would oversee and direct the work of their employees with an eye toward optimization.

Taylor heralded scientific management as "the remedy" for inefficiency in production but promised his methods were "applicable to all kinds of human activities" and that "the same principles can be applied with equal force" elsewhere.[30] Industrialized society, with its plethora of institutions, trades, and constantly evolving fields, required this new approach.

To this end, an American engineer named William Henry Smyth published an article in 1919 calling for a "technocracy," or rule by experts.[31] And though Smyth's appeal was concerned with creating a more level society, the adoption of a technocratic administrative state would be unlikely to reduce inequality. This was most certainly the case with the administrative revolution of the early twentieth century in America.

At the helm was Woodrow Wilson, a virulent white supremacist and classist who spent his time and energy as an academic lionizing the Confederate States of America, excusing the horrors of slavery, and forwarding a new philosophy by which the wealthy could better control the world through administrative means. Wilson waxed poetic about "the great maze of Society," an ever-expanding organism of grand "complexity" that the average citizen had no ability to understand; they needed, instead, to turn to a great "leader" capable of operating the machine.[32]

Wilson embodied the Progressive Era's desire for technocratic control that served the interests of the white middle and upper classes. Staying true to his Southern roots, Wilson's presidency backed continued segregation and apartheid policies, and his interest in a society governed by "experts" helped usher in an era of feverish scientific tyranny. As governor of New Jersey, Wilson had led the way in establishing the legal practice of eugenics and forcible sterilization of American citizens, giving credence to the racist and ignorant theories of men like Charles Davenport, director of the Eugenics Record Office at Cold Spring Harbor Laboratory in New York. A zoologist by trade, Davenport investigated the hereditary stock of America and plotted a path toward a "superior race."

Davenport looked at the prevalent concerns of the white ruling class and touted "recent great advances" in eugenics that might help solve "certain problems of human society," including those "of the unsocial classes, of immigration, of population, of effectiveness, of health and vigor."[33] In pursuit of these solutions, Davenport appealed to the wealthiest strata of Americans to end their efforts "to bolster up the weak and alleviate the suffering of the sick" through charity and instead dedicate their resources to eugenics as a means of purifying society.[34] The robber barons who had amassed unprecedented fortunes through industrialization opened their wallets and embraced the plan. Now an America dominated by the rich and administered by trained and scientifically enlightened managers would take aim at its poor, its people of color, its disabled, and its women. Through forced sterilization, they would begin to weed out the so-called defectives in order to "save and perfect" the race.

Other racists shared concerns about the purity of the gene pool and the risk that populations of color would manage to rise up and trouble white-dominated society. Madison Grant's publication of *The Passing of the Great Race* in 1916 warned that the "altruistic ideals" of America were "sweeping the nation toward a racial abyss."[35] Grant believed that a process of "replacement" was taking place: People of color and immigrants were not just outbreeding white citizens but exercising their democratic rights and causing "a corresponding loss of efficiency in the community as a whole."[36]

Grant was lauded for his work and counseled politicians and government officials in carrying out his prescriptions. American society became enraptured with political and "scientific" solutions to protecting white supremacy and the race. Families dabbled in eugenics, entering their children into hereditary contests. Biased intelligence tests began determining the fates of schoolchildren, and couples were made to undergo blood tests prior to marriage. Religious leaders peppered their sermons with attempts to Christianize eugenics, including Reverend Walter Taylor Sumner, who commanded churches "to take up the questions and problems, not only of local needs, but of needs nationwide," such as "the integrity of the race."[37]

On the hot and muggy night of June 10, 1903, King Alexander I and Queen Draga of Serbia woke to a commotion. Fearing the worst, they sought refuge in a hidden room while a group of military officers tore their palace apart searching for them. An elaborate and far-reaching coup had taken place involving the military, members of the government, and even Alexander's personal guards. By morning, the couple was discovered, dragged out of hiding, shot, beaten, eviscerated, and then flung out a window and onto the lawn "naked, bleeding, and broken."[38]

At the center of the coup was a secret society that came to be known as the Black Hand, a shadowy organization in which each member swore "by the Sun which shineth upon me, by the Earth which feedeth me, by God, by the blood of my forefathers, by my honour and by my life" to bring all Serbs together under a shared banner.[39] Eight years later, the group attempted to assassinate Austrian emperor Franz Josef as part of their plan to "liberate" Serbs from Austria-Hungary, but, having failed, they turned to Archduke Franz Ferdinand, the presumptive heir to the throne. On June 28, 1914, a student named Gavrilo Princip leapt onto the archduke's car and shot and killed both Ferdinand and his wife, Sophie, with a .380 pistol.

At first the assassination was merely a blip on the world stage, but soon a crisis grew from festering tensions. The Concert of Europe and the tentative cooperative frameworks of accords like the Berlin Conference quickly unraveled, proving even the most carefully laid plans were incapable of maintaining peace forever. Germany's emergence as a state and competitor had helped destabilize the order, creating a new competition over colonies, resources, and, ultimately, influence in the industrialized world. Despite promises that capitalism would eliminate the need for warfare and that capable statesmen and institutions, if given overwhelming authority, would usher in endless prosperity, the disruption in Sarajevo proved to be an ideal starting point for one of the most senseless and tragic wars in human history.

The same pan-German proponents who influenced the state's founding welcomed the prospect. Even as Helmuth von Moltke, the chief of the general staff, lamented that the looming war would "destroy civilization in almost all of Europe for decades," reactionary forces savored the prospect of "preventative war" that might provide an "inner cleansing" of socialists, communists, reformers, and detractors of the nationalist project.[40] Hostilities would be a prime opportunity for Germany to disrupt the balance and enable the "overthrow of everything that exists."[41]

Looking back in 1920, British prime minister David Lloyd George characterized England's entry into World War I as "something into which they glided or rather staggered and stumbled."[42] But the lead-up to the war had been long and held considerable sway over the British people. Starting in the waning days of the nineteenth century, Britain and Germany had begun squaring off in a frenzied arms race in the wake of the Franco-Prussian War. That victory over France had placed Germany squarely in the British imagination, casting them as an existential threat and inspiring paranoia that they might soon overtake the empire.

In 1871, British general George Tomkyns Chesney published *The*

Battle of Dorking, a novel imagining a future German invasion that rendered Britain a wasteland, its economy wrecked, "its factories silent, its harbours empty," and its people made "prey to pauperism and decay."[43] In 1897, H. G. Wells's *The War of the Worlds* depicted the invasion and destruction of England by a technologically superior alien force following years of "infinite complacency."[44] William Le Queux's *The Invasion of 1910* predicted a German assault made possible by "the careless insular apathy of the Englishman" and aided by numerous German spies, "bound by their oath to the Fatherland," who had infiltrated British society.[45] If England was to avoid total destruction, these works advised, it had to prepare for inevitable war.

The paranoia fed into a mobilizing effort spearheaded by First Lord of the Admiralty Winston Churchill, who pushed for massive investments as he warned "the whole fortunes of our race and Empire, the whole treasure accumulated during so many centuries of sacrifice and achievement would perish and be swept utterly away" should the country fall behind militarily.[46] As would be the case over and over again, a society obsessed with the prospect of war, having tuned its institutions to enhance its military capabilities, soon found itself drifting closer and closer to the very showdown it had professed it hoped to avoid.

In surveying the scene in February of 1914, months prior to the assassination of Archduke Ferdinand, Foreign Secretary Edward Grey was notably concerned. "Exceptional expenditure in armaments," he mused, "carried to an excessive degree, must lead to catastrophe, and may even sink the ship of European prosperity and civilization."[47] Despite his prophetic fears, Grey recognized the forces that would lead to World War I were already in motion, saying sadly, "I can see very little to be done."

Leftists around the world, including socialists, communists, anarchists, labor unions, and social reformers, marched and protested in an effort to stop the war, denouncing the conflict as being motivated by profit and empire. Among them was French socialist Jean Jaurès, who appealed to the working class of Europe to imagine a future in which "the billions now thrown away in preparation for war are spent on useful things to increase the well-being of the people."[48] Of the saber-rattling political class, Jaurès said, "The fever of imperialism has become a sickness. It is the disease of a badly run society which does not know how to use its energies at home."

Jaurès was hurriedly attempting to organize a mass strike to head off the war when, on July 31, 1914, while dining at a restaurant in Paris, he was shot twice and killed by a man named Raoul Villain. The very next day, calls for mobilization appeared throughout France.

Villain was an ardent French nationalist radicalized by the right-wing trends overtaking the nation. In the wake of the Franco-Prussian War, France had marinated in conspiratorial paranoia and calls for revenge on Germany for the indignity of defeat. This came to a head in 1894 when an army captain named Alfred Dreyfus was accused of being a traitor and spy for Germany, setting off a major social crisis. Though Dreyfus would eventually be cleared and released, the case gripped France and set off anti-Jewish riots, created a bloody culture war between the Left and the Right, and prompted a growing anti-Semitic, antidemocratic, nationalist movement.

This particular anti-Semitic fervor had roots in the work of Édouard Drumont, a writer who papered France with accusations that Jews were a plague afflicting the nation since the French Revolution and howled, "We are being pillaged, dishonored, exploited, and emptied by the Jew . . . the Jew is our master."[49] These accusations, and their reframing of the revolution's overthrow of the king as a Jewish plot, found a home among royalists seeking to reinstall the monarchy.

Charles Maurras, a fixture in France's right wing, leveraged these ideas in forming a movement called Action Française. Maurras warned of "the stranger within," or a Jewish threat in league with international efforts like Freemasonry. Action Française represented, as voiced by member Léon Daudet, a "patriotic stand against the Jews" and sought "benevolent dictatorship" in the form of an installed monarch that would overthrow liberal democracy.[50]

The group pumped out excessive amounts of propaganda framing socialists like Jaurès as traitors and calling on subscribers to fight leftists and dismantle the Jewish/liberal conspiracy. Its members joined paramilitary groups that broke up meetings, intimidated workers, and engaged in reckless violence in the streets. In many ways, Action Française portended the fascist movement that would gain ground in postwar Europe and around the world.

The assassination of Jean Jaurès by a man radicalized by right-wing, anti-Semitic paranoia represented the removal of an impediment to the burgeoning world war. Soon, Europe was plunged into a suicidal abyss that had been predicted by experts in developing warfare. The warnings had begun years before with the writings of Jan Bloch, an expert whose 1899 book *The Future of War in Its Technical, Economic, and Political Relations* forecasted "total mutual annihilation."[51]

Bloch's predictions proved correct. The powerful committed to total war across the world, vaporizing one another with hundreds of millions of artillery shells, tearing each other apart with machine-gun fire, laying waste to each other with noxious gas, and fighting a stalemate of a war that saw armies entrench themselves in the earth, where they suffered untold traumas. By war's end, roughly forty million soldiers and civilians had been killed, tens of millions more wounded, entire landscapes decimated and made uninhabitable, an entire generation murdered.[52] An Indian soldier fighting for the British Empire did not mince words in a letter home: "Do not think that this is war," he wrote. "It is not war. It is the ending of the world."[53]

Once the fighting began and the horror erupted unrestrained, psychologist Sigmund Freud wrestled with the carnage and diagnosed Western society with a death drive. In watching the massacre, Freud commented on a puzzled citizenry who "expected that the great ruling nations of the white race, the leaders of mankind . . . to whom we owe the technical progress in the control of nature . . . would find some other way of settling their differences and conflicting interests."[54] The total meltdown in politics, law, and civility, he believed, constituted "the destruction of an illusion."[55]

Years prior, Irish journalist George Lynch had come to a similar conclusion as he traveled to China during the Boxer Rebellion at the turn of the century and reported on attempts by a coalition of "civilized nations," including Britain, Russia, Germany, America, and France, to put down an uprising that threatened imperial plundering. Watching the alliance commit endless inhumane atrocities, he recoiled in horror. "This Western Civilization of ours," he recorded somberly, "is merely a veneer over savagery."[56]

Jan Bloch's predictions that the war would be brutal were paired with a forecast that, if hostilities were to begin, they would not end until they destabilized nation-states. In addition to destroying the remaining monarchial empires besides England, the war meant sweeping change for Russia, a kingdom reeling from decades of military defeat and subjugation. The gap between its self-told mythology as an unparalleled war machine and its results continually undermined the authority of the ruling regime. Czar Nicholas II legitimized his authority with divine right and the supposed will of God, but if the almighty creator favored Russia, there was no accounting for perpetual failure on the battlefield.

Nicholas had personally taken over the war effort in 1915, leaving his wife, Alexandra, to direct domestic affairs. Both fronts were abject disasters. Russian troops served as cannon fodder and in some cases were rushed to the front lines completely unprepared. One Russian general complained that a "third of the men had no rifles" and "had to wait patiently until their comrades fell before their eyes and they could pick up weapons."[57] Within Russia, deteriorating conditions led to strikes, protests, and the revolutionary circles' gaining momentum.

By February of 1917 the crisis had reached critical mass. An immense wave of strikes in nearly all industries and among every circle of Russian life paralyzed the capital city of Petrograd. No stranger to answering uprisings with bloody crackdowns, Nicholas ordered his forces to "put down the disorders by tomorrow," but he had severely misjudged the enormity of the situation.[58] The very troops tasked with crushing the protests rejected the orders, shot and killed many of their own commanders, and were soon seen marching among the protestors with "red flags fastened to their bayonets."[59] By March 15, Nicholas had no choice but to abdicate.

The resulting struggle centered on whether authority rested with the provisional government or with the soviets. Both made claims to representing the will of the people and promised to chart a new course, but the makeups and philosophies splintered along political, social, and economic lines. The government represented a coalition of the upper and middle classes promising to liberalize the society. The soviets, partnering with the Marxist Bolshevik Party, pushed for a total overhaul of Russia, with ultimate authority supposedly transferring to the working class.

Providing the ideological center for the Bolsheviks was Vladimir Ilyich Ulyanov, a revolutionary called Lenin. Though forced into exile, Lenin had kept close watch on Russia while jockeying with rivals over the legacy of Karl Marx. Lenin believed the world crisis betrayed a larger systemic rot. Leveling his gaze on imperialism, Lenin diagnosed that "capitalism has grown into a world system of colonial oppression and of the financial strangulation of the overwhelming majority of the population of the world by a handful of 'advanced' countries," creating a glut of "superprofits" allowing capitalists to overtake their governments and bribe labor leaders and so-called socialists, thereby preventing Marx's predicted revolution, and, "in a thousand different ways, direct and indirect, overt and covert," enjoy unprecedented power.[60]

The dawning of the twentieth century, Lenin claimed, marked "the turning-point from the old capitalism to the new, from the domination of capital in general to the domination of finance capital."[61] If allowed to continue, the evolution would guarantee more suffering and undoubtedly more world wars. Lenin held that only a complete overthrow of the capitalist system and a worldwide turn to communism could stall this nightmarish turn and believed that Russia had great potential to set off that revolution.

In April of 1917 Lenin arrived in Petrograd by train and was welcomed as a returning hero. Addressing onlookers, he said, "I am happy to greet in your persons the victorious Russian revolution and greet you as the vanguard of the worldwide proletarian army," and promised that they had "prepared the way and opened a new epoch."[62] In his "April Theses," published in *Pravda,* the Bolshevik paper, Lenin notably referred to "the first stage of the revolution" and gestured to a "second stage," or a moment in which the Bolsheviks would launch what comrade Leon Trotsky had called "the permanent revolution" that would spark a worldwide uprising and the end of capitalism.[63]

The Bolshevik plan was ambitious but recognized that Russia presented a unique opportunity and challenge: Its economy had yet to become industrialized or begin passing through capitalism, which meant a liberal bourgeoisie had yet to emerge or really gain a stranglehold over its institutions. But, as Lenin had worried, that lack of development meant class-consciousness had yet to develop. To counteract this, the Bolsheviks believed they must serve as a vanguard protecting Marxist ideas, almost as if functioning as the priest class of a secular religion, while cultivating socialist understanding among the people.

Eventually, the Bolsheviks took over the government. By November 18, Lenin declared, "Behind us are the majority of the people. Behind us are the majority of the toilers and the oppressed of all the world. We are fighting in the cause of justice, and our victory is certain."[64] This victory, however, depended on the purging of opponents.

Faced with a developing civil war and efforts by the Western world to destabilize the new regime, Lenin believed subjugation was required to establish permanent order. After seizing private wealth and property, nationalizing industries, and forbidding the hoarding of resources, on August 11, 1918, he ordered the party to hang "one hundred known kulaks, rich men, bloodsuckers," and to "do it in such a way that . . . the people will see, tremble, know, shout."[65] A month later, he demanded more "emergency measures" and commanded subordinates to "prepare the terror."[66]

From the Bolsheviks' perspective, efforts to dismantle the previous society depended upon a total uprooting of reality through any means necessary. The threat of capitalism, with its exploitation of the working classes and incredible ability to permeate all facets of life, represented a crisis, and so a wave of violence and intimidation was well within rational bounds. In vindicating the oppression, Trotsky cited his bourgeois rivals as "destroying human culture" and warned that capitalism represented an apocalyptic peril and "threatens to drag after it into the abyss the whole of society," likening it to a spreading disease and reasoning, "We are forced to tear it off, to chop it away."[67]

Left-wing critics of the Bolsheviks charged that their doctrine was becoming a religion. Karl Kautsky, who had sparred with Lenin for years over Marx's legacy, condemned the party for holding to "the naïve assumption that there really exists an absolute truth, and that the Communists alone are in possession of that truth."[68] The Polish Marxist Rosa Luxemburg welcomed control by the working class but advocated for its realization through democracy rather than top-down, authoritarian actions. In the Bolsheviks she saw a "little leading minority" that had usurped power from the masses in pursuit of its own agenda.[69]

Just as the Bolsheviks established a political orthodoxy through processes akin to the Inquisition, the party utilized religious mythology as a weapon. While shunning organized religion and destroying idols to the faith and the czar's regime, the party swamped Russia with propaganda depicting itself as affiliated with one spiritual concept after another. Lenin held a deep distaste for the practice, but despite his protests he was continually framed as a secular messiah.

Lenin's discomfort with his developing cult of personality stemmed from his belief that religion represented "spiritual oppression" that troubled a working class "taught to be submissive."[70] The institution, he thundered, amounted to "medieval mildew" that needed to be cleansed from society.[71] This conviction was far from unanimous among Marxists. Within the movement existed a clique called "God-builders" who couched the success of Marxism and the defeat of capitalism in crafting a new faith. As Maxim Gorky, a writer and God-builder, argued, humanity needed to hold on to faith that life "will become a blessing" and required a savior figure, but he rejected "a god in heaven" in favor of a leader "on our dismal earth, someone of great wisdom and monstrous power."[72]

The God-building movement represented a conviction that society required the structure outlined in Plato's Allegory of the Cave: Should communists triumph over capitalism, they would need to capture the shadows in order to guide the masses. Religion had succeeded, they posited, because it gifted people the ability to imagine a future better than the present, allowing leaders to marshal necessary resources and energies.

In years past Lenin had fought with the God-builders and preached unembellished secularism, but, as was the case with every other facet of Russian society, he began to lose control as his life came to an end. With his health fading, Lenin was isolated by his associate Joseph Stalin and Stalin's loyalists, writing with disdain, "I haven't died yet, but under Stalin's supervision they are already trying to bury me."[73] Lenin was disturbed by Stalin's obvious plans to take over following his death and, dictating through his personal secretary, noted his doubts that Stalin would be capable of employing "authority with sufficient caution."[74] As a result, Lenin issued a recommendation: "I suggest that the comrades think about a way of removing Stalin."[75]

Regardless, Stalin shouldered his way into prominence, chasing his rival Trotsky from Russia altogether and into exile. There, Trotsky would decry the resulting regime as the "bureaucratic degeneration of the state" and urge a new revolution until his assassination in 1940.[76] With unparalleled power, Stalin built a dictatorial regime that rejected Trotsky and Lenin's call for worldwide communist revolution. Instead, he envisioned the Soviet Union as a standalone communist state, "a complete socialist society" that placed him at the top of a constructed hierarchy where he and his comrades could enjoy the spoils.[77]

Stalin surrounded himself with a freshly constructed cult of personality that depended on turning Lenin into the messiah he had so desperately refused to be. Following his death, the party heralded his effects and writings as saintly relics for worship. Despite the objections of his widow, Nadezhda Krupskaya, and her request that their mourning not "take the form of external reverence for his person" and that the party instead honor him by building "kindergartens, houses, schools, libraries, medical centres, hospitals, [and] homes for the disabled," Stalin and the party would not squander their opportunity.[78]

After scientists experimented with means to preserve Lenin's body, including a crude attempt at cryogenic freezing, in order to present it as a living memorial serving the communist state, a tomb for public viewing of Lenin's corpse was constructed while propaganda communicated that the great leader was merely "waiting for the science" to develop a cure for mortality and, in his slumber, "dreams of resurrection."[79] The religious was made secular as they promised that science would light the way forward to a future where reason and logic were able to re-create preposterous "miracles" of old and even raise the dead, performing an earthly resurrection that returned Lenin like a material Jesus Christ to the land of the living.

Stalin and his conspirators had managed a bizarre and tremendous feat. By commandeering Lenin's legacy, as well as the worldwide rallying cry for a socialist alternative, they had positioned themselves as the leaders of a new religion.

The Russian Revolution sent a tremor through the established order. Although they were still active on the front lines, America, Great Britain, France, Canada, and other allies sent hundreds of thousands of troops to Russia to aid the counterrevolution in the developing civil war.

Their efforts proved futile and merely reinforced the Bolsheviks' fear that the capitalist order would do anything to destroy them.

Woodrow Wilson believed communism was "lurking everywhere" and that if hostilities continued, Germany itself would "plunge into Bolshevism" and set off a chain reaction.[80] To counteract this, he and his team of advisors penned his famed "Fourteen Points," designed in part by propagandists to emphasize "anti-imperialistic war aims" so that the Allies might strike against Bolshevik rhetoric and bring Germany to the table for peace talks in order to prevent further destabilization.[81]

The appeal was so successful that Wilson was regarded for a brief time as a savior of democracy and the idol of nations looking for both peace and an end to imperialism. This was key, Wilson explained on his voyage to Europe for negotiations, as bolshevism had succeeded because "it is a protest against the way in which the world has worked," and in order for the threat to be neutralized, "a new order" was needed to quell disillusionment around the world.[82]

Unfortunately, the rhetoric was empty. Reflecting on Wilson's participation in the peace conference, British economist John Maynard Keynes lamented that Wilson had "thought out nothing . . . had no plan, no scheme, no constructive ideas whatsoever."[83] The Fourteen Points had been an advertising marvel, a set of slogans and buzzwords designed by America's best marketers. Germans looking for Wilson to save them from crushing repercussions were disappointed, as were the legions of believers hoping for an end to colonization and a future of advertised self-determination.

As the war ended, Wilson saw communism as an existential threat to his beloved project of the administrative state. This "ugly, poisonous thing," he said, subsisted on "the doubt of the man on the street of the essential integrity of the people he is depending on to do his governing," which would challenge technocratic control. It was nothing short of "poison running through the veins of the world," and in a liberal democracy, "all the veins of the world are open and the poison can circulate."[84]

Postwar America could hardly chance that possibility. In its years of neutrality, the United States had served as a banker and merchant for the Allies, using businesses like General Electric, DuPont, and Bethlehem Steel to keep the armies in weapons and goods, and firms like J. P. Morgan to loan in excess of $7 billion in order to keep them afloat.[85] From the beginning, even while the country remained technically "impartial," the prospect of participating in the war business had been too tantalizing to pass up. *The New York Times* covered the initial surge of investment as "pouring into the big financial institutions downtown at a rate that taxed the force of men handling it."[86]

American investment in the war established the nation as the heart of developing international finance and effectively moved the center of gravity from London to New York City. So large was the boom that new structures and administrative bodies that existed beyond representative government, such as the Federal Reserve, were necessary to manage the sheer enormity of transactions and the flow of capital. Economic growth was so substantial and crucial that no interruption could be tolerated.

Wilson's concerns over the threat of bolshevism and the dominance of capitalism meant America's Left would become a target of state power. Foremost among these "enemies" was the Industrial Workers of the World, a revolutionary union dedicated to uniting all of the world's workers into "one big union" in order to realize the "abolition of the wage system" and form "the structure of the new society within the shell of the old."[87] Among its leaders was Eugene V. Debs, a labor activist who, while serving a jail sentence for organizing, found his purpose in the socialist cause. Upon his release, Debs sought to change the established system, charging that both of America's parties served as "the legislative tool of the exploiting class."[88]

The views of Debs and fellow IWW members departed from those of other labor unions, most notably the American Federation of Labor (AFL). Samuel Gompers, the head of the AFL, maintained that while he was "critical of [the US] economic order," he remained "squarely and unequivocally for [its] defense and maintenance . . . and for its development and improvement," meaning that the body sought only to improve its members' financial standing rather than overthrow the capitalist system.[89] In exchange for promises to head off any potential labor disruptions, Gompers earned a spot in Wilson's inner circle and advised him on production and domestic affairs. Gompers warned Wilson that "war weariness" and "Utopian dreams fanned into new life by the Russian revolution" might embolden his rivals in the IWW, firmly tying them to the Bolshevik threat and prompting Wilson to approach them as enemies of the state.[90]

The prospect of the IWW and its associated factions disrupting the war effort and possibly sparking a Russian-style revolution within the United States weighed heavily on American leadership. To counteract them, the Bureau of Investigation (the forerunner to the Federal Bureau of Investigation) raided their offices, illegally confiscated materials, and harassed members, all to the liking of agents like future FBI director J. Edgar Hoover. As had been the case in eighteenth-century England, the fear of revolution inspired a symbiotic relationship between law enforcement and right-wing paramilitary groups, in this case the American Protective League. With the blessing of Wilson's administration and the attorney general, hundreds of thousands of members of the APL engaged in intimidation in disrupting labor strikes and unions, all in defense against a "hidden army of German espionage and German sympathy" they claimed operated within the United States and was funded by millions of dollars from foreign agents.[91]

Soon, copies of *The Protocols of the Elders of Zion,* updated to blame the communist revolution on a partnership between Bolsheviks and a "secret Jewish society" working to "have the whole world . . . in their grip" and destroy Christianity, circulated throughout the Wilson administration.[92] Investigating these claims was a body in the Senate called the Overman Committee. In June of 1919, after hearing testimony from conspiracy theorists and peddlers of *The Protocols of the Elders of Zion,* the committee released a report warning there were "several activities now being carried on in the United States" by "radical revolutionary elements" obsessed with "the overthrow of existing governmental institutions and the complete demoralization of modern society."[93] The conspiracy was widespread, involving labor movements like the IWW as well as European immigrants entering the country with "foreign" and "dangerous" ideas.

One individual who took these paranoid narratives seriously was Attorney General A. Mitchell Palmer, who testified to Congress that he believed the revolutionary element in America was ready to pounce on the Fourth of July and "destroy the government in one fell swoop."[94] The supposed revolution failed to materialize, but Palmer remained convinced. Assisted by agent J. Edgar Hoover, Palmer and the Department of Justice instituted massive raids that targeted socialists, communists, labor members, and leftists, violating their civil liberties and resulting in mass deportations. Following one such raid in January of 1920, *The New York Times* reported on the actions as a strike against a legitimate conspiracy to "make the United States a sister State to Soviet Russia."[95] *The Washington Post* declared there was "no time to waste on hairsplitting over infringement of liberty when the enemy is using liberty's weapons for the assassination of liberty."[96]

Yet again, liberal democracy had been framed as a weakness to be exploited by "enemies" hell-bent on overthrowing the system altogether. Anyone opposing the domination of capital, the extension of finance as an ordering force within the world—anyone even daring to question imperial war, utter a suspect thought, or trouble the prevailing orthodoxy—was considered unworthy of protection or rights.

As an intellectual leader within the Black community, W. E. B. Du Bois struggled with World War I. On one hand, he criticized the clash as an extension of the plundering of Africa, saying that "lying treaties, rivers of rum, murder, assassination, mutilation, rape, and torture" had laid the groundwork for a crisis over "the division of the spoils of trade-empire." On the other, Du Bois recognized an opportunity for

African Americans to "forget our special grievances and close our ranks shoulder to shoulder with our own white fellow citizens" while keeping their eyes "lifted to the hills."[97] If they accepted this fight as their own, Du Bois maintained, it might prove a decisive moment in race relations within the United States and create a future where Black people might emerge "with a right to vote and a right to work and a right to live without insult."[98]

Du Bois was not alone in this prediction. White supremacists had objected to African American soldiers fighting in the war on the grounds that their participation might trouble the apartheid state. Senator James K. Vardaman of Mississippi cried that the situation would "inevitably lead to disaster" and that to "impress the negro with the fact that he is defending the flag, inflate his untutored soul with military airs, teach him that it is his duty to keep the emblem of the Nation flying" was just a "short step to the conclusion that his political rights must be respected."[99]

As a result, many African Americans returned to a cold and tragic welcome and were, much to Du Bois's disappointment, victim to "lynching, disenfranchisement, caste, brutality and devilish insult."[100] Rather than receiving their earned respect and rightful rewards, they were regarded as threats to the status quo. True to his Southern, white supremacist roots, Woodrow Wilson could not find it within himself to be grateful for their service, confiding in an associate that he believed "the American negro returning from abroad" was "our greatest medium in conveying bolshevism to America."[101]

Building off white supremacist beliefs that people of color were easily deceived and controlled, fear spread that African Americans would fall prey to Bolshevik agitators. This manifested as the so-called Negro problem, the concern that the "less informed class of negroes" would make easy pickings for "Bolshevist propaganda."[102] Prominent media outlets covered the events of the infamous "Red Summer" of 1919, which saw widespread violence against African Americans, as a showdown between concerned white patriots and unruly, radicalized Black people, citing "evidence" that "well financed propaganda" spread by the IWW and "certain factions of the radical Socialist elements and Bolsheviki" were effectively turning African Americans into domestic terrorists.[103]

That summer saw dozens of race riots as hordes of white supremacists reacted to cultivated paranoia by lynching, harassing, and oppressing their fellow citizens, culminating in racist attacks in major cities like Chicago, New York City, and the nation's capital. Some even wore their service uniforms and used their military-issued firearms to murder civilians and their fellow veterans. Others joined the resurgent Ku Klux Klan as the paramilitary organization spread beyond the confines of the Confederate South and propagated around the country.

While cities burned, race war raged, and the nation self-destructed, a debate over how modern society should function was taking shape. The crisis of World War I, with its irrational destruction and seemingly inexplicable origins, presented a pressing question of how to move forward. Wilson's concern regarding the faith of the people in their leaders and institutions still proved vexing and, with the collapse of the League of Nations, presented little in the way of answers.

Much as Du Bois had faced a personal crisis in the lead-up to the war, journalist and public intellectual Walter Lippmann wrestled with his own predicament. Lippmann had helped in the war, plying his trade with American propaganda operations and assisting Wilson with the drafting of his Fourteen Points. Watching propaganda efforts firsthand, as well as the results of the mass administrative state, Lippmann entered the postwar era convinced it was "no longer possible . . . to believe in the original dogma of democracy."[104] The world had grown too complex, too specialized, its processes "too numerous, too complicated, too obscure in their effects," for a mass of "busy and tired people" to effectively decide the future for themselves.[105] The only solution lay in a technocracy, or a society led by a "specialized class" of technocrats and the "manufacture of consent" in the public through "psychological research coupled with the modern means of communication."[106]

Lippmann's crisis of faith paralleled what Wilson had envisioned in his outlining of the administrative state but also relied on the psychological appeals used during the war. This propaganda had won the battle and opened the possibility in peacetime for technocratic leaders to appeal to the public at large, feed them a carefully tuned and designed fantasy removed from the complicated nature of governance, and manufacture the necessary consent.

A nephew of Sigmund Freud, Edward Bernays had contributed to the war propaganda effort as well and weaponized his uncle's psychological theories. Now, postwar, he advocated the use of these techniques by an "invisible government" that could "pull the wires which control the public mind" and save society from chaos.[107] Bernays saw opportunities that lay beyond governance, though, and his experience as an advertising agent meant he could utilize these same propaganda tactics in business by manipulating consumers via unconscious appeals.

This revolution of business, coupled with the postwar economic developments, created a boom within the United States wherein the public was largely pacified, their consent manufactured, and their time and money spent surrounding themselves with luxuries they didn't need. The Progressive Age gave way to an era of laissez-faire capitalism emphasizing free markets and vehemently contesting government intervention of any kind. President Warren G. Harding was a champion, disparaging "false economics which lure humanity to utter chaos" and framing labor unions and reformers as impeding "the march of progress."[108]

Harding's pro-capitalist urgings weren't his only fascination. In a speech in Alabama, he recommended a book called *The Rising Tide of Color Against White World-Supremacy* by the racist Lothrop Stoddard, saying that whoever read the tome "must realize that our race problem here in the United States is only a phase of a race issue that the whole world confronts."[109] This book, which would later inspire the Nazi Party in Germany, warned that a "malaise" had overtaken "the white world" and that World War I was "only the beginning of a war-cycle leading to the utter disruption of white solidarity and civilization."[110] Like Madison Grant before him, Stoddard advocated radical action through limitation of immigration, the rejuvenation of white supremacy in practice and action, and the use of eugenics in order to "perfect the race" and eliminate people of color and the so-called lesser elements of society that would soon outnumber the true rulers of the world.

Stoddard's warnings and the needs of the capitalist, white supremacist American system won the day. Eugenicists like Harry Laughlin were consulted by the government in reconsidering immigration policies and evaluating the "blood value" of potential immigrants and their effect on the American race.[111] The result was the Immigration Act of 1924, which effectively closed the doors to certain peoples and races, including those from eastern and southern Europe, which were seen as flooding America with "unworthy" and "radical" actors.[112] Capturing the prevailing sentiment, Representative Carl Vinson of Georgia argued the importance of protecting America as a state dedicated to "the Aryan race . . . the persons who created and now maintain the greatest Nation on the globe."[113]

By November of 1918, the German fantasy of victory in the Great War had all but shattered. A series of demoralizing losses on the front lines, coupled with worsening conditions at home, coalesced into a wave of mutinies and strikes that undermined the autocratic regime. Facing an intractable crisis, Kaiser Wilhelm II abdicated his throne and fled into exile, leaving Germany to decide its fate and contend with a developing revolution.

At the center of the upheaval was the Social Democratic Party (SDP), a socialist body that had, to the horror of leftists like Vladimir Lenin, cooperated with the previous regime and supported the war. Rather than chance a Bolshevik-style revolution, the SDP sought to build the foundations of the nascent Weimar Republic on the remnants of the empire. In this pursuit, the SDP brokered an alliance with the existing power structure and remaining military components.

Others thought the time for moderation had long since passed. A group calling itself the Spartacus League after the fabled Roman slave rebellion agitated for widespread and radical change. Led by Rosa Luxemburg and Karl Liebknecht, the Spartacists touted the disastrous war as proof that "humanity is almost ready to bleed to death from the bloodletting. Victors and vanquished stand at the edge of the abyss."[114] The only solution was "to awaken all the physical and moral energies of humanity, and to replace hatred and dissension with fraternal solidarity" through worldwide revolution and the complete overthrow of the capitalist system.[115]

By January the Spartacists had gained enough support to believe victory might be at hand. Luxemburg addressed the members of her movement on New Year's Day 1919, gestured at the "gigantic heap of ruins" left by the war, and declared, "Today we can seriously set about destroying capitalism once and for all . . . [and] save human society from destruction."[116] The optimism was ill founded. As had been the case in previous uprisings, the Left found itself opposed by a coalition of moderates, liberals, and the far Right. The SDP and wealthy Germans sanctioned a vicious regiment of paramilitary soldiers called the Freikorps to crush the rebellion. Sadistically, they hunted down and murdered the Spartacists, including Luxemburg and Liebknecht, whom they captured, tortured, and assassinated before unceremoniously dumping their bodies.

The alliance between the SPD and the militaristic far Right proved unstable and deadly. While the Freikorps and associated groups murdered and intimidated communists, they continually sought to establish control over the political structures and dispense with representative politics. Hardly a year after the Spartacist uprising, they helped carry out a coup backing the nationalist Wolfgang Kapp and briefly overthrew the republic. Mass action saved the day and rejected his rule, but the majority of participants went unpunished and would continue troubling the precarious order.

Kapp's argument for a dictatorship had been predicated on offering a solution to "the conflict of classes and parties" that plagued the fledgling system.[117] This spoke to a prevailing concern that the tensions within liberal democracy—namely, the process of deliberation, coalition building, and navigating the clashing concerns of disparate peoples, combinations, and interests—had rendered it not only vexing but ultimately futile. The Right recognized that socialists and communists had seized upon the truth that the system had reached a point of crisis and if the work of industrialization was to continue, and the problem of class was to be solved, drastic measures were required.

The fascist movement developed as soldiers returning from the war front gazed upon their homelands through new eyes and desired the discipline and order of the military structure to be imposed on the state, creating what Italian Benito Mussolini, a driver of the new philosophy, called a "trenchocracy."[118] Fascism represented a possible solution to the contradictions of capitalism while rejecting what Mussolini characterized as "Liberalism, Democracy, Socialism and the Masonic bodies."[119] Through an embrace of militarism, an acceptance of struggle as the reality of existence, and the firm belief that liberalism could lead only to "certain ruin," the fascists sought to eradicate the concept of individualism in favor of permitting the state to pursue its goals unimpeded by liberal concerns.[120]

In Italy, Mussolini organized this movement and intimidated his way into absolute power over the government. Watching from Germany, veterans and far-right paramilitary groups lusted after similar arrangements. As they did, a belief spread that their defeat in the war had been the result of a betrayal orchestrated by a "socialist and pacifist press" under the direction of Jewish puppet masters.[121] This conspiracy, they held, riddled the entirety of the Weimar Republic, involving rival socialists, liberals, and a cabal of Jewish traitors, meaning they were justified in any action necessary to "take back" their country.

A chief proponent of this idea was Dietrich Eckart, who devoured *The Protocols of the Elders of Zion* and held it as proof his beloved country had been betrayed. In 1919, he helped found the German Workers' Party, which would soon become the Nazi Party, all while characterizing the struggle against the Jews as inarguably apocalyptic. Eckart declared, "The hour of decision has come: between existence and non-existence, between Germantum and Jewry, between all or nothing."[122] This struggle, which would determine the fate of humanity, amounted to "a war between light and darkness, truth and lies, Christ and Antichrist."

This framing of the fight against the supposed Jewish conspiracy as a religious crusade culminating in an Armageddon-type final battle meant the faith would require a messiah. A prime candidate emerged in veteran Adolf Hitler, a member of the party who had joined to spy on their activities for his military commanders but had come to believe in their mission. Hitler quickly adopted Eckart's vision of the crisis and compared Jews to the biblical Devil while linking them to "Jewish-God-denying Marxists," who, if successful, would crown themselves with "the funeral wreath of humanity."[123]

To set the stage for Hitler's ascent, Eckart and others used propaganda to meticulously construct a cult of personality. They positioned Hitler as a national savior prophesized by the mystic Guido von List, who predicted a *Starke von Ober*, or a "strong one from above," who would rise to lead the Aryan charge against evil and deliver the world to a "new age."[124] Building off the *völkisch* and mystic movements that had made the dream of a unified Germany possible, Eckart and the Nazis imbued Hitler with a sense of destiny and immense, ancient energy, all while casting him as the literal, physical embodiment of the collected mass of German people.

Hitler, like Mussolini, was aided by a feeling among sectors of Western civilization that the collected crises required the rise, as one Italian jurist put it, of an "exceptional man on whom history has conferred the task of creating the new order."[125] In this way, they desired a messiah capable of renewing the world through sheer force of will. It was, as German historian Oswald Spengler argued in his 1918 book *The Decline of the West,* the predictable and inevitable evolution of the present state, a movement favoring "Caesarism," or the welcoming of a dictatorial force that might rectify all the crises emboldened by mass democracy.[126] Disturbingly enough, this belief proliferated around the world, gaining support among the elite.

Helming a cult of personality and a growing movement, Hitler became convinced his time as Caesar had arrived. On November 8, 1923, he and his conspirators attempted to overthrow the republic. Brandishing a pistol in a Munich beer hall, Hitler declared, "The national revolution has broken out," and emotionally informed the assembled crowd of his intention to resurrect "a Germany of power and greatness."[127] His instincts were wrong, however, as the Nazi Party met overwhelming resistance by police and military units loyal to the government. Sixteen Nazis were killed in the fighting and an injured Hitler was arrested and convicted of treason.

He was sentenced to five years in prison, a light punishment by a regime sympathetic to his goals and plight. While imprisoned, Hitler penned *Mein Kampf,* his propagandized memoir that would rally the people to his cause. It was the story of Germany as the victim of a Jewish-Marxist conspiracy that threatened the established order, and the battle to save it from those hellish collaborators. By the time he was pardoned and released in 1924, Hitler had become the savior-in-waiting.

- CHAPTER SEVEN -

Lightning from the Dark Cloud of Man

In his final State of the Union in 1928, American president Calvin Coolidge could not hold back his enthusiasm. After eliminating federal oversight in order to let the economy run wild, he touted the "great wealth created by our enterprise and industry," through which "the requirements of existence have passed beyond the standard of necessity and into the region of luxury."[1] This new era of wealth was lousy with get-rich-quick scams, and promises of markets that would double and triple investments, seducing American citizens into dumping their wealth into an ever-increasing market, often after borrowing to get into the craze.

History guaranteed the party would eventually come to an end. Following what one financial writer called an "orgy of reckless speculation," this bust would have unheralded ramifications as efforts to bring nations together through interlocking markets, not to mention welcoming the population at large into the casino, created a perfect scenario for the house of cards to topple.[2]

The bottom fell out in October of 1929. As "hysteria swept the country" and a "pall of gloom" set in, billions of dollars were erased and scores of Americans and businesses ruined.[3] Despite assurances that "the public was coming somewhat to its senses" and a massive flood of money from luminaries, the damage was done.[4] Shock waves from the collapse radiated throughout the United States and the world, leading to incredible suffering and political discord.

Advising President Herbert Hoover on the developing crisis were capitalists uninterested in alleviating human suffering. Capitalism, after all, had been celebrated as both God's will and a scientific law. Richard Whitney of the stock exchange counseled that the only action necessary was to "let nature take its course."[5] Business leaders cautioned against public programs and "handouts" that might teach Americans to embrace unemployment. Hoover's secretary of the Treasury Andrew Mellon even saw the burgeoning depression as an opportunity. "Liquidate labor, liquidate stocks, liquidate the farmers, liquidate real estate," he recommended. "Let it collapse" and "purge the rottenness out of the system" while separating the strong individuals from the weak.[6]

Unemployment in the United States affected a quarter of the population. Industry that had seemed unstoppable and restless came to a grinding halt. Streets and towns were filled with hollow-eyed people scrounging for food, waiting in bread lines, and losing themselves in misery. America's promise, the highest degree of comfort and security in the history of the world, had been essentially wiped out. The unwillingness by a government in thrall to the wealthy to help the people bred discontent that inevitably fermented into uprisings. In 1932, Father James Renshaw Cox, a preacher from Pittsburgh, marched twenty thousand men to Washington, DC, to "protest against unemployment conditions."[7] Hoover was convinced Cox and his group had been part of a conspiracy between the Vatican, the Democratic Party, and communists seeking to destroy the country.

Months later, with the automobile industry in shambles, thousands of unemployed workers descended on Dearborn, Michigan, to confront magnate Henry Ford and demand he hire more men and end his racist practices. In return, they were attacked by police officers, company guards, and firefighters who opened fire and lashed them with cold water on a freezing day. The streets of Dearborn "were stained with blood" and "littered with broken glass and the wreckage of bullet-riddled automobiles" as five men were killed and dozens more injured.[8]

In July of the same year over forty thousand veterans of World War I marched to Washington, DC, to demand early payment of their promised bonuses. Led by former sergeant Walter W. Waters, this "army of occupation" believed it had earned "the same consideration as the bankers and railroad owners whose property was protected during the late war."[9] After likening the group to Roman legions with an "intent to overthrow the republic and set up a military dictatorship," Congress voted down a resolution to meet their demands.[10] Hoover ordered the protestors dispersed, a task carried out by future World War II generals Douglas MacArthur and George Patton, who used tanks, tear gas, and bayonets against their fellow veterans.

Though the disturbance was quelled, the situation remained tense. The vice president of the American Federation of Labor warned Congress in so many words that year: "There will be a revolution in this country if nothing is done at once to create work for the unemployed or to meet their needs in some other way."[11]

But the system hardly allowed for any measures that would be necessary to curb the suffering. Since Adam Smith had outlined capitalism in 1776, it had theoretically relied on free markets beyond the reach of politics or government—and, its proponents and beneficiaries were quick to note, functioned as a self-sufficient system by harnessing the self-interest of individuals. Any attempt to intervene or relieve the people's suffering, adherents to this belief warned, would not only run counter to over a century's worth of uncontested ideology but imperil the very notions upon which the United States of America had been founded.

Franklin D. Roosevelt staked his career and name on challenging the conventional assumptions of capitalism. In his campaign for the presidency in 1932, Roosevelt identified that the economic system that had replaced feudalism and hereditary wealth had become too concentrated, too monopolized, leading to what he deemed "privileged princes of these economic dynasties" who had fundamentally established a "new industrial dictatorship."[12] Over years of industrialization and modernization, the divide between the haves and have-nots had grown so wide as to throw everything off balance, exactly as Karl Marx had predicted in his critiques of the inherent contradictions of capitalism.

But Roosevelt was not interested in deposing capitalism and realizing a socialist or communist revolution. In answering the "royalists of the economic order" who claimed as much, Roosevelt assured the people that those who "complain that we seek to overthrow the institutions of America" were merely worried "that we seek to take away their power."[13] Instead of replacing it, Roosevelt intended to save capitalism from itself.

While Hoover, his advisors, and the wealthiest Americans insisted on staying the course, Roosevelt recognized this new phase of monopoly capitalism courted disaster and could result in only a few outcomes. If conditions persisted, there would more than likely be a revolution or a coup, leading to something resembling what had occurred in fascist Italy or communist Russia. Roosevelt proposed loosening the wealthy's grip over the government and investing in the people as a means of jump-starting the economy and curbing the growth of the radicalism that had begun to fester. In his Democratic National Convention speech, he pledged to create "a new deal for the American people" and deemed his proposed administration "prophets of a new order of competence and of courage."[14]

The reaction was apoplectic. Hoover peppered his campaign speeches with claims the economic crisis had been "transmitted to the United States" from abroad.[15] Faced with near-certain defeat, he warned that Roosevelt would "destroy the very foundations of the American system of life."[16] The beleaguered president lamented, "This will not be the America which we have known in the past." And as the day of reckoning approached, Hoover left pretense behind, likening

Roosevelt's agenda to "the same philosophy of government which has poisoned all of Europe" and left it reeking of "the fumes of the witch's cauldron which boiled in Russia."[17]

Following Roosevelt's landslide victory, his inaugural address again sounded the call for reform. In addressing the "dark realities of the moment," Roosevelt decried the "rulers of the exchange of mankind's goods" for their greed and lack of flexibility and vision.[18] The new administration would use its mandate to reorder government and hasten relief while challenging the bedrock principle of self-interest in capitalism. "If I read the temper of the people correctly," the new president commented, "we now realize as we have never realized before our interdependence on each other: that we cannot merely take but we must give as well."[19]

The challenge of capitalist orthodoxy stemmed from a developing economic philosophy held by English economist John Maynard Keynes, who had previously criticized Woodrow Wilson's performance at Versailles. Keynes advocated for governments to play a role in navigating the fluctuation the market had traditionally endured. Keynes argued for governments to run deficits in order to stimulate economies and check the interests of employers, who would only exacerbate the destructive tendencies of capitalism.

Roosevelt freed the government from subservience to business, using its resources to reinvigorate the economy, employ people to carry out public works, and provide a measure of security to the elderly and disabled. Faced with the choice between running a deficit and "callous indifference," Roosevelt answered that "humanity came first."[20] Roosevelt's success in navigating the depression rested on his willingness to abandon conventional wisdom.

Regardless, these reforms drew accusations and vilification. Al Smith, who had been the Democratic nominee for president in 1928, continually harangued Roosevelt's New Deal, complaining of "the foul breath of Communistic Russia."[21] Republican senator Thomas Schall called Roosevelt the "first Communist president of the United States" and claimed the country was on its "way to Moscow."[22] Henry D. Hatfield, a Republican senator from West Virginia, went even further, saying in a fundraising call, "This is despotism. This is tyranny. This is the annihilation of liberty . . . [Roosevelt] has not merely signed the death warrant of capitalism, but has ordained the mutilation of the Constitution."[23] Newspaper giant William Randolph Hearst began referring to the president as "Stalin Delano Roosevelt."[24]

By March of 1934 a cadre of wealthy industrialists had had enough. A retired DuPont vice president named R. R. M. Carpenter complained to John Raskob, former head of the Democratic Party and employee of both General Motors and DuPont, that FDR's actions had crossed a line. "Five negroes on my place in South Carolina refused work," he complained before adding, "A cook in my houseboat at Fort Myers quit because the government was paying him a dollar an hour as a painter."[25] Raskob shared his pain and wondered if they might "induce the du Pont and General Motors groups, followed by other big industries, to defiantly organize to protect society from the suffering which it is bound to endure if we allow communistic elements to lead the people to believe that all business men are crooks."[26]

This alliance of moneyed interests created the American Liberty League, an association of wealthy Americans whose public purpose was to "combat radicalism, preserve property rights, [and] uphold and preserve the Constitution," but who set their sights on undermining Roosevelt's agenda.[27] While using the league to fight political battles, many of the members, who would go on to either support outright the Nazi regime or collaborate with it financially, funded and relied on white supremacist paramilitary groups like the Black Legion, a branch of the Ku Klux Klan, who extended their operations to target leftists and union organizers.

In 1934, the year the Liberty League formed, retired major general Smedley Butler testified to Congress that he had been approached to lead a joint military-industrialist coup against Roosevelt. The plan, known as the Business Plot, would allegedly have involved some half a million troops and the backing of some of the richest Americans, who worried that the president might threaten their wealth. Butler asserted this conspiracy constituted an attempt to establish a fascist dictatorship, a claim the committee echoed in its findings, stating, "There is no question but that these attempts were discussed, were planned, and might have been placed in execution when and if the financial backers deemed it expedient."[28]

Challenges to Roosevelt continued throughout his presidency until the outbreak of World War II, including fascist appeals that mirrored the Nazi playbook. Charges of a "Jewish Dictatorship" stemming from Henry Ford's publication of *The International Jew,* a retelling of *The Protocols of the Elders of Zion,* found footing in the halls of Washington, DC.[29] It was a variation on a familiar theme: The country was being brainwashed by Jewish-controlled media that used everything from jazz to changes in baseball to disseminate "psychic poison and visual filth" in an effort to undermine patriotism and spread the evils of communism.[30] In the past, these white supremacists believed, the "Aryan complexion of mind and conscience" in America had inoculated the country against the threat, but changing demographics and the ascendance of racial minorities had endangered the nation.[31]

As the war took shape, Nazi sympathizer and disgraced hero Charles Lindbergh seized the opportunity to perpetuate these conspiracy theories with the America First movement. He claimed that Jews owned Roosevelt and were the "greatest danger" to America with their "large ownership and influence in our motion pictures, our press, and our radio and our government."[32] That influence, he claimed, had been used to push the United States toward communism and leverage it against Nazi Germany. "We, the heirs of European culture," he wrote in one appeal, "are on the verge of a disastrous war, a war within our own family of nations, a war which will reduce the strength and destroy the treasures of the White race."[33]

The bombing of Pearl Harbor on December 7, 1941, rendered Lindbergh and his American fascists momentarily irrelevant. But had Roosevelt not intervened and lowered the temperature on radicalism, and had the efforts of the nation's wealthiest financiers to undermine his efforts and realize a fascist solution succeeded, a glance at the wide-scale human tragedy in Europe would serve to give even the most optimistic person pause.

The meeting took place in the private residence of Hermann Göring, president of the Reichstag, on February 20, 1933. Adolf Hitler entered the room as chancellor of Germany and the head of a coalition government. Since his release from prison in 1924, he had reconstituted the Nazi Party using a mixture of force and fearmongering while exploiting the panic brought on by the onset of the depression. In 1932's election, the Nazis won a plurality of seats in government, but the communists were gaining momentum. Representatives of Germany's largest and wealthiest businesses, many of whom had already exerted their influence in pressuring President Paul von Hindenburg into elevating Hitler to the chancellorship, were ready to hear the fascist pitch.

For over an hour and a half Hitler addressed them, continually promising to respect property but asserting that "private enterprise cannot be maintained in the age of democracy."[34] The situation required an "iron fist" to crush the communists, stave off labor disruptions, and maintain an order conducive to the desires of the wealthy. Hitler vowed to them that the upcoming contest in March would be the "last election" one way or another. But to ensure that desirable result, he would need their financial backing.

They opened their checkbooks without delay.

As the crisis of capitalism worsened, the Nazis and fascists like them built their base on rectifying circumstances and protecting established wealth. In the words of Fritz Thyssen, an enormously wealthy steel mogul who bankrolled Hitler and his associates, the Nazis earned support by proving they were "capable of solving in a new manner the pressing industrial and social problems" of the day.[35] Those wealthy few who had built their fortunes at the expense of the many faced a terrible reckoning. With the collapse of the system and growing unrest, leftist elements threatened to gain ground by harnessing working-class anger and desperation. The capitalists were left scrambling for alternatives, and groups like the Nazis provided them one: the suppression of leftists and reformers by force, widespread intimidation, and a new means of sanctifying the existing system.

The Nazis deployed their troops to occupy existing labor unions and systematically absorbed the bodies into the party, effectively dissolving them. They placed the unions under handpicked "enterprise-Führers," or unquestionable dictators who ensured that "every single individual" would "perform the maximum of work."[36] In this way, Hitler delivered a subjugated workforce to his corporate backers and used the status of an "emergency" to reframe the very concept of the German state.

By presenting every action as a response to this "emergency," Hitler created a state of crisis where the only recourse was the demolition of civil liberties, liberalism, and individualism in totality, and the wiring of society as a constant militaristic defense against the rest of the world. Many Germans were convinced an invisible war was raging and that the threat of Jewish-controlled communism could, according to their new Führer, lead to the "annihilation of the German people."[37]

Fascists took the disaffection of modern life, with its meaningless toil and suffering in the name of production and profit, and transformed it into religious purpose, framing the obliteration of the individual as a sublime sacrifice in a greater war between good and evil. This injection of religion into the public sphere was a conscious assault on the principles of secular liberalism, which had intentionally separated the two worlds. Fascists believed this rebirth of sacredness would solve the problems of capitalism and class and make digestible the murder and cruelty needed to carry out their plans.

In Italy, Mussolini created around himself a cult of personality predicated on the belief that he was leading humanity into a new and necessary phase. This was based on Friedrich Nietzsche's concept of the Übermensch, or superman. Nietzsche had theorized in his 1883 book

Thus Spoke Zarathustra that "man is something which must be surpassed," meaning humanity would have to lift itself out from under the weight of Christian tradition and forge its own system of values, becoming like gods themselves. These Übermenschen would be like "lightning from the dark cloud of man." Not one to be penned in by anything, Mussolini touted the rise of this "new species of 'free spirits'" who would "triumph over God and the Nothingness" and overcome "this anguishing and tragic period of crisis."[38]

Though Mussolini sought to rise above religious convention and had even referred to priests and their teachings as "fatal to mankind as a tuberculosis germ," he was still eager to seek the legitimizing influence of organized religion.[39] To this end, he pursued a mutual understanding with the Catholic Church, which was keen for the dictator to take on the threat of "Freemasonry, tied to communists and Bolsheviks."[40] Satisfied with his willingness to cooperate and serve the church's purposes, it had no issue referring to him as "the Man sent by Providence."[41]

In Germany, where the schism between Catholicism and Protestantism had been birthed, Hitler was less concerned with buy-in from the Catholic Church and boasted, "They will swallow anything in order to keep their material advantages . . . They will know which way the wind blows."[42] The Nazis would sign a concordat with the church and set about co-opting the Protestant denominations by attacking the "degenerate" culture of the Weimar Republic and appealing to conservative values, including the relegation of women to *Kinder, Kirche, Küche,* or "children, church, and the kitchen"; the violent suppression of homosexuals; and the censorship of art and entertainment.[43]

Hitler had invoked Christianity when expressing his anti-Semitism, calling Jews "the personification of the Devil as the symbol of all evil" and extolling himself as "fighting for the work of the Lord."[44] But over time, the writings and speeches of Hitler came to carry the same weight and authority as the Bible, the cross synonymous with the swastika, and Hitler a messiah and "the herald of a new revelation."[45] Soon, young children would be indoctrinated through their lessons to believe "just as Jesus redeemed mankind from sin and hell, so did Hitler rescue the German people from destruction."[46]

The next step was for the Nazis to construct a new religion. Party member Alfred Rosenberg, whose 1930 screed *The Myth of the Twentieth Century* declared Christianity "buried in the bloody chaos of the Great War," prophesized the rise of a "new faith . . . the myth of blood, the faith that the divine essence of mankind is to be defended through blood."[47] This new religious mythology would move beyond the sacrifice and culture of Christian martyrdom and focus on the saintly, supernatural character of the "Aryan" race.

For Germans like philosopher Martin Heidegger, this resurrection of spiritual energy in the midst of industrialization was thrilling. Heidegger believed the modern preoccupation with the material world had resulted in a "dawning spiritlessness" in which humanity had grown more and more lost.[48] He called the process the "darkening of the world," an increase in nihilism leading to what he believed would be "world-midnight," or the darkest moment in the history of humanity.[49] The United States and Russia, with their liberalism and socialism, represented this force in action, and Heidegger held that only something truly revolutionary could unseat them. When Heidegger joined the Nazi Party, he hoped to be part of what he predicted, an event, or an "Ereignis," in which the world reached that midnight, rediscovered spirituality, and, in the process, freed itself from the disastrous confines of modernity.

By cobbling together bits of esoteric nonsense peddled by so-called mystics and incorporating bizarre myths regarding Atlantis and long-forgotten races, the Nazis attempted to manifest a new spirituality and establish their own religion that could both fill the emptiness of modernity and extend their influence into the future. To support these megalomaniacal ends, they relied on mass spectacles of force and numbers, employing fire and symbols and gigantic fields of banners, all to create a sense of awe and supernatural power.

Modern and conventional assessments of the Nazi phenomenon

tend to focus on Hitler's oration and dark charisma as facilitating his rise, predictably nodding to supernatural, occult forces. These narratives underplay key components of what made the Third Reich possible, perhaps because wrestling with the realities reveals that fascism was not a problem isolated in a certain place at a certain time. Fascism was both widespread and a glimpse at what a motivated movement could do with the right propaganda and effective manipulation of mass media.

Nazi domination of German culture was aided by the proliferation of radios to disperse propaganda and establish a weaponized reality. Nazi Albert Speer testified to the practice at the Nuremberg trials, holding that Hitler's dictatorship was the first to use mass media and radios "to mechanize" opinion and deprive the populace of "independent thought."[50] Lead propagandist Joseph Goebbels, who had overseen the development of Nazi radio propaganda and coordinated, consistent messaging, ensured that the devices were widely available and inexpensive. He called them the "spiritual weapon of the totalitarian state."[51]

In the build up to their takeover, Nazis flooded the public sphere with their propaganda, preparing the population for the destruction of the republic. Prior to the fall of the Weimar Republic, art, philosophy, science, and cosmopolitan expression had flourished, creating a vast cultural divide between conservatives favoring traditional German culture and those appreciating pluralism. Nazis dictated nearly every facet of life within the state. The Nazi Party immediately shut down the "offensive" cosmopolitan culture, which they called *Kulturbolschewismus*, or cultural bolshevism. They declared it part of an ongoing conspiracy to undermine the Aryan race and seed future revolution.[52]

Similarly, Goebbels attempted to purge all literature offensive to the regime, burning any books deemed to contain "defective" or "subversive ideas" in a practice reminiscent of past scenes in which the church had destroyed the work of heretics. Speaking at a book burning, Goebbels declared, "Jewish intellectualism is dead," and said, "These flames do not only illuminate the final end of the old era, they also light up the new."[53]

New curricula at every level were designed to revere Hitler, prioritize indoctrination, reaffirm the ever-present propaganda and blossoming religious myths, and assist in the rebirth of the German empire and its military ambitions. Nazi officials sat down college professors and delivered an ultimatum. At the University of Frankfurt, in one meeting, the demand was very clear: "You either do what I tell you or we'll put you into a concentration camp."[54]

All of this was in the pursuit of a solitary goal. It was imperative that Western civilization, with its inherent need for resources, materials, and wealth at the expense of people of color and vulnerable minorities, continue. But only the fascists were willing to carry out the necessary brutality. They took seriously the warnings of writers like Madison Grant and Lothrop Stoddard that, save for a renewal of racial violence and subjugation, a rising tide of color would soon overturn everything that had been accomplished. They considered themselves realists, in contrast to others who were so infected by liberalism that their sensibilities had been dulled by Jewish puppet masters.

As the idea of the individual and liberalism were discarded, Nazis prioritized resources for the war effort over human life, as Karl Binding and Alfred Hoche had predicted when they wrote, in their repulsive 1920 screed *The Destruction of Life Unworthy of Life,* "A new period will come which, on the basis of a higher morality, will cease continually implementing the demands of an exaggerated concept of humanity and an exaggerated view of the value of human life at great cost."[55] A mad rush of murders of the disabled, the mentally ill, the elderly, and children broke out in 1939 as Hitler decreed, "Those suffering from illnesses deemed to be incurable may be granted a mercy death."[56] Hospitals, asylums, and birth wards became akin to slaughterhouses as doctors and nurses secretly carried out a murdering spree, ultimately taking hundreds of thousands of lives.

The Nazis systematically murdered over six million Jews, as well as Roma, Poles, homosexuals, and every person undesirable in the regime's eyes. This "Final Solution of the Jewish Question" was meant to eliminate those Hitler and his conspirators believed would oppose their objectives.[57] Heinrich Himmler, whose position as head of the SS meant overseeing this operation, rationalized that the Nazis enjoyed a "moral right . . . to destroy the people which wanted to destroy [them]," meaning that "the difficult decision had to be taken to have this people disappear from the earth."[58]

This genocide, in philosophy, reflected the actions of past colonizers, but what set it apart was the time and the Nazis' use of industrial methods. Colonial powers had long waged total war against populations of color, had massacred them with swords, guns, even the strategic use of gas, but Hitler leveraged advanced bureaucracy, the mechanics of mass production, and principles of scientific management to unleash unfathomable tragedy. The Nazis wielded science and modernity like weapons of mass destruction, studying the application of force to determine how to carry out the maximum production, applying the scientific method to perfect the most efficient means of mass murder.

The Third Reich in many ways embodied the principles of "Western civilization," with its rationalized genocides, enslavements, plundering, and abject, senseless inhumanity, its basis in absurd religious and mythological narratives about "chosen peoples" and "superiority," enabled by visions of "progress" and science in service of utopia. It can be understood as the logical endpoint of murderous white supremacy. And yet, as soon as the war ended—once Hitler had committed suicide in his dreary bunker and Mussolini's broken body had been dragged through the streets—the victors began telling themselves a new story that hid the brutal past, all while absorbing aspects of fascism into their institutions and strategies.

Fascism was far from a German or Italian phenomenon. In America it flourished as thousands flocked to rallies and the wealthy turned to violence to protect their property. Around the world the crisis of capitalism exacerbated existing prejudices and authoritarian tendencies, provoking politicians and citizens alike to herald as the solution to ongoing problems either fascism or movements that might provide meaning and direction.

The underlying narrative of a Jewish plot against Western civilization was ever present. In 1920s England, a conspiracy theorist named Nesta Helen Webster was a sensation, peddling repurposed *Protocols of the Elders of Zion* narratives for profit and influence. Webster's book tied Jews to the Illuminati, Freemasonry, and liberalism, laying the blame for the French Revolution, World War I, and the rise of the Bolsheviks at their door. The forces of Western civilization, she wrote, were engaged in a fight against a "cult of Satan" wielding "black magic," and "the present world crisis" was in fact "a conflict between the powers of good and evil."[59] The target of these plots was the Christian religion, which had become "a beleaguered citadel surrounded by the dark forces," as well as the British Empire, currently enduring "attempts to poison the life-blood" with "alien germs of corruption."[60]

One admirer was Winston Churchill, secretary of state of war and air. In a glowing review of Webster's white supremacist fever-dream drivel, Churchill told readers "this movement among the Jews is not new" and was part of a "worldwide conspiracy for the overthrow of civilization and for the reconstitution of society on the basis of arrested development, of envious malevolence, and impossible equality."[61] Churchill confirmed that Webster's accusations that Jews had caused the French Revolution were credible and accused them of having "gripped the Russian people by the hair of their heads and have become practically the undisputed masters of that enormous empire."

Churchill's hatred of communism would lead him, and the rest of the world, into dark waters. Having traveled as chancellor of the Exchequer to fascist Italy in 1927, Churchill gushed over Benito Mussolini, freely admitting to having been "charmed" and adding, incredibly, "If I had been an Italian I am sure I would have been wholeheartedly from start to finish with Fascismo's triumphant struggle against the bestial appetites and passions of Leninism."[62] Fascism, he continued, "proved [to be] the necessary antidote to the Communist poison." Even six years later, following incredible tyranny in Italy, Churchill still could not contain his admiration for Mussolini, calling him "the greatest lawgiver among living men" and offering fascism as "a centre of orientation from which countries which are engaged in a hand-to-hand struggle with Socialism must not hesitate to be guided."[63]

When the depression crossed the ocean and hobbled the British economy, many turned to a young politician named Oswald Mosley, who promoted a radical plan for a "Minister" to seize "supreme control" of all facets of life to solve the crisis.[64] Rebuffed in part for the involved costs, Mosley became disillusioned and grew enchanted, much like Churchill, with Mussolini's movement. Forming what he called the New Party and eventually the British Union of Fascists, Mosley called for the development of an "iron core" for the "preservation of England" to survive what he believed to be a coming communist revolution aided by "a state within a nation" and "international Jewish finance."[65] Like others of his poisonous ilk, Mosley blamed "organized corruption of Press, cinema, and Parliament, which is called democracy but which is ruled by alien Jewish finance," an "unclean, alien influence in our national and imperial life."[66]

In France, the German invasion was welcomed by right-wing extremists like Charles Maurras, who called the Nazi victory in the summer of 1940 "a divine surprise."[67] Maurras and his fellow extremists had based their activities on espoused patriotism and nationalism, but the pretense of patriotism and nationalism gave way to a warm embrace of failure, the Right rejoicing over an opportunity to crush their political opposition and forge the despotic France of their wildest dreams.

As the Nazis occupied France, the prime minister resigned and authority transferred to Marshal Philippe Pétain, one of the foremost French heroes of World War I. And though Pétain would later claim to have operated every single day with "a dagger at my throat," he cooperated with the Nazis, accepted dictatorial powers, and, ruling by decree, instituted an oppressive, totalitarian state in Vichy France dedicated to *travail, famille, patrie,* or "work, family, and fatherland."[68] Pétainism, or the radical program pursued by Pétain and the ascendant Right in Vichy France, sought to completely restructure French society, supposedly to "put right" the destructive influence of the Left, purge problematic elements, and reprogram the psyche of the people.

Maurras had called for just this very thing, wishing for "the leader that defends and rebuilds" and "the dictator that decentralizes" as he led France into a future free of liberalism.[69] Pétain's turn as a dictator and supposedly putting to rights the failures of the past, reconditioning society and pulling it back from cosmopolitan, liberal decay, earned him a cult following among segments of the Right as he was heralded as "the way, the truth, the life" and "the Savior of France."[70] Pétain and his allies collaborated with the Nazis while scapegoating the Left and liberal citizens for losing the war, laying blame on a scheme between communists, Freemasons, and the Jews, as well as France's women, who had become, in their eyes, "excessively liberated" to the point that their "exaggerated emancipation has destroyed familial traditions."[71]

Though resistance leader Charles de Gaulle would later claim Vichy's crimes were carried out only by "a handful of scoundrels," the authoritarian state was aided by many different people and groups, ranging from those who reluctantly agreed to participate to those who felt the dictatorship hardly went far enough.[72] Pétain set loose many of the state's officials, declaring an end to the "impotence" caused by "narrow regulations and excessive controls."[73] Technocrats and authoritarians alike used the opportunity to tinker with French society as scores of citizens simply swore allegiance to the new dictator, continued their jobs, and held their posts in the face of an authoritarian takeover.

The Vichy regime worked hand in hand with the Nazis in carrying out their Holocaust, capturing over seventy thousand Jews and sending them to their deaths. Although some would go on to frame this relationship as one of coercion, elements within Vichy France, like Minister of Labor and National Solidarity Marcel Déat, roared that France should "cover itself with concentration camps and execution squads" in order to purge what he believed was an existential threat to the regime.[74]

Fascism had already taken root in Spain, where the right wing had gone to extreme lengths in a struggle against rival socialists. Ideologues had framed this as a war between "construction and destruction, between the Spain of ancient traditions, religious principles and the conservation of society and the anti-Spain of demolition, church burning and the October revolution," and the struggle as nothing short of a holy war.[75]

Spain's radical Right became convinced of the need for civil war as they were drowning in conspiracy theories. They devoured journals and newspapers dedicated to anticommunist, antiliberal ideology, the stories detailing "international communist plans" to seed revolution and overthrow existing structures.[76] One of the most vociferous readers was General Francisco Franco, an officer who oversaw colonizing efforts. Franco grew increasingly paranoid as he consumed this propaganda, coming to believe there existed "precise communist plans" for the "liquidation of all Army officers and men" that would hasten the supposed coming communist revolution in Spain enabled by leftists.[77]

A plot developed to install "a strong and disciplined state" by military coup, and following the death of a right-wing propagandist that plan came to fruition.[78] On July 18, 1936, Franco's voice came over the radio as he declared the beginning of a coup in "defense" of Spain. "To all of you who feel holy love for Spain," the general began, "to all of you who in the ranks of the army and navy have sworn to serve the fatherland, to those of you who swore to defend it from its enemies with your lives, the nation calls you to defend it." He named their enemy and target as "revolutionary hordes obeying the commands they receive from foreign dictators."[79]

The resulting civil war was heralded as a Christian crusade to save the Catholic Church, as well as Western civilization, from "oriental threats and from communism," and received widespread support from conservative and reactionary elements.[80] Religious leaders like Cardinal

Isidro Gomá y Tomás charged that communists, Jews, and Freemasons had corrupted "the national soul" and praised Franco as a champion while advocating the wholesale murder of leftists.[81]

The focus of hostilities was to crush the Left and, as General Emilio Mola put it, "eliminating without scruples everyone who does not think as we do."[82] This designation included "left-wing elements, communists, anarchists, union masters," and anyone so much as perceived as sharing a shred of belief with or containing an ounce of sympathy toward them.[83] To accomplish this, the Nationalists carried out unrestrained violence and used sexual assault as a weapon of terror against their enemies. As women and girls of the opposition were considered subhuman, troops were encouraged to violate and torture them accordingly. General Gonzalo Queipo de Llano boasted that this widespread use of rape would serve as an example to "the Red cowards what it means to be a real man."[84] Having carried out these vile acts and leaving to inflict them on the next round of victims, Nationalists would regularly scrawl, "Your women will give birth to fascists," on the city walls to celebrate their crimes.[85]

Franco's regime used time-tested methods of manipulation. They required books and educational materials to refer to their endeavor as "the Crusade" and "the War of Salvation"; created fake documents that portrayed their leftist rivals as engaged in a conspiracy with the international communist movement; forced Catholic religion upon the populace; and used widespread repression to either silence disagreeable elements or eliminate them altogether.[86] Survivors of the civil war were imprisoned in concentration camps, where they would be either reeducated or purged.

The regime came to define leftist and republican ideals as indicative of mental illness, a status taken advantage of by psychiatrists like Antonio Vallejo-Nájera, who made it an imperative to "save" children "from the degenerative environment of their leftist parents." His solution was to take some thirty thousand of them by force, send them to statist orphanages, and redistribute them to loyalist families.[87] As had been the case in other fascist countries, these brutal actions reflected the same type of activities and measures colonizers had previously inflicted on the colonized abroad, only now they were being implemented in the homeland against their own neighbors and communities.

Franco's reign of terror became a subject of great consternation among the Allies as World War II came to a close and questions turned to what the postwar environment might look like. From Washington, DC, President Franklin D. Roosevelt signaled his discomfort to his ambassador in Spain. "I can see no place," he said, "in the community of nations for governments founded on fascist principles."[88] Circumstances changed, however, following Roosevelt's death and the beginning of the Cold War. Diplomat George Kennan said in October of 1947, with a concerned eye toward Russia, although he considered Franco's rule a "totalitarian regime," "The time has come for a modification of our policy toward Spain," including a "normalization of U.S.-Spanish relations, both political and economic."[89]

Despite warnings from critics like Senator Herbert H. Lehman of New York, who worried an alliance would prove America was "not sincerely democratic, that we are ready to support a Fascist government," the United States and Spain came to an understanding.[90] Soon, Franco cleared the way for technocrats to begin guiding his regime, opening the door for "developmentalism" as international finance worked with him to operate his economy, and Spain grew into a capitalist's dream. Labor disruption was curtailed by fear and coercion, wages were kept low, and democratic representation was nonexistent, allowing economic planning to go forward unhindered and result in the so-called Spanish Miracle.

That "miracle" was built on ground littered with bodies and soaked in blood, proof positive that nations like the United States, who had defeated fascism in the war, were unconcerned with the rights and liberties they espoused as guiding principles and much more interested in economic opportunities—and defense against communism. In this way, the crisis of capitalism and the battle against fascistic aggression gave way to a new era where the ideas of authoritarianism were absorbed and implemented behind the veneer of liberalism and progress.

Since snatching power from a dying Lenin in 1924, Joseph Stalin had wielded a cult of personality to realize supreme power and force out his rivals. Just a few years later, he put into action what he called "the tremendous breakup of the old and the feverish buildup of the new," a campaign to industrialize and modernize the Soviet Union at breakneck speed.[91] Framing the operation as a crusade and mobilization for theoretical war, Stalin sought to move the USSR and its peoples through the stages of industrialization by force.

The results were appalling. "Famine on a colossal scale," as reported by Welsh journalist Gareth Jones, claimed as many as eight million people, many of whom were targets of Stalin's ire and may have been intentionally sacrificed.[92] To solve the problem of labor, Stalin had enthusiastically embraced the recommendations of Naftaly Frenkel, a smuggler who caught the dictator's ear by suggesting the "dazzling prospects for constructing socialism through the use of prison labor." This led to an era of mass incarceration in which tens of millions of Russians were arrested, relocated, and exploited for forced labor.[93] Indifferent to the suffering, Stalin continued pushing his programs regardless of their tragic results.

Behind the dictatorial plans and abuses was a remnant of Lenin's vision for the Soviet project. While he was severely critical of the exploitative nature of capitalism and the age of industry, Lenin had still believed "the possibility of building Socialism" depended on "combining the Soviet power and the Soviet organization of administration with up-to-date achievements of capitalism."[94] Lenin held that humankind had come to be enslaved by the machinery of industrialization, but by co-opting the technology, as well as Frederick W. Taylor's scientific management and Henry Ford's innovations in mass production, communists could achieve dominance.

The idea depended on changing the very notion of what a human was and stripping away the poisonous influences of capitalism. Doing this, Leon Trotsky proposed, might lead to the "New Soviet Man," a "higher social biologic type" that was "immeasurably stronger, wiser, and subtler."[95] This New Soviet Man was to be an unflagging worker devoid of a sense of self and dedicated, in totality, to the cause of communism. Art, mass media, and propaganda depicted workers as heroic, tireless, their bodies and destinies having fused with the industrial moment and desired technology. They became living, breathing monuments to Soviet modernization, possessing, as poet Alexei Gastev wrote, "nerves of steel" and "muscles like iron nails."[96]

Despite his total supremacy over Russian society, Stalin remained paranoid and quick to dispose of rivals both real and perceived. As Stalin's plans wreaked havoc, members of the Communist Party, including Martemyan Ryutin, an original Bolshevik who participated in the 1917 Revolution, sounded an alarm. Ryutin prepared a document titled "Stalin and the Crisis of the Proletarian Dictatorship" in the summer of 1932, denouncing Stalin as "the evil genius" whose "desire for power and revenge" had "brought the Revolution to the verge of ruin."[97] In order to restore sanity, Ryutin forwarded, the only solution was the "liquidation of the dictatorship of Stalin and his clique" of criminal cronies.[98]

Immediately Ryutin and those around him were charged as "degenerate elements who have become enemies of communism and of Soviet power, as traitors to the party and the working class."[99] By April of 1933 a wide-scale purge commenced to calm Stalin's fears. Targeting so-called "anti-state elements, wreckers, and opportunists," this purge reinforced conformity to Stalin's brand of communism, likening any critic to an apostate.[100]

The purge established a general environment of fear and paranoia. Rather than creating the so-called New Soviet Man, this installed in members of the ruling elite a tendency to tell superiors whatever they wanted to hear and transfer blame to other parties lest they suffer the consequences of a mercurial tyrant. As one official noted in a letter to his comrade, "The trouble with Soviet power is the fact that it gives rise to the vilest type of official . . . [who] never tells the truth because he doesn't want to distress the leadership."[101]

Despite all of these abuses and an ill-fated treaty with Nazi Germany, Joseph Stalin still found a place for himself and the USSR among the Allies, creating a partnership between the forces of capitalism and communism to end the fascist threat. At best, it was a tenuous alliance.

At the close of the war, the so-called Big Three assumed the task of constructing the postwar order, a charge ripe with possibilities. Franklin Roosevelt favored a strategy called the world policemen theory, which would have seen America, Great Britain, Russia, and potentially China establishing spheres of influence, leading to "all other nations save the Big Four" disarming in totality.[102] But Churchill and the British were already prepared for their own deep change of policy, sinking time and resources into what would come to be known as Operation Unthinkable, a proposed new war. As World War II came to a conclusion, the operation would "impose upon Russia the will of the United States and the British Empire" and would "[make] use of German manpower and what remains of German industrial capacity."[103]

This concept of co-opting the Nazi war machine against the Soviet Union would prove prophetic: The Allies went on to plunder the Third Reich of its scientists and experts to aid its weapons programs. Similarly, the United States would also strike a deal with Japanese war criminals who had experimented with and tested armaments on civilians and carried out widespread crimes against Chinese populations by dropping bombs laced with bubonic plague.[104]

The Allies began to absorb other Nazi positions, including jurist Carl Schmitt's theories on the legitimacy of dictatorships in the face of imminent crises and a bevy of geopolitical concepts, including the idea that survival depended on geography and the reduction of the world to a chessboard that determined the survival of the fittest. Roosevelt had been a staunch proponent of a continued alliance with Russia, but his death in 1945 cleared the way for this new philosophy to take hold, much to the delight of Churchill and other anticommunist hard-liners. Only a few weeks later, as an in-over-his-head Harry Truman assumed the role of president of the United States, the prime minister hurriedly counseled him to take a tougher stance on Russia, cribbing a phrase from Nazi propagandist Joseph Goebbels: "An Iron curtain is drawn down upon their front."[105]

As vice president, Truman was largely left in the dark, so much so that he had not been kept abreast of Roosevelt's development of the atomic bomb. Following his swearing in, Truman found himself inundated not only with Churchill's counsel but with that of advisors Roosevelt had largely dismissed. The vast majority of these advisors drilled into him that there existed "a basic and irreconcilable difference of objective between the Soviet Union and the United States."[106] Abandoned was Roosevelt's dream of a steady and lasting peace, and in its place developed what George Orwell feared, an "epoch as horribly stable as the slave empires of antiquity" in which the major powers existed "in a permanent state of 'cold war,'" or "a peace that is no peace."[107]

Truman followed his advisors' instruction, and after the dropping of atomic bombs on Hiroshima and Nagasaki, Stalin admitted, "The balance has been destroyed."[108] Convinced that peace with the capitalist countries was impossible, he drew the iron curtain even tighter and prepared for the long haul, telling his people that the "uneven development of capitalist countries" would inevitably lead to further wars.

Apologizing for the "burdening of telegraphic channels," in February of 1946 American diplomat George Kennan wired to Washington, DC, what came to be known as the "Long Telegram." He advised that the contradictions between the United States and Russia were irresolvable and that inevitably "two centers of world significance" would emerge that would "decide the fate of capitalism and communism in the entire world."[109] Kennan's telegram carried another warning, instructing that totalitarianism was far from a Russian phenomenon but was rather a state of mind in which any person or entity could become possessed with a "sense of being the innocent victim of unseen conspirational forces," constituting "a disease to which all humanity is in some degree vulnerable."[110] It was imperative to confront the Soviet Union, he believed, and the most prudent means was a strategy of containment. Still, he stressed that "the greatest danger" was not communism or the spread of its ideals but the possibility "that we shall ourselves become like those with whom we are coping."[111]

Unfortunately, this proved to be the case. In creating a defense against the specter of communism, the United States produced a restrictive order conducive to its own interests while embracing elements of fascism and totalitarianism it claimed to abhor. By portraying the USSR as an existential threat, much like Carl Schmitt had theorized, any action taken in neutralizing that threat was not only justifiable but necessary.

Following the war, the United States pursued a policy that would both reconstruct ravaged Europe and establish itself as the director of postwar capitalism. The Marshall Plan, named after Secretary of State George C. Marshall, provided the funds necessary to rebuild the continent while opening the markets and trade America required; it also used these needed funds as a lever of influence. To ensure "a smooth transition from a wartime to a peacetime economy" and that European currencies were "defined in terms of a common denominator," what came to be called the Bretton Woods system placed the American dollar as the foundation of international finance.[112]

A new system of unelected and unaccountable financial organizations like the International Monetary Fund and the World Bank, helmed by technocrats and economists, would exercise outsized control over the politics and economies of participating nations. The magnitude of these changes was far from lost on British participants; Henry Clay of the Bank of England mourned that they had "cut the heart from Britain's preferential trade system."[113]

Besides dominating the economic sector, leadership forwarded the Truman Doctrine, which the president advocated in 1947, saying, "I believe that it must be the policy of the United States to support free peoples who are resisting attempted subjugation by armed minorities or by outside pressures" and that the United States "must assist free people to work out their own destinies in their own way."[114] Whereas past doctrines had declared American prominence in its own sphere of influence, this more or less established that every corner and every people were under US purview.

As paranoia guided America's foreign relations, fear took hold in the heartland. The Republican Party, long critical of Roosevelt's New Deal and constantly likening it to the communism they opposed and a "totalitarian state," struck against the achieved progress. They dismantled labor unions through the Taft-Hartley Act and rolled back many of the programs that had helped the nation out of the Great Depression.[115] To further their agenda, they leveraged fear of communism, accusing their Democratic rivals of "appeasement of Russia," striking out against what they called the "Communist press in New York," and calling for "a revival of the moral strength of Christianity" in order to make the country great again.[116]

These efforts went into overdrive after the Soviet Union tested its first atomic bomb in August of 1949. Truman announced the news by admitting "the eventual development of this new force by other nations was to be expected."[117] The proliferation of weapons seemed, to many, an opportunity to pause the arms race and finally achieve a semblance of world peace under the threat of collective destruction. Scientist Albert Einstein had called for years for the establishment of a "supranational security system," an arrangement that would end the threat of nuclear weapons, stave off a war "likely to bring destruction on a scale never before held possible and even now hardly conceived, and that little civilization would survive," and finally realize a stable system in which the major states could disarm and enter a new era of armistice and prosperity.[118]

This hope would die on the vine. Any prospect of an international effort to curb nuclear annihilation would be absorbed into nationalist conspiracy theories, painted as a despotic plot, and used by aspiring demagogues to gain power and pad their bank accounts. The paranoid state of the burgeoning Cold War was too good for business to even consider giving up.

- CHAPTER EIGHT -

The Machine

The Twentieth Congress of the Communist Party of the Soviet Union opened nearly three years after Joseph Stalin died. Found by leadership in a pool of his own filth on March 1, 1953, Stalin had experienced a massive cerebral hemorrhage and suffered for days until he finally expired on March 5. Official propaganda painted the death as an ascendance, proclaiming he had become "one with Lenin" as his body was laid to rest next to his predecessor. As the first two Soviet leaders slumbered in the dark of the mausoleum, Nikita Khrushchev took the stage in preparation for bringing the state mythology to its knees.

For over four hours, Khrushchev detailed Stalin's "cruel repression" and aired the dirty secrets of his dictatorial regime.[1] At the heart of his critique was Stalin's betrayal of Marxism-Leninism, to which it was "impermissible . . . to elevate one person, to transform him into a superman possessing supernatural characteristics akin to those of a god."[2] The cult of Stalin, he charged, had violated "the principle of collective direction of the Party," leading to an "accumulation of immense and limitless power in the hands of one person," thereby perverting and endangering the revolution. "We must abolish the cult of the individual," Khrushchev implored, "once and for all."[3]

This "Secret Speech" stunned those in attendance as well as the entire world. Attendees were reportedly so distressed, they fell to the floor and clutched their chests as their hearts betrayed them. When he was finished, Khrushchev set off to forge a new path for the Soviet Union.

Wishing to leave the poisonous legacy of Stalin behind, Khrushchev took the USSR in a new direction and focused on improving material conditions. Whereas Stalin had kept Russia on a permanent war footing to force rapid industrialization and maintain total control, his inheritors relaxed the environment and emphasized a betterment of life. Rather than raising a new generation of humanity that eschewed the trappings of capitalism for collective sacrifice, the Soviet Union instead attempted to prove that its system of economic planning could provide goods and luxuries more efficiently than the capitalist free-market system. Khrushchev dedicated this pursuit to "satisfying the growing material and spiritual needs" of the people, promising that Russia would "overtake and surpass America."[4]

The endeavor was revealing and foolhardy. Since the revolution, Russia had deviated consistently from both Marxism and Leninism. Stalin's construction of a domineering bureaucracy created a culture of corruption and a strict class division hidden behind the thin veneer of ideology. As Emma Goldman observed, "True Communism was never attempted in Russia, unless one considers thirty-three categories of pay, different food rations, privileges to some and indifference to the great mass as Communism."[5] More accurately, Goldman contended, what the Soviets practiced was "the crassest form of state capitalism."[6]

Around this time advances in fields like computer science, beginning with the applications that had helped wage war in Europe, emerged as possible means of determining the future. A few years prior, in 1955, the Soviet All-Union Institute for Scientific Information was already predicting "a new revolution" in "the storage and dissemination of data" and the rise of an era where "all data accumulated by humanity" would be stored and transmitted "within a comparatively brief time interval."[7]

The American mathematician Norbert Wiener had put forward

some incredible technological possibilities in his 1948 book *Cybernetics; or, Control and Communication in the Animal and the Machine.* Wiener, while aiding the Allies in World War II in solving the problems of antiaircraft weapons in predicting behavior, had established what he called "cybernetics," a system of "feedback" that turned the study of behavior into a mathematical science.[8] Wiener saw the system's potential to deal with the problems of labor, remarking that his idea gave "the human race a new and most effective collection of mechanical slaves to perform its labor." Such a development could either free people from their toil, thus creating a new "society based on human values other than buying or selling," or gift capitalists with an opportunity to eliminate jobs and plunge workers into more and more misery.[9]

This seemed tailor-made for the Soviet project, and the technological tools appeared to make a planned economy finally achievable. But instead of throwing their weight fully into the pursuit of Marxism-Leninism through technology, Stalinist Russia had rejected the idea out of hand. The idea that computers might determine the future was treated as nothing more than a "giant-scale campaign of mass delusion."[10] The idea was condemned as a capitalistic reduction of the human mind "to a mechanical connection and to signaling," the entire program in thrall to the American war machine, "the god whom cybernetics serves."[11]

Khrushchev changed course, announcing, "The time has come, comrades, to work on the automation of production processes in earnest."[12] Its use would allow the construction of a communist society and a new system wherein labor would be "replaced by machines" overseen by workers who would manage and "control the correctness of the technological process." Rapidly the culture embraced the idea of "thinking machines." In the United States, such a development would portend "unemployment, exploitation of workers, and fear of the future," but in a socialist world it could free people "from hard, uninteresting work" and "provide an opportunity to focus on something lofty and joyful."[13]

Proponents of cybernetics like Anatoly Kitov and Aleksei Liapunov believed cybernetics could move beyond production and was, in fact, the key "to fully implement the main economic advantages of communism—centralized control and the planned economy."[14]

The United States worried about this development. In 1962, assessing advances in technology and computing, the Central Intelligence Agency sounded the alarm that "tremendous increments in economic productivity as the result of cybernetization of production may permit disruption in world markets," creating in the USSR "a model society" that might cause "the socio-economic demoralization of the West."[15] If the project continued, the military warned, it could lead to a "centralized, cybernated, world-powerful command and control center in Moscow."[16]

But the legacy of Stalin would allow no such thing. Years after his death, the bureaucracy he had crafted remained intact and was in fact growing. Victor Glushkov, a Soviet academic and cybernetics proponent, reportedly believed that the bureaucracy was so self-perpetuating that by 1980 it would require "the services of the entire population" in order to carry out its bloated functions.[17] When an automated system of central planning was presented, the prospect of yielding even a semblance of power was too much for entrenched bureaucrats. Lamenting the failure, Anatoly Kitov wrote his partner Aleksei Liapunov in 1968 that there was "no interest in the automation of management or the optimization of planning," and that the issue wasn't ideology or a dispute over importance but the danger it posed to bureaucrats' "positions."[18]

The technology would not be completely abandoned. Rather than implementing it to automate the processes of communism and the economy, a new regime reimagined the systems as tools of repression. Khrushchev would be pushed out of power and his aspiration to make the Soviet Union an ideal consumerist society would fail. Succeeding him was Leonid Brezhnev, who repurposed cybernetics in the pursuit of "managing society" but failed under the incredible weight of the task and the USSR's bureaucracy.[19] Computers fell out of favor in Russia, and the nation fell far behind America in the realm of technology that would determine the future of the world.

The United States spent these decades shoring up its own power over its citizens and abroad. In the wake of World War II, those charged with military planning were convinced the only way to win a future war was to never stop preparing. George S. Pettee of the Office of War Information espoused this viewpoint in 1946 with *The Future of American Secret Intelligence.* Using British failures as an example of the consequences of poor preparation, Pettee cited the Soviet threat and the possibility of a future showdown with the USSR as a need to continue wartime intelligence efforts "for at least a generation to come."[20] Yale professor Sherman Kent, who would go on to play a vital role in developing the CIA and its processes, agreed, arguing it was in the "grand strategic interest" of the United States to maintain "war potential" through continued intelligence gathering.[21]

President Harry Truman agreed but worried that, if left unchecked, the CIA could become dangerous. Regardless, it was founded in September of 1947 with the charge to "collect intelligence through human sources and by other appropriate means," while Truman claimed it would merely be there "in case of an emergency."[22] Soon Truman's fears would come true as the CIA swelled in scope and consequence, moving from an in-case-of-emergency role to an aggressive and offensive entity that not only directed the actions of government but often acted independently and outside of its oversight.

These developments were spurred in part by Allen Dulles, a veteran of the Office of Strategic Services and the longest-serving and arguably most influential director of the CIA. Even as the agency was being discussed, debated, and designed, Dulles argued that its mission should be more than simply the accumulation of intelligence for advisement of the president. In a memo contending that the agency should fall under civilian command rather than military, Dulles made his case that the

United States "must deal with the problem of conflicting ideologies as democracy faces communism, not only in relations between Soviet Russia and the countries of the west, but in the internal political conflicts within the countries of Europe, Asia, and South America."[23]

The CIA became a force unto itself that acted upon the affairs of the rest of the world, engaging in secret activities that were unknown to its victims, the people of the United States, and even government officials as high-ranking as the president, all of it created, directed, and implemented by individuals who had never been elected and faced no possibility of electoral consequences.

What's more, this transformation affected its intelligence-gathering capabilities and analysis. Harry Rositzke, who led the agency's Russian operations, mournfully reflected that American policy regarding the USSR was predicated on "an almost total ignorance" and "systemized delusions of persecution."[24] It was "an illusion" that the Soviet Union was an all-pervasive threat constantly on the offense and threatening to overtake the world. Instead, it was a "country weakened by war, with a shattered economy, an overtaxed civilian and military bureaucracy, and large areas of civil unrest." That reality, which might have prioritized large-scale demobilization in a rational world, was buried by ideologues and opportunists like Dulles in favor of paranoia and a secular-religious myth of "a holy war against the infidels, a defense of free God-fearing men against the atheistic Communist system."

Acting on biased and flawed intelligence that supported this advantageous mythology, the United States doubled down on its war footing and officially militarized the Cold War. In April of 1950 a report titled NSC-68 presented this farcical mythology as undisputed fact and advised Truman a depleted Russia was actually attempting a "complete subversion or forcible destruction of the machinery of government and structure of society in the countries of the non-Soviet world and their replacement by an apparatus and structure subservient to and controlled from the Kremlin."[25] To counteract this, the report advised, "we must make ourselves strong . . . we must lead in building a successful functioning political and economic system in the free world."[26]

In other words, in order to frustrate the Soviet plot to dominate the world, the United States would be forced to dominate it first.

NSC-68 was considered by its drafters a "psychological scare campaign" for Truman and members of the government in the hopes of spurring them into funding operations, but it was also a radical restructuring of society.[27] As Deputy Secretary of Defense Robert Lovett observed in his assessment of this "mortal conflict," even "the economy of the United States might benefit from this kind of build-up" as government funds were used to continue mobilization, fund research and development, and maintain an endless war footing.[28] While other states took the opportunity in the wake of World War II to improve social services and invest in health care, housing, and infrastructure, the United States eschewed these investments in favor of flooding its defense sectors, creating a war-based economy and dealing a blow to the authority of civilian government in the process.

Under Dulles, the CIA carried out coups and subversive actions, traded in psychological operations that both skewed and obliterated truth, illegally experimented on and surveilled American citizens, orchestrated assassinations, and fought an undeclared secret war in pursuit of strengthening America's political and economic interests, most often in assistance of the aims of wealthy individuals and the nation's corporations.

The battle against Soviet Russia, predicated on false and biased information and in service of the political and economic interests of a privileged few, meant deploying any measures imaginable, including overthrowing democratically elected leaders, carrying out coordinated assassinations, sacrificing entire populations of civilians, and creating wars out of thin air. The CIA was dedicated to achieving its objectives at any cost, all while obfuscating its methods and intentionally casting doubt on the very notion of objective truth. It's hardly any wonder that, in this environment and in these times, paranoia as a cultural state and a political weapon became so omnipresent and so significant.

This defining myth of the Cold War as a battle between good and evil exacerbated a sickness within American society that had permeated it since before its founding. As the Soviet Union was cast as the embodiment of Satan in the modern world, once more Americans saw evil spirits conspiring in the darkness and plotting the nation's destruction. While the military-industrial complex took shape in opposition to these phantoms, perhaps no one saw more opportunity in exploiting the fear than Senator Joseph McCarthy of Wisconsin, who made outrageous claims to discredit his rivals and bolster the political fortunes of the Republican Party.

In 1951, as the Korean War marched on, McCarthy was already charging Secretary of Defense George C. Marshall with being part of "a great conspiracy, a conspiracy on a scale so immense as to dwarf any previous such venture in the history of man."[29] McCarthy alleged that numerous high-ranking officials had intentionally worked to "diminish the United States in world affairs, to weaken us militarily," so that America might "finally fall victim to Soviet intrigue from within and Russian military might from without."

Similar to the paranoia of Stalinist Russia, Cold War conspiracies within the United States were both delusional and windows of opportunity. America was supposedly an invincible champion of moral good, and any setback or struggle must have been part of a larger plot laid by outside enemies and internal traitors. But McCarthyism was more than wild-eyed paranoia. It functioned as a means to deal a deathblow to the New Deal consensus by targeting leftists within government, as well as people of color, women, and gay Americans. All were framed as possible traitors and, as the absurd crusade rolled on, systematically swept out of government.

McCarthyism was incredibly useful for the Republican Party in destroying the New Deal coalition and rolling back its achievements. But despite the stories we tell ourselves in conventional histories, believers of this nonsense were not just limited to members of McCarthy's House Un-American Activities Committee, the Republican Party, and a select few. This paranoia found wide purchase and replaced the egalitarian New Deal with a fearful, pro-business, individualist, and consumerist consensus.

Admirers of McCarthy included J. Edgar Hoover, who cut his teeth oppressing leftists as a young agent and used his perch as director of the Federal Bureau of Investigation to infringe on the civil liberties of Americans and wage ceaseless and unnecessary war on anyone arousing his suspicions. Telling McCarthy and HUAC they rendered "a distinct service" in revealing "the diabolic machinations of sinister figures engaged in un-American activities," Hoover picked up where they left off and gave the paranoia the legitimacy of law enforcement.[30] Explaining that "Communism represents a different kind of enemy," Hoover cautioned that the "ideological infection" had already created "thousands of its agents" throughout the nation, all of them "lying like serpents in ambush."[31]

Hoover used his prized COINTELPRO program to "expose, disrupt, misdirect, discredit, or otherwise neutralize" what he considered dangerous elements, including social reformers, student protestors, labor unions, and the burgeoning civil rights movement. In a COINTELPRO memo following Martin Luther King Jr.'s iconic "I Have a Dream" speech in August of 1963, the address about racial harmony was called a "demagogic speech," MLK was labeled "the most dangerous Negro of the future of this Nation from the standpoint of Communism," and a direction was given to research the "communist influence on the Negro."[32] MLK would be surveilled, harassed, and implored by authorities to kill himself, all while the FBI, believing African Americans were part of a communist plot and represented a national security threat, operated under a mandate to "prevent the rise of a 'messiah' who could unify and electrify the militant Black nationalist movement."[33]

Paranoia was particularly useful in the turbulent sixties and seventies in America as Left and Right clashed in a battle of cultures. Something like the civil rights movement, a legitimate call for equality, could be reduced to a front for communist subversion, with segregationists and white supremacists dismissing Black organizers as Soviet plants and legitimizing violence as a means of "protecting" their communities. Governor George Wallace of Alabama, one of the foremost segregationists, called the movement a "fraud, a sham, and a hoax" perpetrated by a media "run and operated by left-wing liberals, communist sympathizers," and members of "communist front organizations." He declared that Black armies and overreaching, traitorous liberal federal authorities were attempting to overthrow the government, eradicate property, and destroy the Christian religion.[34]

Southern professor Medford Evans was even more explicit, telling an audience at the 1965 Congress of Conservatives in Chicago, "Communism has fostered the civil rights mythology and is vigorously perpetrating the civil rights hoax as a means of destroying the United States," and it was carrying out "the dissolution of Modern European civilization."[35]

Evans was a member of a group calling itself the John Birch Society. Named after an intelligence agent killed by Chinese communists, the Birchers were the brainchild of candy magnate Robert Welch Jr., who founded the group in the fall of 1958 in Indianapolis, Indiana. Welch told prospective members that communist agents had not only infiltrated the US government but taken it over completely. The plan was "to change the economic and political structure" over time so as to avoid detection until America could be "comfortably merged with Soviet Russia" and all of humanity could be subjected to a "one-world socialist government."[36]

Birchers also believed Dwight D. Eisenhower, a five-star general, the original NATO supreme allied commander of Europe, and the sitting president of the United States, was engaged in treason. Charging that Eisenhower was a "dedicated, conscious agent of the Communist conspiracy," the Birchers, with their cross-section of affluent and working-class members, were convinced their president was betraying the country. To them, international entanglements like NATO, the United Nations, and numerous treaties and alliances with other countries only served as proof that the international conspiracy carried out by Jews, communists, the Freemasons, and the Illuminati was winning its invisible war.

The Cold War, with its battle over information and reality, created an environment ripe for distrust and intrigue. Plots to attack America's enemy saw the CIA engage in clandestine operations that spanned multiple presidencies, including the ill-fated Bay of Pigs invasion of Cuba, intended to depose Fidel Castro. President John F. Kennedy accepted the political fallout, stating, "I am the responsible officer of government," but the operation had originated with the Eisenhower administration.[37] Quickly, it became apparent that the state might not have full authority over its own agencies.

As the Bay of Pigs fiasco played out in the United States and Kennedy slowly realized his intelligence agencies might have let themselves loose from their leash, French president Charles de Gaulle faced his own crisis in France when a corps of hard-line retired generals attempted a coup on April 21, 1961. De Gaulle had addressed a crisis concerning the fate of Algeria, declaring the people would "have free choice of their destiny," and had preemptively reminded troops, "It is France that you serve," and ordered them to avoid any plot against their government.[38] That a challenge would be rendered did not surprise him, but nonetheless de Gaulle remained convinced that the United States and the CIA had plotted with the generals.

The coup would fail, but de Gaulle's suspicions and troubles would not end. The reactionaries responsible were part of a paramilitary group calling themselves Organisation armée secrète (OAS), which carried out terror attacks in Algeria and in France, where they attempted to assassinate de Gaulle dozens of times.

The OAS emerged from the Algerian War and France's attempt to maintain its grip on its colonial holdings. In line with most colonial wars, French tactics were particularly cruel. As insurgents hid among the civilian population, the people were victim to "regrouping," or herding into concentration camps, where food and supplies were so scarce that prisoners were "found eating grass" and "infants were often found dead of cold in the mornings."[39] To systematically track down their enemies, French forces divided the landscape into residential areas and "forbidden zones," where troops were free to fire on anyone they saw.[40] In search of information and in pursuit of suppression, the French tortured and raped indiscriminately, the practice of sexual assault becoming so commonplace that there developed a distinction between rape as a tool of war and "rape for comfort."[41]

The Algerian War caused a stark divide within France. Those supporting the viciousness believed the nation held a place of greatness and, through colonization, had traded the wonders of "civilization" for the fealty, resources, and labor of the Algerians. This view carried with it currents of racism and discrimination, against both refugees and the people of Algeria themselves. The designation of "terrorist," they felt, gave France not only carte blanche to kill, maim, torture, and abuse but a moral obligation to hasten victory and restore "order" as quickly as possible.

The Algerian War exposed an ugliness hiding within Western society that horrified French philosopher Jean-Paul Sartre. Living through the Nazi occupation of Paris during World War II, Sartre had reached a moment of clarity. In occupied France, he wrote, he had seen French citizens make "authentic" decisions between right and wrong, moral and immoral choices between resisting Nazis and living alongside them while they carried out their sadistic plans, that made them "freer" than they had ever been before.[42]

So much of living, Sartre felt, was hiding behind expectations and the veneer of polite society. In the case of Algeria, the ones cheering on the oppression were bad enough, but similarly at fault were people "personally implicated" by their inability to embrace the necessary revolutionary actions to end the subjugation they knew was indefensible.[43] This "bad faith," or "playing at *being*," was a condition Sartre chalked up to the modern era, in which most people glided through life performing a version of themselves they believed others expected of them while denying their own personal ethics and morality.

Though de Gaulle solved the crisis by allowing Algeria to chart its own course, the revolt of the OAS, not to mention the destruction they wreaked, would prove that something ugly and possibly irrepressible brewed in the postwar world. The comfort with inflicting intolerable pain and dealing death to entire populations in the name of empire, and the willingness and quickness with which those same individuals would betray the very nation they claimed to cherish, spoke to a rotting danger and a brutal clarity that Sartre had recognized in the faces and actions of his fellow French citizens as the Third Reich despoiled the streets of Paris.

The very same brutishness that aided Western civilization in carrying out the cruelties of empire, in conquering continents and peoples, in securing riches and resources and extracting labor from enslaved people and prisoners, would return to inflict unthinkable suffering on those empires should they ever deviate from their chosen course.

The horrors of the Algerian War broke men on both sides. Treating them was Frantz Fanon, a French West Indian psychiatrist, whose 1961 book *The Wretched of the Earth* detailed his findings on the consequences of both colonization and the process of decolonization. Fanon found that the relationship between the colonizer and the colonized was a violent one, as their "first encounter was marked by violence" and then that relationship was "carried on by dint of a great array of bayonets and cannons" until the colonized freed themselves via cleansing revolt.[44] Colonialism, Fanon argued, had resulted in "a world cut in two" and divided unmistakably into those who had rationalized their actions and those subjugated by laws, customs, and mythologies.[45]

Fanon argued that the Western powers had actually created themselves using riches and resources "plundered from the underdeveloped peoples."[46] In this arrangement, and considering the divide between the colonizer and the colonized, developing countries would be doomed to continual appropriation and languishing in a state of intentional underdevelopment unless they threw off the chains of colonialism and charted their own course.

In the postwar environment, the process of decolonization was feverish. Colonized peoples liberated themselves from their oppressors in starts and stops with a variety of tactics and varying levels of success.

Long oppressed and exploited by Great Britain, India gained independence following the ideas of Mahatma Gandhi, who shunned violence as "a suicidal policy" and instead embraced civil disobedience.[47]

In Cuba, Che Guevara rejected both this approach and the religious concept of martyrdom as a weapon, promising, "I will fight with all the arms within reach instead of letting myself be nailed to a cross."[48]

Resistance to French colonial domination coalesced in Vietnam behind an ideology borrowed from America as "It is better to die for liberty than to live in slavery" became a rallying cry for the rebellion.[49]

In China, Mao Zedong advocated a revolution by citing the "total emptiness and rottenness of the mental universe" of the ruling regime, opting for an uprising of the rural poor, which he believed could lead the way toward a utopian society.[50] Saying, "A clean sheet of paper has no blotches, and so the newest most beautiful words can be written on it," Mao sought to mold the population in preparation for a fulfillment of communist visions, a process that would lead to incredible tragedy.[51]

Regardless of their methods, people freeing themselves at this time faced a cavalcade of decisions, including whether to align with the United States or the Soviet Union—or to remain independent and unaligned. Based on what ideology they embraced or rejected, these movements were either aided or challenged, sometimes through economic pressures and sometimes with the barrel of a rifle. In the eyes of both Cold War belligerents, the people and nations amounted to little more than expendable pawns in a much larger game.

That game was the purview of players who prided themselves on being pragmatists or practitioners of realpolitik, and perhaps no player of the era loomed larger than German-born diplomat Henry Kissinger. A refugee from Nazi Germany, Kissinger dedicated his life to seeking order and balance in international affairs, admiring the work of Klemens von Metternich, the Austrian statesman who picked up the pieces of Europe following the Napoleonic Wars and created a reactionary and oppressive status quo. Kissinger lauded this "balancing act" in which Metternich was able to manage the "conflict between inspiration and organization," a goal of any statesman seeking order.[52]

Indisputably bright and irrepressibly ambitious, Kissinger worked his way up in the ranks of American government and became a national security advisor to President Gerald Ford and then Richard Nixon, with whom Kissinger formed a disastrous relationship. In that position and as secretary of state, Kissinger played out his grand game, carrying out proxy battles with the Soviet Union, orchestrating war crimes, greenlighting genocides, and overthrowing democratically elected leaders.

In 1972, Kissinger turned his attention to the nation of Chile, where socialist Salvador Allende was gaining in the polls and seemed on a path toward winning the presidency, and groused, "I don't see why we need to stand by and watch a country go Communist due to the irresponsibility of its own people."[53] Nixon agreed. If Allende could successfully "set up a Marxist anti-American policy," then other nations would certainly follow.[54] The CIA had undercut Allende's campaigns in the past through psychological operations and propaganda, and now they would either force the government to keep him from taking office or create the circumstances needed to inspire a coup to overthrow him before any damage could be done.

Allende did become president and curtailed the financial ambitions of American corporations, though his agenda was far from the radicalism Nixon and Kissinger feared. Regardless, the United States used international financial bodies to deny Chile loans and aid while providing substantial packages for the military they hoped would depose him. That plan would come to fruition as a military coup launched on September 11, 1973, under the direction of a trio of generals, including Augusto Pinochet.

Pinochet and his conspirators cited a "grave economic, social, and moral crisis . . . destroying the country" and promised "the armed forces and the police" were dedicated to freeing the "country from the Marxist yoke" and reestablishing "order and the rule of law."[55] After overthrowing Allende, forged documents were "uncovered" detailing a "Plan Z" conspiracy into which Allende had supposedly entered with foreign communists from around the world in order to assassinate military and political leaders and "impose a Dictatorship of the Proletariat," providing Pinochet and his plotters more cover for their murderous acts.

Pinochet and his military junta enforced harsh discipline on the Chilean people. The regime cracked down on individual liberties, censored the media, crushed labor unions, and rounded up hundreds of thousands, torturing, beating, and disappearing them. Addressing his subordinates, Kissinger instructed them to "understand our policy—that however unpleasant they act, this government is better for us than Allende was."[56]

This moment in South America saw several military dictators establish authoritarian states that were aggressively anticommunist and anti-leftist. They formed an agreement and partnership: Chile, Argentina, Uruguay, Paraguay, Bolivia, Brazil, Peru, and Ecuador would not only provide information on potential threats but form shared units of assassination and murder squads to eliminate possible opponents. In what would come to be called Operation Condor, these dictatorial states believed they represented the last hope for "Western, Christian civilization," a belief the United States stoked to strike a blow in the

Cold War and eliminate "subversive threats."[57] With America's blessing, the group became one of the largest and most dangerous terrorist networks in the history of the world, operating within the borders of several nations, including the United States, where Chilean dissident Orlando Letelier was assassinated in Washington, DC, by a "time bomb" fastened to his car. The explosion killed him and his assistant, "spraying glass and metal" all over the streets and sidewalks of the capital's Embassy Row.[58]

This support of Operation Condor by the United States was in spite of the fact that proponents knew the alliance was based on absurd fears of communist conspiracies. The international Left was absolutely decimated and posed little threat to the dictators' reigns or the emerging economic order. Those piecing together the operation, analysts confirmed, were possessed of a "siege mentality shading into paranoia" and acting out of irrational fear and anger.[59]

Regardless, practitioners of realpolitik saw an opportunity and took it. The United States provided aid and information, including linking the efforts to an ongoing project called Operation Gladio, a covert anticommunist collection of "stay-behind armies" that remained in Europe as World War II closed in preparation for fighting a future war against the Soviet Union and to ensure leftists were unable to mobilize or gain a foothold.[60] Gladio made use of reactionary elements in these European countries, including former Nazis and fascists who had fought on the side of the Axis Powers in the war. Members of the participating governments' police and military forces and political actors were also utilized, creating in these nations "a state within a state," or what some referred to as a "deep state" that influenced and guided events while remaining in the shadows.

To organize the campaigns, America loaned these dictators state-of-the-art computers and programs that the United States had pioneered in its own counterinsurgency efforts in Vietnam. In seeking to mollify the situation in France's former colony and win another theater in the grand game of realpolitik, America had learned from France's successes and failures in Algeria, implementing the insurgent strategies of torture and pacification techniques, all while feeding masses of data into computers that might make sense of what seemed irrational and random. In what was called the Phoenix Program, American intelligence worked with South Vietnam forces in targeting enemies and civilians alike in order to change the course of the war.

They found, however, that the program turned into an orgy of "indiscriminate killing."[61] Vietcong fighters and villagers with no stake in the war were routinely kidnapped before being sadistically tortured and murdered. Making matters worse, there appeared little in the way of logic behind the brutality. By 1972, estimates placed the number of Vietcong killed by the Phoenix Program at eighty-one thousand and civilians at over twenty-six thousand.[62]

Finger-pointing commenced, but it is clear the computers and thinking machines were not responsible. The programs had been designed and implemented by humans, and their suggestions and prompts were carried out by willing humans. Those pointing to the tools and blaming them for the tragedies in Vietnam and South America and everywhere in the world were desperate to blame anything besides themselves.

On August 25, 1968, eight men and women and one infant sat down in Red Square in Moscow and unfurled banners reading, "Stop Soviet interference in Czechoslovakia."[63] Among them was the poet Natalya Gorbanevskaya, who remembers the protest as lasting only a few moments before a squad of plainclothes Russian agents rushed forward, destroyed their banners, and then began "hitting those sitting down about the face and the head" before dragging them away into custody. For her role in the brief protest, Gorbanevskaya was "declared insane and lodged in a special category psychiatric hospital for compulsory treatment," where Soviet officials and doctors attempted to "cure" her madness.[64]

The demonstration was a response to the crushing of the "Prague Spring" in Czechoslovakia, where Alexander Dubček had been elected in January of 1968 on the promise of creating "socialism with a human face" and reforming the nation into "an advanced socialist society" with "historical democratic traditions."[65] Czechoslovakia began to change, and people embraced their nascent freedoms with unabashed optimism until the Soviet Union flooded the country with over two hundred thousand troops and forcibly rolled back the reforms.

Decades of cold war took a toll on the people. Both the Soviet Union and the United States, along with their assorted allies, had shown themselves to be hypocrites and tyrants and their espoused principles nothing more than a veneer of ideology to conceal a struggle over resources and influence. Following World War II, the defeat of fascism was supposed to have bred a new world of hope, peace, democracy, and equality, but the truth was bitterly disappointing.

American sociologist C. Wright Mills surveyed the landscape at the beginning of the 1960s and saw nothing but "smug conservatives, tired liberals and disillusioned radicals" who had blended and combined into a "bipartisan banality."[66] Within this dull environment, a "power elite" had formed that hoarded wealth and lived in delusional worlds of their own making, leaving most of the population to feel "without purpose in an epoch in which they are without power."[67] Mills believed any hope for change or progress lay with the emergence of a new radical spirit among the younger people, who, if they embraced radicalism and partnered with the oppressed and the working class, might be capable of breaking the stalemate and forging something real and meaningful. By the end of the decade, this seemed possible. The next generation of students, activists, and reformers rose up to challenge the previous generation for their fascistic, patriarchal, racist, elitist beliefs, as well as their vapid consumer dullness and penchant for war making.

On December 2, 1964, student activist Mario Savio took to the steps of Sproul Hall on the campus of the University of California at Berkeley to address a crowd of protestors. The subject was a school controversy regarding free speech and autonomy, but Savio detailed a societal sickness, an authoritarian energy bristling just beneath the surface of polite society that depended on a complex system of laws, customs, and expectations with a momentum all their own and the unquestioning obedience of the masses. This "machine," he held, was inhuman and dangerous. He implored his fellow protestors to resist, saying, "There's a time when the operation of the machine becomes so odious, makes you so sick at heart, that you can't take part . . . And you've got to put your bodies upon the gears and upon the wheels, upon the levers, upon all the apparatus, and you've got to make it stop."[68]

Savio's appeal encapsulated a growing domestic sentiment that the Western world was both vapid and dangerous. Following the defeat of the Nazis and fascists, the crusade for freedom and individual dignity had been quickly replaced with neocolonialism, with warmongering as a political, economic, and social tool, and the search for meaning had been exchanged for mindless consumption. The latter was crystalized by the urging of a business consultant named Victor Lebow, who advocated that, should the economy survive, it was necessary "that we make consumption our way of life, that we convert the buying and use of goods into rituals, that we seek our spiritual satisfactions, our ego satisfactions, in consumption."[69]

The prevailing mode of meaning, in both the capitalist societies and later the twisted Soviet economy, would be through the psychological appeals of consumerist culture, leading people to chase purpose and fulfillment through the purchasing of products and services. The strategy of "planned obsolescence" by General Motors CEO Alfred P. Sloan would ensure consumers would continue to regularly and consistently replace their purchases. At Sloan's GM, new models of cars were slightly different from the previous versions, adding noticeable features that enticed consumers to buy, in the words of industrial designer Brooks Stevens, "something a little newer, a little better, a little sooner than is necessary."[70] This also created, in the consumerist society, an inherent competition between individuals desperate to express their status in comparison to their neighbors, families, friends, and community members, a competition that meant increased sales but escalating alienation.

In his analysis of the developing consumerist society, French philosopher Jean Baudrillard reckoned these advancements had led to "a fundamental mutation" in humankind.[71] The alienation and selfishness encouraged by consumerism, as a function of capitalism, had not only divided humanity and created a ruptured society populated with distinct, opposed individuals but had also plunged them into an unreal world where, "sheltered by signs" in advertising, psychological distortions, and manufactured meaning, those individuals remained perpetually "in the denial of the real" nature of existence.[72]

In revolt against this sordid system that also required institutionalized and weaponized racism, sexism, and colonial war and plunder to continue, a movement arose that circled the globe. While some advocated a Marxist turn or voiced a critique of capitalism, many rejected the programs of both the United States and the Soviet Union, choosing instead to trouble the system in pursuit of something novel and free of the stains and tragedy of the Cold War. In France, graffiti and manifestos made it abundantly clear: "We want a new and original world."[73]

The youth of capitalist West Germany concurred. Despite efforts at denazification and proclamations that the awful past had been buried, all signs indicated that was simply not the case. In the nation's pursuit of moving beyond its ugly legacy and reestablishing the economy and society, something had gone awry. German philosopher Theodor Adorno had spoken to this possibility in a lecture in 1959. Troubled by an inescapable call to "work through the past," Adorno charged that it did not mean an actual reckoning with events but an effort "to close the books on the past and, if possible, even remove it from memory."[74] Adorno believed "National Socialism lives on . . . lingers on after its own death" and worried that "the willingness to commit the unspeakable survives in people as well as in the conditions that enclose them."[75] In fact, the concept of Nazism surviving "*within* democracy" was "potentially more menacing than the survival of fascist tendencies *against* democracy."

These concerns certainly seemed valid as West Germany sleepwalked through disturbingly familiar developments. Former Nazis populated the government, including Chancellor Kurt Georg Kiesinger, who had worked alongside Joseph Goebbels to create and air anti-Semitic propaganda.

In the United States, which had positioned itself as the champion of human liberty following World War II and with the outbreak of the Cold War, the pretense was obviously untrue. A general apartheid existed in the Southern states through codified laws upheld by the Supreme Court, and in the nation's economic and legal structures a definitively white supremacist bias existed just below the surface.

As World War II raged, Black leaders met in Durham, North Carolina, at the Southern Conference on Race Relations. They released a manifesto expressing the "faith to believe . . . that it is possible to evolve in the South a way of life, consistent with the principles for which we as a Nation are fighting throughout the world, that will free us all, white, Negro alike, from want, and from throttling fears."[76]

Frustration built until the movement was ready to unfurl. One of the leaders was A. Philip Randolph, head of the March on Washington, who promised, "We would rather die on our feet fighting for Negroes' rights than to live on our knees as half-men, as semi-citizens, begging for a pittance."[77] That movement, which made history on August 28, 1963, with the March on Washington and rally at the National Mall, was dedicated to "an end to Jim Crow in education, in housing, in transportation, and in every other social, economic and political privilege," as well as an end to lynching and the eradication of the apartheid state.[78]

Challenges to the status quo rippled through American society. Following the Red Scare, McCarthyism, and the resulting conservative reaction that targeted and marginalized specific groups, these populations began reasserting their power. Gay Americans, long discriminated against and persecuted, famously fought back. Following a spate of protests, which included picketing at the White House, the revolutionary energy spilled over on June 28, 1969, as a police raid on the Stonewall Inn in Greenwich Village sparked a firestorm of revolt.

Discrimination was social, economic, and institutionalized. Gay citizens were economically disadvantaged, harassed, and faced with the constant threat of violence or murder. The psychological community had even considered homosexuality a "sexual deviation," labeling it a "sociopathic personality disturbance" and recommending a variety of treatments to cure it, including prescription drugs, aversion therapy, and lobotomies.[79]

Liberation, activists believed, depended on gay people freeing themselves from the prejudices society had heaped upon them, including notions spread by the scientific community that they were mentally ill and needed to be "cured." As Carl Wittman argued in "A Gay Manifesto," the "first job" of revolutionaries was "clearing our heads of that garbage that's been poured into them."[80] The open expression of their selves and their identities in rebellion against imposed societal expectations and pressures would begin that process as revolutionaries like the writer Martha Shelley declared, "Liberalism isn't good enough for us," and warned the elite that the movement was dedicated to "shaking off the chains of self-hatred and marching on your citadels of repression."[81]

In the growing feminist movement, the rejection was of a different sort. The prevailing patriarchal culture prescribed for women a gendered role that hid subordination behind a mythology of "protection" and "reverence." Because of a woman's God-given role as a wife, a mother, and the angel of the household, the culture pretended to venerate her as a means of perpetuating subservience. This gendered existence, as French writer Simone de Beauvoir explained, was an outright construction. "One is not born, but rather becomes a woman," de Beauvoir contended. "It is civilization as a whole that produces this creature."[82]

George Gallup was undoubtedly ignorant of de Beauvoir's work when he published an article in *The Saturday Evening Post* in December of 1962 that presented his findings on the state of the American woman. According to his research, they were among the happiest and most content people because they knew "precisely why they're here on earth . . .

to be either a good mother or a good wife."[83] That delusional assertion was obliterated not long after when journalist Betty Friedan released *The Feminine Mystique,* which investigated what she called "the problem" that had lain "buried, unspoken, for many years in the minds of American women" and troubled the housewife as she "made the beds, shopped for groceries, matched slipcover material, ate peanut butter sandwiches with her children, chauffeured Cub Scouts and Brownies, lay beside her husband at night," and led her to ask, "Is this all?"[84]

This second wave of feminism built off the suffrage movement and pushed for equal rights between the sexes, including the relaxing of spoken and unspoken expectations, equal pay, protection from domestic abuse, and reform of a system tailored to the benefit of men. Its supporters made gains in economic and legal circles but were hampered by conservative reaction, including conservative women, and the deep, interlocking currents of racism, sexism, and classism that flowed through society.

Figures like activist Angela Davis were piecing together the puzzle as the movements fought for reform. At a Black Panther rally in Oakland, California, a twenty-five-year-old Davis connected the antiwar movement to civil rights and to the oppression of all peoples. "We have to talk about what's happening in Vietnam as being a symptom of something that's happening all over the world," she stressed, diagnosing the intersectionality of the struggle shared by Black people, women, queer and trans people, the poor, and Indigenous peoples around the globe.[85]

However, just as the picture was beginning to emerge, the reactionary forces these activists sought to unseat were beginning a counter-revolution of their own to turn the tide of change and secure their continued domination.

In August of 1971, corporate lawyer Lewis Powell was just months away from being nominated to the Supreme Court. There, he would champion corporate rights and whittle away at safeguards of democracy.

Before he was seated, though, he was tasked with forging a defense of the wealthy and the system they believed was in dire danger.

Powell had earned his fortune as a lawyer representing the tobacco company Philip Morris, parrying the blows of critics who asserted that cigarettes were causing an epidemic of cancer in America. Though Powell and his associates fought these accusations tooth and nail, secretly they knew them to be true. As early as 1953 executives had been alerted that cigarettes caused cancer by a doctor named Evarts Graham, who said, "This is no longer merely a possibility. Our experiments have proved it beyond any doubt."[86] Accepting the results, the tobacco companies pooled their resources in creating a "research project" of their own with the express purpose of twisting the scientific consensus and building "a foundation of research sufficiently strong to arrest continuing or future attacks."[87]

This tactic would later be replicated by the oil industry as their own scientists confirmed that the burning of fossil fuels was beginning to endanger the environment and contributed to calamitous global climate change. By 1968 they already knew their businesses were creating "serious world-wide environmental changes" that could lead to "the melting of the Antarctic ice cap, a rise in sea levels, warming of oceans," and a whole host of apocalyptic scenarios.[88] Rather than deal with the looming crisis responsibly or ethically, the oil companies borrowed a page out of Big Tobacco's playbook by using their resources to fund spurious science, often relying on the same individuals and companies to break consensus and inspire falsified skepticism.

Powell understood this strategy all too well, and his drafting of what has come to be called the "Powell Memo" was undoubtedly done with an eye toward that approach. Addressing his friend Eugene B. Sydnor of the US Chamber of Commerce and outlining a strategy for wealthy Americans and their businesses, Powell declared that the "American economic system is under broad attack."[89] This attack, directed by "Communists, New Leftists, and other revolutionaries who would destroy the entire system," was coming from all sectors of American society, including the universities, the media, and the culture.[90] So far the efforts had been gaining ground because, as Powell lamented, "businessmen have not been trained or equipped to conduct guerilla warfare with those who propagandize against the system" and had been unwilling to marshal their resources and step into the arena.[91]

Powell proposed an aggressive investment of funds and resources into the development of a project to replicate the efforts of industries like Big Tobacco to counteract the influence of academics, scientific experts, and persuasive voices in culture by creating their own institutions and organizations. Frightened by democratic and reform movements, the wealthy invested heavily in conservative think tanks to develop strategies and policy to undermine expertise as a means of defusing problematic findings and create a media complex of pundits and personalities to win support in the public and muddle the debate.

These corporate interests were far from the only ones concerned with the backlash against the people's movements of the sixties and seventies. Social conservatives within the evangelical community, economic conservatives fretting over government interference and the looming specter of collectivism, and traditionalists obsessed with maintaining an adherence to days and ideas gone by coalesced to form a counterrevolution that would define the United States and Western civilization for decades to come.

After enjoying a resurgence during the early days of the Cold War as a counterbalance to the "godless atheism" of the Soviets, American evangelical Christians sounded the alarm about the idea that, with social movements and reform, the very soul of the country was at stake. Leaders like preacher Billy Graham called for a "religious revival" in order to "restore our historic heritage, create moral stamina and consciousness, bring back the sanctity of our homes, [and] strengthen the bulwarks of freedom."[92]

As the years rolled on, this "revival" overtook the country and America fashioned itself a Christian state in opposition to Russia's godlessness. Perhaps no one took greater advantage than Jerry Falwell, a

Virginia televangelist who built an empire of wealth and political influence by leveraging his pulpit as a soapbox. Falwell was an aggressive segregationist, proclaiming, "Where God has drawn a line of distinction, we should not attempt to cross that line," and prophesizing that doing so would "destroy our race eventually."[93]

When the issue of segregation lost favor, Falwell capitalized on other divisive social issues. Of the feminist movement, he said that its believers were "in disobedience to God's laws" and practiced a "godless philosophy."[94] Later he would charge that the movement itself was nothing more than a front to "take away the marvelous legal rights of a woman to be a full-time wife and mother," establish a society of "abortion on demand," and gain "privileges for lesbians and homosexuals to teach in the schools and to adopt children." Those gay Americans, Falwell warned his supporters, were "after my children and your children."[95]

In economic circles, free-market proponents pushed for more and more libertarian approaches and the destruction of what little social safety net there was. These trends had taken shape as a backlash to Roosevelt's New Deal and reflected the absurd fear that government investment and regulation amounted to tyranny. One of the most popular and influential voices was the Russian writer Ayn Rand, who preached her philosophy of "objectivism" and the virtues of selfishness.

These elements converged in the presidential election of 1964 and the campaign of Arizona senator Barry Goldwater, a self-styled cowboy who built a financial empire marketing novelty underwear called "Antsy Pants."[96] Backing Goldwater was a network of wealthy businessmen with sanitized segregationist ideals and libertarian rationales parroting concepts of "states' rights" and arguing that the "problem of race relations, like all social and cultural problems, is best handled by the people directly concerned."[97] Anything else "enthrones tyrants and dooms freedom."

In winning the Republican nomination, Goldwater would answer critics who said his views were extreme and that he was unfit for office by declaring, "I would remind you that extremism in the defense of liberty is no vice. And let me remind you also that moderation in the pursuit of justice is no virtue."[98] He claimed the line belonged to the Roman statesman Cicero, but it was actually the work of a speechwriter named Harry V. Jaffa. A disciple of the German political philosopher Leo Strauss, Jaffa believed the United States was founded explicitly on the principles of "natural rights" that lay beyond the realm of the law.

That America was supposedly founded on these ideals meant, for Jaffa, that a line "between civilization on the one hand, and barbarism and savagery on the other" had been drawn; on one side was the proud tradition of conservatism and on the other "the exhibitionism of lesbians, sodomites, abortionists, drug addicts, and pornographers."[99]

The fusion of these interlocking and sometimes contradictory elements into the modern Republican Party and conservative movement proved lucrative and politically beneficial. All of it could function in tandem to counteract calls for progress and reform. Even the absurd beliefs of the John Birch Society and associated groups could be weaponized, as long as their wilder and more controversial elements were hidden from view and distanced from the Birchers themselves. It was an incredibly effective alliance but also immensely tenuous. The varied interests jockeyed for support and control and jostled constantly as the project lumbered on, but as long as they were united in support of a white, evangelical, patriarchal aristocracy, there was hardly any hope of standing in resistance.

After becoming the head of the opposition in British government in 1979, conservative Margaret Thatcher made a point of visiting an Austrian economist named Friedrich Hayek. The meeting took place in London and lasted roughly thirty minutes, but as it came to a close, Hayek grew overwhelmed as he realized Thatcher would be an ideal partner in enacting his economic philosophy and changing the world. When she left, Hayek was stunned. "She's so beautiful," he muttered as he realized his designs would gain traction in England.[100]

Hayek was a prominent proponent of a worldview that had come to be known as neoliberalism. He vehemently opposed any notion of government interference in the economy whatsoever, forwarding the idea that for it to invest in projects, distribute favors or resources to certain groups, or even make value judgments in regard to redistribution of wealth was for it to infringe on the rights of every citizen. This, he posited, amounted to a "totalitarian state" and violated the entire liberal idea of liberty.[101] Democracy was particularly dangerous, as leaving these issues to the public will would almost always lead to tyranny and result in the society destroying itself because of seductive notions of egalitarianism and rumors of greater freedom.

Neoliberalism had emerged in the summer of 1938 as Nazism and fascism gained a foothold in Europe and as the liberal democracies of the world were faltering. Faced with the possibility that the liberal project, with roots tracing back to the eighteenth-century period of Enlightenment, might be reaching its fatal conclusion, French philosopher Louis Rougier summoned the brightest minds he knew to Paris to discuss ways to reinvigorate the philosophy.

For the colloquium the topic du jour was American Walter Lippmann's newest book, *The Good Society,* which attempted to answer the trends of illiberalism and mixed economy solutions by defining "a free society" as one that "does not administer the affairs of men. It administers justice among men who conduct their own affairs."[102] The conference discussed Lippmann's call for a revitalization of traditional liberalism and largely came to an agreement that the answer lay, as German economist Walter Eucken explained, in the state's finding the strength and clarity "to distance itself in one way or another from the economic process."[103] Joining him was Wilhelm Röpke, another German troubled by how democracy had delivered his country to Adolf Hitler and the Nazi Party, who suggested that the answer, "as so much is crumbling and tottering," was for "a genuine *nobilitas naturalis,*" or natural nobility, to rise once more and hold sway over the world and its processes.[104]

These discussions would later lead to the founding of the Mont Pelerin Society in April of 1947, a group of economists and thinkers dedicated to resurrecting traditional liberalism and reinforcing its libertarian core. They released a statement saying that "the central values of civilization are in danger" because of "a decline of belief in private property and the competitive market," necessitating a wide-scale change.[105]

To test neoliberalism's merits, an extraordinary situation would have to present itself. The neoliberals found such a laboratory in Chile, where dictator Augusto Pinochet was struggling with his economy and was more than happy to experiment on his population. A group of Chilean neoliberals had studied in the United States under the economist Milton Friedman at the University of Chicago, learning the ins and outs of this new philosophy. These "Chicago Boys" were given carte blanche by Pinochet to reverse "a half century of errors."[106]

The Chicago Boys administered what has been called "shock treatment." It amounted to the rollback of state assistance that helped the people, the privatization of resources and services, and a tuning of the economy in favor of international markets.[107] As a result, the economic borders collapsed. Businesses either found their place in the international system or were destroyed. The Chilean people suffered terribly, but the results for capitalists in the country and around the world were staggering.

Called "the Chilean Miracle," it was a real-world example of how neoliberalism would function. Ideology would be limited and ideally eliminated. Politics and government would be separated from the economic sphere, which would be left to technocratic "experts." The market would be absolutely free and unrestricted, allowing the people to either prosper or fail without government intervention. Power at the ballot box was replaced with "consumer sovereignty," meaning votes were relatively useless and the consumer made their preferences known with their purchases.

For the market, it was fantastic. For the people, disastrous.

Hayek was overjoyed. The horrors of Pinochet's neofascistic

dictatorship didn't concern him. In fact, he went so far as to claim that in some circumstances personal liberty was "better protected under an authoritarian than a democratic government."[108] To the neoliberal, ethics and morality weren't relevant to the market. Self-interest was the guiding principle, and the only thing that mattered was that the democratic will was thwarted, or at least molded to create as conducive an environment as possible for the flow of capital.

Following advice from Hayek that included Chile as an example of neoliberalism's potential, Margaret Thatcher would win leadership in 1979 by promising to humble labor unions and address the "underlying problems" of the British economy.[109] As had been the case in Chile, Britain was facing a moment of reckoning with its economy and the safety net that had been created. Thatcher used Hayek's and the neoliberals' playbook to get the job done, cutting government investment in human projects and tilting operations in favor of unadulterated business. She demonized labor unions as enemies of the people and appealed to growing white supremacist extremists by capitalizing on xenophobia and immigration fears, saying, "People are really rather afraid that this country might be rather swamped by people with a different culture," which would be a tragedy considering "the British character has done so much for democracy, for law, and done so much throughout the world."[110]

This fearmongering mainstreamed a radicalism that had been growing in Britain. The process had begun with a colleague of Thatcher's named Enoch Powell, who delivered a controversial speech in 1968 that recounted a conversation with a constituent who predicted "in 15 or 20 years' time the black man will have the whip hand over the white man" and likened the nation's acceptance of immigrants to "heaping up its own funeral pyre."[111] Powell would be forced out of his position as shadow defence secretary, but Thatcher recognized the potential in his sentiments and cribbed them for herself to steal support from Britain's growing neofascist population.

Joining her in the neoliberal project was Ronald Reagan, a two-bit actor who established his conservative bona fides serving as governor of California during the counterculture era, cracking down on students and leftists. In the seventies, the economic order was on the fritz and America was suffering stagnation. While President Jimmy Carter called on Americans to reconsider their fulfillment through consumerism and unrestrained individualism, Reagan told the people there was nothing wrong with them and that the problem was "excessive bureaucracy," which he would dismantle in order that he might set loose "the energies and ingenuity of our people."[112]

Reagan's landslide victory was based on this stark contrast in messaging, but it was also aided by his marshaling of conservative trends and appeals to white supremacist extremism. In his speeches and appearances, he spoke constantly of America as God's "Shining City on a Hill" and peppered his remarks with references to God and evangelical principles. The think tanks that had been funded by the nation's wealthiest individuals and corporations handed a clueless Reagan an instruction manual on how to run a government, and he happily took their cues. And with the help of an assortment of dog-whistling racists, he took advantage of white paranoia and anger. As president, Reagan mirrored Thatcher's actions: cutting all social programs to the bone or out of existence, lowering taxes on the wealthy, redirecting state efforts toward deregulation and assistance of the market, and crushing what was left of the American labor movement.

The marked divide between the elite and everyone else inspired a new era of mystification. Neoliberal operations were complicated and specialized, including internal and external forces, international regulatory bodies, and principles that required a lifetime's worth of education and experience to even begin grappling with; as a result, most people lacked a strong understanding of the system in which they lived. From this intentional ignorance grew mythologies of battles between good and evil that determined the fates of the people, rather than market forces and weaponized self-interest, including elements of conspiracy theories that had inspired genocides and the rise of fascism.

Radical and paranoid narratives were peddled by true believers and grifters alike. Conspiracy theorist Lyndon LaRouche built a rabid base for himself by claiming that world affairs were being controlled on behalf of the British royal family, which was hell-bent on destroying the "American system of political-economy."[113] A veteran named Bill Cooper chiseled out a conspiracy theory empire, explaining seemingly nonsensical current events as part of a larger narrative involving a 1954 "treaty" between aliens from outer space and America. To boot, an ongoing plot to subvert America and place it within a one-world tyrannical government was well underway. Gary Allen, a John Birch Society member who had advised the bigoted George Wallace in his 1972 presidential campaign, contributed his own take on what was happening in the world, explaining that a cabal of "insiders," including corporations and political and financial elites, were engaged in a "master conspiracy" to reduce America to a communist state.

There was big money to be had in selling such nonsense. Hal Lindsey capitalized on Christian paranoia in his bestseller *The Late Great Planet Earth,* promising the faithful they were careening toward "the last war of the world, involving all nations," in which Jesus Christ himself would "return to prevent the annihilation of mankind."[114] Similarly, the Swiss author Erich von Däniken cobbled together ludicrous stories of ancient astronauts that simply retold esoteric Nazi mythologies of forgotten races and pseudoarchaeology. Däniken captivated audiences with stories of a past teeming "with unknown gods who visited the primeval earth in manned spaceships," disgustingly discounting the achievements of cultures that predated white Western civilization and attributing them to gods who, he posited, might have judged "the black race a failure" before creating the Aryans via "gene surgery."[115]

Many Americans were primed to believe in anything, no matter how ridiculous or supernatural. Sensing an opening, Jerry Falwell warned that "Satan has mobilized his forces to destroy America" and was thriving due to "inner moral decay."[116] News broadcasts were full of stories of Devil cults and rumors of human and animal sacrifice, a growing danger that lurked around every corner. A wave of anxious parents bought into a panic about sexual abuse in childcare centers around the country, lending credence to stories children told "of being thrown into shark-infested waters, taking trips to outer space, and worshiping the devil," and, in one instance, watching a caregiver fly through the air.[117]

Pat Robertson, another televangelist in the vein of Falwell and a presidential candidate who won four Republican primaries in 1988 against the sitting vice president, took the developing neoliberal, international system and lent it the evil air of satanic conspiracy. Calling it "the New World Order," Robertson warned it was the work of a "tightly knit cabal whose goal is nothing less than a new order for the human race under the domination of Lucifer and his followers."[118] The ongoing process of enforcing austerity, opening international economic markets, and creating the perfect environment for hypercapitalism to gain momentum was transformed from a political and economic issue into a supernatural battle between good and evil. In the process, any rational and helpful explanation of what was happening was obfuscated and blame was transplanted from neoliberals and the wealthy to liberals, the Left, and internal "traitors."

It was the perfect recipe for the Right and the ideal condition for neoliberalism to overtake the United States and then be transmitted through its economic and political channels throughout the rest of the world.

When the Soviet Union collapsed in December of 1991, the Russian people were caught off guard, but perhaps no one was more surprised than the intelligence agents tasked with knowing that such a collapse was about to occur. For all of the millions and millions of dollars, the exhaustive resources, and the unblinking attention dedicated to knowing every solitary detail of Soviet life, one of the most momentous occasions in all of human history came as a complete shock to those who were paid never to be shocked.

Not everyone was, however. Richard Pipes, a professor of Soviet history, maintained that, despite near-universal astonishment, the intelligence reports and details he had viewed "provided a clear description of the USSR's internal crisis."[119] Pipes was used to serving as a contrarian to intelligence consensus and had served as a member of Team B, a group of outside experts who had been brought in during the 1970s to serve as a counterbalance to intelligence agency insiders. Pipes and other analysts delivered a scathing rebuttal to the established perspective that left the regular team "speechless."[120] Confusion broke out as intelligence agents and government officials grappled with how two separate groups poring over the exact same information could come to such radically different conclusions.

Despite the West's inability to grasp its severity, the situation in the Soviet Union had been deteriorating for some time. By the fiftieth anniversary of the 1917 revolution, Polish Marxist Isaac Deutscher gazed at a "mass of accumulated disillusionment and even despair," a culture "fraught with the moral-psychological potentiality of restoration that cannot become a political actuality."[121] By 1970, Soviet dissident Andrei Amalrik was already asking if the USSR could even survive another decade. If it were to continue, he argued, it would have to radically change. He forwarded three competing notions for an alternative course, including a resurrection of "Genuine Marxism-Leninism," "a return to Christian ideas," and "a transition to a Western kind of democratic society."[122]

Amid the wreckage of the failed state, leader Boris Yeltsin delivered solemn news to the Russian people. "Russia is gravely ill," he told them. "The economy is sick."[123] To treat the problem would mean remedies that would be painful but necessary and result in "a certain decline in the standard of living" that he promised would be only temporary.[124] The solution was "shock therapy," the same neoliberal program Chile had undergone before it was transferred around the world and through Great Britain and the United States. Government assistance was cut, price controls lifted, the state's bountiful services and resources privatized, and the international market was welcomed in for the first time since the October Revolution of 1917.

This effort was spearheaded by American officials and international finance projects like the International Monetary Fund. The prescriptions that had worked and produced economic success stories elsewhere, however, landed flat. Flummoxed by a result they hadn't expected, the economists who had treated neoliberalism as a religious faith and indisputable were left searching for answers. They blamed Russian society itself, scapegoating corruption and the remnants of Soviet ideology that hampered the full acceptance of necessary measures.

Their faith in the neoliberal project remained unshakable. It was a religion all of its own, including a priestly class of economists and technocrats armed with specialized knowledge and a ceaseless and tireless dedication to an ideology that had come to replace all other ideologies, a devotion that relied on unquestioning obedience and a belief that all the human suffering and inequality that resulted from their plans, all of the injustices and prejudices their ideology relied on, was justified in the long run if it meant creating the heavenly utopia they believed to exist just ahead.

- CHAPTER NINE -

Flying Ever Closer to the Sun

On the morning of September 11, 2001, at 8:46 a.m., a Boeing 767 from Boston crashed into the side of World Trade Center Tower 1 in New York City. Hopes that it might have simply been an accident evaporated seventeen minutes later when United Airlines Flight 175 raced through the electric-blue sky and slammed into Tower 2. By then, the attention of the world was trained on the scene, bearing witness to the dawning of a terrible new age.

With the fall of the Soviet Union and the relative peace and prosperity of the 1990s, the United States had come to believe, as empires often do, that its rule had achieved a state of permanence. In 1989, Francis Fukuyama had posited that the Cold War had ended with the "unabashed victory of economic and political liberalism" and that humanity had reached the "end of history," wherein American liberal democracy represented "the end point of mankind's ideological evolution" and "the final form of human government."[1]

This notion, while hubristic and retrospectively absurd, held weight among the ruling class. With the aid of burgeoning technologies, the internet, trade deals, deregulation, and the force of international bodies, neoliberalism had crisscrossed the world and intertwined countries both large and small into a system of economic interdependence. Designed as a means of separating markets from democracy and ideology, this

New World Order would not prove as all-encompassing or unassailable as Fukuyama or its architects would have hoped.

The weakness proved to be its attempt to eliminate ideology. Neoliberals had meant to counter the ideologically driven conflicts of the twentieth century and negate the "dangers" of mass democracy and populism. Believing economics were much too important and complex to be left to the people, they designed a system to transfer democratic compulsions to the market and political expression into consumerism, all while disarming the danger of ideas. But that brief respite, in which the political and economic elite came to believe their system would be everlasting, came crashing down with the towers of the World Trade Center, a structure ironically built to embody the neoliberal project.

That such a terrible and gigantic tragedy could have occurred, and that a small cell of terrorists armed with box cutters could change the course of history, was virtually unthinkable. Hubris and incompetence made it possible. Though President George W. Bush and his administration portrayed the event as unpredictable, the now-infamous truth is the administration ignored multiple warnings about an imminent attack. This improbable narrative, that America, the most powerful empire in the history of the world, had been caught unaware in such a way, required some kind of explanation.

As the towers in New York City burned, a conspiracy theorist in Austin, Texas, named Alex Jones held court. Cutting his teeth on public access television, Jones had emerged as one of the country's most influential paranoia peddlers, treating his audience to visions of a New World Order hellscape populated with jackbooted storm troopers, barbed-wire concentration camps, and a coming apocalyptic assault by satanic forces that would result in the murder and enslavement of all humankind. His narrative merged the Book of Revelation with Third Reich retroism and pandered to America's paranoid militias and separatist groups, creating a daily broadcast that played like a dispatch from the end of the world.

September 11 was ripe material for Jones. Listeners could watch the carnage in New York while their fears multiplied via the gravelly voice of their chosen prophet of doom and destruction. "Well, I've been warning you about it for at least five years," Jones began his broadcast, detailing how the despotic American government had perpetrated one fake terror attack after another, including the calamitous bombing in Oklahoma City in 1995.[2] "They need this as a pretext to bring you and your family martial law. They're either using provocateur Arabs and allowing them to do it or this is full complicity with the federal government." The event had been "orchestrated" by the "New World Order system that has taken control of our government."

The attack presented a political Rorschach test. For Jones, whose worldview had been influenced by the John Birch Society and Bill Cooper, it signified yet another in a long line of operations carried out by a shadowy cabal obsessed with world domination. Anti-Semites blamed the Jews. In an interview with Pat Robertson, Jerry Falwell laid the blame on "pagans and the abortionists, the feminists, and the gays and the lesbians," who had drawn the ire of God and caused the deity "to lift the curtain and allow the enemies of America to give us, probably, what we deserve."[3]

While Falwell was criticized, his perspective was echoed in religious and political discourses. British prime minister Tony Blair, a fervent neoliberal, penned a furious memo to President Bush that the West had "pussyfooted around" the threat of terrorism and allowed evildoers to use liberal values against them.[4] In this new world, Blair believed, the very fate of Western civilization would "require action that some will baulk at."[5] There was no choice. "These groups don't play by liberal rules," Blair wrote, "and we can't either."

Though the perpetrators of the attacks were a small band of extremists, the threat of Islamic terrorism was quickly framed as an apocalyptic battle the likes of which Christianity had been anticipating for millennia. It was considered "a war to reverse the triumph of the West," and the only possible response was to leave behind liberal concepts like justice, freedom of expression, privacy, and human rights in order to form a crusade to protect Western civilization through religious struggle.[6]

Reactionary paranoia kicked into high gear. As America had become the center of the white Christian world, the attack was dressed in all the vestments of martyrdom and holy war. The ongoing fear of an outside force conspiring with internal traitors inspired a venomous suspicion of Muslim Americans and people of color acting as deadly fifth columns. Politicians and personalities decried Islam as a murderous faith, creating an environment of distrust, anger, discrimination, and racism. Four days after the attacks, a man named Frank Roque told a server in Mesa, Arizona, he was "going to go out and shoot some towelheads" before killing Balbir Singh Sodhi, a Sikh gas station owner, and attempting to murder a man of Lebanese descent.[7] When he was finally apprehended, Roque exclaimed, "I am a patriot! I stand for America . . ."

Unfortunately, America's grief and anger in the wake of September 11 led to tragedy on a worldwide scale and a slew of events and consequences that would bring Western civilization to a new and blistering crisis. The plan for al-Qaeda, the perpetrators of the attack, was to provoke America to "act chaotically against those who attacked" and carry out a massive campaign of war and destruction that would undermine its professed values and set off a cycle of self-destruction.[8] The United States did just that. The resulting War on Terror would cause more than nine hundred thousand deaths, cost nearly $8 trillion, and lead to an ever-expanding campaign within nearly eighty separate countries. American leaders would operate with breathless and remarkable cruelty that exposed the nation's hypocrisy, all while militarizing American society and arresting anything approaching necessary reform and progress.

History would prove to be far from over.

In the wake of the tragedy, members of both parties coalesced behind a Manichean mindset that the coming war was a battle between good and evil. They granted the administration authority to wage war abroad and circumvent civil liberties on American soil. While George W. Bush spoke of crusades against malevolent forces, the more dispassionate members of his administration capitalized on the crisis and, in doing so, began toying with reality itself. Dismissing a journalist as a member of the "reality-based community" where "solutions emerge from . . . judicious study of discernible reality," one official explained, "That's not the way the world really works anymore. We're an empire now, and when we act we create our own reality."[9]

September 11 opened a window of opportunity. As the Cold War ceased, neoliberalism had effectively frozen the state of things, theoretically preventing wars and blocking any shifting of territory. Free markets and economic transactions steered world events but maintained a general equilibrium. The attacks constituted a shocking interruption—and, more so, an invitation for the United States to take advantage in reasserting its status as the world's defining actor, acquiring resources and establishing new military and economic centers, all under the auspices of self-defense, moral impunity, and martyrdom.

Operations began in Afghanistan, where a coalition force led by the United States sought to replace the al-Qaeda–friendly Taliban with their rivals, the Northern Alliance. Once established, the Northern Alliance perpetrated horrific war crimes, leaving in their wake mass graves littered with "pieces of white bone" and reeking of the "smell of decaying bodies."[10] Asked about these atrocities, Bush returned to his uncomplicated narrative, waxing poetic about "a wonderful, joyous occasion as the citizens were free, free from repression, free from a dictatorial government."[11] Later, US forces were stunned to find their new allies engaging in other crimes, including the widespread, ritual rape and abuse of children. Writing home, one marine told his father, "At night we can hear them screaming, but we're not allowed to do anything about it." Another service member was even more explicit: "We were putting people into power who would do things that were worse than the Taliban did."[12]

Soon America would turn to Iraq, a favorite target of the neoconservatives in Bush's administration. There, American forces would yet again underestimate the realities on the ground in favor of a naïve and damning belief that its status and reputation ensured victory and a population that would, as Vice President Dick Cheney bragged, greet them "as liberators."[13]

Cheney's claim proved as ludicrous and tragic as the US government's allegation that Iraq harbored weapons of mass destruction. In March of 2003, the United States invaded Iraq under fallacious auspices and waged an illegal war. American forces decimated Iraq's infrastructure and brutalized its people, violating the very laws the major powers had created and vowed to uphold. At the same time, American troops on the ground faced an insurgency they were unprepared to meet. When Cheney's promise of a joyful welcoming turned sour, troops were instructed to follow the same anti-insurgency tactics the French pioneered in their cruel oppression of the Algerians. Torture became just another tool for the United States, as did a willingness to extradite belligerents and civilians in order to bypass laws. Very quickly, America's self-perceived moral imperative and impunity conferred by the September 11 attacks wore thin.

As the war ground on, America relied on private entities to carry out operations and provide services. This pivot was symbolic of the larger restructuring taking place: The Iraq War predictably served as a launching pad for neoliberalism. Iraq had been a closed, socialist society prior to the invasion; as warfare loomed, institutions like the Heritage Foundation salivated over the potential economic benefits and advised the Bush administration to "develop a modern legal system that recognizes property rights and is conducive to privatization," "prepare state assets" for private interests, and "liberalize and expand trade" as a means of offering the country to the market.[14] Sure enough, the administration followed its instructions.

As former US ally Saddam Hussein was toppled, the scene in Iraq grew surreal. American forces were soon joined by private interests profiting off repairing the ongoing destruction and carrying out plans to sell state assets to corporations. *The Economist* gushed in September

2003: "If it all works out, Iraq will be a capitalist's dream."[15] America's chosen administrator in Iraq, a man named Paul Bremer, based the success of his tenure on his ability to establish the principles of private property, much as colonizers had done centuries prior, reasoning that "a free economy and a free people go hand-in-hand" and saying, "Building such prosperity in Iraq will be a key measure of our success here."[16]

The execution of the so-called War on Terror had a spate of insidious consequences. Considering it was an all-encompassing crusade and that "defeating terrorism," as a concept, relied on both preventing violence and accessing the very thoughts of the individual, a massive surveillance system was considered necessary. In 1999, such a system had been proposed by the military-industrial complex. Called Total Information Awareness, the system would take advantage of electronic communications and artificial intelligence to "solve the problems that every law enforcement agency has" through predictive policing.[17] Prior to September 11, this idea seemed confined to the realm of science fiction and was a precursor to future efforts, including the PRISM program, which consisted primarily of information provided by private companies like Yahoo, Google, and Microsoft.[18]

Harnessing the internet was key to security in this new world. As an individual surfed the web, sent emails, and purchased items, they provided to companies a collectible summary of their thoughts, interests, goals, and habits, a novel state of affairs that proved both incredibly lucrative for companies and advantageous for nation-states desperate to surveil citizens. In carrying these operations out, however, the impetus had again shifted from the public to the private: Governments were heavily relying on tech companies both to handle this gathering and to construct the technological apparatuses of the state.

Under Bush, the United States carried out operations using boots on the ground, but as President Barack Obama took the reins, a significant portion of these duties turned to remote-controlled drones.

These drones were designed and constructed by corporations, and in some cases the administration depended on these same companies to sort the accompanying data necessary to carry out missions.[19] Drone warfare was beneficial to US interests for a variety of reasons, not the least of which was the political toll of sending troops into combat and suffering losses. These strikes could occur anywhere in the world at any moment and Americans would only very rarely see them covered in the media. Over the course of his presidency, Obama would order over five hundred drone strikes, killing more than three thousand "terrorists" and costing the lives of hundreds of civilians.[20]

The problem of a war to defeat terrorism was clear. "We can't possibly kill everyone who wants to harm us," a senior official in the Obama administration would say.[21] In truth, killing one "terrorist" would often produce two or three more. What had begun as a crusade against evil turned into a chore. An advisor to Obama summed it up by likening drone strikes to lawn maintenance: "You've got to mow the lawn all the time. The minute you stop mowing, the grass is going to grow back."

This chore grew so large and complicated that the United States once more turned to artificial intelligence to carry out the functions, creating a "disposition matrix" that echoed the disastrous Phoenix Program in Vietnam in determining who needed to be killed and when the killing was to be done.

These wars and operations carried on over the course of four presidencies, leading to incredible death tolls around the world, a generation of wounded and traumatized soldiers, geopolitical instability, a massive loss of global trust in the United States, and a hemorrhaging of resources. In the past, such imperialism might have filled the coffers of the aggressor nation, but now the state was enriching private interests. Instead of creating a modern health care system, providing necessary updates to infrastructure, housing citizens, and fully funding the educational system, America transferred its wealth to the military-industrial complex, including the new architects of its digital necessities, and a handful of private firms.

In 2020, after years of nonexistent progress, the story grew even more senseless as President Donald Trump struck a deal with the very Taliban that American forces had unseated nearly two decades prior. "I really believe the Taliban wants to do something to show that we're not all wasting time," Trump reasoned before adding, "They will be killing terrorists."[22] A year later, President Joe Biden honored this deal and the standing Afghanistan government collapsed immediately, allowing the Taliban to return. Addressing the nation following a bloody and chaotic retreat, Biden stood firm: "I was not going to extend this forever war."[23]

His remarks were less than reassuring.

"This is a new world," he said. "The terror threat has metastasized across the world, well beyond Afghanistan." There were still battles to fight, brewing tensions with Russia and China. History had come roaring back and caught the era's dominant empire unaware.

The forever wars were coming to a close, but their fallout raged on.

On August 29, 2005, Hurricane Katrina made landfall in Louisiana and brought with it all the fury of a climate readied for destruction. With winds exceeding a hundred miles per hour, the storm lashed New Orleans, breaching its floodwalls and swamping the city. Over a thousand people would die.[24] The tragedy that ensued was a terrible conflagration of interlocking failures and crises, a perfect mixture of America's weaknesses and mistakes that could no longer be ignored.

When the sheer size and scope of the storm was realized, a mandatory evacuation was ordered, but poverty exacerbated by socioeconomics and the inherent racism of the capitalist order stranded many in the majority-Black city. By the time the eye had passed, citizens were left to fend for themselves, to climb atop their roofs as the water rose higher and higher, to hope against hope that a helicopter or boat might rescue them, while others struggled to survive on dwindling resources.

President George W. Bush was on a long vacation, and members of his administration were more concerned with protecting the power infrastructure than saving American lives. The Federal Emergency Management Agency, under the management of Michael D. Brown—whose relevant experience prior to his appointment included work with the International Arabian Horse Association—botched nearly every responsibility, leaving the people of New Orleans to die and suffer while the nation watched.

This glaring incompetence exposed something that had been fundamentally true for years. While the United States had enjoyed a measure of economic success and relative stability, the neoliberal system had been eating away at the authority of the state, systematically transferring power from the federal government to the domain of the market and corporations. A president and government could marshal forces to take the country to war in order to pursue new markets, but the talent, attention, and especially resources needed to protect citizens and respond to their needs had simply been plundered.

The grand administrative state and the powerful presidency had been co-opted, transitioned from doing the business of the nation to overseeing the health of the market and its myriad corporate benefactors. Bush won office because of his ability to play the character of a "compassionate conservative" and brush-clearing Texas cowboy rather than his ideas or ability to govern. He served as a catastrophic figurehead incapable of doing much of anything beyond spouting platitudes about "freedom" and the crusades of the good, all while serving as the faithful steward of capital.

As his ruinous presidency came to a close, Bush was faced once again with a crisis a long time coming. Gambling in the American housing market set off a chain reaction in the fall of 2008 that threatened to reverberate through the global system and possibly destroy Western capitalism in totality. All of the growth and accumulation of the past half century was being rapidly erased. At the Federal Hall National Memorial in New York City, the original home of the United States government, Bush admitted, "I'm a market-oriented guy, but not when I'm faced with the prospect of a global meltdown."[25] Bush advocated addressing the situation but balked at the prospect of any real change. "The answer is not to try and reinvent the system. It is to fix the problems we face, make the reforms we need, and move forward with the free market principles that have delivered prosperity and hope to people all across the globe."

Unfortunately, this very attitude had led to the collapse. Neoliberalism had prioritized both deregulation as the necessary mantra of government and an environment of extreme risk-taking among the capitalist class. Governments had receded from their role of overseeing the markets in favor of allowing them to regulate themselves. This led predictably to a series of escalating risks that grew and grew and grew until the entire financial structure of the known world was wired to an unstable bomb.

Most Americans did not realize the economic system had largely been transferred to the digital realm and entrusted to artificial intelligence. Investment firms and traders had used their immense wealth to build networks to handle their trading and investments, relying on the technology to find opportunities human actors might miss or never even imagine, leading to what one writer described as "financial arrangements so complex that only machines can make, derive, and trade them."[26]

An outsized cause of the apocalyptic meltdown of the world's financial system was an algorithm created by an analyst named David X. Li. Called the Gaussian copula function, Li's "beautiful" and "simple" calculations were wielded by unscrupulous investors and their arsenal of computer systems to create new and riskier investment opportunities in the housing market, birthing volatile assets that only a handful of experts could even fully understand.[27] The lure of exorbitant new wealth and fresh prospects for new markets was too much for a system primed to reward unrestrained greed.

One of the prophets of unrestrained markets was former chair of the Federal Reserve Alan Greenspan, a devotee of Ayn Rand's philosophy of unrepressed selfishness and a chief architect of the neoliberal state in America. By 2008, however, witnessing the collapse of the financial world, Greenspan was mystified. "I made a mistake," he testified to Congress, "in presuming that the self-interests of organizations, specifically banks and others, were such as that they were best capable of protecting their own shareholders and their equity in the firms."[28]

As the fate of the capitalist world teetered, Barack Obama was elected the forty-fourth president of the United States on his promise to bring hope and change to the American people. His first test, however, would be shoring up the system and avoiding a full-scale meltdown. In meetings with the individuals and firms responsible for the crisis, Obama cautioned, "My administration is the only thing between you and the pitchforks."[29] Despite this warning, the government gave the firms what they wanted in the form of nearly a trillion-dollar bailout that purchased toxic assets, averted acute financial catastrophe, and rescued a number of "too big to fail" institutions.[30]

A government inquiry into the disaster found that "the captains of finance and the public stewards of our financial system ignored warnings and failed to question, understand and manage evolving risks within a system essential to the well-being of the American public."[31] Turning to mythology, the report mourned, "Like Icarus, they never feared flying ever closer to the sun." Despite the flourishing rhetoric, business largely returned to the conditions that had facilitated the problem.

Obama was left to both explain the government's decision and attempt to ease anger. "One of the most important lessons to learn from this crisis," he said, "is that our economy only works if we recognize that we're all in this together, that we all have responsibilities to each other and to our country."[32] To avoid future meltdowns would take a reconsideration of how the economy functioned, but, Obama maintained, nothing too radical, as the country could not "afford to demonize every investor or entrepreneur who seeks to make a profit."

By 2010, with the financial world saved and the fallout of the collapse resting squarely on the backs of the American people, Greenspan revisited his existential dilemma that had bloomed as the markets crashed. In a 2010 study nicknamed "the Crisis Paper," Greenspan announced his "doubt that stability is achievable in capitalist economies" and belief that the promised "equilibrium" of neoliberalism was probably impossible.[33] To maintain the system meant risking periodic collapses that could throw the world into chaos and doom regular people to incredible suffering. Any effort to reform or create a new, sustainable system was "infeasible," but luckily the governments of the world were there to provide the necessary resources to stave off total collapse.[34] Of these predictable and cyclical disasters, which neoliberalism would inevitably cause, Greenspan conceded, "Assuaging their aftermath seems to be the best we can hope for."

As the effects of the recession reverberated through the country, anger and frustration toward political and economic elites were harnessed by the same people who had been following the advice laid out by Lewis Powell in his 1971 memo. Exploiting the moment, wealthy entities and individuals funding think tanks, institutes, and academic research and bankrolling politicians in order to further deregulation and dismantle government as a public good set their sights on harvesting populist and racist rage against the first Black president.

Soon, grassroots organizers consolidated under the banner of the upstart Tea Party, and libertarian-minded wealthy donors flooded their coffers with overwhelming resources and used them as a mobilized force to change the political environment. The phenomenon could never have happened without the help of cable news as a mass medium and deliverer of propaganda. Fox News had premiered in 1996 as the brainchild of Roger Ailes, a media consultant for Republicans like Richard Nixon, Ronald Reagan, and George H. W. Bush, and was intended to serve as a communications hub for the GOP. In the press conference for the launch of the network, Ailes had told reporters he had found a "marketing niche" of viewers who believed the media had a liberal bias and that Fox would fill that vacuum.[35] Ailes remained convinced that Nixon's presidency had been done in by Republicans' failure to dominate the media narrative, and Fox would never allow that to happen again.

The Tea Party was a perfect product for Fox. Coverage of the group obfuscated the wealthy donors pulling the strings and touted it as an organic, grassroots movement by the people rejecting Obama's "radical" agenda. Rallies received round-the-clock airtime, hosts were dispatched to events, and segments were dedicated to aggrandizing their efforts while demonizing Obama's every movement. Over time, the Republican Party, faced with a possible political challenge, chose to absorb the Tea Party into itself, officially embracing its toxic stew of white supremacist paranoia, all while Fox News aired New World Order conspiracy theories twenty-four hours a day.

Obama was a moderate neoliberal president who idolized Ronald Reagan and touted policies designed by Republicans in coordination with corporations, but in his opponents' eyes he was "an international socialist" who "envisions a one-world government."[36] Randy Weber, a Republican representative from Texas, labeled him a "socialist dictator."[37] Always one to recognize an opportunity, Alex Jones released a documentary calling Obama "the elite's puppet of choice" and "a betrayer, a liar, a Judas goat, a Trojan horse to bring in the one world government."[38] Reality TV star and failed businessman Donald Trump got in on the action, making one appearance after another on Fox News to further the racist conspiracy theory that Obama had not been born in the United States, making him ineligible for the presidency, and claiming that somebody told him that Obama was secretly a Muslim.[39]

The national conversation was effectively hijacked by a concentrated effort by the wealthy to take advantage of widespread frustration over the financial crisis and push their own agenda. It was supported by a biased propaganda network, embraced by one of the two major political parties, and trumpeted by a repulsive cast of opportunists and grifters. Millions of Americans were shoved into an alternate reality populated by white supremacist paranoid fantasies, leftover demons of the War on Terror, and Christian fears of persecution and apocalypse, set within the frame of the New World Order narrative that diverted blame from neoliberalism to shadowy, evil forces lurking behind every corner. By the spring of 2010, the consequences were already becoming apparent. Nearly a quarter of Republicans believed Obama was the Antichrist and an overwhelming majority were confident he was a secret Muslim socialist with plans to take their guns before handing America over to a one-world government.[40]

While millions were told to chase shadows, circumstances for Americans deteriorated by the day. Neoliberalism, with its austerity, hollowing out of meaning, relentless stressing of individual striving, and interpersonal economic competition, soured existence and resulted in incredible suffering. A trend had emerged that political scientist Robert D. Putnam chronicled in his work *Bowling Alone.* Putnam noted that "striking evidence" pointed to a distressing fact: "The vibrancy of American civil society has notably declined."[41] Americans were spending less time together, community groups were losing members, and civic organizations and governmental bodies were experiencing incredible deterioration.

Neoliberalism had infected the populace, encouraging Americans to view their neighbors, families, and fellow citizens as competitors. Government operated according to technocratic experts and dominated by the economic elite had alienated the people to such a degree that voter turnout plunged and participation in local governance decreased. Trust in government crashed.

Conditions necessitated an explanation, and absent the specialized understanding of economics, politics, and history neoliberalism relegated, like hierarchical regimes of old, to the technocratic elite, the people were willing consumers when corporations and the wealthy sold them stories capitalizing on their inherent prejudices and religious fears. These stories maintained the long-held mythology of American exceptionalism communicated in their educations and through mass culture, political leaders, and commercial appeals that had been supercharged during the War on Terror. Rather than wrestling with the fact that neoliberalism and the economic policies it dictated had redistributed roughly

$50 trillion to the wealthiest 10 percent of the country, racist and xenophobic stories built on religious and cultural narratives were weaponized by the beneficiaries of the new order to tell the people the decimation was the result of conspiracies carried out by evil forces lurking in the dark.[42]

Globalism as a neoliberal project to break down borders and free capitalists from regulation, minimum wages, and labor unions, while prioritizing cheap, imported goods requiring constant replacement, led to mass deindustrialization and the destruction of local economies. Those profiting from these changes shifted the blame away from the economic system and, instead, substituted a story of good versus evil, of satanic conspiracies. Capitalism's workings and consequences were attributed to malevolent beings and sinister machinations. The same conspiracy theories that led to the murdering of the Jews throughout the ages, the overthrow of governments, the rise of fascism and Nazism—the same authoritarian narratives that had plagued America from its very beginning—again took hold of the culture. Those profiting wildly off the destruction sold back to the people this same story, that evil puppet masters outside of the United States were conspiring with internal traitors and making use of minorities to carry out an insidious plot to destroy the nation and enslave its people.

Rigging the economy to favor the wealthy at the expense of everyone else and the wasting of resources on the War on Terror meant general austerity and a population increasingly incapable of affording the necessities of life. In regard to health care, America lagged far behind the other industrialized nations, and any effort to either update the system or make it even the least bit more affordable was met with conservative and corporate accusations of socialist conspiracies. Education was continually and intentionally underfunded by forces desperate to destroy the public funding and carry out what former lobbyist Charles Siler characterized as the "incremental march to full privatization."[43] As deindustrialization shifted the economy to information, technology, and skilled labor, capitalists took advantage of a captive market by invading higher education, making tuition skyrocket and forcing tens of millions to assume insurmountable debt. By 2021, that debt had grown to over $1.7 trillion and remained a burden on the people that has prevented them from buying homes and having children. Meanwhile, it kept them in such precarity that often they were too terrified to leave their jobs and accepted less in wages and benefits.[44]

Among the most telling problems plaguing American society is the scourge of gun violence, particularly the epidemic of mass shootings that has touched every corner of public life. In December of 2012, a man named Adam Lanza walked into the Sandy Hook Elementary School in Newtown, Connecticut, with an AR-15–style semiautomatic rifle and murdered twenty-seven people, including twenty children aged seven or younger. In the wake of the tragedy, President Barack Obama called for commonsense reform but was headed off by members of the Republican Party, the conservative National Rifle Association, and members of his own party, like West Virginia senator Joe Manchin, who assured his "friends in the NRA" there would "not be an encroachment on your Second Amendment rights."[45] The conspiracy theory world did its part: Famously, Alex Jones took to the airwaves and told his audience it was yet another false flag to take their guns, saying, "Sandy Hook is a synthetic, completely fake with actors, in my view manufactured."[46]

Even the most unthinkable and ghastly crime imaginable was not enough to spur the machine to take action.

Kept by design from carrying out any effort to make the people's lives better, the state instead focused on one of the few responsibilities neoliberalism continued to afford it: the protection of private property and the operation of law enforcement. As the neoliberal order came to fruition, progressive politicians faced gridlock on anything that didn't free the markets, cut taxes on the wealthy, slash social programs, disrupt regulation, and push more and more resources into policing.

President Bill Clinton's tenure had served as a preview of what was to come. After finishing Ronald Reagan and George H. W. Bush's push for neoliberal free trade, Clinton had attempted to slightly reform health care, only to meet incredible opposition in the form of paranoia pushed by the Republican Party and intense lobbying by corporations. With that put to bed and his political fortunes embattled, Clinton embraced a continued centrist approach that prioritized deregulation and financial growth and found common ground in law enforcement. Backed by Democratic allies like senator and future president Joe Biden, who warned of "predators" who so threatened public safety "we have no choice but to take them out of society," a new and expansive crime bill proved a political success at the time.[47] Declaring, "Gangs and drugs have taken over our streets," Clinton signed the bill in 1994 and flooded police departments with the people's money and gave the judicial system the green light to deal with crime more aggressively.[48]

Rather than investing in social programs to reduce crime, the United States punished the poor and the desperate. An obscenely well-funded army of police officers, armed with a surplus of weaponry left over from the Cold War, fought a war against their own people and came to believe they were the only thing standing between civilization and chaos. The supposed beacon of freedom and liberty became the home of the world's largest system of incarceration, with over two million of its citizens locked up in prisons costing the state more than $80 billion a year.[49] As the laws and the institutions are themselves riddled with white supremacy, this national disgrace weighs exponentially more heavily on people of color, populations that have already been subject to generations of prejudice in the country's economic, political, and social affairs.

The postwar American dream collapsed. The myth that each succeeding generation would have better lives than the last fell by the wayside, leaving the population to suffer austerity. Wages stagnated and reliable employment more or less disappeared. Save for a select few, people came to realize the promises of a better future were, and always had been, nothing more than lies.

Providing the necessary tech support for the growing security state and empire was lucrative work. Beginning in 2004, Big Tech companies were paid nearly $45 billion by the United States government to assist with the War on Terror, handling the technologies associated with its prosecution and crafting surveillance the government deemed necessary to protect the state.[50] Many of those same companies were also awarded thousands of contracts to assist with law enforcement and data storage. The scope of the surveillance amounted to a changing of the definition of the military-industrial complex and a massive redistribution of income from the people to a privileged group of specialized corporations.[51]

This sudden sea change and redistribution of wealth resembled the post–Civil War boom, in which a handful of robber barons and their businesses industrialized the nation, building railroads, telegraph networks, and the logistical systems necessary to carry out mass production. And, as in that era, the concentration of wealth resulted in vast inequality and the co-opting of government.

The roots of the modern digital age extend back to the 1990s, when the government-created internet became widely available, but the evolution from the initial project to what would come to be called Web 2.0 was dramatic and world shaping. In this new era, individuals, through their posts and original content, would mean an exponential increase in traffic and commerce, and drive profits for corporations. This would be previewed at the 2004 Web 2.0 Conference by John Battelle and Tim O'Reilly, who told capitalists the future lay in a system where customers would "build your business for you."[52]

Identity played a massive role in the new system as consumerism had trained people to express themselves through products. The website BuzzFeed, which came online in 2006, gained much of its original audience by pandering to these expressions and recognizing that, rather than seeking mass appeal, finding "a niche audience" based on a "specific identity" paid dividends.[53] This phenomenon reached an enormous audience on February 25, 2015, the same day Donald Trump told *The Washington Post* he was "more serious" about running for president than ever before.[54] That afternoon, Cates Holderness of BuzzFeed posted a photo of a dress asking viewers to weigh in on its color. Some saw it as white and gold while others swore it was blue and black. The image went super-viral around the world as the two camps squared off, both sides vehemently certain they were correct. Holderness was shocked as she saw "the comments were all people just screaming at each other—just losing their minds."[55] This seemingly random moment was enough to supercharge profit.

Other applications of consumer identity were much more directly lucrative. Though reliant on the same psychological techniques that had enabled consumerism since World War I, Web 2.0 companies had access to an unprecedented amount of information that allowed them to scrutinize, analyze, and guide their users, directing them to products that matched their chosen personalities, and occasionally even effectively changing consumers' own perceptions of themselves.[56] Dubbed "surveillance capitalism" by social psychologist Shoshana Zuboff, this process was incredibly profitable for the tech companies that "tracked, parsed, wired, and modified" the information, and the many companies that relied on that data for sales.[57]

This new system changed the very nature of consumerism. Marketing strategies came to depend on extended engagement and expression of identity. And the information communicated by these platforms, whether in the form of articles, content, or psychological appeals, could dramatically affect how an individual experienced the world. Even as sales soared, it seemed entirely possible that all of this influence conferred by the new medium could, much like the printing press and mass media had led to tragedy, prove disastrous if it fell into the wrong hands. Central to the emergence of Big Tech as one of the defining deciders of the future was a philosophy that came to be known as the Californian Ideology. Defined by Richard Barbrook and Andy Cameron, this mindset merged "the free-wheeling spirit of the hippies and the entrepreneurial zeal of the yuppies," an amalgamation made possible by "a profound faith in the emancipatory potential of the new information technologies."[58] Included in this is a counterculture belief that the traditional structures of society are constrictive, reactionary, and outdated, but also that free-market principles are the essential essence of freedom. When combined, these seemingly contradictory ideals form the basis of a movement infused with a faith that the digital world holds the key to freedom and that the market will lead the way while archaic concepts like the nation-state fall by the wayside.

This was a continuation of the ideology of science that emerged as the medieval age gave way to the Scientific Revolution. Its adherents, like Francis Bacon and his contemporaries did, hold that knowledge and rationality will lead humanity to utopia—an ascent that requires dispensing with tradition, including established morals and ethics. The defining actors also see themselves as a priestly class of sorts, their wealth testament to their mastery and status as the chosen few.

In carrying out the grotesque business of hyperaccumulation of capital and influence, billionaires like Elon Musk embrace titles like "technoking" and practice a sort of neo-feudalism.[59] Discussing their grandiose ideas, including either colonizing Mars or transferring humanity to space, Musk and rival Jeff Bezos flaunt a vision that transcends the political and economic concepts that define the moment. When asked how normal people could afford the pilgrimage to the red planet, Musk has posited an indentured-servant-style arrangement where loans would be issued and recipients could work off their debts on Mars.[60] Bezos, who made his historic fortune defining online commerce, believes his wealth makes him capable of defining the fate of our planet itself, telling reporters that once humanity leaves on his spaceships they'll be able to "visit Earth the way you visit Yellowstone National Park."[61]

Megalomania goes hand in hand with the Californian Ideology, and its leaders' mastery of the infrastructure of the digital world has situated them to define the future of humanity: Their obscene riches can influence politics, culture, and science itself on a massive scale. In crude ways this absurdity has made itself known, like the fact that Musk and

Bezos can afford space programs that dwarf NASA or that social media sites such as Facebook and Twitter have effectively corporatized the public square, where ideas, relationships, and rights have traditionally been defined.

Facebook's venture into this territory has proven cataclysmic. Founder Mark Zuckerberg described the company as having a "social mission" to "make the world more open and connected" and "strengthen how people relate to each other."[62] That noble goal, however, hid the commodified nature of the meeting space, as well as the recklessness with which Zuckerberg operated. Telling his people to "move fast and break things," he prioritized hurried disruption over measured action, creating a myriad of crises, including genocide, attacks on democracy, the straining of social ties, and the obliteration of shared reality.[63]

With Facebook, a service based on an expertly devised program, tended to by the best and brightest minds and tuned to prioritize meaningful interactions and relationships, Zuckerberg hoped to revolutionize the world. His plans resembled, to an extent, something that neoliberal architect Friedrich Hayek termed "extended order," or a "great framework" that would form the basis of a stable society and "of which we are largely unaware."[64] In many ways, Hayek's idea would function as a proliferation of the "invisible hand" of Adam Smith's capitalist vision across every stratum of existence, guiding ignorant humans toward a more productive life.

Facebook tested this algorithm constantly and decided to favor "meaningful social interactions," a designation that would actually prioritize anger and division over intimacy and joy by a measure of five to one.[65] Soon, users were being guided by these invisible hands toward contentious material, misinformation, propaganda, conspiracy theories, and adversarial content. In some cases, without so much as cursory awareness, people were being aggressively radicalized by extremists and foreign actors, their inherent prejudices exacerbated and amplified, all while their relationships with their friends, families, and reality itself were being torn to shreds.

This heavily contributed to political radicalization and crises in the United States, but the consequences of social media were global. In Brazil, YouTube was co-opted by right-wing elements airing radicalizing misinformation, turning the site into what women's rights advocate Debora Diniz called an "ecosystem of hate" and preparing the country to elect an extreme right-wing star on the platform named Jair Bolsonaro.[66] Facebook would be used in Myanmar by the government and military to seed a bloody genocide that began in 2016 and for which inquiries have laid the blame with the social media company. "I'm afraid," United Nations investigator Yanghee Lee would report, "that Facebook has now turned into a beast."[67]

Rather than pause and reflect on what damage has been done, Zuckerberg has sprinted forward into the future. As whistleblowers inside the company alerted the public in 2021 to the company's unwillingness to reform or step in and curtail the destruction it causes, Zuckerberg announced that Facebook would change its name to Meta in anticipation of unveiling a virtual reality he has come to call "the Metaverse." In describing the project, Zuckerberg has promised, "You're going to be able to do almost anything you can imagine," and has claimed it would come to encompass almost everything, providing a platform for work, commerce, and daily life.[68]

As envisioned, the Metaverse would be another plane in which users could live and where the laws of physics don't apply and the restrictions of normal existence have vanished, giving way to a glittery digital world designed, controlled, and populated by corporations, with every experience optimized for marketing and consumer possibilities. True to the Californian Ideology, it would be, in effect, an escape from the groaning, aging edifices of the old, material world, and probably its legal and political institutions as well, but also tuned to the liking of businesses and the wealthy, who are already gobbling up its virtual real estate and preparing for the implications of a second existence where people will have to pay for virtual clothes, virtual goods, and virtual media.[69]

In yet another nod to pre-capitalist conditions, this new world would be lorded over by an unquestionable sovereign, the very nature of reality subject to his whims, his kingdom a sparkling fantasy designed to hold the user's attention as long as humanly possible in spite of the consequences, their decisions and communications surveilled and cataloged for maximum use of data and harnessed for cutting-edge psychological appeals to sell anything and everything.

An escape from apocalypse, if only in the eyes of the beholder.

True to the Californian Ideology and the neoliberal worldview, Big Tech has been more than happy to work with antidemocratic entities and authoritarian states if it means profit. Just as Hayek prized Augusto Pinochet and the stability his iron fist guaranteed the market, companies like Google have cooperated with dystopian states like China in censoring the internet and continually limiting what its citizens can view. This "Great Firewall" represents one of the most restrictive forces in human history, and companies desperate to gain access to the country's markets are quite willing to lend a hand in the censorship.[70]

That China has become such a desired market for capitalist entities is a bizarre twist. Its espoused status as the last remaining communist superpower hides the contradiction that China is competing with the United States to define what capitalism and state authority will look like in the future. Over the past few decades, however, China has become something entirely new and novel.

Following the Chinese Revolution, Mao Zedong remade the country according to his ideology, but by 1966 disagreements among members of the ruling party fueled his paranoia. He called for a "cultural revolution," warning that "counterrevolutionary revisionists" had "sneaked into the party, the government, the army and various spheres of culture" in order to "seize political power and turn the dictatorship of the proletariat into a dictatorship of the bourgeoisie."[71] The only solution was more bloody struggle, the interrogation of "suspicious actors," widespread revival of Maoist principles, and the reaffirmation of the defining cult of personality.

A decade later, following Mao's death, power in China moved from his closest clique of allies, called the Gang of Four, to many of the individuals Mao had been suspicious of in the first place. These opponents would use economic difficulties to blame the Gang of Four and accuse them of "sabotage" and using the cult's ideology to their "advantage."[72] The Gang of Four, including Mao's widow Jiang Qing, would be arrested, making room for new leaders promising a policy of Boluan Fanzheng, or to "bring order out of chaos."[73]

Chief among them was Deng Xiaoping, a rival Mao had targeted multiple times and criticized openly, saying, "Xiaoping does not care for class struggle . . . Capitalism or Marxism, it makes no difference to him."[74] He had a point. Deng was proudly ideologically malleable, declaring, "We don't care if it is a black cat or a yellow cat; as long as it catches mice."[75] Under this new regime, China moderately reformed its political and economic practices, affording some individual rights to its citizens while toying with the concept of limited, controlled capitalism. This merging of markets with state domination of society meant the centralized command could strategize, organize, and then use its resources and businesses as weapons.

This liberalization was marginal as the state maintained its authoritarian nature. In 1989, as its citizens flooded Tiananmen Square in Beijing to demand more freedom, the regime blamed America and other rival states, claiming they were attempting to "sow dissension among the people, plunge the whole country into chaos, and sabotage the political situation of stability and unity."[76] Before cracking down on the protestors and killing an untold number of them, Chinese authorities rolled out new surveillance measures to study and ultimately undermine the movement. In the past, the revolutionary ideology of Mao had inspired communities to police themselves, but in the dawning age of technology, new innovations could be employed to ensure total dominance.

Experiments with "special economic zones" and controlled capitalism would come to a head with the emergence of the neoliberal globalist age. Leadership in China had long considered economics a means of soft warfare, and the new system was an incredible opportunity. Announcing it would "have a significant impact on China's economic development," the state joined the World Trade Organization in 2001.[77] The United States and other Western countries believed the tide had changed and free markets would not only liberalize China but turn it into a massive new market for their products. Instead, China took advantage of their consumerist desire for cheap imported goods. Calling it "the China Shock," experts have recognized this as an "epochal shift in patterns of world trade" in which jobs and industries have simply disappeared with no replacement in sight.[78]

Rather than China liberalizing, their authoritarianism spread through the system. In subjugating vulnerable populations such as the Uighurs, putting them in "re-education camps," forcibly sterilizing them, subjecting them to compulsory labor, and arguably carrying out a genocide marked by enslavement, China has not only benefited from the explicit exploitation but has found willing partners in the so-called liberal nations around the world in the form of corporations like Nike, Adidas, and Apple, which benefit from reduced labor costs.[79] Though companies like Apple have publicly claimed they are "dedicated to ensuring that everyone in our supply chain is treated with dignity and respect," they have repeatedly lobbied the United States government against any restrictions on forced labor.[80]

What's more, the surveillance technologies used to create this system have been finding favor in the Western world. Governments including those of the United States, Britain, and scores of their cities and towns, not to mention their militaries, have bought these tools of repression for their own use and, following China's lead, have begun implementing them as further protection against their own people.[81]

As the process of neoliberalism continues on, it seems as if exploitation is taking a new turn. Originally, following the leadership of "First

World" nations, the machine had operated with those states atop an interlocked system wherein "Second" and "Third World" states provided the resources, cheap labor, and production for the consumerist societies to enjoy. The management of these systems, in their innovation and development, was the purview of a new managerial class educated in universities in countries like the United States, which was intended by its leaders to become the hub of the new information society. But the drain of industry and production disturbed this equilibrium, creating in America a society increasingly divided between those capable of joining the managerial class and those left behind, the latter only able to continue consuming via ever-increasing loads of debt.

China's rising portended another epochal change. Similar to the way the business of colonization during the lamentable "Age of Discovery" had exported oppression to distant shores before returning to its lands of origin in order to quell and exploit their populaces, neoliberalism now seemed to be entering a new and familiar phase. As it twisted, convulsed, and turned inward and backward, and as history rushed back to assert itself, nations recognized it might be time to enforce discipline on their peoples and benefit from a renaissance of cheap, controllable labor.

- CHAPTER TEN -

Almost Midnight

In America, some believed the end was at hand. "The floodwaters are upon us," wrote right-wing author Rod Dreher in his 2017 book *The Benedict Option*.[1] According to Dreher, liberalism's assault on religion and traditional values had eradicated America's Christian foundation, plunging Western civilization into "barbarism" that had "exchanged the animal pelts and spears of the past for designer suits and smartphones."[2]

For Dreher and similar minds, the death knell first rang in 2015. That spring, the state of Indiana pushed a "religious freedom" bill designed to allow businesses to discriminate according to the tenets of their faith. Signing the bill in March, Governor Mike Pence qualified the need for it, saying, "Many people of faith feel their religious liberty is under attack by government action."[3] There was immediate pushback, however, as corporations in Indiana suffered consumer backlash. The tide turned as these companies, worried over boycotts and publicity that might hurt their brands, compelled the state and Republicans to change course.

Then, in June, the Supreme Court legalized same-sex marriage in *Obergefell v. Hodges* by a vote of five to four, bestowing what Justice Anthony M. Kennedy called "equal dignity in the eyes of the law."[4] Opponents considered it liberalism run amok and, for some, a victory for supernatural evil. Religious leaders like Pat Robertson had warned supporters for years that if this came to pass, it would be a "long downward slide in relation to all the things we consider morally abhorrent," including the legalization of bestiality and pedophilia.[5] Barry Goldwater's speechwriter Harry Jaffa, who had become a leading intellectual in the conservative movement, claimed the fight for gay rights presented "the most complete repudiation . . . of all objective standards of human conduct" and "the ultimate repudiation of nature."[6]

These twin events were proof for some that not only had liberalism triumphed, but the project of conservative fusion during the Cold War era had ultimately failed. Pairing economic libertarianism with movements dedicated to championing Christianity, "traditional values," and patriarchal white culture resulted in scores of Republicans getting elected, while it also birthed neoliberalism. Along with its push for unrestricted profit, it also undermined the power of the state, nationalism, and religious ideologies, and brought along with it an environment at least superficially conducive to multiculturalism and tolerance.

Dreher's despondency led him to advocate briefly for Christians to leave the "barbarian" culture behind and escape like refugees from Sodom and Gomorrah to their own cloistered communities, where they might rediscover themselves and prepare for the future. This call for departure would soon be replaced by a new energy and direction, one that rejected the conservative fusion project and liberalism in totality and offered a new way forward.

Or, rather, backward.

A search for answers led to Hungary, where right-wing extremist Viktor Orbán caught the interest of desperate Americans. After Orbán cut his teeth opposing communists, he helmed a conservative movement that dominated his country and changed it in disturbing ways. Having achieved this, Orbán beckoned disillusioned American conservatives like Dreher to consider Hungary their "intellectual home."[7]

Orbán leveraged conservative anger, pioneering what he came to call the "illiberal state."[8] Like authoritarians before him, Orbán warned of "foreign attempts to gain influence" within the nation, as well the failures of liberal democracy to protect culture, and promoted a new path that outright rejected liberalism. He drew upon a new so-called crisis of immigration in Europe following the War on Terror and political unrest in Syria. Waves of refugees terrified a population convinced by demagogues that these people constituted a cultural, democratic threat carried out by sinister forces. George Soros, a Hungarian-born Jewish billionaire, became a favorite stand-in for these "puppet masters" among right-wingers, once more energizing anti-Semitic conspiracy theories.

Globalism, Orbán told his supporters in an anti-Semitic rant, was a plot to replace the nations and the cultures of the world with a multicultural coalition directed by these forces and susceptible to their machinations. "We are fighting an enemy that is different from us," he said. "Not open, but hiding; not straightforward but crafty; not honest but base; not national but international; does not believe in working but speculating with money; does not have its own homeland but feels it owns the whole world."[9] Orbán utilized the New World Order narrative, accusing a "George Soros–style network" of working "to create open societies of mixed ethnicity through acceleration of migration, to dismantle national decision-making and hand it over to the global elite."[10]

Orbán's proposed solution was to reject liberalism out of hand, thus eliminating democracy. "We need to say it loud because you can't reform a nation in secrecy," Orbán said. "The era of liberal democracy is over. Rather than try to fix a liberal democracy that has run aground, we will build a 21st-century Christian democracy."[11]

Security against "invasion" meant building a border wall and implementing restrictive immigration policies; manipulating the voting system to advantage Orbán's movement; and enacting a constitution that made official "the role of Christianity in preserving nationhood," institutionalized "promoting and safeguarding [Hungary's] heritage, [its] unique language," and diagnosed a "state of moral decay" that necessitated "spiritual and intellectual renewal."[12] His government legalized discrimination against gay people and banned depictions of them in the media and educators from mentioning them. All of society was aggressively reconfigured to promote the idea that Hungary was a homogeneous, Christian state and that democracy and multiculturalism were insidious weapons.

The specter of "replacement" drew on dangerous ideas of the past, including those of protofascist Charles Maurras, who had helped create the anti-Semitic royalist group Action Française before welcoming Nazi-collaborating Vichy France. More recently, another French thinker named Renaud Camus coined what he called *le Grand Remplacement,* or "the Grand Replacement," which amounted to a "loss of . . . cultural identity through multiculturalism."[13] With twisted reasoning, Camus argued this was colonization in reverse, with colonized peoples coming to dominate their oppressors, believing that to oppose it was tantamount to an "anti-colonist struggle" by the original colonizers.[14]

In France, the National Front party surged in popularity by promising to "reverse the flow" of immigration, "defend our roots," and "safeguard our heritage" from the dangers of "a multiracial, multicultural society."[15] Across the channel, reactionary movements in Great Britain gained favor. Building off the influence of Enoch Powell, the disgraced politician who had once given the disturbing "Rivers of Blood" speech that had caught Margaret Thatcher's attention, conservatives used growing anger and fear to mount a successful campaign to leave the European Union.

The Great Replacement narrative found purchase in white communities around the world where people struggled to understand how their economic, political, and cultural fortunes had so dramatically changed. This new story once more diverted anger from the forces of capitalism that were responsible and redirected it to evil forces, internal liberal traitors, and vulnerable populations of color. Making matters worse, the innovation of the internet drove many of these individuals further and further down the rabbit hole of radicalization: In the pursuit of engagement, tech companies pushed users toward ever more extreme content and communities.

Dylann Roof was one of these users. At twenty-one years old, he searched for answers online and became convinced an invisible war was raging. Already primed by his own prejudices, Roof came to believe there was a massive conspiracy against white Americans. Believing Jews controlled world events and carried out their plans through "Jewish agitation of the black race," he became convinced somebody had to do something.[16] "Nobody else is brave enough to do anything about it," he told interrogators after he walked into the Emanuel African Methodist Episcopal Church in Charleston, South Carolina, on June 17, 2015, and murdered nine worshippers.[17] "I had to do it."

Roof's massacre stunned mainstream America but proved great entertainment and inspiration for some of those lurking in the darkest recesses of the internet and a nihilistic, angry subculture where death and destruction were considered pastimes. On forums like 4chan and its more extreme successor 8chan, users traded vile racist, fascist, misogynistic memes and child sex abuse materials, all while stewing in rage and sneering cynicism.

In March of 2019, a twenty-eight-year-old named Brenton Harrison Tarrant from New South Wales posted a manifesto on 8chan before livestreaming his pair of attacks on mosques in Christchurch, New Zealand; he murdered fifty-one people. Tarrant's screed cribbed Camus's Great Replacement theory for its title, declaring there was a "war upon my people" being carried on through "an invasion on a level never seen before in history."[18] This was a plan by "state and corporate entities," supported by the "global and corporate run press" and the "anti-white media machine," to "ethnically replace" cultures. It was, Tarrant believed, nothing short of "white genocide."

At the same time, something strange was happening between the former blood rivals of the Cold War. Though the modern right wing in America had defined itself by its opposition to the Soviet Union, in the 2010s they had grown suspiciously fonder of Russia. Bizarre polls were suddenly appearing showing that, even while Russian operations antagonized American interests and seeded misinformation determined to harm democracy, Republicans favored authoritarian Vladimir Putin over Democratic presidents like Barack Obama and then Joe Biden.[19] The entire political spectrum seemed tossed upside down.

Since the shock therapy of the 1990s had been deployed to transfer Russia from its failed communist state to a modern, purportedly free market, the country had been shaped by the fallout. Hampered by corruption, the privatization of state assets had been a disaster. Organized crime rings seized the industries, creating a new and largely unelected oligarchical class with almost total control over the new nation. Vladimir Putin, a former KGB agent with a penchant for cold-blooded, dictatorial rule, emerged as the nation's new leader and helmed an autocratic, illiberal state that served as a vehicle for furthering the enrichment of the oligarchs and himself. Elections were held, but the results were predetermined. There existed a "free market" built and tailored to the criminals' needs. Day-to-day life was manipulated as misinformation was pumped into the society. Citizens had "rights" but knew, after years of violent, murderous crackdowns, that any attempt to assert them would mean risking their own lives.

As the Soviet Union fell, conspiracy theories had run rampant, filling the need to explain how the utopian project could have failed. Men like Oleg Platonov spread the New World Order narrative, claiming that the Russian Revolution itself had been a Jewish plot for world domination and that humanity was being prepared for a dark future in which the world would be "transformed into a giant concentration camp" and the people either eliminated or enslaved.[20] Liberalism, with its "universal human values," was the means by which this dark plot would be carried out.[21] Slowly but surely, multiculturalism and neoliberal globalism would erase national cultures, destroy sovereignty, and plunge the world into chaos.

Putin positioned himself as the only thing standing between the Russian people and oblivion. He explained his extreme powers as necessary against such awesome forces, his control over politics and culture as weapons in defiance of an "amoral international" effort to undermine Russia's heritage in preparation for its destruction.[22] Conservative, reactionary policies targeting vulnerable populations like gay Russians and supporting Christians were rationalized as defenses against the conspiracy. This, Putin told the people, was essential should they survive the global elite's plan to erase "moral and ethical norms" and "national traditions" as part of a larger plot to enslave humanity.

Tragically, Putin's story worked. The dictator and his chosen clique of oligarchs held almost complete sway over the fates of the Russian people and continually grew their wealth. And although he based his rule on opposition to neoliberal globalism, Putin was welcomed into the international community, his and his oligarchs' poisonous blood money happily accepted and circulated through the world economic system. All the while, neoliberalism continued to appreciate the stability provided by an authoritarian strongman.

But within Putin's circle there grew an alternative vision. Holding Putin and the Russian leadership's attention was a strange philosopher named Aleksandr Dugin, a self-styled revolutionary and neofascist. In his youth, Dugin had spent his time fetishizing the beliefs and iconography of the Nazi Party. He later attempted to synthesize National Socialism and the Soviet Union into a bizarre amalgamation called National Bolshevism. Over time, however, Dugin's ideas would mutate and grow in their scope before he earned a position of influence within Russia's twisted regime.

Dugin believed that the ideologies of the twentieth century had lost "the ability to explain contemporary reality" and were "incapable of responding to the new global challenges."[23] This included liberalism, communism, and fascism, and their failures meant a new, so-called Fourth Political Theory would need to arise to set the world right again. Neoliberalism constituted a corruption of the world, an utter abomination that Dugin likened to "the kingdom of the Antichrist" as foretold in the Book of Revelation.[24] With an eye toward Martin Heidegger,

Dugin heralded this new theory as hastening the "return of Being," its appointment with fate set for "midnight of the world's night—at the darkest moment in history."[25]

Heidegger's ideas played a central role in Dugin's philosophy. In his exhaustive plundering of the German thinker's oeuvre, Dugin insisted that humanity was nearing Heidegger's "midnight," the moment in which "the historic-philosophic process of the European man has exhausted itself, and the era of total nihilism has arrived," and what came next was the heralded "Ereignis," or event, which Heidegger believed would lead to the "immediate transition from the inauthentic mode of existence to the authentic kind."[26] Dugin needed a new race of Friedrich Nietzsche's fabled Übermensch to capture history and guide it away from the midnight kingdom and back to meaning.

Arrogantly, Dugin believed he was among the chosen and that this "global rehabilitation," and the destruction of "all of modernity," would require the adoption of his own Fourth Political Theory.[27] He held that the birth of liberalism—and accordingly the abandonment of a hierarchical social structure supported by a priestly class that supplied discipline—had been a mistake. Now, he posited, liberalism had become "so rotten within" that there was a chance to destroy it once and for all and seek out "global rehabilitation of Tradition, the sacred, the religious, the caste-related . . . the hierarchical and not equality, justice, or freedom."

To counteract neoliberal globalism, Dugin prescribed that the nations of the world retreat within their own borders; rediscover their national traditions and cultures; reject multiculturalism, plurality, and democracy; and emerge into a new world ruled by these antiquated ideas. At the heart of this worldview was an ideology called Traditionalism, a hodgepodge of esoteric concepts that harkened back to Spiritualism, Madame Blavatsky, and the sources of pseudophilosophy and pseudohistory that had inspired the Fascists and Nazis, including superior Aryan races and mythical cycles of evolution.

Traditionalism itself can be traced back to René Guénon, a French philosopher who synthesized Eastern and Western esoteric concepts. At the dawning of the twentieth century, Guénon had declared that "the modern world is in the throes of a crisis," that history was made up of repeatable cycles of growth and decay, and that presently humanity was suffering through a "dark age" at the end of a cycle.[28] This dark age represented a "monstrosity" marked by a "refusal" to "admit any authority higher than the individual." These ideas continued to evolve with Julius Evola, an Italian philosopher who participated in the construction of fascism but left Italy for Nazi Germany as Benito Mussolini's regime was not pure or extreme enough for his liking. In Germany, even the Nazis were disturbed by Evola's beliefs, deciding "the ultimate and secret motivation" for his theories was "a revolt of the old aristocracy against today's world."[29]

Evola greeted the convulsions of the twentieth century and the rise of fascism as a possible means of reestablishing traditional control but was disappointed by what he perceived as compromises with capitalism and industrialization and their ultimate failures. Angered and disillusioned, Evola spent the rest of his life inspiring neofascists who carried out terror attacks and detailing what he believed could be the solution to the crisis of modernity. Writing that humanity was nearing the "terminal and twilight phase of the Western cycle," Evola predicted a time was coming in which modernity might become vulnerable.[30] Using an old proverb, Evola likened corrupting liberal systems to a deadly tiger that could be ridden until it grew weak and weary enough that the rider might dismount and then "get the better of it."[31]

Though Traditionalism's esoteric and fascistic nature might have made it a hard sell, it held sway over those who fashioned themselves opponents of modernity. Among them was Steve Bannon, a former investment banker turned right-wing media mogul, who considered the 2008 financial crisis the beginning of the end of neoliberalism. Bannon was convinced the only answer was to "bring everything crashing down."[32] In a 2014 address to a conference at the Vatican, Bannon nodded toward the growing synchronicity developing between American conservatives and Putinist Russia, telling attendees, "We the Judeo-

Christian West really have to look at what [Aleksandr Dugin's] talking about as far as Traditionalism goes."[33] Moving forward, Bannon would meet with Dugin and other traditionalists around the world, laying the groundwork for ongoing collaboration.

Like Dugin and the thinkers they both held in esteem, Bannon was convinced liberalism and multiculturalism had hollowed out the world, reduced humanity to cogs in a larger machine, destroyed national and cultural traditions, and represented the last stage in a cycle of decay and degeneration. And, like Dugin, Bannon fashioned himself as a member of the class of men who would seize history and restore meaning at humanity's darkest hour.

The answer was simple: a rejuvenation of hierarchical structures, the replenishment of the sovereignty and unique cultures of nations, and the reestablishment of discipline and faith through religious orthodoxy. Bannon sought out partners around the world, including Viktor Orbán in Hungary and Jair Bolsonaro in Brazil, to seed right-wing antidemocratic movements around the globe.

But he would need to find just the right individual within the United States to make his plan feasible. It was a tall order: Bannon required a figure who could embody the anger of America's aggrieved population while taming the other shareholders of the fusion project that had helped birth neoliberalism. An individual possessing wealth that kept them outside the party's influence and allowed them to disregard political norms. A demagogue who could take off on their own path while remaining virtually without personal principle—and therefore vulnerable to the manipulations and guidance of ideologues like Steve Bannon.

Strangely enough, all Bannon needed to do to find this elusive person was turn on his television.

For a nation reeling from the election of Donald Trump as the forty-fifth president of the United States, the soul-searching required would be wrenching and surreal. As a figure in popular culture, Trump had been ubiquitous, appearing in television shows and movies, programs glamorizing the rich and famous; commodifying the sink-or-swim, ruthless nature of the neoliberal era; and representing the worst aspects of American capitalism and conspicuous consumption.

The campaign was built off appearances on Fox News where Trump questioned Barack Obama's citizenship and right to the presidency while satisfying his own slavish addiction to the medium. Trump lived, breathed, and spoke fluent cable news, and by the time he announced his candidacy at a 2015 press conference in Trump Tower in New York City, he was more than ready to embody the alternate reality created by the network. But what Trump profited from the most was his willingness not to skirt around the ugliest parts of the narrative.

Among his primary rivals, Trump stood out as the lone candidate willing to stray outside the lines of expected behavior. He bullied. He disparaged. Like the internet trolls who supported him, he casually dispensed racist, misogynist poison without so much as an apology or second thought. His ramblings were lousy with the same New World Order conspiracy theories spread by the likes of Alex Jones, on whose show he appeared, telling the host, "Your reputation is amazing. I will not let you down."[34]

Trump was Steve Bannon's ideal candidate and Bannon jumped at the opportunity. Joining the campaign as chief executive, he steered Trump toward a populism that capitalized on the anger and frustration of white Americans who had suffered the brunt of neoliberalism. To these people, the promise of a return to America's greatness, combined with continued references to the conspiracy theories they had been primed to believe, not to mention opposition to a cultural and economic elite they despised and resented, would prove an incredibly potent proposition.

Bannon made use of widening gaps present in American culture but also fissures around the world. The new economy had created classes of winners and losers with very little in between while disabling the government's ability or desire to intervene or lessen the resulting suffering.

Globalism meant industry fleeing the nation for cheaper labor, leaving communities, cities, and even states to rust and rot. The economic arrangement of the postwar era was destroyed. Americans could no longer depend on traditional careers to stay afloat, and higher education, as a captive market, grew so expensive that to attend meant either having the resources required already or amassing massive debt. This left populations to resent experts and the educated, a resentment corporations used to continue polluting and destroying the environment and selling hazardous products, all to the tune of Lewis Powell's prescribed methods.

The nature of the language and behavior necessitated by new work environments, including political correctness and tolerance, was recognized as the hallmark of this world they could not enter and rejected as networks like Fox vilified it. Movies, television shows, and commercials produced by liberal creators and prized by corporations worried only about capturing certain markets of the consumer population played on their screens, reinforcing an imagined notion that their world was being encroached upon in accelerating fashion. To boot, Trump's sleazy background as a two-bit salesman happy to put his name on anything to make a buck resulted in a flood of MAGA-themed products, taking his upstart, racist campaign and turning it into a consumer identity.

Not to mention, white, patriarchal Christianity was being challenged like never before. The electorate was growing more secular and diverse, and calls for needed reform were repackaged by Fox and right-wing voices as an insidious plot against white Americans. Originally dismissed as a sideshow, Trump's candidacy was soon recognized for its potential to help the disgruntled members of the fusion of American conservatism.

Despite Trump's violations of "traditional values," the right wing, facing its own apocalypse, recognized the advantages of looking the other way. Religious leaders who had lectured for decades about moral decline fell behind him, telling their flocks that God worked in mysterious ways, just as their predecessors had when Constantine delivered them power. Republicans who had criticized Trump as a cancer on conservatism quickly changed their tune as they realized their fortunes could rise or fall based on Trump's direction and that his ascendance might allow them to fully secure the Supreme Court and further the process of neoliberalism.

Their rivals in the conservative movement, those most concerned with Traditionalism, recognized in the moment a precious and fleeting opportunity to roll back the floodwaters of liberalism. Calling it the "Flight 93 Election" after the September 11 flight on which passengers challenged the hijackers and crashed the plane into the ground in Pennsylvania to prevent another tragedy, a man named Michael Anton, who would later serve in the Trump administration, published an appeal to those people under the pen name "Publius Decius Mus." Anton was a part of Harry Jaffa's Claremont Institute, an enclave that had grown sick of Republican compromises and the neoliberal age. Anton made his argument in no uncertain terms: "Charge the cockpit or you die."[35] The liberal agenda, with its individualism, tolerance of gay people, and acceptance of immigration, was "the mark of a party, a society, a country, a people, a civilization that wants to die." And though Trump was "worse than imperfect," there was no choice if conservatives wanted to survive.

Thanks to this total abdication of principles, the inherent racism, sexism, and xenophobia of America, the environment of suffering and despair caused by neoliberalism, a general distrust in institutions and politicians, the insidious influence of social media and foreign actors interfering in the national discourse, and nearly $5 billion in free advertising by media that understood the danger of a Trump presidency but couldn't help but cash in on the easy ratings and clicks, Trump would garner the nomination of the party.[36] At the Republican National Convention, he promised the "forgotten men and women" of America that he would be their voice and that, as president, "Americanism, not globalism, will be our credo."[37] These were Bannon's promises, appeals tailored to the people he believed would break the stranglehold of decaying liberalism and deliver humanity to its next stage.

When Trump won, the inaugural continued the message. "Politicians prospered," a newly sworn-in Trump said, "but the jobs left, and the factories closed. The establishment protected itself, but not the citizens of our country."[38] Notably, Trump, a prodigious liar, was telling the truth. Neoliberalism had done just that, and this struck a chord with a portion of the electorate that had been waiting to hear even a semblance of something that reflected their experiences. Unfortunately, as he continued, the truth quickly dried up and the lies began.

"This American carnage stops right here and stops right now," Trump continued. "I will fight for you with every breath in my body, and I will never, ever let you down. America will start winning again, winning like never before. We will bring back our jobs. We will bring back our borders. We will bring back our wealth. And we will bring back our dreams."

Steve Bannon's tenure in the Trump administration was relatively short. As chief strategist, Bannon was only briefly able to hold court directly with the most powerful man in the world. In August of 2017, white supremacist groups that had supported Trump and enjoyed ties to Bannon converged on Charlottesville, Virginia, to protest the proposed removal of a statue of Confederate general Robert E. Lee. On August 11, they marched by torchlight, chanting slogans on loan from Renaud Camus and referencing his Replacement theory, repeatedly screaming, "You will not replace us! Jew will not replace us!"[39] The next day, violent skirmishes with counterprotestors scandalized the nation and culminated in one of the white nationalists driving their car into a crowd of people, killing one woman and injuring several others.

In his usual repulsive manner, Trump defended the white supremacists, infamously insisting that there were "very fine people" on both sides of the fight.[40] Despite his connections with these groups, Bannon probably would have survived the scandal had he not displeased Trump with comments to the press and his constant infighting with other members of his administration, including Jared Kushner, Trump's son-in-law and advisor. Bannon was out within the week and free to travel the world and build his movement while Trump got to work betraying his followers.

Instead of confronting neoliberalism and dismantling it, Trump fell into it and gave neoliberals the keys to the kingdom. Like other Republican presidents, even those he had continually criticized and lambasted, Trump followed the Heritage Foundation's "Mandate for Leadership" agenda to a T, obeying directions from the country's wealthiest individuals and instituting proposals to further tune the government toward "free enterprise" and "limited government," allowing the infection of neoliberalism to grow exponentially.[41] His cabinet was filled by appointees intent on destroying the agencies they led, including Secretary of Education Betsy DeVos, one of the nation's leading opponents of public education. Over the course of his presidency, the nation's billionaires expanded their wealth by over $1 trillion.[42]

Despite all this, Trump's base remained true and convinced he worked on their behalf. In part, this came from the white evangelical community's undying support. Building off the lies about Barack Obama, Trump became something like a savior in opposition to Obama's Antichrist, a chosen instrument of God's will in the fight against evil. In 2016, Trump had won the vote of roughly 80 percent of all white evangelicals, owing a debt to their sense of cultural and political persecution, not to mention their leaders' praising Trump as being heaven-sent.[43]

The need to reconcile Trump's actions with his promises and overcome the contradictions would have a startling solution. A bizarre posting appeared on 4chan, the site that nurtured white supremacist mass shooters, in October 2017. Claiming to originate with an anonymous figure with "Q level security clearance," the post communicated that clandestine operations to arrest Hillary Clinton were "already in motion" and that a secret plan being carried out by Trump and America's intelligence and military was underway.[44]

This phenomenon would come to be called "QAnon" and provided an alternate reality in which Trump was an unrelenting warrior on behalf of the people. A secret war was being waged by the forces of good against a satanic cabal of global elites manipulating every facet of the world. Building off past paranoid rumors used against Christians in Rome and then Jews throughout history, a narrative emerged that these elites sexually abused children, harvested their blood and fluids for the dark arts, and planned the destruction of America and the world. It was a retelling of the anti-Semitic conspiracy theories of *The Protocols of the Elders of Zion,* a new version of the Book of Revelation and the New World Order, only this time adherents could lend a hand. The "Deep State" was everywhere, and believers were invited to search for clues in television shows, movies, and everyday life that would unravel the mystery and defeat the enemy, an echo of the same idea that enabled Web 2.0's content creation economy that saw QAnon's followers piece together their own narratives and establish an entire ecosystem of minor celebrities, influencers, and associated content.

QAnon became disturbingly popular and infected the minds of people unaware of what it was or what it entailed. Over time, "Q" even advised followers to stop referring to the name or its associated catchphrases in order to aid the spread. By 2021, over thirty-one million Americans had come to believe "the government, media, and financial worlds in the U.S." were "controlled by a group of Satan-worshipping pedophiles who run a global child sex trafficking operation."[45] Forty-two million believed "a storm" was coming that would "sweep away the elites in power and restore the rightful leaders," another promise conveyed by "Q."

This "storm" was believed to be the final victory of good over evil. Within the QAnon mythos, it is envisioned as a military coup punishing the guilty while returning the righteous to their rightful place. Following that, a "great awakening" is prophesized, a new beginning that alarmingly sounds a lot like Aleksandr Dugin's "event." The spread of these fearful ramblings, aided by social media companies that prized the level of engagement they inspired, and their merging with American white evangelicals' faith, has prepared adherents to welcome a violent coup and the purging of their political enemies.

Even though posts attributed to "Q" abruptly ended in December 2020, the reverberations continue. Scores of QAnon believers have run for office and won, and even more continue to crawl out of the woodwork. While the Republican Party has absorbed these ideas, much as it did with the Tea Party in 2010, the cult of Q grows, which has allowed wealthy donors to capitalize on the conspiracy theories and spread fear of "groomers" preying on children in schools in an effort to destroy public education, all the while vilifying gay and trans Americans and turning them into scapegoats. More and more people believe the prophesized storm is imminent, that it will bring a higher state of being in which the paradise promised by God in the Bible will come to pass. It is the same story told by prophets of old, an appeal to hold on to faith, to wait out the apocalypse and prepare for the end of the old world.

It's hard to imagine a worse president during the COVID-19 pandemic than Donald Trump. As his sole concern was his own fate and self-interest, Trump approached the burgeoning crisis as a threat to his own presidency instead of a problem for humanity. As this novel virus reared its head and presented the prospect of a worldwide pandemic that would disrupt life in totality and lead to incredible suffering and death, Trump worried about the numbers' affecting his chances of being reelected in 2020.

Under Trump, the federal government turned the response almost entirely over to the states and private entities, creating an absolute mess of the developing crisis. In true neoliberal fashion, states were forced to bid against one another for supplies, doctors and health care workers went without necessary lifesaving equipment, and citizens went without masks, as globalized production had created a shortage within the United States. Trump's son-in-law, Jared Kushner, led the administration's response without so much as a hint of experience or expertise. "Free markets will solve this," he told bewildered onlookers in strategy sessions. "That is not the role of government."[46]

Neoliberalism had relegated the government to serve as a relief fund in the case of financial emergencies, and with the pandemic wearing on and interfering in business, once more Congress was permitted to act. Minuscule aid allowed Americans to go on consuming, but over $600 billion of funds took the shape of tax relief for companies that were either unaffected or went on to lay off employees.[47] As federal funds were handed over to corporations and the wealthy, they took the opportunity to restructure their business models, laying off workers without taking a public relations hit, eliminating the overhead of office space, pioneering work-from-home strategies that obliterated the forty-hour workweek and kept employees from engaging in solidarity and organizing, and continued to force the working class to labor in deadly conditions, as they were deemed "essential workers."

The right-wing forces that supported Trump played their part. Fox News repeated whatever talking point the administration wanted. Billionaires financed astroturf groups that protested to end mandated lockdowns. Grifters hawked snake oil products to cure the disease. As a vaccine was rolled out, more conspiracy theories were proliferated, including rumors it was made from fetal tissues, contained microchips, was a depopulation weapon created by the New World Order, and amounted to the "mark of the beast" from the Book of Revelation.[48]

This pandemic proved to be a perfect storm. The assault on science and experts carried out by wealthy Americans led to a situation where public health experts and epidemiologists were not only discredited but became targets of derision and harassment. A health care system held in check by markets thirsty for profits was overwhelmed, the comorbidities exacerbated by a lack of preventative care adding to the overall tragedy. Social media designed to profit off engagement at any cost supercharged QAnon and commodified misinformation. The drive for a free market without ethics or morals or concern for the well-being of others gave Fox News incentive to pander to a consumer base hungry to deny that anything was happening or even consider for a moment the fates of their family members, neighbors, or communities.

It was a damning indictment of the world as it stood, proof positive that government lacking strong, unquestionable leadership could stand up to novel threats of the moment. Russian authorities considered the pandemic "a fortuitous harbinger of the end of the post–Cold War liberal order."[49] Aleksandr Dugin called it a "sign of the end of times" and a "kind of punishment for globalization" that signaled America would have to "choose now between life and liberalism."[50]

Certainly, for a world looking at what the United Nations calls a "code red for humanity" in the form of looming climate catastrophe, the pandemic made obvious that collective action in the face of an existential threat would be almost unthinkable in the current environment. Liberal democracy had become so overrun with corruption and greed, so bought out by special interests and riddled with weaponized conspiracy theories, that the idea of coming together to answer that issue, created by generations' worth of industrialization, is almost unthinkable.

Considering that fact, the very prospect of climate change, with its disruption, guarantee of displacement, and shrinking of land and resources, seems to guarantee that the current problems of polarization and radicalization will continue and worsen, leading Western civilization closer and closer to the striking of midnight.

As the pandemic was merely beginning and America remained largely shut down, George Floyd was murdered by police in Minneapolis, Minnesota, on May 25, 2020. Repulsive footage of Floyd's killing showing police officer Derek Chauvin driving his knee into Floyd's neck inspired immense outrage, leading the people into the streets in protests around the country and hinting at a dormant potential for mass political action.

Just as conservatives had claimed movements for reform throughout the twentieth century were plots carried out by sinister foreign influences, the Black Lives Matter protests were framed as an attempt to destroy America. As the default target of modern anti-Semitic conspiracy theories, George Soros was called a "domestic terrorist" and accused of paying and transporting protestors and providing them with weapons and bricks to smash windows.[51] Former New York City mayor turned Trump stooge Rudy Giuliani told Republicans that BLM harbored a "Marxist agenda," saying, "Black Lives Matter wants to come and take your house away from you. They want to take your property away from you."[52] This Marxist "threat," others believed, originated from China and was part of a larger plot to tear America apart.

Donald Trump's attorney general William Barr used the tumult to forward his own agenda. A stalwart evangelical, Barr told Republicans they were facing a Bolshevik-style revolution that intended to replace religion after a "steady erosion of our traditional Judeo-Christian moral system and a comprehensive effort to drive it from the public square."[53] As chief law-enforcement official in the nation, Barr held that "man is fallen" and that the Christian religion was the best way to not only live life but discipline society. If law and order were to be restored, it would only come through that faith.

Barr was behind Trump as he made a show of taking the public square on June 1. After declaring himself the "president of law and order," Trump marched with his cabinet in tow across Lafayette Square in Washington, DC, once protestors had been tear-gassed and dispersed.[54] His destination was St. John's Church, which had been boarded up following a small fire. Trump displayed a copy of the Christian Bible as television cameras beamed the image around the world. In a particularly odious and sanctimonious photo-op, Trump was declaring himself a Christian president in a life-or-death struggle with evil.

That framing carried over to the 2020 presidential election. As Trump neared his date with electoral destiny, he continually seeded the discourse with the idea that if he were to lose it would only be because the election was stolen through fraud. After a long and arduous process of counting the votes, Democratic candidate Joe Biden bested Trump by seven million in the popular count and seventy-four votes in the Electoral College. True to his threats, Trump refused to concede and raged about plots carried out in the middle of the night and foreign interference.

The accusations were ludicrous, involving computer hacks and plots from every corner of the globe, and reeked of a QAnon-style choose-your-own narrative. In the contested state of Arizona, auditors searched for traces of bamboo in the ballots after being told China had rigged the election.[55] One grifter after another peddled these stories to either gain more followers or raise huge sums of money from true believers buying their pitch that they would fight to unravel the plot.

But it wasn't just crackpots who got involved. The lie that the 2020 election had been stolen emboldened the Republican Party to ramp up its crackdown on voting rights and enact the illiberal restructuring they needed to remain competitive as their popularity dwindled to record lows. The same think tanks in thrall to the same wealthy individuals and corporations funded these antidemocratic initiatives while using the conspiracy theory as cover.

Things escalated in the white evangelical world as well. Trump's spiritual advisor Paula White preached it was a satanic plot to "hurt this nation," utilizing "witchcraft," spells, and "demonic manipulation," before calling on the "blood of Jesus" to protect Trump and commanding "all satanic pregnancies to miscarry."[56] Televangelist Kenneth Copeland told his followers "the wisdom of God has been functioning in Donald John Trump" and that Satan himself had been conspiring with the Democrats to "steal this election so he can continue to kill babies and destroy the youth of this nation."[57] Churches throughout America struggled with QAnon and election conspiracy theories, creating unmanageable situations for pastors and leaders and an exodus of some to so-called Patriot Churches practicing Christian nationalism that considered America God's chosen nation. Criticizing "weak and spineless" preachers, Patriot pastor Ken Peters framed his ministry as a necessary revolutionary body, saying, "We can't be so afraid of a violent outcome that we allow the left to cheat their way to destroying the country."[58]

The radicalization exacerbated a growing rift in the country and primed the population for violence. By December of 2020, as Trump's term was coming to an end, less than a quarter of Republicans accepted the results of the election.[59] Another poll showed that 39 percent of them believed that violence might be necessary given current political conditions.[60] Among Trump voters, a stunning 84 percent considered their political rivals "a clear and present danger to American democracy," and 82 percent felt the "country needs a powerful leader in order to destroy the radical and immoral currents prevailing in society."[61]

On January 6, 2021, Donald Trump stood behind a pane of bulletproof glass and addressed an angry mob that had gathered at his invitation. In a few hours, Congress would meet to certify the results of the 2020 election, and Trump's supporters were hoping Vice President Mike Pence, serving in his official capacity overseeing the process, would carry out some maneuver to save the day. "If Mike Pence does the right thing," Trump said, "we win the election . . . He has the absolute right to do it."[62] Trump reiterated his claims that the contest had been stolen, blaming criminal Democrats and "weak . . . pathetic Republicans," telling those assembled, "We're going to walk down to the Capitol."

Trump was lying. Returning to the White House, he clicked on his television and watched as his supporters clashed with overwhelmed police, forced their way inside the Capitol, interrupted the certification, clamored to execute Pence for his "betrayal," and searched room by room for the politicians they had come to hate. While mainstream America looked on in abject horror, Trump was gleeful as he rewound the footage and watched it over again.[63]

The events of that day were not only appalling but a fitting representation of the ongoing unraveling of America. It aired live on every channel, the coverage replete with multiple angles, reckless speculation, and endless misinformation. Even as it occurred, many people attempted to pretend it wasn't that momentous of an event, that a literal coup wasn't playing out on television.

On the ground, the makeup of the crowd was an overwhelmingly white mixture of different groups with intertwined interests. Supporters of Trump like Jenna Ryan, a real estate agent from Texas, brandished their MAGA merchandise and livestreamed their participation to potential customers.[64] Also in attendance were QAnon adherents like Ashli Babbitt, who before being shot and killed by a Capitol Police officer—and turned into a martyr by extremists—declared online, "Nothing will stop us . . . the storm is here."[65] Alex Jones was there as well, joined by other paranoia peddlers looking to make a buck and build their prestige. And then there were extremists like the Oath Keepers, a paramilitary group dedicated to warring against a "communist/Deep State coup" while serving as Trump confidant and provocateur Roger Stone's bodyguards.[66]

As the chaos of the day subsided, Congress regrouped to finish counting the votes, even as Republicans continued to challenge them. Two weeks later, Joe Biden was sworn in as president of the United States, promising an end to the chaos and a return to normalcy. But while many wanted to believe the event was the end of a terrible story, it was only a chapter in an ongoing tragedy.

After the smoke had dissipated, military leaders like Chairman of the Joint Chiefs General Mark Milley admitted they had worried Trump might attempt a coup by invoking the Insurrection Act, an action Milley compared to the Reichstag fire in Weimar Germany.[67] This fell in line with revelations that plans circulated throughout the Republican Party and Trump's circle in advance of January 6 to do just that. An executive order had even been drafted for Trump to "seize, collect, retain and analyze all" voting machines used in disputed elections, citing a national security threat by "foreign agents, countries, and interests" that had supposedly interfered.[68] Extremists like the Oath Keepers had been of the same mind. After being charged with seditious conspiracy, details of their plans emerged that showed the group had stockpiled weapons and practiced military maneuvers in preparation for Trump invoking the Insurrection Act and calling on them to serve as a "quick reaction force."[69]

What was missing from much of the coverage, however, were the concealed elements that made January 6 possible: the crucial support of wealthy donors and forces that funded the Big Lie that the election was stolen and mobilized supporters to travel to Washington, DC. Plans to utilize Pence's role and potentially steal the election through underhanded means in Congress were cooked up by think tanks awash in donations from the richest Americans.

Rather than recognizing January 6 and the bygone Trump presidency as a moment to reflect and repent, the Republican Party doubled down. QAnon principles became party orthodoxy. Attention-seeking politicians like Marjorie Taylor Greene built their brands on flaunting semiautomatic rifles and promising to fight a war against the "Deep State." Rehabilitation of the January 6 coup attempt began almost immediately, led by conspiracy theorists who attempted to sell a narrative that those arrested were political prisoners.

This pivot required incredibly contradictory ideas. Initially, right-wing media underplayed the significance of the day and likened the participants to tourists, but then, within a few months, following the lead of actors like Alex Jones, Fox News and Republican politicians claimed the entire event had been a false-flag operation created by federal authorities looking to entrap Trump supporters and make an excuse to oppress them. Fox News host Tucker Carlson used his prime-time show to push this theory, explicitly calling it a false flag to launch a "new war on terror" against patriots using "soldiers and paramilitary law enforcement, guided by the world's most powerful intelligence agencies" and focused on "hunting down American citizens" and "purging them from society."[70] In a shocking turn, Carlson even came to endorse Alex Jones as a "better journalist than mainstream" sources, adding that his screeds detailing New World Order, thinly veiled anti-Semitic, and fascistic conspiracy theories constituted "a far better guide to reality in recent years" than established journalists and networks.[71]

These were far from the only disturbing trends in Carlson's post–January 6 product. At the urging of conservatives like Rod Dreher, Carlson traveled to Hungary and broadcast from Budapest, telling his audience, "If you care about Western Civilization and democracy and families and the ferocious assault on all three of those things by leaders of our global institutions, you should know what is happening here, right now."[72] Carlson aired a fawning interview with Viktor Orbán, selling him and his illiberal state to his viewers as a potential solution to America's woes, all while airing a cleaned-up version of the Great Replacement theory. He warned his viewers of an alleged plan to "change the racial mix of the country . . . to reduce the political power of people whose ancestors lived here, and dramatically increase the proportion of Americans newly-arrived from the third world."[73]

Proponents of traditional conservatism asserted there was "no returning to the pre-Trump conservative consensus" and that the future depended on opposing "tyrannical liberalism" and "poisonous and censorious multiculturalism."[74] Calling itself "National Conservatism," the idea percolated and found purchase as it focused on opposition to neoliberalism and liberalism in totality, advocating for a society not based on democracy or individualism but ordered by "natural" hierarchies and the Christian religion.

Strikingly similar to Aleksandr Dugin and Steve Bannon's Traditionalism, this National Conservative movement was a strange incorporation of contradictory elements. At its heart was white American paranoia in the face of demographic change, a malleable belief in capitalism tinged with socialist protections for favored groups, a return to industrialization at all costs, a reaffirmation of patriarchal dominance, and the refortification of religion as a guiding force in all facets of life, including its usage as a means of sanctifying exploitation in labor and political oppression. Its believers mostly recognized Trump as buffoonish but incredibly helpful in breaking the dominance of neoliberalism within the conservative fusion consensus. In the resulting upheaval, they have a chance to overtake the political system and create a new order, this one resembling what Orbán and Putin had with their illiberal states and achieving what traditionalists and neofascists so desire: a world in which liberalism is finally deposed.

This movement reflects a larger trend around the world. The wealthy have corrupted and co-opted governments, leading to a plummeting of trust among the people and a desire for something different and a solution to the pressing problems of the moment. We've seen this before with one reactionary movement after another. The tactics are depressingly familiar.

It is infuriating, but unsurprising, that a stolen Supreme Court in the United States is hell-bent on erasing the progress of the twentieth century. The overturning of a woman's right to reproductive choice in the summer of 2022 was a result of decades of a well-funded and restless project, and now the rights of LGBTQ+ people, communities of color, and other vulnerable populations, not to mention protections for workers, are on the chopping block as well. Meanwhile, legislators in conservative strongholds are disenfranchising voters, rigging their systems of power, and attempting to turn public schools into for-profit hubs of aggressive indoctrination.

It's depressingly obvious that existing and constantly improving systems of surveillance—utilizing everything from cameras to algorithms that often seem to know us better than we know ourselves—are poised to not only enforce these draconian laws but ward off any attempt to protest, organize, or trouble the developing order. And past events show how reactionaries will not hesitate to make use of these tools in disciplining the population.

It's by no means unexpected that right-wing conspiracy theories capitalizing off white supremacist paranoia are both inspiring mass shootings and radicalizing the population toward further violence. The narrative that this is a battle between good and evil, God and Satan, a religious crusade necessitating any means for capturing victory, all while emphasizing that failure means eradication and a nightmarish future, only makes it a certainty that more blood will be shed.

And it's no surprise that demagogues are on the rise, consolidating power and strength by relying on the same narratives and frustrations that fueled their predecessors. Or that a dictator like Vladimir Putin, having bought his way into the system, is now challenging it by seeding discontent in seemingly every corner of the globe and pushing his forces into sovereign nations like Ukraine while claiming he is warring against a worldwide conspiracy. The status quo, which many believed might be permanent and unassailable, is now buckling as nations are once more replenishing their arsenals and preparing for a conflict that might represent the long-fabled and feared World War III.

After decades of austerity and corruption, the neoliberal system is under political and financial duress. Just as previous systems—including the Roman Empire, feudalism, and even the post-Napoleon European concert—lost their power and gravity, we are again coming to a moment in which a new direction is almost assured. And, having defeated leftists and all but made collective action seemingly impossible, the only alternatives and solutions are being posed by the authoritarian right. The threat to liberal democracy, though largely unrecognized or ignored by those trusted to protect it, is very real.

The American order appears to be approaching some kind of crossroads as the centuries-long battle between liberalism and conservatism once more reaches a fever pitch. This moment is strange and horrifying, but it is undeniable that with every passing second it becomes more and more obvious that the clock does seem to be ticking toward midnight.

- EPILOGUE -

Digging out of the End of the World

Strangely enough, when I lose hope, I turn back to my grandma. Her apocalyptic stories and tales of satanic conspiracies were terrifying, but sometimes her hellfire would calm and give way to joyful nostalgia. Though her childhood in the Great Depression had been horrific and marked with terrible tragedy, she liked to reminisce on exactly how her family had survived, how they had closed ranks together and worked with their neighbors to weather the storm. It was acts of kindness that made the difference. The sharing of food. Quiet and unconditional charity. The way a community would gather to help move an evicted family back into their home once the police had left the scene.

Aleksandr Dugin and Steve Bannon are right about some things. Neoliberalism and this hypercapitalist state have left humanity desperate for meaning. But the last thing we need is more lies about history and the nature of power. Plato's Cave was and has always been a prison. That fact doesn't change regardless of who controls the shadows on the wall. Anyone erecting their new order on a foundation of myths is only doing so to replace one hierarchy with another.

If Vladimir Putin, Viktor Orbán, Dugin, Bannon, or any of these authoritarians manage to seize control and determine a post-neoliberal future, it will be a humanitarian tragedy on a scale that boggles the mind. We already know how the rich would react. Concentrated wealth has no problem working with despots and fascistic movements, and, if faced with a developing crisis, that willingness could turn to full-fledged support. Global climate change would exacerbate this worst-case scenario, and an era of diminishing resources, vanishing territory, and cultures thrown into chaos is sure to make everything exponentially worse. What we saw with the Trump administration and its treatment of refugees on the southern border, including imprisonment, gleeful abuse, and forced sterilization, could with these elements and supercharged white supremacy create a historic disaster. With no frontier to escape to, no means of venting internal frictions, we might see a breakdown of open society, widespread civil war, or the type of desperate struggle with enemies real or imagined that gives new meaning to "total warfare."

The self-styled messiahs of Big Tech offer digital and futuristic salvation, but that's only another mythology. Promising a future in the cosmos or in a virtual world is just distracting from the pressing problems and allowing the concentration of wealth and extracting of resources to continue unabated. Looking back on catastrophes enabled by developing technologies, it's clear that relying on algorithms or machine learning to determine the future and ensure law and order would be disastrous. And aggressive surveillance, accelerated during the War on Terror and employed to protect property and serve as a panopticon to discipline the people, could create an unthinkable dystopia.

These untenable solutions proliferate what I've come to think is a very general but costly mistake. The concept of sin powered Christianity, led to systems of spiritual and economic domination, rationalized war and slavery and genocide and inequality, supplied the self-interested core of capitalism, and inspired conspiracy theories and a general distrust that makes collective action nearly impossible.

But it was never real.

Like the Devil, which I learned to fear as a supernatural, external threat, it was a projection of internal guilt. The powerful who manipulated the world and engaged in endless cruelties for their own benefit laid their own shame upon the rest of us and designed the systems that continued to benefit them accordingly around that lie. That frame contorted us, perverted us, turned us into twisted versions of them, and with that twisting we projected it outward again and again and again.

It is a generational trauma. A legacy of guilt and suffering that continues to echo throughout time. But it can be overcome. We can recognize these burdens were never ours to begin with and choose something better. This current system, riddled with this poisonous lie, is failing, and our ability to choose an alternative will be either aided or hindered by our ability to lay those burdens down.

My grandma was unable to heal from that trauma. She had no doubt that the Devil troubled the world and that humanity was sick and evil. And yet, her conviction of humanity's wickedness receded when she talked about the solidarity of suffering. When she stopped with tales of supernatural battles and the armies of good and evil clashing at Armageddon, when she shifted from wild conspiracies to critiques of power and wealth, something changed in her. She could, if only for a moment, believe in a different reality in which the people came together to help one another, where people of all races and creeds could transcend their supposed differences and make the world, or at least their small corner of it, a better place.

We are facing the prospect of a new day. There are battles to fight and choices to make in determining what dawn might bring. That choosing will require faith. Forces are hard at work to try to rewind time and reinstall theocratic, authoritarian rule based on weaponized faiths that once ruled the world. To defeat them will take a new faith that transcends the divisions of old and centers on a belief and trust in one another.

Movements that have shaped history began with this faith. They started small and, much like the organizing and unionizing movements currently taking shape, gained in size because liberation is intoxicating. Hopelessness is not only illusory but easily dismissible. Change begins with a small step and, in this case, a recognition of where we are and how we have arrived at this moment of crisis. Then it is dependent on our ability to reinvigorate faith in one another and to determine our own destinies and reassert the power of the people. The corruption and ravages of neoliberalism must be addressed, and as we have seen, it is not merely enough to wait for elected representatives to take action. Time and time again, progress originates with the people pressuring the system to change.

Neoliberalism, with its distrust of people and religious faith in wealth and rule by elites, must give way. The past is littered with these trends that should seem disturbingly familiar. Corporations that overtook nations. Concentrated wealth that threatens democracy. Neoliberal austerity is radicalizing, its treatment of peoples and cultures is indefensible, and its inability to address the pressing issues of the present is damning. Either it will reinforce itself with additional despotism, as the system has done before, or it will break and give way to something else.

Any alternative must begin with a deep and honest reckoning with the tides of history and the influence of wealth and the combating of misinformation designed to appeal to our worst instincts, obscure the truth, and exonerate the guilty parties. It is no coincidence that reactionary, entrenched power has always attempted to suppress information and wield it as a weapon. By piecing together the puzzle of time and events, humanity was miraculously able to escape domination by theocratic institutions enforcing bloody orthodoxy and the senseless tyranny of kings.

We have done this before, and now, rapidly approaching midnight, we have no choice but to do it again.

- ACKNOWLEDGMENTS -

This project would not have been possible had it not been for the energy and direction of Marya Pasciuto and the support of Ross Harris. Many, many thanks to Cassidy Sachs and John Parsley. Thank you to the wonderful team at Dutton for all your hard work. And all the thanks I can muster to my family, loved ones, friends, colleagues, students, and members of the *Muckrake* community. Always, always.

- NOTES -

CHAPTER 1: BY THIS, CONQUER

1. Tacitus, *The Annals: The Reigns of Tiberius, Claudius, and Nero,* trans. J. C. Yardley (Oxford, UK: Oxford University Press, 2008), 357.
2. C. Suetonius Tranquillus, *The Lives of the Twelve Caesars,* trans. Alexander Thomson (New York: R. Worthington, 1883), 371.
3. Suetonius, *Lives of the Twelve Caesars,* 372.
4. Juvenal, *The Satires of Juvenal: A Verse Translation,* trans. Christopher Kelk (Lewiston, NY: Edwin Mellen Press, 2010), 371.
5. Suetonius, *Lives of the Twelve Caesars,* 294.
6. Flavius Josephus, *The Death of Caligula,* trans. T. P. Wiseman (Liverpool: Liverpool University Press, 2013), 30.
7. Suetonius, *Lives of the Twelve Caesars,* 270.
8. Mary Beard, *SPQR: A History of Ancient Rome* (New York: Liveright, 2015), 391.
9. Suetonius, *Lives of the Twelve Caesars,* 292.
10. Tacitus, *Annals,* 357.
11. Tacitus, *Annals,* 359.
12. Tacitus, *Annals,* 360.
13. Beard, *SPQR*, 477.
14. Robert Louis Wilken, *The Christians as the Romans Saw Them* (1984; repr., New Haven: Yale University Press, 2003), 19.
15. Augustus Neander, *The Emperor Julian and His Generation: A Historical Picture,* trans. G. V. Cox (New York: J. C. Riker, 1850), 59.
16. Neander, *Emperor Julian,* 58.
17. A. N. Wilson, *Paul: The Mind of the Apostle* (New York: Norton, 1997), 9.
18. Marta Sordi, *The Christians and the Roman Empire,* trans. Annabel Bedini (Norman: University of Oklahoma Press, 1986), 173.
19. Thomas C. Patterson, *Inventing Western Civilization* (New York: Monthly Review Press, 1997), 91.
20. George Hart, *The Routledge Dictionary of Egyptian Gods and Goddesses,* 2nd ed. (New York: Routledge, 2005), 79.
21. Elizabeth McCabe, *An Examination of the Isis Cult with Preliminary Exploration*

into New Testament Studies (Lanham, MD: University Press of America, 2008), 19 and 110.

22. Suetonius, *Lives of the Twelve Caesars,* 398.
23. Suetonius, *Lives of the Twelve Caesars,* 388.
24. John Floyer, ed., *The Sibylline Oracles* (London: R. Bruges, 1713), 95.
25. Floyer, *Sibylline Oracles,* 41.
26. Cassius Dio, *Roman History,* vol. 3 (London: Loeb Classical Library Edition, 1923).
27. The Holy Bible, King James Version (Nashville: Thomas Nelson Inc., 1973), 1830.
28. Holy Bible, KJV, 1831.
29. Holy Bible, KJV, 1821–23.
30. Aurelius Augustine, *The Works of Aurelius Augustine, Bishop of Hippo,* ed. Marcus Dods, vol. 2, *City of God* (Edinburgh: T. & T. Clark, 1871), 382.
31. William Amherst, Bernard P. Grenfell, and Arthur S. Hunt, eds., *The Amherst Papyri* (London: Oxford University Press, 1900), 17.
32. William C. Weinrich, ed. and trans., *Ancient Christian Texts: Latin Commentaries on Revelation* (Downers Grove, IL: IVP Academic, 2011), 18.
33. Leonard L. Thompson, *The Book of Revelation: Apocalypse and Empire* (New York: Oxford University Press, 1997), 25.
34. Paul D. Hanson, *The Dawn of Apocalyptic: The Historical and Sociological Roots of Jewish Apocalyptic Eschatology* (Philadelphia: Fortress Press, 1979), 2.
35. Thompson, *Book of Revelation,* 25.
36. Jeffrey Burton Russell, *Satan: The Early Christian Tradition* (Ithaca, NY: Cornell University Press, 1981), 28.
37. Thompson, *Book of Revelation,* 28.
38. Walter Burkert, *Ancient Mystery Cults* (Cambridge, MA: Harvard University Press, 1987), 48.
39. Holy Bible, KJV, 125 and 131.
40. Holy Bible, KJV, 152.
41. Michael Gaddis, *There Is No Crime for Those Who Have Christ: Religious Violence in the Christian Roman Empire* (Berkeley: University of California Press, 2005), 41.
42. Holy Bible, KJV, 1450–51.
43. Judith Perkins, *Roman Imperial Identities in the Early Christian Era* (London: Routledge, 2009), 5.
44. Holy Bible, KJV, 11.
45. Dionysius of Halicarnassus, *The Roman Antiquities,* trans. Earnest Cary (Cambridge, MA: Harvard University Press, 1937), 383.
46. Holy Bible, KJV, 8.
47. R. E. Witt, *Isis in the Graeco-Roman World* (Ithaca, NY: Cornell University Press, 1971), 22.
48. Jan Assmann, "Monotheism and Polytheism," in *Ancient Religions,* ed. Sarah Iles Johnston (Cambridge, MA: Belknap Press of Harvard University Press, 2004), 29.
49. Kyle Harper, *The Fate of Rome: Climate, Disease, and the End of an Empire* (Princeton, NJ: Princeton University Press, 2017), 155.

50. Eusebius Pamphilus, *The Ecclesiastical History*, trans. Christian Frederic Crusé (Philadelphia: J. B. Lippincott & Co., 1860), 320.
51. Eusebius, *Ecclesiastical History*, 320 and 328.
52. Bill Leadbetter, *Galerius and the Will of Diocletian* (London: Routledge, 2009), 224.
53. Abraham Gross, *Spirituality and Law: Courting Martyrdom in Christianity and Judaism* (Lanham, MD: University Press of America, 2005), 3.
54. G. W. Bowersock, *Martyrdom and Rome* (New York: Cambridge University Press, 1995), 1.
55. Bowersock, *Martyrdom and Rome*, 315.
56. Adrastos Omissi, *Emperors and Usurpers in the Later Roman Empire: Civil War, Panegyric, and the Construction of Legitimacy* (Oxford: Oxford University Press, 2018), 138.
57. Mary Beard, John North, and Simon Price, *Religions of Rome*, vol. 1 (Cambridge: Cambridge University Press, 1998), 366.
58. H. A. Drake, *A Century of Miracles: Christians, Pagans, Jews, and the Supernatural, 312–410* (New York: Oxford University Press, 2017), 61.
59. Lactantius, *The Minor Works*, trans. Mary Francis McDonald (Washington, DC: The Catholic University of America Press, 1965), 197.
60. Socrates, *History of the Church* (London: George Bell & Sons, 1897), 48.
61. Guido M. Berndt and Roland Steinacher, *Arianism: Roman Heresy and Barbarian Creed* (London: Routledge, 2014), 9.
62. Jonathan Kirsch, *God Against the Gods: The History of the War Between Monotheism and Polytheism* (New York: Viking Compass, 2004), 173.
63. A. H. M. Jones, *Constantine and the Conversion of Europe* (1962; repr., Toronto: University of Toronto Press, 2003), 195.
64. Philostorgius, *Church History*, trans. Philip R. Amidon (Atlanta: Society of Biblical Literature, 2007), 32.
65. Timothy D. Barnes, *Constantine and Eusebius* (Cambridge, MA: Harvard University Press, 1981), 162.
66. Eusebius, *Church History* (New York: The Christian Literature Company, 1890), 372.
67. Eusebius Pamphilus, *The Ecclesiastical History*, trans. Isaac Boyle (Philadelphia: J. B. Lippincott & Co., 1860), 437.
68. Eusebius, *The Life of the Blessed Emperor Constantine* (London: S. Bagster and Sons, 1845), 32.
69. Eusebius, *Life of the Blessed Emperor Constantine*, 27.
70. Philip Schaff and Henry Wace, eds., *A Select Library of Nicene and Post-Nicene Fathers of the Christian Church*, vol. 1, *Eusebius* (New York: The Christian Literature Company, 1890), 522.
71. Christopher Bush Coleman, *Constantine the Great and Christianity* (New York: Columbia University Press, 1914), 147–48.
72. Noel Lenski, *Constantine and the Cities: Imperial Authority and Civic Politics* (Philadelphia: University of Pennsylvania Press, 2016), 231.

73. Kevin W. Kaatz, *Early Controversies and the Growth of Christianity* (Santa Barbara: Praeger, 2012), 128.
74. Gaddis, *There Is No Crime for Those Who Have Christ,* 185.
75. Catherine Nixey, *The Darkening Age: The Christian Destruction of the Classical World* (New York: Houghton Mifflin Harcourt, 2018), 19.
76. A. D. Lee, *Pagans and Christians in Late Antiquity: A Sourcebook* (London: Routledge, 2000), 121.
77. John Chrysostom, *The Homilies,* pt. 3 (London: Walter Smith, 1885), 949 and 1013.
78. Guy G. Stroumsa, *The End of Sacrifice: Religious Transformations in Late Antiquity* (Chicago: University of Chicago Press, 2009), 154.
79. Socrates, *History of the Church,* 287 and 349–50.
80. Tamara M. Green, *The City of the Moon God: Religious Traditions of Harran* (Leiden, the Netherlands: Brill, 1992), 114.
81. Gaddis, *There Is No Crime for Those Who Have Christ,* 92.
82. Firmicus Maternus, *The Error of the Pagan Religions,* trans. Clarence A. Forbes (New York: Newman Press, 1970), 89.
83. Aurelius Augustine, *The Works of Aurelius Augustine, Bishop of Hippo,* vol. 3, trans. Marcus Dods (Edinburgh: T. & T. Clark, 1919), 484.
84. Augustine, *Works of Aurelius Augustine,* vol. 3, 488.
85. St. Augustine, *Letters,* vol. 2, trans. Wilfried Parsons (Washington, DC: Catholic University of America Press, 1953), 58 and 59.
86. Ariel G. Lopez, *Shenoute of Atripe and the Uses of Poverty: Rural Patronage, Religious Conflict and Monasticism in Late Antique Egypt* (Berkeley: University of California Press, 2013), 24.
87. Nixey, *Darkening Age,* 170.
88. Nixey, *Darkening Age,* 173.
89. Eberhard Sauer, *The Archaeology of Religious Hatred: In the Roman and Early Medieval World* (Stroud, UK: Tempus Publishing, 2003), 157.
90. Sauer, *Archaeology of Religious Hatred,* 75.
91. Sauer, *Archaeology of Religious Hatred,* 176.
92. Kenneth Atkinson, *Empress Galla Placidia and the Fall of the Roman Empire* (Jefferson, NC: McFarland, 2020), 57.
93. Philip Schaff and Henry Wace, eds., *A Select Library of Nicene and Post-Nicene Fathers of the Christian Church*, vol. 6, *St. Jerome* (New York: The Christian Literature Company, 1893), 500.
94. Augustine, *The City of God,* vol. 2, trans. Marcus Dods (Edinburgh: T. & T. Clark, 1871), 177.
95. Ramsay MacMullen, *Christianity and Paganism in the Fourth to Eighth Centuries* (New Haven: Yale University Press, 1997), 15; Soraya Field Fiorio, "The Killing of Hypatia," *Lapham's Quarterly,* January 16, 2019, laphamsquarterly.org /roundtable/killing-hypatia.
96. MacMullen, *Christianity and Paganism in the Fourth to Eighth Centuries*, 28.

Notes

CHAPTER 2: THE GREAT CHAIN OF BEING

1. Stuart Airlie, "Charlemagne and the Aristocracy," *Charlemagne: Empire and Society,* ed. Joanna Story (Manchester, UK: Manchester University Press, 2005), 95.
2. Bernard S. Bachrach, *Charlemagne's Early Campaigns (768–777): A Diplomatic and Military Analysis* (Leiden, the Netherlands: Brill Publishers, 2013), 238.
3. Bernhard Walter Scholz and Barbara Rogers, trans., *Carolingian Chronicles: Royal Frankish Annals and Nithard's Histories* (Ann Arbor: University of Michigan Press, 1972), 49.
4. Eginhard, *Life of Charlemagne,* trans. Samuel Epes Turner (New York: American Book Company, 1880), 27.
5. Dana Carleton Munro, *The Laws of Charles the Great* (Philadelphia: University of Pennsylvania, 1900), 3.
6. Scholz and Rogers, *Carolingian Chronicles,* 61.
7. Charles Oman, *The Dark Ages, 476–918* (London: Rivingtons, 1908), 355.
8. Roger Collins, *Charlemagne* (Toronto: University of Toronto Press, 1990), 95.
9. Eginhard, *Life of Charlemagne,* 65; Collins, *Charlemagne,* 142.
10. Collins, *Charlemagne,* 146.
11. Herwig Wolfram, *History of the Goths,* trans. Thomas J. Dunlap (1979; repr., Berkeley: University of California Press, 1988), 104 and 11.
12. Rosamond McKitterick, "Political Ideology in Carolingian Historiography," in *The Uses of the Past in the Early Middle Ages,* eds. Yitzhak Her and Matthew Innes (Cambridge: Cambridge University Press, 2000), 173.
13. Charles E. Schrader, "The Concept of World Unity in Patristic Literature During the First Five Centuries," in *The Quest for Political Unity in World History,* ed. Stanley Pargellis (Washington, DC: American Historical Association, 1944), 34.
14. Aristotle, *History of Animals,* trans. Richard Cresswell (London: George Bell & Sons, 1897), 6.
15. Arthur O. Lovejoy, *The Great Chain of Being: A Study in the History of an Idea* (Cambridge, MA: Harvard University Press, 2001), 67.
16. Thomas Aquinas, *On Kingship,* trans. Gerald B. Phelan (1949; repr., Toronto: Pontifical Institute of Mediaeval Studies, 1982), 12.
17. Brett Edward Whalen, *Dominion of God: Christendom and Apocalypse in the Middle Ages* (Cambridge, MA: Harvard University, 2009), 40.
18. Benjamin Garstad, ed. and trans., *"Apocalypse of Pseudo Methodius" and "An Alexandrian World Chronicle"* (Cambridge, MA: Harvard University Press, 2012), 47.
19. Oliver J. Thatcher and Edgar H. McNeal, eds., *A Source Book for Mediaeval History* (New York: Charles Scribner's Sons, 1905), 518.
20. Thatcher and McNeal, *A Source Book for Mediaeval History,* 519.
21. Jill Claster, *Sacred Violence: The European Crusades to the Middle East, 1095–1396* (Toronto: University of Toronto Press, 2009), xv.
22. Thomas Head and Richard Landes, eds., *The Peace of God: Social Violence and*

Religious Response in France Around the Year 1000 (Ithaca, NY: Cornell University Press, 1992), 1.

23. Edward Peters, ed., *The First Crusade: "The Chronicle of Fulcher of Charles" and Other Source Materials* (1971; repr., Philadelphia: University of Pennsylvania Press, 2011), 39.
24. Carl Erdmann, *The Origin of the Idea of Crusade,* trans. Marshall W. Baldwin and Walter Goffart (Princeton, NJ: Princeton University Press, 1977), 339.
25. Erdmann, *Origin of the Idea of Crusade,* 338.
26. Jonathan Riley-Smith, *The Knights of St. John in Jerusalem and Cyprus, 1050–1310* (1967; repr., Houndmills and New York: Palgrave Macmillan, 2002), 8.
27. Thatcher and McNeal, *Source Book for Mediaeval History,* 519.
28. Carole Hillenbrand, *The Crusades: Islamic Perspectives* (New York: Routledge, 2000), 49.
29. Jonathan Lyons, *The House of Wisdom: How the Arabs Transformed Western Civilization* (New York: Bloomsbury Press, 2009), 20.
30. Léon Poliakov, *The History of Anti-Semitism,* vol. 1, *From the Time of Christ to the Court Jews,* trans. Richard Howard (New York: Vanguard Press, 1965), 48.
31. Norman Golb, *The Jews in Medieval Normandy: A Social and Intellectual History* (Cambridge: Cambridge University Press, 1998), 117.
32. Thomas Asbridge, *The First Crusade: A New History* (New York: Oxford University Press, 2004), 85 and 88.
33. Asbridge, *First Crusade,* 101.
34. Jonathan Phillips, *Holy Warriors: A Modern History of the Crusades* (New York: Random House, 2009), 27.
35. F. E. Peters, *Jerusalem: The Holy City in the Eyes of Chroniclers, Visitors, Pilgrims, and Prophets from the Days of Abraham to the Beginnings of Modern Times* (Princeton, NJ: Princeton University Press, 2017), 288.
36. Adrian J. Boas, *Jerusalem in the Time of the Crusades: Society, Landscape and Art in the Holy City Under Frankish Rule* (London: Taylor & Francis, 2001), 13.
37. Henry Betterson, *Documents of the Christian Church* (1943; repr., Oxford: Oxford University Press, 1967), 106.
38. Leo D. Lefebure, ed., *Religion, Authority, and the State: From Constantine to the Contemporary World* (London: Palgrave Macmillan, 2016), 12.
39. Cullen Murphy, *God's Jury: The Inquisition and the Making of the Modern World* (Boston: Houghton Mifflin, 2012), 31.
40. Christopher Tyerman, *God's War: A New History of the Crusades* (Cambridge, MA: Harvard University Press, 2006), 591.
41. Murphy, *God's Jury,* 33.
42. R. I. Moore, *The War on Heresy* (Cambridge: Belknap Press of Harvard University Press, 2012), 241.
43. E. Vacandard, *The Inquisition: A Critical and Historical Study of the Coercive Power of the Church* (London: Longman, Green, and Company, 1915), 108.
44. Vacandard, *Inquisition,* 109–10.

45. F. M. Powicke, "The Culmination of Medieval Papacy," in *Philip the Fair and Boniface VIII: State vs. Papacy,* ed. Charles T. Wood (New York: Holt, Rinehart, and Winston, 1967), 109.
46. John Julius Norwich, *Absolute Monarchs: A History of the Popes* (New York: Random House, 2011), 199.
47. James C. Robertson, *History of the Christian Church,* vol. 6 (London: John Murray, 1904), 336.
48. Robertson, *History of the Christian Church,* vol. 6, 338.
49. Philip Schaff, *History of the Christian Church,* vol. 5, pt. 2 (New York: Scribner's, 1924), 25–26.
50. Robertson, *History of the Christian Church,* vol. 6, 339.
51. M. Guizot and Madame Guizot de Witt, *France,* vol. 1, trans. Robert Black (New York: Peter Fenelon Collier & Son, 1900), 479.
52. Robertson, *History of the Christian Church,* vol. 6, 354.
53. Sophia Menache, *Clement V* (Cambridge: Cambridge University Press, 1998), 58.
54. G. Mollat, *The Popes at Avignon* (1949; repr., Nashville: Thomas Nelson and Sons, 1963), 247.
55. Mollat, *Popes at Avignon,* 248.
56. Malcolm Barber, *The Two Cities: Medieval Europe, 1050–1320* (London: Routledge, 1992), 460.
57. Lorenzo Valla, *The Treatise of Lorenzo Valla on the Donation of Constantine,* trans. Christopher B. Coleman (New Haven, CT: Yale University Press, 1922), 27.
58. Marsilius of Padua, *The Defensor Pacis,* ed. C. W. Previté-Orton (Cambridge: Cambridge University Press, 1928), xv and xix.
59. Bernard McGinn, "Angel Pope and Papal Antichrist," *Church History* 47, no. 2 (June 1978), 166.
60. Philip C. Almond, *The Antichrist: A New Biography* (Cambridge: Cambridge University Press, 2020), 181.
61. Bernard McGinn, *Visions of the End: Apocalyptic Traditions in the Middle Ages* (1979; repr., New York: Columbia University Press, 1998), 237.
62. Dante, *De Monarchia,* trans. F. J. Church (London: Macmillan & Co., 1879), 1 and 116.
63. John de Wycliffe, *Tracts and Treatises,* ed. Robert Vaughan (London: Blackburn and Pardon, 1845), 165.
64. Mandell Creighton, *A History of the Papacy During the Period of the Reformation,* vol. 1 (Boston: Houghton Mifflin, 1882), 341.
65. Jules Michelet, *Joan of Arc, or The Maid of Orleans* (Boston: Houghton Mifflin Company, 1858), 25 and 41.
66. Michelet, *Joan of Arc,* 26.
67. Michelet, *Joan of Arc,* 226.
68. Daniel Hobbins, trans., *The Trial of Joan of Arc* (Cambridge, MA: Harvard University Press, 2005), 211 and 228.

69. Barbara Tuchman, *A Distant Mirror: The Calamitous 14th Century* (New York: Alfred A. Knopf, 1978), 102.
70. Brian Wilkie and James Hunt, eds., *Literature of the Western World: The Ancient World Through the Renaissance* (London: Macmillan, 1992), 1833.
71. Tuchman, *A Distant Mirror,* 103.
72. Léon Poliakov, *The History of Anti-Semitism,* vol. 1, *From the Time of Christ to the Court Jews,* trans. Richard Howard (New York: Vanguard Press, 1965), 112.
73. Laura A. Smoller, "Plague and the Investigation of the Apocalypse," in *Last Things: Death and the Apocalypse in the Middle Ages,* eds. Caroline Walker Bynum and Paul Freedman (Philadelphia: University of Pennsylvania Press, 2000), 162.
74. Thomas of Monmouth, *The Life and Miracles of St. William of Norwich* (Cambridge: Cambridge University Press, 1896), 21.
75. Jacob Rader Marcus, ed., *The Jew in the Medieval World, A Source Book: 315–1791* (1990; repr., Cincinnati: Hebrew Union College Press, 1999), 53.
76. Rosemary Horrox, ed., *The Black Death* (Manchester, UK: Manchester University Press, 2013), 72–73.
77. Rodney Hilton, *Bond Men Made Free: Medieval Peasant Movements and the English Rising of 1381* (1973; repr., London: Routledge, 2003), 29.
78. Thomas Wright, *The History of France,* vol. 1 (London: The London Printing and Publishing Company, 1856), 392.
79. Tuchman, *A Distant Mirror,* 181–82.
80. R. B. Dobson, *The Peasants' Revolt of 1381* (1970; repr., London: Macmillan, 1989), 375.
81. Juliet Barker, *1381: The Year of the Peasants' Revolt* (Cambridge, MA: Belknap Press of Harvard University Press, 2014), 251.
82. Barker, *Year of the Peasants' Revolt,* 255.
83. William Urwick, *Nonconformity in Herts* (London: Hazell, Watson, and Viney, 1884), 29.

CHAPTER 3: THE EMPIRE OF MAN OVER INFERIOR CREATURES

1. William F. Keegan and Lisabeth A. Carlson, *Talking Taíno: Essays on Caribbean Natural History from a Native Perspective* (Tuscaloosa: University of Alabama Press, 2008), 8.
2. José R. Oliver, "The Taíno Cosmos," in *The Indigenous People of the Caribbean,* ed. Samuel M. Wilson (Gainesville: University Press of Florida, 1997), 141.
3. Nicholas Terpstra, ed., *Lives Uncovered: A Sourcebook of Early Modern Europe* (Toronto: University of Toronto Press, 2019), 206.
4. Christopher Columbus, *The Journal of Christopher Columbus,* trans. Cecil Jane (New York: Bonanza Books, 1960), 4.
5. John Boyd Thacher, *Christopher Columbus: His Life, His Work, His Remains,* vol. 3 (New York: G. P. Putnam's Sons, 1904), 661.

6. Frank Graziano, *The Millennial New World* (New York: Oxford University Press, 1999), 28.
7. Christopher Columbus, *The Book of Prophecies,* ed. Roberto Rusconi, trans. Blair Sullivan (1997; repr., Eugene, OR: Wipf & Stock, 2004), 137.
8. Columbus, *Journal of Christopher Columbus,* 194.
9. Columbus, *Journal of Christopher Columbus,* 200.
10. Luis N. Rivera, *A Violent Evangelism: The Political and Religious Conquest of the Americas* (Louisville: Westminster/Knox Press, 1992), 94.
11. James Carson, *The Columbian Covenant: Race and the Writing of American History* (New York: Palgrave Macmillan, 2015), 5.
12. Alexander Koch, Chris Brierley, Mark M. Maslin, and Simon L. Lewis, "Earth System Impacts of the European Arrival and Great Dying in the Americas After 1492," *Quaternary Science Reviews* 207 (2019), 13–36.
13. Ken Coates, *A Global History of Indigenous Peoples: Struggle and Survival* (London: Palgrave Macmillan, 2004), 130.
14. Sheldon Watts, *Epidemics and History: Disease, Power and Imperialism* (New Haven, CT: Yale University Press, 1999), 93.
15. Laurence Bergreen, *Columbus: The Four Voyages, 1492–1504* (New York: Penguin, 2011), 204.
16. M. Lindsay Kaplan, *Figuring Racism in Medieval Christianity* (Oxford: Oxford University Press, 2018), 156.
17. Thomas Southey, *Chronological History of the West Indies,* vol. 1 (London: Longman, Rees, Orme, Brown, and Green, 1827), 22.
18. Helen M. Kinsella, *The Image Before the Weapon: A Critical History of the Distinction Between Combatant and Civilian* (Ithaca, NY: Cornell University Press, 2011), 58.
19. D. A. Brading, *The First America: The Spanish Monarchy, Creole Patriots and the Liberal State, 1492–1867* (Cambridge: Cambridge University Press, 1991), 144.
20. José Barreiro, "Survival Stories," in *The Cuba Reader: History, Culture, Politics,* eds. Aviva Chomsky, Barry Carr, and Pamela Maria Smorkaloff (Durham, NC: Duke University Press, 2003), 35.
21. Bartolomé de las Casas, *The Devastation of the Indies: A Brief Account,* trans. Herma Briffault (1974; repr., Baltimore: The John Hopkins University Press, 1992), 32.
22. De las Casas, *Devastation of the Indies,* 34.
23. Juan Ginés de Sepúlveda, "Democrates Alter," in *Chapters in Western Civilization,* vol. 1 (New York: Columbia University Press, 1954), 495.
24. Sepúlveda, *Chapters in Western Civilization,* vol. 1, 497.
25. Louise A. Breen, *Converging Worlds: Communities and Cultures in Colonial America; A Sourcebook* (New York: Routledge, 2012), 42.
26. De las Casas, *Devastation of the Indies,* 131–32.
27. Hugh Thomas, *The Slave Trade: The Story of the Atlantic Slave Trade, 1440–1870* (New York: Simon & Schuster, 1997), 92.

28. Joseph E. Inikori and Stanley L. Engerman, *The Atlantic Slave Trade: Effects on Economies, Societies, and Peoples in Africa, the Americas, and Europe* (Durham, NC: Duke University Press, 1998), 6.
29. The Holy Bible, King James Version (Nashville: Thomas Nelson Inc., 1973), 19.
30. Gomes Eanes de Zurara, *The Chronicle of the Discovery and Conquest of Guinea,* vol. 1, trans. Charles Raymond Beazley and Edgar Prestage (London: Hakluyt Society, 1896), 54.
31. Zurara, *Discovery and Conquest of Guinea,* vol. 1, 84.
32. Zurara, *Discovery and Conquest of Guinea,* vol. 1, 19.
33. Desmond Manderson, *Danse Macabre: Temporalities of Law in the Visual Arts* (Cambridge: Cambridge University Press, 2019), 110.
34. John Shaw, ed., *Charters Relating to the East India Company, from 1600 to 1761* (Madras: Government Press, 1887), 71.
35. Theodore E. Mommsen, "Petrarch's Conception of the 'Dark Ages,'" *Speculum* 17, no. 2. (1942), 227; Mary Roper Price and Donald Lindsay, *A Portrait of Europe, 1300–1600: Authority and Challenge* (Oxford: Oxford University Press, 1972), 176.
36. Plato, *The Republic,* trans. Raymond Larson (Wheeling, IL: Harlan Davidson, 1979), 175.
37. Plato, *Republic,* 176.
38. Plato, *Republic,* 180.
39. Niccolò Machiavelli, *The Prince,* trans. Luigi Ricci (1952; repr., New York: New American Library, 1999), 94.
40. Plato, *Republic,* 203.
41. Plato, *Republic,* 151.
42. Niccolò Machiavelli, *Discourses on the First Decade of Titus Livius* (London: Kegan Paul, Trench, & Co., 1883), 327.
43. Robert Boyle, *The Works of the Honourable Robert Boyle,* vol. 3 (London: W. Johnston, 1772), 402.
44. O. R. Dathorne, *Imagining the World: Mythical Belief Versus Reality in Global Encounters* (Westport, CT: Bergin & Garvey, 1994), 61 and 59.
45. Thomas More, *Utopia* (New York: Columbia Publishing, 1891), 37–38.
46. Francis Bacon, *Essays* (London: Oxford University Press, 1921), 85–86.
47. Tommaso Campanella, *The City of the Sun* (New York: Cosimo Classics, 2007), 15.
48. Eric Lund, ed., *Documents from the History of Lutheranism, 1517–1750* (Minneapolis: Fortress Press, 2002), 28–29.
49. K. R. Hagenbach, *History of the Reformation in Germany and Switzerland Chiefly,* vol. 1, trans. Evelina Moore (Edinburgh: T. & T. Clark, 1878), 129.
50. Martin Luther, *First Principles of the Reformation,* trans. Henry Wace (London: John Murray, 1883), 3.
51. Martin Luther, *Works of Martin Luther,* vol. 2 (Philadelphia: A. J. Holman Company, 1915), 303–4.
52. Kenneth R. Bartlett and Margaret McGlynn, eds., *The Renaissance and Reformation in Northern Europe* (Toronto: University of Toronto Press, 2014), 64.

53. Ronald J. Deibert, *Parchment, Printing, and Hypermedia: Communication in World Order Transformation* (New York: Columbia University Press, 1997), 71.
54. Thomas Müntzer, *Revelation and Revolution: Basic Writings of Thomas Müntzer,* trans. Michael G. Baylor (Bethlehem, PA: Lehigh University Press, 1993), 145.
55. Friedrich Engels, *The German Revolutions: "The Peasant War in Germany" and "Germany: Revolution and Counter-Revolution"* (Chicago: University of Chicago Press, 1967), 49.
56. John A. Wagner, ed., *Voices of the Reformation: Contemporary Accounts of Daily Life* (Santa Barbara, CA: Greenwood, 2015), 48–49.
57. Hans J. Hillerbrand, ed., *The Protestant Reformation* (London: Palgrave Macmillan, 1968), 83.
58. Preserved Smith, *The Life and Letters of Martin Luther* (Boston: Houghton Mifflin Company, 1914), 162.
59. Ernest Belfort Bax, *German Culture: Past and Present* (London: George Allen and Unwin, 1915), 198.
60. Bax, *German Culture,* 197.
61. Max Weber, *The Protestant Ethic and the Spirit of Capitalism,* trans. Talcott Parsons (1992; repr., London: Routledge, 2001), 65.
62. Pierre Nicole, *Moral Essays* (London: Sam. Manship, 1696), 79–80.
63. Nicole, *Moral Essays,* 79.
64. Peter H. Wilson, *The Thirty Years War: Europe's Tragedy* (Cambridge, MA: Belknap Press of Harvard University, 2009), 787.
65. John Theibault, "Destruction in the Thirty Years War," *Journal of Social History* 27, no. 2 (Winter 1993), 277.
66. *The Articles of the Treaty of Peace* (London: W. Onley, 1697), 1–2.
67. Henry Bettenson, ed., *Documents of the Christian Church* (London: Oxford University Press, 1943), 303–4.
68. Hugo Grotius, *De jure belli ac pacis libri tres,* vol. 2, trans. Francis W. Kelsey (Oxford: Clarendon Press, 1925), 20.
69. Geoffrey Treasure, *The Huguenots* (New Haven, CT: Yale University Press, 2013), 169.
70. George Buchanan, *A Dialogue Concerning the Due Priviledge of Government in the Kingdom of Scotland* (London: Richard Baldwin, 1689), 5 and 20.
71. James I, *The Political Works of James I* (Cambridge, MA: Harvard University Press, 1918), 307.
72. Estelle Ross, *Oliver Cromwell* (New York: Frederick A. Stokes Company, 1915), 110.
73. Charles Macfarlane, *The Comprehensive History of England,* vol. 2 (London: Blackie and Son, 1876), 576–77.
74. *The Parliamentary History of England,* vol. 3 (London: T. C. Hansard, 1808), 1267.
75. Christopher Hill, *God's Englishman: Oliver Cromwell and the English Revolution* (New York: Dial Press, 1970), 144.
76. T. B. Howell, ed., *Complete Collection of State Trials,* vol. 6 (London: T. C. Hansard, 1816), 814.

77. Titus Oates, *A True Narrative of the Horrid Plot and Conspiracy of the Popish Party Against the Life of His Sacred Majesty* (London: Thomas Parkhurst and Thomas Cockerill, 1679), page b.
78. David Hume, *The History of England,* vol. 8 (Oxford: D. A. Talboys, 1826), 70.
79. E. N. Williams, ed., *The Eighteenth Century Constitution: Documents and Commentary* (Cambridge: Cambridge University Press, 1978), 8.
80. David Hughes, *The British Chronicles,* vol. 1 (Westminster, MD: Heritage Books, 2007), 350.

CHAPTER 4: TO BEGIN THE WORLD OVER AGAIN

1. Mary Newton Stanard, *The Story of Bacon's Rebellion* (New York: Neale Publishing Company, 1907), 13.
2. Stanard, *Story of Bacon's Rebellion,* 13–14.
3. Fred Albert Shannon, *American Farmers' Movements* (New York: Van Nostrand, 1957), 113.
4. James D. Rice, *Tales from a Revolution: Bacon's Rebellion and the Transformation of Early America* (New York: Oxford University Press, 2012), 44.
5. David Saville Muzzey, *Readings in American History* (Boston: Ginn & Company, 1921), 33.
6. Frank E. Grizzard Jr. and D. Boyd Smith, *Jamestown Colony: A Political, Social, and Cultural History* (Santa Barbara, CA: ABC Clio, 2007), 250.
7. Grizzard and Smith, *Jamestown Colony,* 250.
8. Thomas Hariot, *A Briefe and True Report on the Found Land of Virginia* (Manchester, UK: A. Brothers, 1888), 7; Karen Ordahl Kupperman, *The Jamestown Project* (Cambridge, MA: Belknap Press of Harvard University Press, 2007), 253.
9. Linda M. Heywood and John K. Thornton, *Central Africans, Atlantic Creoles, and the Foundations of the Americas, 1585–1660* (Cambridge: Cambridge University Press, 2007), 7.
10. William Hand Browne, ed., *Proceedings of the Council of Maryland, 1667-8–1693* (Baltimore: Maryland Historical Society, 1887), 134.
11. Browne, *Proceedings of the Council of Maryland,* 137, 134, and 147.
12. Helen Ainslie Smith, *The Thirteen Colonies,* pt. 2 (New York: G. P. Putnam's Sons, 1901), 127.
13. J. Thomas Scharf, *History of Maryland,* vol. 1 (Baltimore: John B. Piet, 1879), 369.
14. Cotton Mather, *The Wonders of the Invisible World* (London: John Russell Smith, 1862), 61.
15. Mather, *Wonders of the Invisible World,* 78.
16. Francis J. Bremer, *John Winthrop: America's Forgotten Founding Father* (New York: Oxford University Press, 2003), 179.
17. David Hume, *Dialogues Concerning Natural Religion* (Edinburgh: William Blackwood and Sons, 1907), 37.

18. Thomas Jefferson, *The Thomas Jefferson Bible,* ed. Henry E. Jackson (New York: Boni and Liveright, 1923), 132.
19. Thomas Jefferson, *Memoir, Correspondence, and Miscellanies,* vol. 4, ed. T. J. Randolph (Charlottesville, VA: F. Carr and Co., 1829), 223.
20. Paul Henri Thiry, *The System of Nature,* vol. 1 (London: William Hodson, 1817), 17.
21. Immanuel Kant, *Perpetual Peace,* trans. Benjamin F. Trueblood (Boston: The American Peace Society, 1897), 6.
22. Benjamin Franklin, *The Select Works of Benjamin Franklin,* ed. Epes Sargent (Boston: Phillips, Sampson and Company, 1855), 192 and 193.
23. Franklin, *Select Works of Benjamin Franklin,* 192.
24. J. A. Leo Lemay, *The Life of Benjamin Franklin,* vol. 2, *Printer and Publisher, 1730–1747* (Philadelphia: University of Pennsylvania Press, 2006), 207.
25. Lisa Smith, *The First Great Awakening in Colonial American Newspapers* (Lanham, MD: Lexington Books, 2012), 16.
26. Jonathan Edwards, *Edwards on Revivals* (New York: Dunning & Spalding, 1832), 33.
27. Edwards, *Edwards on Revivals,* 89.
28. Adam Smith, *An Inquiry into the Nature and Causes of the Wealth of Nations* (Edinburgh: University Press, 1827), 169.
29. Adam Smith, *Essays* (London: Alex Murray & Co., 1872), 383–84; Smith, *Wealth of Nations,* 184.
30. Ruth Bloch, *Visionary Republic: Millennial Themes in American Thought, 1756–1800* (Cambridge: Cambridge University Press, 1985), 54.
31. Thomas Paine, *Common Sense* (New York: Peter Eckler, 1918), 57.
32. Paine, *Common Sense,* 1.
33. Paine, *Common Sense,* 36.
34. J. William Harris, *The Hanging of Thomas Jeremiah: A Free Black Man's Encounter with Liberty* (New Haven, CT: Yale University Press, 2009), 88.
35. James Iredell, *The Life and Correspondence of James Iredell,* vol. 1, ed. Griffith J. McRae (New York: D. Appleton and Co., 1857), 321.
36. T. S. Arthur and W. H. Carpenter, *The History of Georgia, from Its Earliest Settlement to the Present Time* (Philadelphia: Lippincott, Grambo & Co., 1852), 56.
37. Lawrence Celani, "'No Scheme More Monstrous Could Have Been Invented': Slave Election Ceremonies and the New York Slave Conspiracy of 1741," in *Black Resistance in the Americas,* eds. D. A. Dunkley and Stephanie Shonekan (New York: Routledge, 2019), 91 and 86.
38. *The Declaration of Independence and Constitution of the United States of America* (New York: R. Spalding, 1868), 15.
39. Benjamin H. Irwin, *Clothed in Robes of Sovereignty: The Continental Congress and People Out of Doors* (New York: Oxford University Press, 2014), 141.
40. Ignatius Sancho, *Letters of the Late Ignatius Sancho, an African,* vol. 1 (Dublin: Pat. Byrne, 1784), 271.
41. René Huchon, *George Crabbe and His Times, 1754–1832,* trans. Frederick Clarke (New York: Dutton and Co., 1907), 103.

42. Cesare Beccaria, *An Essay on Crimes and Punishments* (Philadelphia: Philip H. Nicklin, 1819), 15.
43. Beccaria, *Essay on Crimes and Punishments,* 16.
44. Jeremy Bentham, *The Works of Jeremy Bentham,* pt. 2 (Edinburgh: William Tait, 1843), 563.
45. Jeremy Bentham, *An Introduction to the Principles of Morals and Legislation* (Oxford: Clarendon Press, 1879), 70.
46. Jeremy Bentham, *Panopticon* (Dublin: Thomas Byrne, 1791), 3.
47. Bentham, *Panopticon,* 2.
48. *Historical Records of New South Wales,* vol. 1, pt. 2 (Sydney: Charles Potter, 1892), 17.
49. Alan Frost, *Dreams of a Pacific Empire: Sir George Young's Proposal for a Colonization of New South Wales* (Sydney: Resolution Press, 1980), 41.
50. James Cook, *Captain Cook's Voyages Round the World* (London: Thomas Nelson and Sons, 1897), 170.
51. James Bonwick, *First Twenty Years of Australia* (London: Sampson Low, Marston, Searle, & Rivington, 1882), 181.
52. Anil Chandra Banerjee, *The Agrarian System of Bengal: 1582–1793* (Calcutta: K. P. Bagchi, 1980), 114.
53. *The Parliamentary History of England from the Earliest Period to the Year 1803,* vol. 17 (London: T. C. Hansard, 1813), 835.
54. George Bruce Malleson, *Life of Warren Hastings* (London: Chapman & Hall, 1894), 475.
55. Edmund Burke, *The Speeches of the Right Hon. Edmund Burke* (Dublin: James Duffy, 1853), 84.
56. Burke, *Speeches of the Right Hon. Edmund Burke,* 122 and 80.
57. Edmund Burke, *The Correspondence of Edmund Burke,* vol. 7, eds. P. J. Marshall and John A. Woods (Cambridge: Cambridge University Press, 1968), 170 and 489.
58. Mary Wollstonecraft, *A Vindication of the Rights of Men* (London: J. Johnson, 1790), 8 and 18.
59. Edmund Burke, *Reflections on the Revolution in France* (London: Macmillan and Co., 1890), 66.
60. Burke, *Reflections on the Revolution in France,* 165.
61. John Robison, *Proofs of a Conspiracy Against All the Religions and Governments of Europe* (London: T. Cadell, 1798), 11 and 103.
62. Augustin Barruel, *Memoirs, Illustrating the History of Jacobinism* (London: T. Burton and Co., 1797), xvi.
63. Barruel, *Memoirs,* xviii, 24.
64. Edmund Burke, *The Correspondence of Edmund Burke,* vol. 10 (Cambridge: Cambridge University Press, 1978), 39.
65. Historical Manuscripts Commission, *Fourteenth Report, Appendix, Part V: The Manuscripts of J. B. Fortescue,* vol. 2 (London: Her Majesty's Stationery Office, 1894), 315.

66. *The Reports of the Committee of Secrecy of the House of Commons,* vol. 2 (Edinburgh: Bell & Bradfute, 1794), 76–77.
67. William David Evans, ed., *A Collection of Statutes Connected with the General Administration of the Law,* vol. 5 (London: Saunders and Benning, 1829), 108.
68. Adrian Shubert, "Private Initiative in Law Enforcement: Association for the Prosecution of Felons, 1744–1856," in *Policing and Punishment in Nineteenth Century Britain,* ed. Victor Bailey (New Brunswick, NJ: Rutgers University Press, 1981), 28, 34.
69. Elizabeth Sparrow, "Secret Service Under Pitt's Administrations, 1792–1806," *History* 83, no. 270 (April 1998), 283.
70. Elizabeth Sparrow, *Secret Service: British Agents in France, 1792–1815* (Woodbridge, UK: Boydell Press, 1999), 19.
71. John Reeves, *Thoughts on the English Government* (London: J. Owen, 1795), 6.
72. Reeves, *Thoughts on the English Government,* 2.
73. *Proceedings of the Association for Preserving Liberty and Property Against Republicans and Levellers* (London: J. Sewell, 1793), 3.
74. *Proceedings of the Association for Preserving Liberty and Property,* 2.
75. Charles K. McHarg, *Life of Prince Talleyrand* (New York: C. Scribner, 1857), 77, 74, and 76.
76. Simon Schama, *Citizens: A Chronicle of the French Revolution* (New York: Alfred A. Knopf, 1989), 511.
77. William Doyle, *The Oxford History of the French Revolution* (Oxford: Clarendon Press, 1989), 16; Matilda Betham-Edwards, ed., *Arthur Young's Travels in France During the Years 1787, 1788, 1789* (London: George Bell & Sons, 1892), 27.
78. Steven L. Kaplan, *The Famine Plot Persuasion in Eighteenth Century France* (Philadelphia: American Philosophical Society, 1982), 1 and 6.
79. Alison Johnson, *Louis XVI and the French Revolution* (Jefferson, NC: McFarland & Co., 2013), 76.
80. *Translations and Reprints from the Original Sources of European History,* vol. 1 (Philadelphia: University of Pennsylvania, 1902), 6, 7.
81. Mary Wollstonecraft, *A Vindication of the Rights of Woman* (London: J. Johnson, 1792), 2 and 6.
82. Dominique Gondineau, *The Women of Paris and Their French Revolution,* trans. Katherine Streip (Berkeley: University of California Press, 1988), 170.
83. Marie-Olympes de Gouges, "Declaration of the Rights of Women and Citizens," in *Princeton Readings in Political Thought,* ed. Mitchell Cohen (Princeton, NJ: Princeton University Press, 2018), 342.
84. Sanja Perovic, *The Calendar in Revolutionary France: Perceptions of Time in Literature, Culture, Politics* (Cambridge: Cambridge University Press, 2012), 112.
85. Perovic, *Calendar in Revolutionary France,* 113.
86. Noah Webster, *A Collection of Papers on Political, Literary and Moral Subjects* (New York: Webster & Clark, 1843), 33.

87. Hermann Lieb, *The Foes of the French Revolution* (Chicago: Belford, Clarke & Co., 1889), 198.
88. George Henry Allen, *The French Revolution,* vol. 2 (Philadelphia: George Barrie's Sons, 1923), 283; William Doyle, *The Oxford History of the French Revolution* (Oxford: Clarendon Press, 1989), 192; Ernest Belfort, *Jean Paul Marat* (London: Charing Cross Publishing, 1879), 58.
89. F. Bayford Harrison, *The Contemporary History of the French Revolution* (London: Rivington's, 1889), 146.
90. Graeme Fife, *The Terror: The Shadow of the Guillotine: France 1792–1794* (New York: St. Martin's Press, 2004), 415.
91. George Henry Lewes, *The Life of Maximilien Robespierre* (London: Chapman and Hall, 1899), 327.
92. Jonathan Israel, *Revolutionary Ideas: An Intellectual History of the French Revolution from "The Rights of Man" to Robespierre* (Princeton, NJ: Princeton University Press, 2015), 569.
93. Lewes, *Life of Maximilien Robespierre,* 337.
94. Lewes, *Life of Maximilien Robespierre,* 338.
95. Lewes, *Life of Maximilien Robespierre,* 341.
96. Adolphe Thiers, *The History of the French Revolution,* trans. Frederick Shoberl, vol. 3 (Philadelphia: Carey and Hart, 1842), 13.
97. Lewes, *Life of Maximilien Robespierre,* 346–47.
98. Schama, *Citizens: A Chronicle of the French Revolution*, 834.
99. Doyle, *Oxford History of the French Revolution*, 277.
100. Jan Ten Brink, *Robespierre and the Red Terror,* trans. J. Hedeman (London: Hutchinson & Co., 1899), 34.
101. John S. C. Abbott, *The French Revolution of 1789,* vol. 2 (New York: Harper & Brothers, 1887), 388.
102. Terry Pinkard, *Hegel: A Biography* (Cambridge: Cambridge University Press, 2000), 228.
103. G. W. F. Hegel, *The Philosophy of History,* trans. J. Sibree (New York: American Home Library Company, 1902), 64.
104. Hegel, *Philosophy of History,* 77–78.
105. Clive Emsley, *Napoleon: Conquest, Reform, Reorganisation* (London: Routledge, 2015), 129.
106. David P. Jordan, *Napoleon and the Revolution* (New York: Palgrave Macmillan, 2012), 71.
107. Napoleon Bonaparte, *Napoleon: In His Own Words,* ed. Jules Bertaut, trans. Herbert Edward Law and Charles Lincoln Rhodes (Chicago: A. C. McClurg & Co., 1916), 48–49.
108. Bonaparte, *Napoleon,* 49–50.
109. J. S. C. Abbott, *Life of Napoleon Bonaparte* (London: Beeton, 1860), 266.
110. Napoleon Bonaparte, *The Bonaparte Letters and Despatches,* vol. 1 (London: Saunders & Otley, 1846), 330.

111. Bonaparte, *Bonaparte Letters,* vol. 1, 279.
112. Mary H. Allies, *Pius the Seventh, 1800–1823* (London: Burns & Oates, 1897), 54.
113. Napoleon Bonaparte, *The Mind of Napoleon,* ed. J. Christopher Herold (New York: Columbia University Press, 1955), 106; J. Holland Rose, *Napoleon Studies* (London: George Bell and Sons, 1906), 107.
114. Martyn Lyons, *Napoleon Bonaparte and the Legacy of the French Revolution* (New York: Macmillan, 1994), 82.
115. Cecil B. Hartley, *Life of the Empress Josephine* (Philadelphia: Porter & Coates, 1870), 246.
116. Carolyn E. Fick, *The Making of Haiti: The Saint Domingue Revolution from Below* (Knoxville: University of Tennessee Press, 1990), 93.
117. Merry Wiesner-Hanks, *Early Modern Europe, 1450–1789* (Cambridge: Cambridge University Press, 2013), 509.
118. Caryn Cossé Bell, *Revolution, Romanticism, and the Afro-Creole Protest Tradition in Louisiana, 1718–1868* (Baton Rouge: Louisiana State University Press, 1997), 20.
119. Voltaire, *The Works of M. de Voltaire,* vol. 19 (London: S. Crowder, 1780), 89.
120. Voltaire, *The Whole Prose Romances of François-Marie Arouet de Voltaire,* vol. 2 (London: Walpole Press, 1900), 40.
121. Johann Friedrich Blumenbach, *The Anthropological Treatises of Johann Friedrich Blumenbach,* trans. Thomas Bendyshe (London: Longman, Green, Longman, Roberts, & Green, 1865), 269.
122. George Louis Leclerc, *Buffon's Natural History,* vol. 5 (London: The Proprietor, 1797), 130; Georges Louis Leclerc, *A Natural History of the Globe and of Man,* vol. 1 (London: Thomas Tegg, 1831), 175 and 177.
123. Laurent Dubois, *Avengers of the New World: The Story of the Haitian Revolution* (Cambridge, MA: Belknap Press of Harvard University Press, 2004), 95.
124. George Washington, *The Papers of George Washington: September 1791–February 1793* (Charlottesville: University Press of Virginia, 2000), 339; Timothy M. Matthewson, "George Washington's Policy Toward the Haitian Revolution," *Diplomatic History* 3, no. 3 (1979), 321.
125. George Washington, *The Writings of George Washington,* vol. 10, ed. Jared Sparks (Boston: Russell, Shattuck, and Williams, 1836), 194.
126. Jean-Bertrand Aristide, ed., *The Haitian Revolution* (London: Verso Books, 2019), 47.
127. Philippe R. Girard, *The Slaves Who Defeated Napoleon: Toussaint Louverture and the Haitian War of Independence, 1801–1804* (Tuscaloosa: University of Alabama Press, 2011), 46.
128. Napoleon Bonaparte, *Memoirs of the History of France,* vol. 1 (London: Henry Colburn and Co., 1823), 202.
129. Percy Waxman, *The Black Napoleon: The Story of Toussaint Louverture* (New York: Harcourt, Brace, 1931), 289; Girard, *Slaves Who Defeated Napoleon,* 210.
130. J. N. Leger, *Haiti: Her History and Her Detractors* (New York: Neale Publishing Company, 1907), 182.

131. Mary A. Renda, *Taking Haiti: 1915–1940* (Chapel Hill: University of North Carolina Press, 2001), 99.
132. Brenda Gayle Plummer, *Haiti and the United States: The Psychological Moment* (Athens: University of Georgia Press, 1992), 108.

CHAPTER 5: A MAN IS BUT A MACHINE FOR CREATING VALUE

1. Alan Palmer, *Alexander I: Tsar of War and Peace* (London: Weidenfeld & Nicholson, 1974), 126.
2. Jose de Maistre, *Considerations on France,* trans. Richard A. Lebrun (Cambridge: Cambridge University Press, 2003), 41.
3. William Howitt, "The Baronness Barbara Juliana von Krüdener," *Spiritual Magazine* 4 (1869), 16.
4. Jovan Byford, *Conspiracy Theories: A Critical Introduction* (Basingstoke, UK: Palgrave Macmillan, 2011), 47.
5. Paula E. Hyman, *The Jews of Modern France* (Berkeley: University of California Press, 1998), 46.
6. Prince Metternich, *Memoirs of Prince Metternich, 1815–1829,* vol. 3 (New York: Charles Scribner's Sons, 1881), 537–38.
7. Metternich, *Memoirs of Prince Metternich,* 538.
8. Metternich, *Memoirs of Prince Metternich,* 471.
9. Mack Walker, ed., *Metternich's Europe* (London: Macmillan & Co., 1968), 64.
10. Walker, *Metternich's Europe,* 65.
11. Robert J. Goldstein, *Political Repression in 19th Century Europe* (New York: Routledge, 2010), 36.
12. Adam Zamoyski, *Phantom Terror: The Threat of Revolution and the Repression of Liberty, 1789–1848* (London: William Collins, 2014), 210.
13. James Harvey Robinson, *The Restoration and the European Policy of Metternich, 1814–1820* (Philadelphia: Dept. of History of the University of Pennsylvania, 1820), 17.
14. *Restoration and the European Policy of Metternich,* 18.
15. Walker, *Metternich's Europe,* 71.
16. Andrew C. Isenberg, *The Destruction of the Bison: An Environmental History, 1750–1920* (Cambridge: Cambridge University Press, 2000), 106.
17. J. M. Baltimore, "In the Prime of the Buffalo," *Overland Monthly* 14, no. 83 (November 1889), 515.
18. Donna Feir, Rob Gillezeau, and Maggie Jones, "The Slaughter of the Bison and Reversal of Fortunes on the Great Plains," University of Victoria Economics Department Discussion Paper DDP1701, July 31, 2017, https://www.uvic.ca/socialsciences/economics/assets/docs/discussion/DDP1701.pdf; Isenberg, *Destruction of the Bison,* 12.
19. John Stuart Mill, *Principles of Political Economy* (New York: D. Appleton and Co., 1891), 516.
20. Mill, *Principles of Political Economy,* 126.

21. David Ricardo, *On the Principles of Political Economy and Taxation* (London: John Murray, 1821), 468.
22. Andrew Ure, *The Philosophy of Manufactures* (London: Charles Knight, 1835), 368–69.
23. Frederick Engels, *The Condition of the Working-Class in England in 1844* (London: Swan Sonnenschein & Co., 1892), 24.
24. Engels, *Condition of the Working-Class in England*, 26.
25. Engels, *Condition of the Working-Class in England*, 31.
26. Alexander Hamilton, *Report on the Subject of Manufactures* (Philadelphia: William Brown, 1827), 21.
27. John Brown, *A Memoir of Robert Blincoe, an Orphan Boy* (Manchester, UK: J. Doherty, 1832), 26.
28. Ure, *Philosophy of Manufactures*, 301.
29. Ure, *Philosophy of Manufactures*, vii.
30. John McVickar, *Outlines of Political Economy* (New York: Wilder & Campbell, 1825), 187.
31. Stewart Davenport, *Friends of the Unrighteous Mammon: Northern Christians and Market Capitalism, 1815–1860* (Chicago: University of Chicago Press, 2008), 94.
32. John Ellis, *The Social History of the Machine Gun* (Baltimore: Johns Hopkins Press, 1986), 86.
33. Ernest N. Bennett, *The Downfall of the Dervishes* (London: Methuen & Co., 1898), 167 and 172.
34. Evelyn Ashley, ed., *The Life of Henry John Temple, Viscount of Palmerston: 1846–1865*, vol. 1 (London: Richard Bentley and Son, 1877), 62–63.
35. Ashley, *Life of Henry John Temple*, 109.
36. *The Treaty of Nanking* (Macao: Office of the Chinese Repository, 1844), 6.
37. James Rochfort Maguire, *Cecil Rhodes: A Biography and Appreciation* (London: Chapman Hall, 1897), 50.
38. F. Verschoyle, *Cecil Rhodes: His Political Life and Speeches* (London: George Bell and Sons, 1900), 380–83.
39. Winston Churchill, *The Boer War* (New York: Rosetta Books, 2013), 60–61.
40. Churchill, *Boer War*, 99.
41. John Boje, *An Imperfect Occupation: Enduring the South African War* (Urbana: University of Illinois Press, 2015), 108.
42. Emily Hobhouse, *The Brunt of the War and Where It Fell* (London: Methuen & Co., 1902), 123.
43. W. de Puy, *Louis Napoleon and the Bonaparte Family* (New York: Miller, Orton, and Mulligan, 1856), 291.
44. De Puy, *Louis Napoleon and the Bonaparte Family*, 378–79.
45. De Puy, *Louis Napoleon and the Bonaparte Family*, 378.
46. Henry Blumenthal, *A Reappraisal of Franco-American Relations, 1830–1871* (Chapel Hill: University of North Carolina Press, 1959), 166.
47. Otto von Bismarck, *Bismarck: The Man and the Statesman* (London: Smith, Elder, and Co., 1898), 56.

48. Jonathan Steinberg, *Bismarck: A Life* (Oxford: Oxford University Press, 2011), 181.
49. Auguste Blanqui, *The Blanqui Reader: Political Writings, 1830–1880* (London: Verso Books, 2018), 223.
50. Frank Jellinek, *The Paris Commune of 1871* (New York: Grosset & Dunlap, 1965), 174.
51. Karl Marx, *The Paris Commune* (New York: New York Labor News Company, 1902), 80.
52. Karl Marx, *Capital,* vol. 1 (New York: The Modern Library, 1906), 784.
53. Karl Marx and Frederick Engels, *Manifesto of the Communist Party* (Chicago: Charles H. Kerr, 1906), 12.
54. Marx and Engels, *Manifesto of the Communist Party,* 19.
55. Marx and Engels, *Manifesto of the Communist Party,* 21–22.
56. Johann Georg Hamann, *Writings on Philosophy and Language,* trans. Kenneth Haynes (Cambridge: Cambridge University Press, 2007), 207.
57. Mary Shelley, *Frankenstein, or The Modern Prometheus* (Boston: Sever, Francis, and Co., 1869), 45.
58. William Blake, *Milton* (London: W. Blake, 1907), xix.
59. Emma Hardinge, *Modern American Spiritualism* (New York: Emma Hardinge, 1870), 9.
60. H. P. Blavatsky, *The Secret Doctrine,* vol. 2 (Point Loma, CA: Aryan Theosophical Press, 1909), 421.
61. Charles Darwin, *The Descent of Man,* vol. 1 (New York: D. Appleton and Company, 1872), 193.
62. Darwin, *Descent of Man,* vol. 1, 161–62.
63. Darwin, *Descent of Man,* vol. 1, 162.
64. T. R. Malthus, *An Essay on the Principle of Population,* vol. 2 (London: J. Johnson, 1806), 95.
65. Herbert Spencer, *The Man Versus the State* (New York: Mitchell Kennerley, 1916), 68–69.
66. Francis Galton, *Inquiries into Human Faculty and Its Development* (London: Macmillan & Co., 1883), 2.
67. George Washington, *The Diaries of George Washington, 1748–1799,* vol. 4, ed. John C. Fitzpatrick (Boston: Houghton Mifflin Company, 1925), 215.
68. Aleine Austin, *Matthew Lyon, New Man of the Democratic Revolution, 1749–1822* (University Park: Pennsylvania State University Press, 1981), 80.
69. Carol Sue Humphrey, *The Revolutionary Era: Primary Documents on Events from 1776 to 1800* (Westport, CT: Greenwood Press, 2003), 236.
70. George Washington, *The Writings of George Washington,* vol. 12, ed. Worthington Chauncey Ford (New York: G. P. Putnam's Sons, 1891), 491.
71. Washington, *Writings of George Washington,* vol. 12, 486.
72. Marilyn Michaud, *Republicans and the American Gothic* (Cardiff: University of Wales Press, 2009), 110.

73. Vernon Stauffer, *New England and the Bavarian Illuminati* (New York: Russell & Russell, 1967), 230–31.
74. Timothy Dwight, *The Duty of Americans, at the Present Crisis* (New Haven, CT: Thomas and Samuel Green, 1798), 8.
75. Dwight, *Duty of Americans*, 18.
76. Brian Farmer, *American Conservatism: History, Theory, and Practice* (Newcastle, UK: Cambridge Scholars Press, 2005), 147.
77. Thomas Jefferson, *The Writings of Thomas Jefferson*, vol. 4 (New York: John C. Riker, 1854), 472.
78. Jefferson, *Writings of Thomas Jefferson*, vol. 4, 472–73.
79. Jefferson, *Writings of Thomas Jefferson*, vol. 4, 475.
80. Wendell H. Oswalt, *This Land Was Theirs: A Study of the North American Indian* (New York: John Wiley & Son Inc., 1967), 521.
81. Andrew Jackson, *Annual Messages, Veto Messages, Protest & c. of Andrew Jackson* (Baltimore: Edward J. Coale, 1835), 20.
82. Lewis H. Morgan, *League of the Ho-De-No-San-Nee*, vol. 2 (New York: Dodd, Mead and Company, 1901), 108.
83. Morgan, *League of the Ho-De-No-San-Nee*, vol. 2, 109.
84. Mahmood Mamdani, *Neither Settler nor Native: The Making and Unmaking of Permanent Minorities* (Cambridge, MA: Harvard University Press, 2020), 58.
85. John Corrigan and Lynn S. Neal, eds., *Religious Intolerance in America* (Chapel Hill: University of North Carolina Press, 2010), 141.
86. *Fifty-Seventh Annual Report of the Commissioner of Indian Affairs* (Washington, DC: US Government Printing Office, 1888), lxxxix.
87. Tyler Anbinder, *Nativism and Slavery: The Northern Know Nothings and the Politics of the 1850s* (New York: Oxford University Press, 1992), 46.
88. Maria Monk, *Awful Disclosures* (New York: Maria Monk, 1836), 156.
89. Matthew J. Clavin, *Toussaint Louverture and the American Civil War: The Promise and Peril of a Second Haitian Revolution* (Philadelphia: University of Pennsylvania Press, 2010), 18.
90. Hannah Spahn, *Thomas Jefferson, Time, and History* (Charlottesville: University of Virginia Press, 2011), 178.
91. David Walker, *Appeal in Four Articles, Together with a Preamble, to the Coloured Citizens of the World* (Boston: David Walker, 1830), 5.
92. Walker, *Appeal in Four Articles*, 5–6.
93. Lucretia Mott, *Discourse on Woman* (Philadelphia: T. B. Peterson, 1850), 14.
94. Booker T. Washington, *Frederick Douglass* (Philadelphia: George W. Jacobs & Company, 1907), 136.
95. Edward Alfred Pollard, "Hints on Southern Civilization," *Southern Literary Messenger* 32, no. 4 (April 1861), 309–10.
96. James Henry Hammond, *Remarks of Mr. Hammond of South Carolina* (Washington, DC: Duff Green, 1836), 5.
97. Hammond, *Remarks of Mr. Hammond*, 11.

98. Emerson David Fite, *The Presidential Campaign of 1860* (Port Washington, NY: Kennikat Press, 1911), 165.
99. Henry Ward Beecher, *Patriotic Addresses* (New York: Fords, Howard, and Hulbert, 1887), 168.
100. James Henley Thornwell, *The Collected Writings of James Henley Thornwell,* vol. 4 (Bedford, MA: Applewood Books, 1871), 414.
101. Thornwell, *Collected Writings,* vol. 4, 405.
102. Stephen V. Ash, *When the Yankees Came: Conflict and Chaos in the Occupied South, 1861–1865* (Chapel Hill: University of North Carolina Press, 1995), 69.
103. Ash, *When the Yankees Came,* 8, 11.
104. S. F. Platanov, *History of Russia,* trans. E. Aronsberg (New York: Macmillan, 1928), 359.
105. Nicholas V. Riasanovsky, *Nicholas I and Official Nationality in Russia, 1825–1855* (Berkeley: University of California Press, 1959), 74.
106. Friedrich Nietzsche, *The Will to Power,* vol. 1, trans. Anthony M. Ludovici (New York: Macmillan, 1924), 5.
107. Martin Katz, *Mikhail N. Katkov: A Political Biography, 1818–1887* (The Hague: Mouton & Co., 1966), 75.
108. Nikolai G. Tchernuishevsky, *A Vital Question; or, What Is to Be Done?* (New York: Thomas Y. Crowell & Co., 1886), 460.
109. Mikhail Bakunin, *God and the State* (New York: Cosimo Classics, 2008), 16; Carl Landauer, *European Socialism,* vol. 1 (Berkeley: University of California Press, 1960), 403.
110. Sergey Nechayev, *Catechism of a Revolutionist* (Pattern Books, 2020), 6.
111. Warren Bartlett Walsh, *Russia and the Soviet Union: A Modern History* (Ann Arbor: University of Michigan Press, 1958), 264.
112. Richard Pipes, *The Russian Revolution* (New York: Vintage Books, 1991), 142.
113. S. M. Dubnow, *History of the Jews in Russia and Poland,* vol. 2 (Philadelphia: Jewish Publication Society of America, 1918), 261.
114. Dubnow, *History of the Jews in Russia and Poland,* 270.
115. Charters Wynn, *Workers, Strikes, and Pogroms: The Donbass-Dnepr Bend in Late Imperial Russia, 1870–1905* (Princeton, NJ: Princeton University Press, 1992), 218.
116. Michael F. Hamm, *Kiev: A Portrait, 1800–1917* (Princeton, NJ: Princeton University Press, 1996), 125.
117. Simon Rabinovitch, *Jewish Rights, National Rights: Nationalism and Autonomy in Late Imperial and Revolutionary Russia* (Stanford, CA: Stanford University Press, 2014), 36.
118. Sergei Nilus, *Protocols of the Learned Elders of Zion,* trans. Victor E. Marsden (Reedy, WV: Liberty Bell Publications, 1970), 19.
119. Nilus, *Protocols of the Learned Elders of Zion,* 48, 16, and 24.
120. Shlomo Lambroza, "The Pogroms of 1903–1906," in *Pogroms: Anti-Jewish Violence in Modern Russian History,* eds. John D. Klier and Shlomo Lambroza (Cambridge: Cambridge University Press, 1992), 225.

121. David Cannadine, *Ornamentalism: How the British Saw Their Empire* (Oxford: Oxford University Press, 2002), 111.
122. Rudyard Kipling, *The Five Nations* (New York: Doubleday, Page & Company, 1914), 214–15.
123. "America at the Jubilee," *New York Times,* June 24, 1897, 6.
124. Sam W. Haynes, *James K. Polk and the Expansionist Impulse* (New York: Longman, 1997), 102.
125. Charles Darwin, *The Descent of Man,* vol. 1 (New York: D. Appleton and Company, 1871), 172.
126. Darwin, *Descent of Man,* vol. 1, 173.
127. John R. Dickinson, ed., *Speeches; Correspondence, Etc. of the Late Daniel S. Dickinson,* vol. 1 (New York: G. P. Putnam & Sons, 1867), 233 and 349.
128. Josiah Strong, *Our Country: Its Possible Future and Its Present Crisis* (New York: The Baker & Taylor Co., 1885), 159.
129. Kipling, *The Five Nations,* 79.
130. Stuart Creighton Miller, *Benevolent Assimilation: The American Conquest of the Philippines, 1899–1903* (New Haven, CT: Yale University Press, 1982), 24.
131. Albert J. Beveridge, *The Meaning of the Times* (Indianapolis: Bobbs-Merrill Company, 1908), 42.
132. Beveridge, *Meaning of the Times,* 43.
133. Beveridge, *Meaning of the Times,* 43–44.
134. Cecil Rhodes, *The Last Will and Testament of Cecil Rhodes,* ed. W. T. Stead (London: "Review of Reviews" Office, 1907), 98.
135. Rhodes, *Last Will and Testament,* 59.
136. Rhodes, *Last Will and Testament,* 73.
137. H. G. Wells, *Anticipations* (New York: Harper & Brothers, 1902), 299.
138. Wells, *Anticipations,* 340.
139. Wells, *Anticipations,* 342.
140. John R. Dos Passos, *The Anglo-Saxon Century* (New York: G. P. Putnam's Sons, 1903), ix–x.
141. Dos Passos, *Anglo-Saxon Century,* x.

CHAPTER 6: A VENEER OVER SAVAGERY

1. Demetrius C. Boulger, *The Congo State* (London: W. Thacker & Co., 1898), 393.
2. Maurizio Viroli, *For Love of Country: An Essay on Patriotism and Nationalism* (Oxford: Clarendon Press, 2003), 117–18.
3. Viroli, *For Love of Country,* 122.
4. Christopher J. Berry, *Hume, Hegel and Human Nature* (The Hague: Martinus Nijhoff Publishers, 1982), 41.
5. Houston Stewart Chamberlain, *The Foundations of the Nineteenth Century,* vol. 1, trans. John Lees (New York: John Lane, 1911), 494–95.
6. Chamberlain, *Foundations of the Nineteenth Century,* vol. 1, 351.

7. Ramesh Dutta Dikshit, *Political Geography: The Spatiality of Politics* (New Delhi: Tata McGraw-Hill Publishing, 2000), 19.
8. Jeremy Noakes, "Hitler and 'Lebensraum' in the East," BBC, March 30, 2011, https://www.bbc.co.uk/history/worldwars/wwtwo/hitler_lebensraum_01.shtml.
9. Lawrence Sondhaus, *World War One: The Global Revolution* (Cambridge: Cambridge University Press, 2001), 10.
10. Mahmood Mamdani, *When Victims Become Killers: Colonialism, Nativism, and the Genocide in Rwanda* (Princeton, NJ: Princeton University Press, 2001), 11.
11. Jeremy Sarkin, *Germany's Genocide of the Herero: Kaiser Wilhelm II, His General, His Settlers, His Soldiers* (Cape Town: UCT Press, 2011), 127.
12. Sarkin, *Germany's Genocide of the Herero,* 137.
13. Sarkin, *Germany's Genocide of the Herero,* 132.
14. Mohammad Shahabuddin, *Ethnicity and International Law: Histories, Politics and Practices* (Cambridge: Cambridge University Press, 2016), 75.
15. Clarence Lusane, *Hitler's Black Victims: The Historical Experiences of Afro-Germans, European Blacks, Africans, and African Americans in the Nazi Era* (New York: Routledge, 2003), 45.
16. Kent Redding, *Making Race, Making Power: North Carolina's Road to Disfranchisement* (Urbana: University of Illinois, 2003), 128.
17. J. G. de Roulhac Hamilton, *History of North Carolina,* vol. 3 (Chicago: Lewis Publishing Company, 1919), 293.
18. Charles H. Pearson, *National Life and Character: A Forecast* (London: Macmillan and Co., 1893), 31.
19. Pearson, *National Life and Character,* 223.
20. Marilyn Lake and Henry Reynolds, *Drawing the Global Colour Line: White Men's Countries and the International Challenge of Racial Equality* (Cambridge: Cambridge University Press, 2008), 112.
21. Theodore Roosevelt, "Duties of the Citizen," *Independent* 68 (January–June 1910), 894.
22. Betsy L. Nies, *Eugenic Fantasies: Racial Ideology in the Literature and Popular Culture of the 1920's* (New York: Routledge, 2002), 70.
23. John A. Mallory, ed., *United States Compiled Statutes,* vol. 10 (St. Paul, MN: West Publishing Co., 1917), 12762.
24. Susan Ware, ed., *American Women's Suffrage* (New York: Library of America, 2020), 283.
25. John Tracy Ellis, *The Life of James Cardinal Gibbons: Archbishop of Baltimore, 1834–1921,* vol. 2 (Milwaukee: Bruce Publishing Company, 1952), 540.
26. *The Case Against Woman Suffrage: A Manual* (New York: The Man-Suffrage Association, 1915), 3.
27. *Case Against Woman Suffrage,* 12.
28. Ida Husted Harper, *The Life and Work of Susan B. Anthony,* vol. 2 (Indianapolis: Hollenbeck Press, 1898), 984.

29. *An Account of the Proceedings on the Trial of Susan B. Anthony* (Rochester, NY: Daily Democrat and Chronicle Book Print, 1874), 83.
30. Frederick Winslow Taylor, *The Principles of Scientific Management* (New York: Harper & Brothers, 1911), 7–8.
31. Michael Kimaid, *Modernity, Metatheory, and the Temporal-Spatial Divide* (New York: Routledge, 2015), 90.
32. Woodrow Wilson, *The Essential Political Writings,* ed. Ronald J. Pestritto (Lanham, MD: Lexington Books, 2005), 229.
33. Charles Benedict Davenport, *Heredity in Relation to Eugenics* (New York: Henry Holt and Company, 1911), iii.
34. Charles Benedict Davenport, *Eugenics: The Science of Human Improvement by Better Breeding* (New York: Henry Holt and Company, 1910), 34.
35. Madison Grant, *The Passing of the Great Race* (New York: Charles Scribner's Sons, 1919), 263.
36. Grant, *Passing of the Great Race,* 5 and 47.
37. Christine Rosen, *Preaching Eugenics: Religious Leaders and the American Eugenics Movement* (Oxford: Oxford University Press, 2004), 60.
38. Chedomille Mijatovich, *A Royal Tragedy* (New York: Dodd, Mead & Co., 1907), 207.
39. Gordon Martel, *Origins of the First World War* (London: Routledge, 2003), 103.
40. Frank C. Zagare, *The Games of July: Explaining the Great War* (Ann Arbor: University of Michigan Press, 2011), 26; Holger H. Herwig, "Germany," in *The Origins of World War I,* eds. Richard F. Hamilton and Holger H. Herwig (Cambridge: Cambridge University Press, 2003), 172.
41. Herwig, "Germany," 177.
42. A. W. Ward and G. P. Gooch, eds., *The Cambridge History of British Foreign Policy, 1783–1919,* vol. 3 (New York: Macmillan, 1923), 507.
43. George Tomkyns Chesney, *The Battle of Dorking* (Edinburgh: William Blackwood and Sons, 1871), 62.
44. H. G. Wells, *The War of the Worlds* (Leipzig: Bernhard Tauchnitz, 1898), 11.
45. William Le Queux, *The Invasion of 1910* (London: Eveleigh Nash, 1906), 356 and 395.
46. Winston Churchill, *The World Crisis* (New York: Charles Scribner's Sons, 1923), 102.
47. Arthur Marder, *From the Dreadnought to Scapa Flow: The Royal Navy in the Fischer Era,* vol. 1 (Annapolis, MD: Naval Institute Press, 2013), 272.
48. Ishaan Tharoor, "The Other Assassination That Led Up to World War I," *Washington Post,* July 31, 2014, https://www.washingtonpost.com/news/world views/wp/2014/07/31/the-other-assassination-that-led-up-to-world-war-i/.
49. Frederick Brown, *For the Soul of France: Culture Wars in the Age of Dreyfus* (New York: Knopf, 2010), 173.
50. Léon Daudet, *Memoirs,* trans. Arthur Kingsland Griggs (New York: Dial Press, 1925), 271 and 288.

51. Jan Bloch, *The Future of War in Its Technical, Economic, and Political Relations* (Boston: Ginn & Company, 1982), 6.
52. Adam Hochschild, *To End All Wars: A Story of Loyalty and Rebellion, 1914–1918* (Boston: Houghton Mifflin Harcourt, 2011), xii.
53. George Robb, *British Culture and the First World War* (London: Palgrave Macmillan, 2002), 110.
54. Sigmund Freud, *Reflections on War and Death* (New York: Moffat, Yard and Company, 1918), 4–5.
55. Freud, *Reflections on War and Death,* 16.
56. George Lynch, *The War of the Civilisations* (London: Longmans, Green, and Co., 1901), 142.
57. Robert K. Massie, *Nicholas and Alexandra: The Fall of the Romanov Dynasty* (New York: The Modern Library, 2012), 331.
58. Catherine Merridale, *Red Fortress: History and Illusion in the Kremlin* (New York: Metropolitan Books, 2013), 270.
59. Massie, *Nicholas and Alexandra,* 425.
60. Vladimir Lenin, *Lenin on Politics and Revolution: Selected Writings,* ed. James E. Connor (New York: Pegasus, 1965), 113–15.
61. Lenin, *Lenin on Politics and Revolution,* 126.
62. E. Victor Wolfenstein, *Revolutionary Personality: Lenin, Trotsky, Gandhi* (Princeton, NJ: Princeton University Press, 1971), 243.
63. August H. Nimtz, *Lenin's Electoral Strategy from 1907 to the October Revolution of 1917* (London: Palgrave Macmillan, 2014), 115.
64. Vladimir Lenin and Leon Trotsky, *The Proletarian Revolution in Russia* (New York: The Communist Press, 1918), 295.
65. Michael Brie, *Rediscovering Lenin: Dialectics of Revolution and Metaphysics of Domination* (Cham, Switzerland: Palgrave Macmillan, 2019), 70.
66. Richard Pipes, ed., *The Unknown Lenin: From the Secret Archive* (New Haven, CT: Yale University Press, 1998), 56.
67. Leon Trotsky, *Dictatorship vs. Democracy* (New York: Workers Party of America, 1922), 64.
68. Karl Kautsky, *Terrorism and Communism* (London: Routledge, 2011), 176.
69. Michael Brie and Jörn Schütrumpf, *Rosa Luxemburg: A Revolutionary Marxist at the Limits of Marxism* (Cham, Switzerland: Palgrave Macmillan, 2021), 181.
70. James Thrower, *Marxist-Leninist "Scientific Atheism" and the Study of Religion and Atheism in the USSR* (Berlin: Mouton Publishers, 2011), 114.
71. Thrower, *Marxist-Leninist "Scientific Atheism,"* 117.
72. Maxim Gorky, *Fragments from My Diary* (New York: Robert M. P. McBride & Co., 1924), 275–76.
73. Alexei Yurchak, "Bodies of Lenin: The Hidden Science of Communist Sovereignty," *Representations* 129, no. 1 (2015), 120.
74. Tom Rockmore and Norman Levine, eds., *The Palgrave Handbook of Leninist Political Philosophy* (London: Palgrave Macmillan, 2018), 269.

75. Rockmore and Levine, *Palgrave Handbook of Leninist Political Philosophy,* 270.
76. Leon Trotsky, *The Revolution Betrayed* (Detroit: Labor Publications, 1991), 144.
77. Joseph Stalin, *Leninism,* vol. 1 (New York: International Publishers, 1931), 304.
78. Gwendolyn Leick, *Tombs of the Great Leaders* (London: Reaktion Books, 2013), 37–38.
79. Vladislav Todorov, *Red Square, Black Square: Organon for Revolutionary Imagination* (Albany: State University of New York Press, 1995), 93.
80. Kyle M. Lascurettes, *Orders of Exclusion: Great Powers and the Strategic Sources of Foundational Rules in International Relations* (New York: Oxford University Press, 2020), 150.
81. C. K. Cumming and Walter W. Pettit, eds., *Russian-American Relations, March 1917–March 1920* (New York: Harcourt, Brace and Howe, 1920), 67.
82. Ray Stannard Baker, *Woodrow Wilson and World Settlement,* vol. 1 (Gloucester, MA: Peter Smith, 1960), 93.
83. Theodore P. Greene, ed., *Wilson at Versailles* (Boston: D. C. Heath and Company, 1957), 30.
84. Hamilton Foley, ed., *Woodrow Wilson's Case for the League of Nations* (Princeton, NJ: Princeton University Press, 1923), 169.
85. Allan H. Meltzer, *A History of the Federal Reserve,* vol. 1 (Chicago: University of Chicago Press, 2003), 84.
86. Richard Drake, *The Education of an Anti-Imperialist: Robert La Follette and US Expansion* (Madison: University of Wisconsin Press, 2013), 149.
87. Vincent St. John, *The IWW* (Cleveland: IWW Publishing Bureau, 1913), 9.
88. St. John, *IWW,* 18.
89. Kim Scipes, *AFL-CIO's Secret War Against Developing Country Workers: Solidarity or Sabotage* (Lanham, MD: Lexington Books, 2010), 35.
90. Carl J. Richard, *When the United States Invaded Russia: Woodrow Wilson's Siberian Disaster* (Lanham, MD: Rowman & Littlefield Publishers, 2013), 33.
91. Emerson Hough, *The Web* (Chicago: Reilly & Lee Co., 1917), 26.
92. Robert Singerman, "The American Career of the 'Protocols of the Elders of Zion,'" *American Jewish History* 71, no. 1 (September 1981), 52.
93. "Senators Tell What Bolshevism in America Means," *New York Times,* June 15, 1919, 40.
94. Beverly Gage, *The Day Wall Street Exploded: A Story of America in Its First Age of Terror* (Oxford: Oxford University Press, 2001), 179.
95. "500 Reds at Ellis Island," *New York Times,* January 4, 1920, 1.
96. Laura Weinrib, *The Taming of Free Speech: America's Civil Liberties Compromise* (Cambridge, MA: Harvard University Press, 2016), 117.
97. W. E. B. Du Bois, "The African Roots of War," *Atlantic,* May 1915, https://www.theatlantic.com/magazine/archive/1915/05/the-african-roots-of-war/528897/; W. E. B. Du Bois, "Close Ranks," *Crisis* 16, no. 3 (July 1918), 6.
98. Mark Ellis, "'Closing Ranks' and 'Seeking Honors': W. E. B. Du Bois in World War I," *Journal of American History* 79, no. 1 (June 1992), 100.

99. Chad L. Williams, *Torchbearers of Democracy: African American Soldiers in the World War I Era* (Chapel Hill: University of North Carolina Press, 2010), 31–32.
100. W. E. B. Du Bois, "Returning Soldiers," *Crisis* 18, no. 1 (May 1919), 13.
101. Lloyd E. Ambrosius, *Woodrow Wilson and American Internationalism* (Cambridge: Cambridge University Press, 2017), 111.
102. "For Action on Race Riot Peril," *New York Times,* October 5, 1919, 112.
103. "Reds Try to Stir Negroes to Revolt," *New York Times,* July 28, 1919, 4.
104. Walter Lippmann, *Public Opinion* (New York: Harcourt, Brace and Company, 1922), 248.
105. Walter Lippman, *The Phantom Public* (New York: Harcourt, Brace and Company, 1925), 41; Walter Lippman, "The Basic Problem of Democracy," *Atlantic Monthly,* November 1919, https://www.theatlantic.com/magazine/archive/1919/11/the-basic-problem-of-democracy/569095/.
106. Lippmann, *Public Opinion,* 248 and 310.
107. Edward Bernays, *Propaganda* (New York: IG Publishing, 2005), 37–38.
108. Frederick E. Schortemeier, *Rededicating America: Life and Recent Speeches of Warren G. Harding* (Indianapolis: Bobbs-Merrill Company, 1920), 224 and 43.
109. Thomas F. Gossett, *Race: The History of an Idea in America* (New York: Oxford University Press, 1997), 404–5.
110. Lothrop Stoddard, *The Rising Tide of Color Against White World-Supremacy* (New York: Charles Scribner's Sons, 1921), 170 and 207.
111. *Hearings Before the Committee on Immigration and Naturalization in the House of Representatives,* March 8, 1924 (Washington, DC: US Government Printing Office, 1924), 1263.
112. Thomas C. Leonard, *Illiberal Reformers: Race, Eugenics, and American Economics in the Progressive Era* (Princeton, NJ: Princeton University Press, 2016), 142.
113. "The Immigration and Naturalization Systems of the United States," in *Report to the 81st Congress* (Washington, DC: US Government Printing Office, 1950), 63–64.
114. Anton Kaes, Martin Jay, and Edward Dimendberg, eds., *The Weimar Republic Sourcebook* (Berkeley: University of California Press, 1994), 37.
115. Kaes et al., *Weimar Republic Sourcebook,* 38.
116. Rosa Luxemburg, *The Rosa Luxemburg Reader,* eds. Peter Hudis and Kevin B. Anderson (New York: Monthly Review Press, 2004), 364.
117. Robert Leeson, *Hayek: A Collaborative Biography,* pt. 8 (Cham, Switzerland: Palgrave Macmillan, 2019), 510.
118. Robert Wohl, *The Generation of 1914* (Cambridge, MA: Harvard University Press, 1979), 173.
119. Jeffrey H. Jackson and Robert Francis Saxe, eds., *The Underground Reader: Sources in the Transatlantic Counterculture* (New York: Berghahn, 2015), 44–46.
120. Mussolini, *The Political and Social Doctrine of Fascism* (London: Hogarth Press, 1933), 18.
121. George S. Vascik and Mark R. Sadler, eds., *The Stab-in-the-Back Myth and the Fall of the Weimar Republic* (London: Bloomsbury, 2016), 83.

122. David Redles, *Hitler's Millennial Reich: Apocalyptic Belief and the Search for Salvation* (New York: New York University Press, 2005), 56.
123. Steven T. Katz, *Historicism, the Holocaust, and Zionism: Critical Studies in Modern Jewish Thought and History* (New York: New York University Press, 1992), 85–86.
124. Nicholas Goodrick-Clarke, *The Occult Roots of Nazism: Secret Aryan Cults and Their Influence on Nazi Ideology* (New York: New York University Press, 2004), 86 and 88.
125. Emilio Gentile, *The Struggle for Modernity* (Westport, CT: Praeger, 2003), 138.
126. Oswald Spengler, *Decline of the West: Perspectives of World History* (New York: Knopf, 1966), 464.
127. James Cross Giblin, *The Life and Death of Adolf Hitler* (New York: Clarion Books, 2002), 37–38.

CHAPTER 7: LIGHTNING FROM THE DARK CLOUD OF MAN

1. Alan Lawson, *A Commonwealth of Hope: The New Deal Response to Crisis* (Baltimore: Johns Hopkins University Press, 2006), 10.
2. David M. Kennedy, *Freedom from Fear: The American People in Depression and War, 1929–1945* (New York: Oxford University Press, 1999), 39.
3. "Closing Rally Vigorous," *New York Times,* October 30, 1929, 1.
4. "Leaders See Fear Waning," *New York Times,* October 30, 1929, 3.
5. Richard Striner, *Hard Times: Economic Depressions in America* (Lanham, MD: Rowman & Littlefield, 2018), 77.
6. John Marsh, *The Emotional Life of the Great Depression* (New York: Oxford University Press, 2019), 33.
7. Matt Perry, *Break and Work: The Experience of Unemployment, 1918–39* (London: Pluto Press, 2000), 299.
8. "Four Killed in Riot at Main Ford Plant as 3,000 Idle Fight," *New York Times,* March 8, 1932, 1.
9. "Defends Bonus Army," *New York Times,* June 10, 1932, 1.
10. "Capital Asks States to Halt Bonus Trek," *New York Times,* June 10, 1932, 12.
11. Robert S. McElvaine, *The Great Depression: America, 1929–1941* (New York: Times Books, 1993), 91.
12. Franklin Delano Roosevelt, *Great Speeches,* ed. John Grafton (Mineola, NY: Dover Publications, 2012), 49.
13. Roosevelt, *Great Speeches,* 50.
14. Roosevelt, *Great Speeches,* 17.
15. Roosevelt, *Great Speeches,* 580.
16. Roosevelt, *Great Speeches,* 657–58.
17. Arthur M. Schlesinger, *The Age of Roosevelt: The Crisis of the Old Order, 1919–1933* (Boston: Houghton Mifflin Company, 1957), 437.
18. Franklin D. Roosevelt, *Inaugural Address of 1933* (Washington, DC: National Archives and Records Administration, 1988), 3.
19. Roosevelt, *Inaugural Address of 1933,* 9.

20. William E. Leuchtenburg, *The American President: From Teddy Roosevelt to Bill Clinton* (New York: Oxford University Press, 2015), 178.
21. Jonathan Michaels, *McCarthyism: The Realities, Delusions, and Politics Behind the 1950s Red Scare* (New York: Routledge, 2017), 83.
22. Michaels, *McCarthyism,* 77.
23. Sally Denton, *The Plots Against the President: FDR, a Nation in Crisis, and the Rise of the American Right* (New York: Bloomsbury Press, 2012), 156.
24. Denton, *Plots Against the President,* 155.
25. Frederick Rudolph, "The American Liberty League, 1934–1940," *American Historical Review* 56, no. 1 (October 1950), 19.
26. David Farber, *Everybody Ought to Be Rich: The Life and Times of John J. Raskob, Capitalist* (New York: Oxford University Press, 2013), 295–96.
27. "League Is Formed to Scan New Deal, 'Protect Rights,'" *New York Times,* August 23, 1934, 1.
28. *Hearings, United States Congress, House Committee of the Judiciary* (Washington, DC: US Government Printing Office, 1935), 77.
29. *The International Jew: Jewish Activities in the United States,* vol. 2 (Dearborn, MI: Dearborn Publishing Company, 1921), 67.
30. *International Jew,* 121.
31. *International Jew,* 119.
32. "Des Moines Speech," CharlesLindbergh.com, http://www.charleslindbergh.com/americanfirst/speech.asp.
33. Max Wallace, *American Axis: Henry Ford, Charles Lindbergh, and the Rise of the Third Reich* (New York: St. Martin's Griffin, 2004), 212.
34. William L. Shirer, *The Rise and Fall of the Third Reich* (New York: Simon & Schuster, 1990), 190.
35. James Pool, *Who Financed Hitler* (New York: Pocket Books, 1997), 114.
36. *Trials of War Criminals Before the Nuernberg Military Tribunal,* vol. 8 (Washington, DC: US Government Printing Office, 1952), 977; Shirer, *Rise and Fall of the Third Reich,* 263.
37. Lucy S. Dawidowicz, ed., *A Holocaust Reader* (West Orange, NJ: Behrman House, 1976), 32.
38. Simonetta Falasca-Zamponi, *Fascist Spectacle: The Aesthetics of Power in Mussolini's Italy* (Berkeley: University of California Press, 1997), 44–45.
39. Peter Neville, *Mussolini* (London: Routledge, 2004), 85.
40. David Kertzer, "Pictro Tacchi Venturi, Mussolini, Piux XI, and the Jews," in *"The Tragic Couple": Encounters Between Jews and Jesuits,* eds. James Bernauer and Robert A. Maryks (Leiden: Brill, 2014), 269.
41. David I. Kertzer, *The Pope and Mussolini: The Secret History of Pius XI and the Rise of Fascism in Europe* (New York: Random House, 2014), 118.
42. Guenter Lewy, *The Catholic Church and Nazi Germany* (Cambridge, MA: Da Capo Press, 2000), 26.

43. Jean-Denis G. G. LePage, *Hitler Youth, 1922–1945: An Illustrated History* (Jefferson, NC: McFarland & Company, 2008), 38.
44. Stephen R. Haynes, *Jews and the Christian Imagination* (New York: Macmillan, 1995), 60.
45. Shirer, *Rise and Fall of the Third Reich*, 225.
46. Uriel Tal, *Religion, Politics, and Ideology in the Third Reich* (London: Routledge, 2004), 179.
47. Gregers Einer Forssling, *Nordicism and Modernity* (Cham, Switzerland: Palgrave Macmillan, 2020), 156; Richard Steigmann-Gall, *The Holy Reich: Nazi Conceptions of Christianity, 1919–1945* (Cambridge: Cambridge University Press, 2003), 94.
48. Martin Heidegger, *Introduction to Metaphysics* (New Haven, CT: Yale University Press, 2014), 50.
49. Heidegger, *Introduction to Metaphysics,* 49.
50. Aristotle Kallis, *Genocide and Fascism: The Eliminationist Drive in Fascist Europe* (London: Routledge, 2007), 142.
51. David Welch, *The Third Reich: Politics and Propaganda* (London: Routledge, 2008), 43.
52. Jean-Yves Camus and Nicolas Lebourg, *Far-Right Politics in Europe,* trans. Jane Marie Todd (Cambridge, MA: Belknap Press of Harvard University, 2017), 26.
53. Molly Guptill Manning, *When Books Went to War: The Stories That Helped Us Win World War II* (Boston: Houghton Mifflin Harcourt, 2014), 3.
54. Bernard Harrison, *Blaming the Jews: Politics and Delusion* (Bloomington: Indiana University Press, 2020), 403.
55. Debórah Dwork and Robert Jan van Pelt, *Holocaust: A History* (New York: W. W. Norton, 2002), 261.
56. Dwork and Jan van Pelt, *Holocaust,* 263.
57. Dwork and Jan van Pelt, *Holocaust,* 281.
58. Judith Hughes, *The Holocaust and the Revival of Psychological History* (New York: Cambridge University Press, 2015), 33.
59. Nesta H. Webster, *World Revolution: The Plot Against Civilization* (Boston: Small, Maynard & Company, 1921), 326–27.
60. Webster, *World Revolution,* 327.
61. Nick Toczek, *Haters, Baiters, and Would-Be Dictators: Anti-Semitism and the UK Far Right* (London: Routledge, 2015), 235.
62. "Churchill Extols Fascismo for Italy," *New York Times,* January 21, 1927, 7.
63. A. N. Wilson, *After the Victorians: The Decline of Britain in the World* (New York: Picador, FSG, 2005), 229.
64. Robert Skidelsky, *Oswald Mosley* (London: Macmillan, 1975), 196.
65. Skidelsky, *Oswald Mosley,* 257; Anthony Julius, *Trials of the Diaspora: A History of Anti-Semitism in England* (Oxford: Oxford University Press, 2010), 306–7.
66. Colin Holmes, *Anti-Semitism in British Society, 1876–1939* (London: Routledge, 2016), 177.

67. Julian Jackson, *The Fall of France: The Nazi Invasion of 1940* (Oxford: Oxford University Press, 2003), 227.
68. Robert O. Paxton, *Vichy France: Old Guard and New Order, 1940–1944* (New York: Columbia University Press, 2001), 47; Robert B. Bruch, *Pétain: Verdun to Vichy* (Washington, DC: Potomac Books, 2008), 101.
69. Stephen Steele, "Memories of the Comtesse de Die: Maurras, Mistral, and Medievalists," in *Studies in Medievalism,* vol. 9, eds. Leslie J. Workman, Kathleen Verduin, and David D. Metzger (Cambridge: D. S. Brewer, 1998), 173.
70. Miranda Pollard, *Reign of Virtue: Mobilizing Gender in Vichy France* (Chicago: University of Chicago Press, 1998), 100.
71. Sarah Fishman, *From Vichy to the Sexual Revolution: Gender and Family Life in Postwar France* (Oxford: Oxford University Press, 2017), 5 and 7.
72. Robert Gildea, *Fighters in the Shadows: A New History of the French Resistance* (Cambridge, MA: Belknap Press of Harvard University Press, 2015), 409.
73. Julian Jackson, *France: The Dark Years, 1940–1944* (Oxford: Oxford University Press, 2001), 252.
74. Jonathan Fenby, *The General: Charles de Gaulle and the France He Saved* (New York: Skyhorse, 2013), 217.
75. Mary Vincent, "The Spanish Church and the Popular Front," in *The French and Spanish Popular Fronts: Comparative Perspectives,* eds. Martin S. Alexander and Helen Graham (New York: Cambridge University Press, 2002), 80.
76. Southworth, *Conspiracy and the Spanish Civil War,* 186.
77. Southworth, *Conspiracy and the Spanish Civil War,* 189.
78. Stanley G. Payne, *The Spanish Civil War* (Cambridge: Cambridge University Press, 2012), 67.
79. John Cowans, ed., *Modern Spain: A Documentary History* (Philadelphia: University of Pennsylvania Press, 2003), 177.
80. Herbert R. Southworth, *Conspiracy and the Spanish Civil War* (London: Routledge, 2001), 58.
81. George Hills, *Franco: The Man and His Nation* (New York: Macmillan, 1967), 302.
82. Christopher Read, *Stalin: From the Caucasus to the Kremlin* (New York: Routledge, 2017), 223.
83. Antony Beevor, *The Battle for Spain* (New York: Penguin, 2006), 88.
84. Francisco Ferrándiz, "Mass Graves, Landscapes of Terror: A Spanish Tale," in *Necropolitics: Mass Graves and Exhumations in the Age of Human Rights,* ed. Francisco Ferrándiz and Antonius C. G. M. Robben (Philadelphia: University of Pennsylvania Press, 2015), 98.
85. Omar G. Encarnación, *Democracy Without Justice in Spain: The Politics of Forgetting* (Philadelphia: University of Pennsylvania Press, 2014), 34.
86. Encarnación, *Democracy Without Justice in Spain,* 43.
87. Encarnación, *Democracy Without Justice in Spain,* 40.
88. Philip J. Briggs, *Making American Foreign Policy* (Lanham, MD: Rowman & Littlefield, 1994), 48.

89. *Foreign Relations of the United States, 1947,* vol. 3 (Washington, DC: US Government Printing Office, 1972), 1092–94.
90. Briggs, *Making American Foreign Policy,* 62.
91. Hiroaki Kuromiya, *Stalin's Industrial Revolution: Politics and Workers, 1928–1932* (Cambridge: Cambridge University Press, 1990), 108.
92. Timothy Snyder, *Bloodlands: Europe Between Hitler and Stalin* (New York: Basic Books, 2010), 47.
93. Elisa Kriza, *Alexander Solzhenitsyn: Cold War Icon, Gulag Author, Russian Naturalist?* (New York: Columbia University Press, 2014), 206.
94. Zenovia A. Sochor, *Revolution and Culture: The Bogdanov-Lenin Controversy* (Ithaca, NY: Cornell University Press, 1988), 115.
95. Rolf Hellebust, *Flesh to Metal: Soviet Literature and the Alchemy of Revolution* (Ithaca, NY: Cornell University Press, 2003), 59.
96. Thomas P. Hughes, *American Genesis: A Century of Innovation and Technological Enthusiasm, 1870–1970* (Chicago: University of Chicago Press, 2004), 257.
97. Robert Conquest, *The Great Terror: A Reassessment* (Oxford: Oxford University Press, 1990), 24.
98. Richard Overy, *The Dictators: Hitler's Germany, Stalin's Russia* (New York: W. W. Norton and Company, 2004), 42.
99. Roy Medvedev, *Let History Judge: The Origins and Consequences of Stalinism* (New York: Columbia University Press, 1989), 297.
100. Sarah Davies and James Harris, *Stalin's World: Dictating the Soviet Order* (New Haven, CT: Yale University Press, 2014), 53.
101. Lewis Siegelbaum and Andrei Sokolov, eds., *Stalinism as a Way of Life: A Narrative in Documents* (New Haven, CT: Yale University Press, 2000), 124.
102. Frank Costigliola, *Roosevelt's Lost Alliances: How Personal Politics Helped Start the Cold War* (Princeton, NJ: Princeton University Press, 2013), 169.
103. Julian Lewis, *Changing Direction: British Military Planning for Post-War Strategic Defence, 1942–1947* (London: Frank Cass Publishers, 2002), xxxii.
104. Jeanne Guillemin, *Hidden Atrocities: Japanese Germ Warfare and American Obstruction of Justice at the Tokyo Trial* (New York: Columbia University Press, 2018), 262.
105. Victor Sebestyen, *1946: The Making of the Modern World* (New York: Vintage Books, 2016), 163.
106. Walter Isaacson and Evan Thomas, *The Wise Men: Six Friends and the World They Made* (New York: Simon & Schuster, 1986), 262.
107. George Orwell, *Collected Essays,* vol. 4 (Boston: Nonpareil Books, 2000), 9–10.
108. Simon Sebaj Montegiore, *Stalin: The Court of the Red Tsar* (New York: Vintage Books, 2003), 502.
109. David Felix, *Kennan and the Cold War* (London: Routledge, 2017), 44–45.
110. Stefan Rossbach, "The Cold War, the Decline of the West, and the Purpose of 'Containment,'" in *Politics, Order and History,* eds. Glenn Hughes, Stephen

A. McKnight, and Geoffrey L. Price (Sheffield, UK: Sheffield Academic Press, 2001), 174.

111. Felix, *Kennan and the Cold War*, 47.
112. *Proceedings and Documents of the United Nations Monetary and Financial Conference*, vol. 1 (Washington, DC: US Government Printing Office, 1948), 368; Dean Acheson, *The Place of Bretton Woods in Economic Collective Security* (Washington, DC: US Government Printing Office, 1945), 6.
113. Anastasia Xenias, "Wartime Financial Diplomacy and the Transition to the Treasury System, 1939–1947," in *Orderly Change: International Monetary Relations Since Bretton Woods*, ed. David M. Andrews (Ithaca, NY: Cornell University Press, 2008), 49.
114. James T. Patterson, *Grand Expectations: The United States, 1945–1974* (New York: Oxford University Press, 1996), 128.
115. Robert A. Taft, *The Papers of Robert A. Taft*, vol. 3 (Kent, OH: Kent State University Press, 2003), 388.
116. Taft, *Papers of Robert A. Taft*, vol. 3, 175, 183.
117. Harry S. Truman, *Public Papers, 1949*, vol. 5 (Washington, DC: US Government Printing Office, 1964), 485.
118. Albert Einstein, "Atomic War or Peace," *Atlantic*, November 1947, https://www.theatlantic.com/magazine/archive/1947/11/atomic-war-or-peace/305443/.

CHAPTER 8: THE MACHINE

1. *Speech of Nikita Khrushchev Before a Closed Session of the XXth Congress of the Communist Party of the Soviet Union* (Washington, DC: US Government Printing Office, 1957), 28.
2. *Speech of Nikita Khrushchev Before a Closed Session*, 23.
3. *Speech of Nikita Khrushchev Before a Closed Session*, 65.
4. Harry Schwartz, "Khrushchev Orders Help for Consumer," *New York Times*, October 11, 1964, 202; Jamil Hasanli, *Khrushchev's Thaw and National Identity in Soviet Azerbaijan, 1954–1959* (Lanham, MD: Lexington Books, 2014), 210.
5. Emma Goldman, *1917: Revolution in Russia and Its Aftermath* (Montreal: Black Rose Books, 2018), 207.
6. Patrick G. Zander, *The Rise of Communism* (Santa Barbara, CA: ABC-Clio, 2018), 178.
7. *U.S. Congress, Reports and Documents of 85th Congress*, vol. 28 (Washington, DC: US Government Printing Office, 1957), 182.
8. Norbert Wiener, *Cybernetics; or, Control and Communication in the Animal and the Machine* (Cambridge, MA: MIT Press, 1985), 6.
9. Wiener, *Cybernetics*, 27–28.
10. Benjamin Peters, *How Not to Network a Nation: The Uneasy History of the Soviet Internet* (Cambridge, MA: MIT Press, 2016), 30.

11. Slava Gerovitch, *From Newspeak to Cyberspeak: A History of Soviet Cybernetics* (Cambridge, MA: MIT Press, 2004), 125.
12. United States Department of State, *Soviet World Handbook* (Washington, DC: US Government Printing Office, 1959), 135.
13. Gerovitch, *From Newspeak to Cyberspeak,* 160.
14. Gerovitch, *From Newspeak to Cyberspeak,* 253.
15. Vincent Mosco, *To the Cloud: Big Data in a Turbulent World* (New York: Routledge, 2014), 23.
16. Mosco, *To the Cloud,* 24.
17. Leon Smolinski, "What Next in Soviet Planning," *Foreign Affairs* 42, no. 3 (April 1964), 603.
18. Gerovitch, *From Newspeak to Cyberspeak,* 277.
19. David Holloway, "The Political Uses of Scientific Models," in *The Use of Models in the Social Sciences* (London: Routledge, 2013), 111.
20. Rhodri Jeffreys-Jones, *The CIA and American Democracy* (New Haven, CT: Yale University Press, 1989), 25.
21. Sherman Kent, *Strategic Intelligence for American World Policy* (Princeton, NJ: Princeton University Press, 2015), 42.
22. Harry Truman, *Public Papers of the President of the United States: Harry S. Truman, 1946* (Washington, DC: US Government Printing Office, 1962), 86.
23. Jeffreys-Jones, *The CIA and American Democracy,* 39.
24. Stephen Kinzer, *The Brothers: John Foster Dulles, Allen Dulles, and Their Secret World War* (New York: Henry Holt and Company, 2013), 105.
25. S. Nelson Drew, ed., *NSC-68: Forging the Strategy of Containment* (Washington, DC: National Defense University, 1996), 39.
26. Drew, *NSC-68,* 42.
27. John Lewis Gaddis, *Strategies of Containment* (Oxford: Oxford University Press, 2005), 105.
28. *Foreign Relations of the United States, 1950,* vol. 1 (Washington, DC: US Government Printing Office, 1977), 197 and 199.
29. *Investigation of Senator Joseph R. McCarthy,* pt. 1 (Washington, DC: US Government Printing Office, 1952), 29.
30. Jonathan Michaels, *McCarthyism: The Realities, Delusions and Politics Behind the 1950s Red Scare* (New York: Routledge, 2017), 124.
31. William A. Donahue, *The Politics of the American Civil Liberties Union* (New Brunswick, NJ: Transaction Publishers, 2009), 184.
32. Curt Gentry, *Hoover: The Man and His Secrets* (New York: Norton, 1991), 528.
33. *Investigation of the Assassination of Martin Luther King, Jr.,* vol. 6 (Washington, DC: United States Congress, 1979), 89.
34. Dan T. Carter, *The Politics of Rage: George Wallace, the Origins of the New Conservatism, and the Transformation of American Politics* (Baton Rouge: Louisiana State University, 2000), 217.

35. Medford Evans, *Civil Rights Myths and Communist Realities* (New Orleans: Conservative Society of America, 1965), 18 and 21.
36. Robert Welch, *The Blue Book of the John Birch Society* (Hauraki Publishing, 2015), 30–31 and 79.
37. Thomas J. Whalen, *JFK and His Enemies: A Portrait of Power* (Lanham, MD: Rowman & Littlefield, 2014), 107.
38. Charles de Gaulle, *Major Addresses, Statements, and Press Conferences, May 19, 1958–January 31, 1964* (New York: French Embassy, 1964), 71–73.
39. Irwin M. Wall, *France, the United States, and the Algerian War* (Berkeley: University of California Press, 2001), 161.
40. David L. Schalk, *War and the Ivory Tower: Algeria and Vietnam* (Lincoln: University of Nebraska Press, 2005), 32.
41. Marnia Lazreg, *Torture and the Twilight of Empire* (Princeton, NJ: Princeton University Press, 2008), 159.
42. Jean-Paul Sartre, "Paris Alive," *Atlantic Monthly* 174, no. 6 (December 1944), 39.
43. David Drake, "Sartre, Camus, and the Algerian War," *Sartre Studies International* 5, no. 1 (1999), 21.
44. Frantz Fanon, *Wretched of the Earth,* trans. Constance Farrington (New York: Grove Press, 1963), 36.
45. Fanon, *Wretched of the Earth,* 38.
46. Fanon, *Wretched of the Earth,* 58.
47. Richard L. Johnson, ed., *Gandhi's Experiments with Truth* (Lanham, MD: Lexington Books, 2006), 229.
48. Michael J. Casey, *Che's Afterlife* (New York: Knopf, 2012), 54.
49. James P. Harrison, *The Endless War: Vietnam's Struggle for Independence* (New York: Columbia University Press, 1989), 138.
50. Mao, *Mao's Road to Power: Revolutionary Writings,* vol. 1 (London: Routledge, 2015), xxxv.
51. Stuart Schram, *The Thought of Mao Tse-Tung* (Cambridge: Cambridge University Press, 1989), 128.
52. Henry Kissinger, *A World Restored: Metternich, Castlereagh, and the Problems of Peace, 1812–22* (Friedland Books, 2017), 61 and 281.
53. Lois Hecht Oppenheim, *Politics in Chile* (New York: Routledge, 2007), 91.
54. *Foreign Relations of the United States, 1969–1976,* vol. 21, *Chile, 1969–1973* (Washington, DC: US Government Printing Office, 2014), 453.
55. Ian Roxborough, Philip O'Brien, and Jackie Roddick, *Chile: The State and Revolution* (London: Palgrave Macmillan, 1977), 228.
56. Peter Kornbluh, *The Pinochet File* (New York: The New Press, 2013), 211.
57. J. Patrice McSherry, *Predatory States: Operation Condor and Covert War in Latin America* (Lanham, MD: Rowman & Littlefield, 2005), 22.
58. David Binder, "Opponent of Chilean Junta Slain in Washington by Bomb in His Auto," *New York Times,* September 22, 1976, 9.

59. Thomas C. Wright, *State Terrorism in Latin America* (Lanham, MD: Rowman & Littlefield, 2007), 27.
60. McSherry, *Predatory States,* 51.
61. Alfred W. McCoy, *A Question of Torture: CIA Interrogation, from the Cold War to the War on Terror* (New York: Metropolitan Books, 2007), 67.
62. McCoy, *A Question of Torture,* 68.
63. Natalia Gorbanevskaya, *Red Square at Noon* (New York: Holt, Rinehart and Winston, 1970), 28.
64. Gorbanevskaya, *Red Square at Noon,* 69.
65. Anna J. Stoneman, "Socialism with a Human Face: The Leadership and Legacy of the Prague Spring," *History Teacher* 49, no. 1 (November 2015), 64.
66. Jan-Werner Müller, "What Did They Think They Were Doing?," in *Promises of 1968,* ed. Vladimir Tismaneanu (Budapest: Central European University Press, 2011), 101.
67. C. Wright Mills, *The Power Elite* (New York: Oxford University Press, 2000), 3.
68. Robert Cohen, *Freedom's Orator: Mario Savio and the Radical Legacy of the 1960s* (Oxford: Oxford University Press, 2009), 327.
69. Victor Lebow, "Price Competition in 1955," *Journal of Retailing* 3, no. 1 (Spring 1955), 3.
70. Brooks Stevens, "Planned Obsolescence," *Rotarian,* February 1960, 12.
71. Jean Baudrillard, *The Consumer Society* (London: SAGE Publications, 1998), 25.
72. Baudrillard, *Consumer Society,* 34.
73. Jeanne Haffner, *The View from Above* (Cambridge, MA: MIT Press, 2013), 131.
74. Theodor W. Adorno, *Critical Models* (New York: Columbia University Press, 1998), 89.
75. Adorno, *Critical Models,* 90.
76. Southern Conference on Race Relations, *Statement of Purpose* (Durham, NC: Southern Conference on Race Relations, 1942), 6.
77. Ai-min Zhang, *The Origins of the African-American Civil Rights Movement* (New York: Routledge, 2002), 112.
78. Zhang, *Origins of the African-American Civil Rights Movement,* 116.
79. Heather Wyatt-Nichol, "Sexual Orientation and Mental Health: Incremental Progression or Radical Change?," *Journal of Health and Human Services Administration* 37, no. 2 (Fall 2014), 228.
80. Carl Wittman, "A Gay Manifesto," in *Out of the Closets: Voices of Gay Liberation,* eds. Karla Jay and Allen Young (New York: New York University Press, 1992), 330.
81. Martha Shelley, "Gay Is Good," in *After Homosexual: The Legacies of Gay Liberation,* eds. Carolyn D'Cruz and Mark Pendleton (Crawley, Australia: UWA Publishing, 2014), 142.
82. Simone de Beauvoir, *The Second Sex,* trans. H. M. Parshley (New York: Vintage Books, 1989), 267.

83. Stephanie Coontz, *A Strange Stirring: "The Feminine Mystique" and American Women at the Dawn of the 1960s* (New York: Basic Books, 2011), 2.
84. Betty Friedan, *The Feminine Mystique* (New York: W. W. Norton & Company, 1963), 15.
85. Angela Davis, "Speech at a Black Panther Rally," EastBay.org, November 12, 1969, https://www.indybay.org/newsitems/2009/04/15/18589458.php.
86. Allan Brandt, *The Cigarette Century: The Rise, Fall, and Deadly Persistence of the Product That Defined America* (New York: Basic Books, 2008), 161.
87. Brandt, *Cigarette Century,* 175.
88. E. Robinson and R. C. Robbins, *Sources, Abundance, and Fate of Gaseous Atmospheric Pollutants* (Menlo Park, CA: Stanford Research Institute, 1968), 108–10.
89. Lewis F. Powell, "Confidential Memorandum: Attack on American Free Enterprise System," August 23, 1971, 1, https://scholarlycommons.law.wlu.edu/powellmemo.
90. Powell, "Memorandum," 2.
91. Powell, "Memorandum," 8.
92. Lee Canipe, "Under God and Anti-Communist," *Journal of Church and State* 45, no. 2 (Spring 2003), 312–13.
93. Max Blumenthal, "Agent of Intolerance," *Nation,* May 16, 2007, https://www.thenation.com/article/archive/agent-intolerance/.
94. Jerry Falwell, "The Feminist Movement," in *Reaction to the Modern Women's Movement, 1963 to the Present,* eds. Angela Howard and Sasha Ranaé Adams Tarrant (New York: Garland Publishing, 1997), 136.
95. Walter Frank, *Law and the Gay Rights Story* (New Brunswick, NJ: Rutgers University Press, 2014), 64.
96. Donald T. Critchlow, *Republican Character: From Nixon to Reagan* (Philadelphia: University of Pennsylvania Press, 2018), 83.
97. Barry Goldwater, *The Conscience of a Conservative* (Shepherdsville, KY: Victor Publishing Company, 1960), 37.
98. Rich Shumate, *Barry Goldwater, Distrust in Media, and Conservative Identity* (Lanham, MD: Lexington Books, 2021), 3.
99. Harry V. Jaffa, "The American Founding as the Best Regime," *Claremont Review of Books,* July 4, 2007, https://claremontreviewofbooks.com/digital/the-american-founding-as-the-best-regime/.
100. Alan Ebenstein, *Friedrich Hayek: A Biography* (Chicago: University of Chicago Press, 2003), 291.
101. F. A. Hayek, *Law, Legislation, and Liberty* (Chicago: University of Chicago Press, 2021), 7.
102. Walter Lippmann, *The Essential Lippmann,* eds. Clinton Rossiter and James Lare (Cambridge, MA: Harvard University Press, 1982), 19.
103. Jeremy Leaman, *The Bundesbank Myth: Towards a Critique of Central Bank Independence* (New York: Palgrave, 2001), 47.

104. Jeremy Leaman, *The Political Economy of Germany Under Chancellors Kohl and Schroder* (New York: Berghahn Books, 2009), 86.
105. David Harvey, *A Brief History of Neoliberalism* (Oxford: Oxford University Press, 2007), 20.
106. Peter Winn, "The Pinochet Era," in *Victims of the Chilean Miracle,* ed. Peter Winn (Durham, NC: Duke University Press, 2004), 27.
107. Winn, "Pinochet Era," 26.
108. Birsen Flip, *The Rise of Neo-Liberalism and the Decline of Freedom* (Cham, Switzerland: Palgrave Macmillan, 2020), 97.
109. Margaret Thatcher, "Conservative Party Political Broadcast," MargaretThatcher .org, January 17, 1979, https://www.margaretthatcher.org/document/103926.
110. Daniel Kilvington and Amir Saeed, "Inscriptions and Depictions of Race," in *Routledge Companion to British Media History,* eds. Martin Conboy and John Steel (London: Routledge, 2014), 115.
111. Clare Hanson, *Eugenics, Literature and Culture in Post-War Britain* (New York: Routledge, 2013), 107.
112. Ronald Reagan, "Election Eve Address: A Vision for America," Ronald Reagan Library, November 3, 1980, https://www.reaganlibrary.gov/archives/speech /election-eve-address-vision-america.
113. Helen Gilbert, *Lyndon LaRouche: Fascism Restyled for the New Millennium* (Seattle: Red Letter Press, 2003), 11.
114. Hal Lindsey, *The Late Great Planet Earth* (Grand Rapids, MI: Zondervan, 1970), 71.
115. Erich von Däniken, *Chariots of the Gods,* trans. Michael Heron (New York: Bantam Books, 1973), vii; Erich von Däniken, *Signs of the Gods?,* trans. Michael Heron (New York: Berkley Books, 1979), 70.
116. David Farber, *The Rise and Fall of Modern American Conservatism* (Princeton, NJ: Princeton University Press, 2010), 188.
117. Mark Pendergrast, *The Repressed Memory Epidemic* (Cham, Switzerland: Springer, 2017), 195.
118. David S. New, *Holy War: The Rise of Militant Christian, Jewish and Islamic Fundamentalism* (Jefferson, NC: McFarland & Co., 2002), 90.
119. David Arbel and Ran Edelist, *Western Intelligence and the Collapse of the Soviet Union* (London: Frank Cass, 2003), 206.
120. David Binder, "New CIA Estimate Finds Soviet Seeks Superiority in Arms," *New York Times,* December 26, 1976, 1.
121. Isaac Deutscher, *The Unfinished Revolution: Russia 1917–1967* (Oxford: Oxford University Press), 105.
122. Andrei Amalrik, *Will the Soviet Union Survive Until 1984?* (New York: Harper & Row, 1970), 11–12.
123. Serge Schmemann, "Yeltsin Tells Russia of Hardship to Come," *New York Times,* December 30, 1991, 3.
124. Serge Schmemann, "Yeltsin Is Telling Russians to Brace for Sharp Reform," *New York Times,* October 29, 1991, 1.

CHAPTER 9: FLYING EVER CLOSER TO THE SUN

1. Francis Fukuyama, "The End of History?," *National Interest* 16 (1989), 3–4.
2. TruthandFreedom 101, "Alex Jones Show 9 11 2011, Full 5 Hours," YouTube, October 18, 2012, https://www.youtube.com/watch?v=H5I98d60GIc.
3. PFAWdotorg, "Jerry Falwell and Pat Robertson Blame 9/11 on Organizations like People for the American Way," YouTube, April 2, 2010, https://www.youtube.com/watch?v=kMkBgA9_oQ4.
4. Tony Blair, "Note for the President," National Archives (UK), archived on November 23, 2017, 3.
5. Blair, "Note for the President," 4.
6. George F. Will, "A Strike at the Pillars," *Washington Post,* September 14, 2001, https://www.washingtonpost.com/archive/opinions/2001/09/14/a-strike-at-the-pillars/cc30cddb-cbb0-4b8f-9ea4-2f0343ee9690/.
7. Anthea Butler, *White Evangelical Racism: The Politics of Morality in America* (Chapel Hill: University of North Carolina Press, 2021), 108.
8. Lawrence Wright, "The Master Plan," *New Yorker,* September 3, 2006, https://www.newyorker.com/magazine/2006/09/11/the-master-plan.
9. Ron Suskind, "Faith, Certainty and the Presidency of George W. Bush," *New York Times,* October 17, 2004, https://www.nytimes.com/2004/10/17/magazine/faith-certainty-and-the-presidency-of-george-w-bush.html.
10. Carlotta Gal, "Study Hints at Mass Killing of the Taliban," *New York Times,* May 1, 2002, 8.
11. George W. Bush, *Public Papers of the Presidents: George W. Bush, 2001,* bk. 2 (Washington, DC: US Government Printing Office), 1395.
12. Joseph Goldstein, "U.S. Soldiers Told to Ignore Sexual Abuse of Boys by Afghan Allies," *New York Times,* September 20, 2015, https://www.nytimes.com/2015/09/21/world/asia/us-soldiers-told-to-ignore-afghan-allies-abuse-of-boys.html.
13. "Transcript for September 14," NBC News, September 14, 2003, https://www.nbcnews.com/id/wbna3080244.
14. Ariel Cohen and Gerald Driscoll, "The Road to Economic Prosperity for a Post-Saddam Iraq," Heritage Foundation, March 5, 2003, https://www.heritage.org/middle-east/report/the-road-economic-prosperity-post-saddam-iraq.
15. "Let's All Go to the Yard Sale," *Economist,* September 27, 2003, https://www.economist.com/middle-east-and-africa/2003/09/25/lets-all-go-to-the-yard-sale.
16. Robert Looney, "The Neoliberal Model's Planned Role in Iraq's Economic Transition," *Middle East Journal* 57, no. 4 (Autumn 2003), 574.
17. Robert O'Harrow Jr., *No Place to Hide* (New York: Free Press, 2006), 210.
18. Barton Gellman and Laura Poitras, "U.S., British Intelligence Mining Data from Nine U.S. Internet Companies in Broad Secret Program," *Washington Post,* June 7, 2013, https://www.washingtonpost.com/investigations/us-intelligence-mining-data-from-nine-us-internet-companies-in-broad-secret-program/2013/06/06/3a0c0da8-cebf-11e2-8845-d970ccb04497_story.html.

19. Abigail Fielding-Smith, Crofton Black, Alice Ross, and James Ball, "Revealed: Private Firms at Heart of US Drone Warfare," *Guardian,* July 30, 2015, https://www.theguardian.com/us-news/2015/jul/30/revealed-private-firms-at-heart-of-us-drone-warfare.
20. Micah Zenko, "Obama's Embrace of Drone Strikes Will Be a Lasting Legacy," *New York Times,* January 12, 2016, https://www.nytimes.com/roomfordebate/2016/01/12/reflecting-on-obamas-presidency/obamas-embrace-of-drone-strikes-will-be-a-lasting-legacy.
21. Greg Miller, "Plan for Hunting Terrorists Signals U.S. Intends to Keep Adding Names to Kill Lists," *Washington Post,* October 23, 2012, https://www.washingtonpost.com/world/national-security/plan-for-hunting-terrorists-signals-us-intends-to-keep-adding-names-to-kill-lists/2012/10/23/4789b2ae-18b3-11e2-a55c-39408fbe6a4b_story.html.
22. Mujib Mashal, "Taliban and U.S. Strike Deal to Withdraw American Troops from Afghanistan," *New York Times,* February 29, 2020, https://www.nytimes.com/2020/02/29/world/asia/us-taliban-deal.html.
23. Joseph Biden, "Remarks by President Biden on the End of the War in Afghanistan," White House, August 31, 2021, https://www.whitehouse.gov/briefing-room/speeches-remarks/2021/08/31/remarks-by-president-biden-on-the-end-of-the-war-in-afghanistan/.
24. Kenneth T. Walsh, "The Undoing of George W. Bush," *US News & World Report,* August 28, 2015, https://www.usnews.com/news/the-report/articles/2015/08/28/hurricane-katrina-was-the-beginning-of-the-end-for-george-w-bush.
25. "President Bush Addresses Financial Markets and World Economy," Bush White House, National Archives, November 13, 2008, https://georgewbush-whitehouse.archives.gov/news/releases/2008/11/20081113-4.html.
26. Richard Dooling, "The Rise of the Machines," *New York Times,* October 11, 2008, https://www.nytimes.com/2008/10/12/opinion/12dooling.html.
27. Felix Salmon, "Recipe for Disaster: The Formula That Killed Wall Street," *Wired,* February 23, 2009, https://www.wired.com/2009/02/wp-quant/.
28. Michael M. Grynbaum, "Greenspan Concedes Error on Regulation," *New York Times,* October 23, 2008, https://www.nytimes.com/2008/10/23/business/worldbusiness/23iht-24greenspan.17202367.html.
29. Eamon Javers, "Inside Obama's Bank CEO Meeting," Politico, April 3, 2009, https://www.politico.com/story/2009/04/inside-obamas-bank-ceos-meeting-020871.
30. Tam Harbert, "Here's How Much the 2008 Bailouts Really Cost," MIT Sloan School, February 21, 2019, https://mitsloan.mit.edu/ideas-made-to-matter/heres-how-much-2008-bailouts-really-cost.
31. Sewell Chan, "Financial Crisis Was Avoidable, Inquiry Finds," *New York Times,* January 25, 2011, https://www.nytimes.com/2011/01/26/business/economy/26inquiry.html.

32. Barack Obama, *Public Papers of the Presidents of the United States: Barack Obama, 2009,* bk. 1 (Washington, DC: US Government Printing Office, 2010), 330.
33. Alan Greenspan, "The Crisis," Brookings Papers on Economic Activity (Washington, DC: Brookings Institute, Spring 2010), 218.
34. Greenspan, "The Crisis," 243.
35. Gabriel Sherman, *The Loudest Voice in the Room: How the Brilliant, Bombastic Roger Ailes Built Fox News—and Divided a Country* (New York: Random House, 2014), 197.
36. "Tea Party Movement Is Full of Conspiracy Theories," *Newsweek,* February 8, 2010, https://www.newsweek.com/tea-party-movement-full-conspiracy-theories-75153.
37. Aaron Blake, "GOP Congressman Calls Obama a 'Socialist Dictator,'" *Washington Post,* January 28, 2014, https://www.washingtonpost.com/news/post-politics/wp/2014/01/28/gop-congressman-calls-obama-a-socialist-dictator/.
38. *The Obama Deception,* dir. Alex Jones (Austin, TX: Jones Productions: Infowars.com), 2009.
39. Gregory Krieg, "14 of Trump's Most Outrageous 'Birther' Claims," CNN, September 16, 2016, https://www.cnn.com/2016/09/09/politics/donald-trump-birther/index.html.
40. Robert Schlesinger, "Party of Nuts: Poll Shows GOP Thinks Obama Is Muslim, Socialist," *US News & World Report,* March 24, 2010, https://www.usnews.com/opinion/blogs/robert-schlesinger/2010/03/24/party-of-nuts-poll-shows-gop-thinks-obama-is-muslim-socialist.
41. Robert D. Putnam, "Bowling Alone," *Journal of Democracy,* January 1995, 65.
42. Carter C. Price and Kathryn A. Edwards, "Trends in Income from 1975 to 2018," RAND Corporation, 2020, https://www.rand.org/pubs/working_papers/WRA516-1.html.
43. Valerie Strauss, "Former Lobbyist Details How Privatizers Are Trying to End Public Education," *Washington Post,* April 16, 2021, https://www.washingtonpost.com/education/2021/04/16/former-lobbyist-details-how-privatizers-are-trying-to-end-public-education/.
44. Abigail Johnson Hess, "The U.S. Has a Record-Breaking $1.73 Trillion in Student Debt," CNBC, September 9, 2021, https://www.cnbc.com/2021/09/09/america-has-1point73-trillion-in-student-debtborrowers-from-these-states-owe-the-most.html.
45. "NRA Says Congress Will Not Pass Weapons Ban," *USA Today,* January 14, 2013, https://www.usatoday.com/story/news/politics/2013/01/14/nra-weapons-ban/1832137/.
46. Jesse Singal, "After Alex Jones, Bracing for the Next Deranged Conspiracy Theory," *Boston Globe,* August 8, 2018, https://www.bostonglobe.com/opinion/2018/08/08/after-alex-jones-bracing-for-next-deranged-conspiracy-theory/1FCvk0n7p7nzhTGqCDnnpI/story.html.
47. Andrew Kaczynski, "Biden in 1993 Speech Pushing Crime Bill Warned of 'Predators

on Our Streets' Who Were 'Beyond the Pale,' " CNN, March 7, 2019, https://www.cnn.com/2019/03/07/politics/biden-1993-speech-predators/index.html.

48. Bill Clinton, *Public Papers of the Presidents of the United States: William J. Clinton, August 1–December 31, 1994* (Washington, DC: US Government Printing Office, 1995), 1540.
49. "Mass Incarceration," American Civil Liberties Union, https://www.aclu.org/issues/smart-justice/mass-incarceration/mass-incarceration-animated-series.
50. Edward Ongweso Jr., "Big Tech Has Made Billions Off the 20-Year War on Terror," Vice, September 9, 2021, https://www.vice.com/en/article/4aveeq/big-tech-has-made-billions-off-the-20-year-war-on-terror.
51. April Glaser, "Thousands of Contracts Highlight Quiet Ties Between Big Tech and U.S. Military," NBC News, July 8, 2020, https://www.nbcnews.com/tech/tech-news/thousands-contracts-highlight-quiet-ties-between-big-tech-u-s-n1233171.
52. Francesca Coppa, "Pop Culture, Fans, and Social Media," in *The Social Media Handbook,* ed. Jeremy Hunsinger and Theresa Senft (New York: Routledge, 2013), 86.
53. Chris Byrene, "4 Things BuzzFeed Has Learned About Content—Identity, Social and Why EQ Matters More Than IQ," *Marketing,* https://www.marketingmag.com.au/news-c/4-things-buzzfeed-has-learned-about-content-identity-social-and-why-eq-matters-more-than-iq/.
54. Robert Costa, "Trump Says He Is Serious About 2016 Bid, Is Hiring Staff and Delaying TV Gig," *Washington Post,* February 25, 2015, https://www.washingtonpost.com/politics/trump-says-he-is-serious-about-2016-bid-is-hiring-staff-and-delaying-tv-gig/2015/02/25/4e9d3804-bd07-11e4-8668-4e7ba8439ca6_story.html.
55. Charlie Warzel, "2/26: How Two Llamas and a Dress Gave Us the Internet's Greatest Day," BuzzFeed, February 26, 2016, https://www.buzzfeednews.com/article/charliewarzel/226-how-two-runaway-llamas-and-a-dress-gave-us-the-internets.
56. Rebecca Walter Reczek, Christopher Summers, and Robert Smith, "Targeted Ads Don't Just Make You More Likely to Buy—They Can Change How You Think About Yourself," *Harvard Business Review,* April 4, 2016, https://hbr.org/2016/04/targeted-ads-dont-just-make-you-more-likely-to-buy-they-can-change-how-you-think-about-yourself.
57. Shoshana Zuboff, *The Age of Surveillance Capitalism: The Fight for a Human Future at the New Frontier of Power* (New York: Public Affairs, 2019), 11.
58. Richard Barbrook and Andy Cameron, "The Californian Ideology," *Imaginary Futures,* www.imaginaryfutures.net/2007/04/17/the-californian-ideology-2/.
59. Chris Isidore, "Elon Musk Is Now 'Technoking' of Tesla. Seriously," CNN, March 15, 2021, https://www.cnn.com/2021/03/15/investing/elon-musk-technoking-of-tesla/index.html.
60. Tim Levin, "Elon Musk's Last Remaining Home, a 47-acre Bay Area Estate, Hits the Market for $37.5 million," Yahoo, June 17, 2021, https://sports.yahoo.com/elon-musks-last-remaining-home-142858274.html.

61. Brian Kahn, "Jeff Bezos: Future Humans Will Visit the Earth the Way You Visit Yellowstone," Gizmodo, November 16, 2021, https://gizmodo.com/jeff-bezos-future-humans-will-visit-the-earth-the-way-1848065795.
62. Nicholas A. John, *The Age of Sharing* (Cambridge: Polity Press, 2017), 65.
63. Reka Patricia Gal, "Machines of Liberation, Machines of Control," in *Algorithmic Culture,* eds. Stefka Hristova, Soonkwan Hong, and Jennifer Daryl Slack (Lanham, MD: Lexington Books, 2020), 91.
64. F. A. Hayek, *The Fatal Conceit* (Chicago: University of Chicago Press, 1988), 14.
65. Jeremy B. Merrill and Will Oremus, "Five Points for Anger, One for a Like," *Washington Post,* October 26, 2021, https://www.washingtonpost.com/technology/2021/10/26/facebook-angry-emoji-algorithm/.
66. Max Fisher and Amanda Taub, "How YouTube Radicalized Brazil," *New York Times,* August 11, 2019, https://www.nytimes.com/2019/08/11/world/americas/youtube-brazil.html.
67. Tom Miles, "U.N. Investigators Cite Facebook Role in Myanmar Crisis," Reuters, March 12, 2018, https://www.reuters.com/article/us-myanmar-rohingya-facebook/u-n-investigators-cite-facebook-role-in-myanmar-crisis-idUSKCN1GO2PN.
68. Meta, "The Metaverse and How We'll Build It Together," YouTube, October 28, 2021, https://www.youtube.com/watch?v=Uvufun6xer8.
69. Debra Kamin, "Investors Snap Up Metaverse Real Estate in a Virtual Land Boom," *New York Times,* November 30, 2021, https://www.nytimes.com/2021/11/30/business/metaverse-real-estate.html.
70. Ryan Gallagher, "Inside Google's Effort to Develop a Censored Search Engine in China," Intercept, August 8, 2018, https://theintercept.com/2018/08/08/google-censorship-china-blacklist/.
71. James T. Myers, Jürgen Domes, and Milton D. Yeh, eds., *Chinese Politics: Documents and Analysis,* vol. 2 (Columbia: University of South Carolina Press, 1989), 63.
72. Fox Butterfield, "China Is Linking 'Gang of 4' to Its Economic Troubles," *New York Times,* November 22, 1976, 10, https://www.nytimes.com/1976/11/22/archives/china-is-linking-gang-of-4-to-its-economic-troubles.html.
73. Yitao Tao and Zhiguo Lu, *Special Economic Zones and China's Development Path* (Singapore: Springer, 2018), 109.
74. Kwok-sing Li, *A Glossary of Political Terms of the People's Republic of China,* trans. Mary Lok (Hong Kong: Chinese University Press, 1995), 13.
75. Li, *Glossary of Political Terms of the People's Republic of China,* 12.
76. A. James McAdams, *Vanguard of the Revolution: The Global Idea of the Communist Party* (Princeton, NJ: Princeton University Press, 2019), 459.
77. "China Joins W.T.O. Ranks," *New York Times,* December 12, 2001, 7, https://timesmachine.nytimes.com/timesmachine/2001/12/12/631477.html?pageNumber=7.
78. David H. Autor, David Dorn, and Gordon H. Hanson, "The China Shock:

Learning from Labor-Market Adjustment to Large Changes in Trade," *Annual Review of Economics* 8 (October 2016), 205.

79. Matthew Hill, David Campanale, and Joel Gunter, "'Their Goal Is to Destroy Everyone': Uighur Camp Detainees Allege Systematic Rape," BBC, February 2, 2021, https://www.bbc.com/news/world-asia-china-55794071; "China Cuts Uighur Births with IUDs, Abortion, Sterilization," Associated Press, June 29, 2020, https://apnews.com/article/ap-top-news-international-news-weekend-reads-china-health-269b3de1af34e17c1941a514f78d764c; Simina Mistreanu, "Study Links Nike, Adidas, and Apple to Forced Uighur Labor," *Forbes,* March 2, 2020, https://www.forbes.com/sites/siminamistreanu/2020/03/02/study-links-nike-adidas-and-apple-to-forced-uighur-labor/.
80. Reed Albergotti, "Apple Is Lobbying Against a Bill Aimed at Stopping Forced Labor in China," *Washington Post,* November 20, 2020, https://www.washingtonpost.com/technology/2020/11/20/apple-uighur/.
81. Zack Whittaker, "US Towns Are Buying Chinese Surveillance Tech Tied to Uighur Abuses," TechCrunch, May 24, 2021, https://techcrunch.com/2021/05/24/united-states-towns-hikvision-dahua-surveillance/?guccounter=1; Avi Asher-Schapiro, "Exclusive: Half London Councils Found Using Chinese Surveillance Tech Linked to Uighur Abuses," Reuters, February 18, 2021, https://www.reuters.com/article/us-britain-tech-china/exclusive-half-london-councils-found-using-chinese-surveillance-tech-linked-to-uighur-abuses-idUSKBN2AI0QJ; Sam Biddle, "U.S. Military Bought Cameras in Violation of America's Own China Sanctions," Intercept, https://theintercept.com/2021/07/20/video-surveillance-cameras-us-military-china-sanctions/.

CHAPTER 10: ALMOST MIDNIGHT

1. Rod Dreher, *The Benedict Option: A Strategy for Christians in a Post-Christian Nation* (New York: Sentinel, 2018), 8.
2. Dreher, *Benedict Option,* 17.
3. Tony Cook, "Gov. Mike Pence Signs 'Religious Freedom' Bill in Private," *Indianapolis Star,* March 25, 2015, https://www.indystar.com/story/news/politics/2015/03/25/gov-mike-pence-sign-religious-freedom-bill-thursday/70448858/.
4. Adam Liptak, "Supreme Court Ruling Makes Same-Sex Marriage a Right Nationwide," *New York Times,* June 26, 2015, https://www.nytimes.com/2015/06/27/us/supreme-court-same-sex-marriage.html.
5. Matt Corley, "Pat Robertson: Gay Marriage Is 'the Beginning in a Long Downward Slide' to Legalized Child Molestation," Think Progress, May 7, 2009, https://archive.thinkprogress.org/pat-robertson-gay-marriage-is-the-beginning-in-a-long-downward-slide-to-legalized-child-molestation-ceee34cd2f6e/.
6. Nathan Robinson, "Conservative Hero's Dark Side: How an "Intellectual' Icon's Real Legacy Got Sanitized," Salon, January 20, 2015, https://www.salon.com

/2015/01/20/conservative_heros_dark_side_how_an_intellectual_icons_legacy_got_sanitized/.

7. Rod Dreher, "Light from the East," *American Conservative,* May 31, 2021, https://www.theamericanconservative.com/dreher/collegium-intermarium-light-from-the-east-mcc/.
8. Csaba Tóth, "Full Text of Viktor Orbán's Speech at Băile Tuşnad," *Budapest Beacon,* July 29, 2014, https://budapestbeacon.com/full-text-of-viktor-orbans-speech-at-baile-tusnad-tusnadfurdo-of-26-july-2014/.
9. Zack Beauchamp, "Hungary Just Passed a 'Stop Soros' Law That Makes It Illegal to Help Undocumented Migrants," Vox, June 22, 2018, https://www.vox.com/policy-and-politics/2018/6/22/17493070/hungary-stop-soros-orban.
10. Viktor Orbán, "PM Orbán in Magyar Nemzet: Together We Will Succeed Again," About Hungary, September 21, 2020, https://abouthungary.hu/prime-minister/pm-orban-in-magyar-nemzet-together-we-will-succeed-again.
11. Marc Santora and Helene Bienvu, "Secure in Hungary, Orban Readies for Battle with Brussels," *New York Times,* May 11, 2018, https://www.nytimes.com/2018/05/11/world/europe/hungary-victor-orban-immigration-europe.html.
12. "Hungary's Constitution of 2011," Constitute Project, August 26, 2021, https://www.constituteproject.org/constitution/Hungary_2011.pdf.
13. Norimitsu Onishi, "The Man Behind a Toxic Slogan Powering White Supremacy," *New York Times,* September 20, 2019, https://www.nytimes.com/2019/09/20/world/europe/renaud-camus-great-replacement.html.
14. Sasha Polakow-Suransky, "The Inspiration for Terrorism in New Zealand Came from France," *Foreign Policy,* March 16, 2019, https://foreignpolicy.com/2019/03/16/the-inspiration-for-terrorism-in-new-zealand-came-from-france-christchurch-brenton-tarrant-renaud-camus-jean-raspail-identitarians-white-nationalism/.
15. Peter Davies, *The Extreme Right in France, 1789 to the Present* (London: Routledge, 2002), 136–39.
16. Dylann Roof, "The Last Rhodesian," https://archive.org/stream/the-last-rhodesian-edited/The%20Last%20Rhodesian-%20Edited_djvu.txt.
17. Kevin Sack and Alan Blinder, "Jurors Hear Dylann Roof Explain Shooting in Video: 'I Had to Do It,'" *New York Times,* December 9, 2016, https://www.nytimes.com/2016/12/09/us/dylann-roof-shooting-charleston-south-carolina-church-video.html.
18. Brenton Harrison Tarrant, "The Great Replacement," https://img-prod.ilfoglio.it/userUpload/The_Great_Replacementconvertito.pdf.
19. Rob Crilly, "Vladimir Putin Has a HIGHER Approval Rating Than Joe Biden Among Republicans," *Daily Mail,* June 18, 2021, https://www.dailymail.co.uk/news/article-9702447/Vladimir-Putin-HIGHER-approval-rating-Biden-Republicans-new-poll-reveals.html.
20. Keith Livers, *Conspiracy Culture: Post-Soviet Paranoia and the Russian Imagination* (Toronto: University of Toronto Press, 2020), 141.
21. Livers, *Conspiracy Culture,* 152.

22. Alec Luhn, "President Vladimir Putin Hails Russia's 'Defence of Traditional Values' in His State of the Nation Speech," *Independent,* December 12, 2013, https://www.independent.co.uk/news/world/europe/president-vladimir-putin-hails-russia-s-defence-of-traditional-values-in-his-state-of-the-nation-speech-9001470.html.
23. Alexander Dugin, *The Fourth Political Theory* (London: Arktos, 2012), 19.
24. Dugin, *Fourth Political Theory,* 27.
25. Dugin, *Fourth Political Theory,* 29.
26. Alexander Dugin, *Martin Heidegger: The Philosophy of Another Beginning,* trans. Nina Kouprianova (New York: Radix, 2014), 144 and 148.
27. "Dugin: The Alternative to Liberalism Is Returning to the Middle Ages," The Fourth Revolutionary War, February 18, 2017, https://4threvolutionarywar.wordpress.com/2017/02/18/dugin-the-alternative-to-liberalism-is-returning-to-the-middle-ages/.
28. René Guénon, *The Crisis of the Modern World,* trans. Arthur Osborne (London: Luzac & Co., 1942), 3 and 10.
29. Julius Evola, *Men Among the Ruins* (Rochester, VT: Inner Traditions, 2016), 62.
30. Julius Evola, *Riding the Tiger* (Rochester, VT: Inner Traditions, 2003), 143.
31. Evola, *Riding the Tiger,* 12.
32. Jennifer Cohn, "Steve Bannon Isn't Just a Problem for America. He Is an International Menace," *Independent,* November 17, 2021, https://www.independent.co.uk/voices/steve-bannon-court-case-vatican-brexit-posobiec-b1959471.html.
33. J. Lester Feder, "This Is How Steve Bannon Sees the Entire World," BuzzFeed, November 15, 2016, https://www.buzzfeednews.com/article/lesterfeder/this-is-how-steve-bannon-sees-the-entire-world.
34. Eric Bradner, "Trump Praises 9/11 Truther's Amazing Reputation," CNN, December 2, 2015, https://www.cnn.com/2015/12/02/politics/donald-trump-praises-9-11-truther-alex-jones/index.html.
35. Michael Anton, "The Flight 93 Election," *Claremont Review of Books,* September 5, 2016, https://claremontreviewofbooks.com/digital/the-flight-93-election/.
36. Emily Stewart, "Donald Trump Rode $5 Billion in Free Media to the White House," TheStreet, November 20, 2016, https://www.thestreet.com/politics/donald-trump-rode-5-billion-in-free-media-to-the-white-house-13896916.
37. "Donald Trump's Speech at the Republican Convention As Prepared for Delivery," CNN, July 22, 2016, https://www.cnn.com/2016/07/22/politics/donald-trump-rnc-speech-text/index.html.
38. "Donald Trump's Inaugural Speech, Annotated," *New York Times,* January 20, 2017, https://www.nytimes.com/interactive/2017/01/20/us/politics/donald-trump-inauguration-speech-transcript.html.
39. Haws Spencer and Sheryl Gay Stolberg, "White Nationalists March on University of Virginia," *New York Times,* August 11, 2017, https://www.nytimes.com/2017/08/11/us/white-nationalists-rally-charlottesville-virginia.html.

40. Rosie Gray, "Trump Defends White-Nationalist Protesters: 'Some Very Fine People on Both Sides,'" *Atlantic,* August 15, 2017, https://www.theatlantic.com/politics/archive/2017/08/trump-defends-white-nationalist-protesters-some-very-fine-people-on-both-sides/537012/.
41. "Trump Administration Embraces Heritage Foundation Policy Recommendations," Heritage Foundation, January 23, 2018, https://www.heritage.org/impact/trump-administration-embraces-heritage-foundation-policy-recommendations.
42. Ben Steverman, "US Billionaires Got $1 Trillion Richer During Trump's First Term," *Bloomberg,* October 30, 2020, https://www.bloomberg.com/news/articles/2020-10-30/u-s-billionaires-got-1-trillion-richer-in-trump-s-first-term.
43. Sarah Pulliam Bailey, "'Their Dream President': Trump Just Gave White Evangelicals a Boost," *Washington Post,* May 4, 2017, https://www.washingtonpost.com/news/acts-of-faith/wp/2017/05/04/their-dream-president-trump-just-gave-white-evangelicals-a-big-boost/.
44. Anonymous, "HRC extradition already in motion . . . ," October 28, 2017, https://archive.4plebs.org/pol/search/uid/BQ7V3bcW/order/asc.
45. David Gilbert, "Over 30 Million Americans Believe in QAnon's Most Outrageous Conspiracy," Vice, May 27, 2021, https://www.vice.com/en/article/4avx99/over-30-million-americans-believe-in-qanons-most-outrageous-conspiracy.
46. Katherine Eban, "That's Their Problem," *Vanity Fair,* September 17, 2020, https://www.vanityfair.com/news/2020/09/jared-kushner-let-the-markets-decide-covid-19-fate.
47. Peter Whoriskey, Douglas Macmillan, and Jonathan O'Connell, "'Doomed to Fail': Why a $4 Trillion Bailout Couldn't Revive the American Economy," *Washington Post,* October 5, 2021, https://www.washingtonpost.com/graphics/2020/business/coronavirus-bailout-spending/.
48. Elizabeth Dwoskin, "On Social Media, Vaccine Misinformation Mixes with Extreme Faith," *Washington Post,* February 16, 2021, https://www.washingtonpost.com/technology/2021/02/16/covid-vaccine-misinformation-evangelical-mark-beast/.
49. Chloe Taylor, "Putin Seeking to Create New World Order with 'Rogue States' Amid Coronavirus Crisis, Report Claims," CNBC, April 2, 2020, https://www.cnbc.com/2020/04/02/putin-seeks-to-create-new-world-order-amid-coronavirus-crisis-report.html.
50. Benjamin Teitelbaum, "Covid-19 Is the Crisis Radical 'Traditionalists' Have Been Waiting For," *Nation,* April 8, 2020, https://www.thenation.com/article/politics/covid-traditionalist-bannon-putin/.
51. David Klepper and Lori Hinnant, "George Soros Conspiracy Theories Surge as Protests Sweep U.S.," Associated Press, June 21, 2020, https://apnews.com/article/ap-top-news-racial-injustice-mn-state-wire-united-states-us-news-f01f3c405985f4e3477e4e4ac27986e5.

52. Cheryl Corley, "Black Lives Matter Fights Disinformation to Keep Movement Strong," NPR, https://www.npr.org/2021/05/25/999841030/black-lives-matter-fights-disinformation-to-keep-the-movement-strong.
53. William P. Barr, "Remarks to the Law School and the de Nicola Center for Ethics and Culture at the University of Notre Dame," Department of Justice, October 11, 2019, https://www.justice.gov/opa/speech/attorney-general-william-p-barr-delivers-remarks-law-school-and-de-nicola-center-ethics.
54. Tom Gjelten, "Peaceful Protesters Tear-Gassed to Clear Way for Trump Church Photo-Op," NPR, June 1, 2020, https://www.npr.org/2020/06/01/867532070/trumps-unannounced-church-visit-angers-church-officials.
55. Sam Levine, "Arizona Republicans Hunt for Bamboo-Laced China Ballots in 2020 'Audit' Effort," *Guardian,* May 6, 2021, https://www.theguardian.com/us-news/2021/may/06/arizona-republicans-bamboo-ballots-audit-2020.
56. Right Wing Watch, "Presidential spiritual adviser Paula White . . . ," Twitter, January 24, 2020, https://twitter.com/RightWingWatch/status/1220740601781608448?ref_src=twsrc%5Etfw%7Ctwcamp%5Etweetembed%7Ctwterm%5E1220740601781608448%7Ctwgr%5E%7Ctwcon%5Es1_&ref_url=https%3A%2F%2Fwww.washingtonpost.com%2Freligion%2F2020%2F01%2F26%2Fpaula-white-miscarry-metaphor%2F.
57. Rebecca Speare-Cole, "Pro-Trump Evangelist Kenneth Copeland Says Devil Is Trying to Steal the Election, Kill Babies," *Newsweek,* December 21, 2020, https://www.newsweek.com/trump-televangelist-kenneth-copeland-devil-steal-election-kill-babies-1556305.
58. David Gilbert, "These Pastors Are Telling People Trump Is Still President and Are Ready for War," Vice, October 25, 2021, https://www.vice.com/en/article/y3vmnb/these-pastors-are-telling-people-trump-is-still-president-and-are-ready-for-war.
59. Domenico Montanaro, "Poll: Just a Quarter of Republicans Accept Election Outcome," NPR, December 9, 2020, https://www.npr.org/2020/12/09/944385798/poll-just-a-quarter-of-republicans-accept-election-outcome.
60. Tom Gjelten, "A 'Scary' Survey Finding: 4 in 10 Republicans Say Political Violence May Be Necessary," NPR, February 11, 2021, https://www.npr.org/2021/02/11/966498544/a-scary-survey-finding-4-in-10-republicans-say-political-violence-may-be-necessa.
61. "New Initiative Explains Deep, Persistent Divides Between Biden and Trump Voters," Sabato's Crystal Ball, University of Virginia Center for Politics, September 30, 2021, https://centerforpolitics.org/crystalball/articles/new-initiative-explores-deep-persistent-divides-between-biden-and-trump-voters/.
62. Brian Naylor, "Read Trump's January 6 Speech, a Key Part of Impeachment Trial," NPR, February 10, 2021, https://www.npr.org/2021/02/10/966396848/read-trumps-jan-6-speech-a-key-part-of-impeachment-trial.

63. Jamie Ross, "Trump Enjoyed Riot So Much He Rewound TV to Watch It Twice, Ex-Aide Says," Daily Beast, https://www.thedailybeast.com/trump-enjoyed-riot-so-much-he-rewound-tv-to-watch-it-twice-says-stephanie-grisham.
64. Pilar Melendez, "Two More Texas Real Estate Agents Who Took Private Jet to Riot Are Charged," Daily Beast, February 4, 2021, https://www.thedailybeast.com/two-more-texas-real-estate-agents-who-took-private-jet-to-riot-with-jenna-ryan-are-charged.
65. Daniel Trotta, Gabriella Borter, and Jonathan Allen, "Woman Killed in Siege of U.S. Capitol Was Veteran Who Embraced Conspiracy Theories," Reuters, January 7, 2021, https://www.reuters.com/article/uk-usa-election-death-idUKKBN29C2NX.
66. "Elmer Stewart Rhodes," Southern Poverty Law Center, https://www.splcenter.org/fighting-hate/extremist-files/individual/elmer-stewart-rhodes-0.
67. Jamie Gangel, Jeremy Herb, Marshall Cohen, Elizabeth Stuart, and Barbara Starr, "'They're Not Going to F**king Succeed': Top Generals Feared Trump Would Attempt a Coup After Election, According to New Book," CNN, July 14, 2021, https://www.cnn.com/2021/07/14/politics/donald-trump-election-coup-new-book-excerpt/index.html.
68. Betsy Woodruff Swan, "Read the Never-Issued Trump Order That Would Have Seized Voting Machines," Politico, January 21, 2022, https://www.politico.com/news/2022/01/21/read-the-never-issued-trump-order-that-would-have-seized-voting-machines-527572.
69. Sergio Olmos, "Guns, Ammo, Even a Boat . . ." *Guardian*, January 14, 2022, https://www.theguardian.com/us-news/2022/jan/14/oath-keepers-leader-charges-armed-plot-us-capitol-attack.
70. Bill McCarthy, "Tucker Carlson's 'Patriot Purge' Film on Jan 6 is Full of Falsehoods, Conspiracy Theories," Politifact, November 5, 2021, https://www.politifact.com/article/2021/nov/05/tucker-carlsons-patriot-purge-film-jan-6-full-fals/.
71. Justin Baragona, "Tucker Gushes over Conspiracist Alex Jones: 'Better Journalist' Than NBC and CBS Reporters," Daily Beast, December 1, 2021, https://www.thedailybeast.com/tucker-carlson-gushes-over-conspiracist-alex-jones-says-hes-a-better-journalist-than-nbc-and-cbs-reporters.
72. Jared Yates Sexton, "Tucker Carlson's Orban Lovefest Is a Dark Glimpse of the Future MAGA Wants," Daily Beast, August 4, 2021, https://www.thedailybeast.com/tucker-carlsons-orban-lovefest-is-a-dark-glimpse-of-the-future-maga-wants.
73. "Tucker Carlson Calls Biden's Immigration Policy 'the Great Replacement' and 'Eugenics,'" Media Matters for America, September 22, 2021, https://www.mediamatters.org/tucker-carlson/tucker-carlson-calls-bidens-immigration-policy-great-replacement-and-eugenics.
74. "Against the Dead Consensus," First Things, March 21, 2019, https://www.firstthings.com/web-exclusives/2019/03/against-the-dead-consensus.

- INDEX -

abolitionists, 138–140
abortion rights, 297
Abraham, 37
Action Française, 162–163, 275
Ad extirpanda decree (Innocent IV), 47
Adam, 22, 32, 111–112
Adams, John, 133
Adorno, Theodor, 229
Africa
  Germany and, 149, 151–152
  Rhodes and, 123–124, 146–147
Against the Murderous, Thieving Hordes of Peasants (Luther), 76
Agreement of the People, An, 79
Ailes, Roger, 257–258
Alaric I, 34
Albigensian Crusade, 46–47
Alexander I, Czar, 115–116, 141
Alexander I, King, 159
Alexander II, Czar, 143
Alexander III, Czar, 143
Alexander VI, Pope, 59–60, 63
Algeria, 219–221
Alhambra Decree, 60
Allegory of the Cave, 70, 168, 299
Allen, Gary, 241
Allende, Salvador, 223–224
al-Qaeda, 248
Altman, Rick, 17
Amalrik, Andrei, 243
Ambrose of Milan, Bishop, 33
America First movement, 188
American Civil War, 137–138, 140
American exceptionalism, 146, 259
American Federation of Labor (AFL), 171–172, 184
American Liberty League, 187
American Protective League (APL), 172
American Rule (Sexton), 7
American War of Independence, 92, 97–98, 131–132
Anglo-Saxon Century, The (Dos Passos), 147–148
Anthony, Susan B., 156
Antichrist
  as false prophet, 51
  Maxentius as, 29
  Napoleon as, 115–116
  Nero as, 20
  North as, 140
  Obama as, 259, 286
Anti-Masonic Party, 136
antiwar movement, 232
Anton, Michael, 284
apocalypticism, 1, 20–21, 26, 41, 92
Apollo, 26, 29
Appeal . . . to the Coloured Citizens of the World (Walker), 138
Apple, 270
"April Theses" (Lenin), 166
Arian sect, 27
Aristotle, 40, 65, 69
artificial intelligence, 251–252, 255
"Aryans," 129–130
Association for Preserving Liberty and Property Against Republicans and Levellers, 101

Index

Association for the Prosecution of Felons, 100
atomic bombs, 205, 207
August Decrees, 103
Augustine of Hippo, 20, 31, 34–35, 40
Australia, 96
Awful Disclosures (Monk), 136

Babbitt, Ashli, 294
Bacon, Francis, 72–73, 265
Bacon, Nathaniel, 83–84
Bakunin, Mikhail, 142
Ball, John, 56–57
Bannon, Steve, 12, 280–281, 282, 284–286, 296, 299
barbarian, term origin/definition, 17
Barbrook, Richard, 264
Barr, William, 291
Barruel, Augustin, 99, 116
Battelle, John, 263
Battle of Dorking, The (Chesney), 160–161
Baudrillard, Jean, 229
Bay of Pigs invasion, 219
Beccaria, Cesare, 95
Beecher, Henry Ward, 140
Beliar, 20
Benedict Option, The (Dreher), 272
Bengal Famine, 96–97
Bennett, Ernest, 122
Bentham, Jeremy, 95–96
Berlin Conference, 149
Bernays, Edward, 176
Beveridge, Albert J., 146
Bezos, Jeff, 265–266
Bible, 1, 3, 7–8, 52, 67. *See also* Revelation, Book of
Biden, Joe, 253, 262, 277, 292, 294
Binding, Karl, 194
birtherism, 258, 282
Bismarck, Otto von, 126, 149
bison, 118
Black Death, 54–55
Black Hand, 159
Black Hundreds, 143
Black Legion, 187
Black Lives Matter, 291
Black Panthers, 232
Blair, Tony, 247
Blake, William, 129
Blavatsky, Helena, 129–130, 279
Bloch, Jan, 163, 164
Blumenbach, Johann Friedrich, 112
Boers, 124
Bois Caïman, 110, 112
Bolshevik Party, 165–168, 170, 174, 196
Bolsonaro, Jair, 267, 281
Boluan Fanzheng, 269
Bonaparte, Louis-Napoleon, 125–127
Bonaparte, Napoleon, 108–110, 113, 115–116, 134
Boniface VIII, Pope, 48–50, 51
Boukman, Dutty, 110–111
"Bowling Alone" (Putnam), 259
Boxer Rebellion, 151, 164
Boyle, Robert, 72, 73
Brafman, Jacob, 143
Brazil, 267
Breckinridge, John, 139
Bremer, Paul, 251
Bretton Woods system, 206
Brezhnev, Leonid, 212
Britain/England
  Brexit and, 275
  French Revolution and, 99–101
  immigration and, 239
  imperialism and, 122–124, 145
  Suez Canal and, 122
  unrest in, 98
  war with France and, 52–54
  World War I and, 160–161
British Union of Fascists, 197
Britten, Emma Hardinge, 129
Brown, Michael D., 254
bubonic plague, 54–55
Buchanan, George, 78–79
Bülow, Bernhard von, 151
Bureau of Investigation, 172
Burke, Edmund, 97–99
Burkert, Walter, 21
Bush, George H. W., 257, 261
Bush, George W., 246, 247, 248–249, 253–255
Business Plot, 187–188

Index

Butler, Smedley, 187–188
BuzzFeed, 263–264

Californian Ideology, 264–265, 267–268
Caligula, Emperor, 14
Calvinism, 76–77
Cameron, Andy, 264
Campanella, Tommaso, 73
Camus, Renaud, 275, 276, 285
capitalism
  American colonies and, 91–92
  Bolsheviks and, 165–168, 202–203
  China and, 268–270
  class conflict and, 125
  communism and, 168
  consumerism and, 228–229
  Darwin's theories and, 130
  development of, 9–10
  Great Depression and, 183, 184–186
  humanism and, 69
  Industrial Revolution and, 119–121
  laissez-faire, 176
  Marx on, 127–128
  natural law and, 130–131
  Nazi Party and, 189–190
  Protestantism and, 76–77
  shift from feudalism to, 86, 129
  Spanish Miracle and, 201–202
  Spartacus League and, 178
  surveillance, 264
  Westphalian sovereignty and, 78
capitalist meritocracy, 127–128
Capitol insurrection, 293–294
Carlson, Tucker, 295–296
Carolingian dynasty, 39, 41
Carpenter, R. R. M., 187
Carter, Jimmy, 240
caste system, 40
Castro, Fidel, 219
Cathars, 46–47
Catholic Church. *See also* Christianity/Christians
  conspiracy theories and, 80, 84–86, 136
  Luther and, 74–75
  Mussolini and, 191
  Napoleon and, 109–110
  Roman Empire and, 37
Celestine V, 48, 49
cemísm, 59
Central Intelligence Agency (CIA), 212, 213–214, 215, 219
Chamberlain, Houston Stewart, 150
Champ de Mars, 102, 107
Charlemagne, 36–39, 41
Charles I, 79
Charles II, 80–81
Charlottesville, Virginia, 6, 285–286
Chauvin, Derek, 290–291
Cheney, Dick, 250
Chernyshevsky, Nikolai, 142
Chesney, George Tomkyns, 160–161
Chicago Boys, 238
child labor, 120–121
Chile, 223–224, 238–239
China, 222, 268–271
Christianity/Christians. *See also* Revelation, Book of
  apocalypticism and, 20–21
  Barr and, 291
  Charlemagne and, 36–38
  church division and, 27–28
  Crusades and, 43–47
  evangelical, 234
  Hitler and, 191
  Luther and, 74–76
  martyrdom and, 24–25
  in Orbán's Hungary, 274–275
  persecution based on, 15, 24
  persecution by, 30–32, 35
  power of, 8–10
  as *religio licita*, 25
  Roman legacy and, 38–39
  in Rome, 8, 15–17, 22–35, 30, 32
  Trump and, 283–284
  white supremacy and, 112
Chronicle of the Discovery and Conquest of Guinea, The (Zurara), 67–68
church and state, separation of, 50–52, 87, 104–107
Churchill, Winston, 124, 161, 196–197, 204–205
Cicero, 236
City of God, The (Augustine), 34–35
City of the Sun, The (Campanella), 73

Index

civil disobedience, 222
civil rights movement, 218, 230, 232
Civilization Fund Act (1819), 134
Claremont Institute, 284
Clay, Henry, 206
Clement V, 50
Clermont, Council of, 41–42
Cleveland, Grover, 155
climate change, 233, 290, 300
Clinton, Bill, 261–262
Clinton, Hillary, 286
COINTELPRO program, 217
Cold War, 201, 208, 214–216, 219, 225, 245
colonization, 9, 65–66, 70, 72–73, 84, 96, 221–222. *See also* imperialism; Indigenous people
Columbian Exchange, 66
Columbus, Christopher, 60–62
Common Sense (Paine), 92
communism, 165–166, 169–170, 205–206, 207, 209–210, 217
Complaint from Heaven with a Hue and Crye, A, 84–85
computer science, 210–213
Comstock Laws, 155
concentration camps, 124, 151
Concert of Europe, 125
Concordat of 1801, 109
Condition of the Working-Class in England, The (Engels), 120
Confederacy, 140, 157
Congress of Conservatives, 218
conspiracy theories
- American War of Independence and, 92
- Catholic Church and, 84–86, 136
- Jewish people and, 143–144, 162–163, 180, 188, 196, 197
- 9/11 attacks and, 247
- Popish Plot and, 80
- presidential election of 2020 and, 292–295
- radicalization and, 4–5
- United States and, 241
- white supremacy/white nationalism and, 6, 93

Constans, 30
Constantine, Emperor, 25–29, 45
constitutional monarchy, 81–82
consumer identity, 263–264
consumer sovereignty, 238
consumerism, 120, 212, 228–229, 240, 246, 263–264, 270–271
contraception, 154–155
Cook, James, 96
Coolidge, Calvin, 182
Cooper, Bill, 241, 247
Copeland, Kenneth, 292
corporations
- rights of, 78
- slavery and, 69

COVID-19 pandemic, 288–290
Cox, James Renshaw, 183
Cox, Jesse, 140
crime bill, Clinton and, 262
Crimean War, 141
"Crisis Paper" (Greenspan), 256–257
Crispus, 29
Cromwell, Oliver, 79–80
Cromwell, Richard, 80
Crusades, 42–47
Cuba, 219, 222
Cult of Reason, 105
Cult of the Supreme Being, 107
cultural revolution, 268
cybernetics, 211–212
Cybernetics; or, Control and Communication in the Animal and the Machine (Wiener), 211
Czechoslovakia, 226–227

Däniken, Erich von, 241
Dante Alighieri, 51–52
Darwin, Charles, 130–131, 145, 150
Daudet, Léon, 162
Davenport, Charles, 158
David, 37
Davis, Angela, 232
De Beers, 123
de Beauvoir, Simone, 231
de Gaulle, Charles, 198, 219–220, 221
de las Casas, Bartolomé, 65–66
Déat, Marcel, 198–199
Debs, Eugene V., 171
Declaration of Independence, 93

Index

Declaration of the Rights of Man and of the Citizen, 103, 111
Decline of the West, The (Spengler), 181
decolonization, 221–223
"deep state," 225, 287, 295
deindustrialization, 260
Deism, 87
Democratic Party, 135, 136
Democratic-Republican Party, 133
demonization, 21
denazification, 229
Deng Xiaoping, 269
deregulation, 255, 262
Destruction of Life Unworthy of Life, The (Binding and Hoche), 194
Deutscher, Isaac, 243
Devastation of the Indies, The (de las Casas), 65
DeVos, Betsy, 286
Diggers, 79
dignitas, 69–70
Diniz, Debora, 267
Diocletian, Emperor, 24, 25
Divine Comedy, The (Dante Alighieri), 51–52
Domitian, Emperor, 19
Dos Passos, John Randolph, 147–148
Douglass, Frederick, 138
Draga, Queen, 159
Dreher, Rod, 272, 273, 296
Dreyfus, Alfred, 162
drone warfare, 251–252
Drumont, Édouard, 162
Du Bois, W. E. B., 173–174
Dubček, Alexander, 227
Dubrovin, Aleksandr, 143
Dugin, Aleksandr, 12, 278–279, 281, 287, 290, 296, 299
Dulles, Allen, 213–214, 215
Dum diversas, 63
Dutch East India Company, 69, 78
Dwight, Timothy, IV, 133

East India Company (EIC), 69, 73, 96–97
Eckart, Dietrich, 180
education costs, 260–261
Edwards, Jonathan, 90
8chan, 276
Einstein, Albert, 207
Eisenhower, Dwight D., 218–219
Emanuel African Methodist Episcopal Church, 276
encomienda system, 61, 66
Engels, Friedrich, 120, 128
England, war with France and, 52–54. *See also* Britain/England
Enlightenment, 86–89, 98–99, 102, 103, 105, 111–112, 128–129
"Ereignis," 279, 287
Eucken, Walter, 237
eugenics, 158–159, 177
Eusebius of Caesarea, 28–29
Eusebius of Nicomedia, Bishop, 28
evangelical Christians, 234
Evans, Medford, 218
Eve, 22, 32, 111–112
Evola, Julius, 280
Exsurge Domine, 74

Facebook, 266–267
Falwell, Jerry, 234–235, 241, 247
Famine Plot, 103
Fanon, Frantz, 221–222
fascism, 179, 190, 193–199, 237, 280
Fatiman, Cécile, 110
Fausta, 29
Federal Bureau of Investigation (FBI), 217
Federal Emergency Management Agency, 254
Federal Reserve, 171
Federalists, 132–133
Feminine Mystique, The (Friedan), 232
feminist movement, 231–232, 235
Ferdinand II, 59–60, 63, 67
Festival of the Supreme Being, 107
Fête de la Fédération, 102
feudalism, 40–41, 56–57, 61, 103
Fichte, Johann Gottlieb, 150
Final Solution of the Jewish Question, 194–195
finance capital, 165
financial crisis (2008), 255–257, 280
First Virginia Charter, 84
Fischer, Eugen, 152
Floyd, George, 290–291

Index

Ford, Gerald, 223
Ford, Henry, 183–184, 188, 202
Four Horsemen of the Apocalypse, 19
4chan, 276, 286
"Fourteen Points" (Wilson), 170
Fourth Political Theory, 278–279
Fox News, 257–258, 282, 283, 289–290, 295
France
  coup attempt in, 219–220
  National Front party in, 275
  unrest in, 98
  Vichy regime in, 197–198
  war with England and, 52–54
Franciscans, 51
Franco, Francisco, 199–201
Franco-Prussian War, 126–127, 149, 160, 162
Frankenstein; or, The Modern Prometheus (Shelley), 129
Franklin, Benjamin, 89–90
Franks, 36–37, 38–39
Franz Ferdinand, Archduke, 159–160
Franz Josef, 159
Freemasons, 89, 99, 116, 136, 162, 191, 196
Freikorps, 178
French and Indian War, 90–91
French Revolution, 99–104, 111, 115–116, 196
French Wars of Religion, 77, 78
Frenkel, Naftaly, 202
Freud, Sigmund, 163
Friedan, Betty, 232
Friedman, Milton, 238
Fukuyama, Francis, 245
Future of American Secret Intelligence, The (Pettee), 213
Future of War in Its Technical, Economic, and Political Relations, The (Bloch), 163

Galerius, 24, 25
Galton, Francis, 131
Gandhi, Mahatma, 222
Gang of Four, 269
Garden of Eden, 22, 32
Gastev, Alexei, 203
Gaussian copula function, 255
gay Americans. *See* LGBTQ+ community
"Gay Manifesto, A" (Wittman), 231
General Motors (GM), 228
Genesis, Book of, 67
genetic manipulation, 73
genocide, 151, 195, 267
Gentz, Friedrich von, 117–118
George III, 93
German Workers' Party, 180
Germany
  Indigenous people and, 151–152
  World War I and, 160–161
Germany, World War I and. *See* Hitler, Adolf; Nazi Party/Nazism
Gibbons, James, 155
Giuliani, Rudy, 291
globalism, 260, 274, 283
Glorious Revolution, 85
Glushkov, Victor, 212
God-builders, 168
Goebbels, Joseph, 193, 205, 230
Golden House, 15
Goldman, Emma, 210
Goldwater, Barry, 235–236, 273
Gomá y Tomás, Isidro, 200
Gompers, Samuel, 171–172
Good Society, The (Lippman), 237
Gorbanevskaya, Natalya, 226
Göring, Hermann, 189
Gorky, Maxim, 168
Gouges, Marie-Olympe de, 104
Graham, Billy, 234
Graham, Evarts, 233
Grant, Madison, 158–159, 194
Great Awakening, 90
Great Chain of Being, 40–41, 48, 50, 55–56, 57–58, 76, 93, 110
Great Depression, 182–183, 186
Great Dying, 62, 66
Great Fire of London, 80
Great Fire of Rome, 13, 14–15
Great Firewall, 268
Great Replacement narrative, 275–276, 296. *See also* replacement theory
Great Rising, 56–57
Greene, Marjorie Taylor, 295
Greenspan, Alan, 255–257
Gregory VII, Pope, 45

Grey, Edward, 161
Grotius, Hugo, 78
Guénon, René, 279–280
Guevara, Che, 222
gun violence, 261
Gutenberg, Johannes, 75

Haiti, revolt in, 110–114, 137
Ham, 67, 111
Hamann, Johann Georg, 128–129
Hamilton, Alexander, 120
Hammond, James Henry, 139
Harding, Warren G., 176
Hastings, Warren, 97
Hatfield, Henry D., 187
Hatuey, 65
Hayek, Friedrich, 236–237, 238–239, 266, 268
Hayes, Rutherford B., 153
health care, 260, 261–262, 289
Hearst, William Randolph, 187
Hegel, Georg Wilhelm Friedrich, 108
Heidegger, Martin, 192, 278–279
Henry VI, 53
Herder, Johann Gottfried, 149–150
Herero people, 151–152
Heritage Foundation, 250, 286
Himmler, Heinrich, 195
Hindenburg, Paul von, 189
Hiroshima, 205
Hispaniola, 61
Hitler, Adolf, 180–181, 189–190, 191–195, 237
Hobhouse, Emily, 124
Hoche, Alfred, 194
Holderness, Cates, 263–264
Holocaust, 194–195, 198
Honorius, 33, 34
Hoover, Herbert, 183, 184, 185–186
Hoover, J. Edgar, 172, 173, 217
House Un-American Activities Committee (HUAC), 217
housing market, 254–255
Huguenots, 78
Hume, David, 87
Hundred Years' War, 52, 56
Hungary, 273–274, 296
Hurricane Katrina, 253–254
Hussein, Saddam, 250
Hypatia, 35

"I Have a Dream" speech (King), 217
identification, malleability of, 38–39
Ignatyev, Nikolay Pavlovich, 143
illiberal state, 273
Illuminati, 89, 99, 116, 133, 196
immigration, 239, 274, 275, 300
Immigration Act (1924), 177
imperial cult, 16, 27
imperialism, 123–124, 131, 145–147, 162, 165. *See also* colonization
India, 96–97, 222
Indigenous people
  bison and, 118
  colonization and, 62–63, 63–66
  Columbus and, 61–62
  fear of, 83
  Germany and, 151–152
  Great Dying and, 62
  Jackson and, 134–135
  Jefferson and, 134
  reservations for, 135
indulgences, selling of, 74
Industrial Revolution, 118–122
Industrial Workers of the World (IWW), 171–172, 175
Inferno, The (Dante Alighieri), 51–52
Innocent I, Pope, 34
Innocent III, Pope, 45–46
Innocent IV, Pope, 47
Innocent X, Pope, 78
Inquiry into the Nature and Causes of the Wealth of Nations, An (Smith), 91
Inquisition, 46–47, 60
Insurrection Act, 294–295
intelligent design, 87
Inter caetera, 63
International Jew, The, 188
International Monetary Fund, 206, 244
Invasion of 1910, The (Le Queux), 161
"invisible things of God," 50, 266
Iraq War, 249–251
Iredell, James, 92
Irminsul, 36–37

Index

Iron Curtain, 205
Isabella I, 59–60, 63
Isis, cult of, 17–18, 22–23
Islam, 37, 42–45, 247–248, 276

Jackson, Andrew, 134–135, 136
Jacquerie movement, 56, 103
Jaffa, Harry V., 236, 273, 284
James I, 79
James II, 81
Jamestown, 83–84
January 6 insurrection, 293–294
Jaurès, Jean, 161–163
Jay, John, 132
Jefferson, Thomas, 87, 93, 103–104, 133–134, 137
Jerome, St., 34
Jerusalem, Crusades and, 45
Jesus Christ, 18, 24, 26–27, 37, 72, 87
Jewish people
- apocalypticism and, 20
- Christian persecution of, 30–31
- conspiracy theories and, 162–163, 180, 188, 196, 197
- conspiracy theories regarding, 143–144
- Crusades and, 44–45
- Dreyfus and, 162
- expulsion of from Spain, 60
- Hitler and, 191
- Napoleon and, 116
- plague and, 54–55
- pogroms and, 143, 144
- vilification of, 55

Jiang Qing, 269
Jim Crow, 230
Joan of Arc, 53
John Birch Society, 218–219, 236, 241, 247
John of Patmos, 19
John of Salisbury, 50
Jones, Alex, 246–247, 258, 261, 282, 294, 295–296
Jones, Gareth, 202
Jones, J., 140
Julio-Caludian dynasty, 13–14

Kant, Immanuel, 88
Kapp, Wolfgang, 178–179
Kautsky, Karl, 167
Kennan, George, 201, 205–206
Kennedy, Anthony M., 272
Kennedy, John F., 219
Kent, Sherman, 213
Keynes, John Maynard, 170, 186
Khrushchev, Nikita, 209–210, 211, 212
Kiesinger, Kurt Georg, 230
King, Martin Luther, Jr., 217
Kipling, Rudyard, 145, 146
Kissinger, Henry, 223–224
Kitchin, William W., 152
Kitov, Anatoly, 212
Knights of the Golden Circle, 139
Know Nothings, 136
Korean War, 216
Kotzebue August von, 117
Krüdener, Barbara von, 115–116
Krupskaya, Nadezhda, 169
Ku Klux Klan, 175, 187
Kulturbolschewismus, 193
Kushner, Jared, 286, 288–289
kyklos, 71

labor unions, 239
Lafayette, 103
Lanza, Adam, 261
LaRouche, Lyndon, 241
Last Emperor prophecy, 41, 60
Late Great Planet Earth, The (Lindsey), 241
Laughlin, Harry, 177
law enforcement, 101, 251, 261–263
Le Queux, William, 161
League of Nations, 175
Lebensraum, 150
Lebow, Victor, 228
Leclerc, Georges-Louis, 112
Lee, Yanghee, 267
legal reform, 95
Lehman, Herbert H., 201
Lenin, Vladimir (Vladimir Ilyich Ulyanov), 165–169, 202
Leo III, Pope, 37–39, 41
Leo X, Pope, 74
Letelier, Orlando, 225
Levellers, 79

Index

LGBTQ+ community, 230–231, 235, 272–273, 274–275, 297
Li, David X., 255
Liapunov, Aleksei, 212
Liberty, concept of, 105
Library of Alexandria, 35
Liebknecht, Karl, 178
Lincoln, Abraham, 139
Lindbergh, Charles, 188
Lindsey, Hal, 241
Lippman, Walter, 175–176, 237
List, Guido von, 180
Lloyd George, David, 160
"Long Telegram" (Kennan), 205–206
Louis XVI, 102, 105–106
Lovett, Robert, 215
Luther, Martin, 74–76
Luxemburg, Rosa, 167, 178
Lynch, George, 164
Lyon, Matthew, 132

MacArthur, Douglas, 184
Machiavelli, Niccolò, 70–71, 80
Malthus, Thomas Robert, 130
Manchin, Joe, 261
"Mandate for Leadership" agenda, 286
Manifest Destiny, 135, 145
Man-Suffrage Association, 155
Mao Zedong, 222, 268–269
March on Washington, 230
Marie Antoinette, 102
Marshall, George C., 206, 216
Marshall Plan, 206
Marsilius of Padua, 50–51
martyrdom, 24–25
Marx, Karl, 127–128, 165, 185
Mary (daughter of James II), 81–82
Mary of Modena, 81
mass incarceration, 262
mass shootings, 261, 297
Massacre of Verden, 37
Mather, Cotton, 85
Mather, Increase, 85
Maurras, Charles, 162, 197–198, 275
Maxentius, 25–26, 29
McCarthy, Joseph, 216–217
McKinley, William, 146
McKitterick, Rosamond, 39
McVickar, John, 121
Mein Kampf (Hitler), 181
Mellon, Andrew, 183
Memoirs, Illuminating the History of Jacobinism (Barruel), 99, 116
Meta/Metaverse, 267–268
Metternich, Klemens von, 117–118, 125, 128, 141, 223
Michael the Archangel, 53
Milan, Edict of, 26
Mill, John Stuart, 119
Milley, Mark, 294
Mills, C. Wright, 227
Milvian Bridge, Battle of the, 25–26, 29
Mola, Emilio, 200
Moltke, Helmuth von, 160
Monk, Maria, 136
monotheism, 21. *See also individual religions*
Mont Pelerin Society, 238
More, Thomas, 72, 73
Morgan, Lewis Henry, 135
Morgan, William, 136
Morse, Jedidiah, 133
Mosley, Oswald, 197
Mott, Lucretia, 138
Müntzer, Thomas, 75
Musk, Elon, 265–266
Mussolini, Benito, 179, 190–191, 196–197, 280
Myanmar, 267
Myth of the Twentieth Century, The (Rosenberg), 192

Nagasaki, 205
National Conservatism, 296
National Front party, 275
National Life and Character (Pearson), 153–154
National Rifle Association (NRA), 261
Nationalists (Spain), 200
NATO, 219
natural law, 130–131
"natural rights," 236
natural selection, 145
Nazi Party/Nazism, 176–177, 180–181, 189–190, 191–195, 197, 220, 229–230, 237, 278, 280

Index

Nechayev, Sergey, 142
Negro Act (1740), 93
neocolonialism, 228
neofascism, 12
neoliberalism, 237–242, 244–246, 249–250, 255–261, 270–271, 273, 278–286, 289, 298, 302
Nero, Emperor, 14–15, 17, 18–19, 20
Nero Redivivus legend, 18–19
New Atlantis, The (Bacon), 72
New Deal, 186, 217, 235
"New Laws of the Indies for the Good Treatment and Preservation of the Indians," 65–66
New Model Army, 79–80
New Party, 197
New Soviet Man, 203
New World Order, 3, 242, 246–247, 258–259, 274, 277, 282, 287
Newgate Prison, 94
Newton, John, 68
Newtown, Connecticut, 261
Nicaea, First Council of, 27
Nicholas I, Czar, 141
Nicholas II, Czar, 164–165
Nicholas V, Pope, 63
Nicole, Pierre, 77
Nietzsche, Friedrich, 142, 190–191, 279
nihilism, 142, 192
Nilus, Sergei, 143
9/11 attacks, 245, 246–249
Nineteenth Amendment, 156
Ninety-Five Theses, 74
Nixey, Catherine, 32
Nixon, Richard, 223–224, 257–258
Noah, 37, 67
North America
- Columbus and, 60–62
- *Inter caetera* and, 63

Northern Alliance, 249
NSC-68, 214–215
nuclear weapons, 205, 207–208
Nuremberg trials, 193

Oates, Titus, 80–81
Oath Keepers, 294–295
Obama, Barack, 251–252, 256, 257–258, 261, 277, 282, 286
Obergefell v. Hodges, 272–273
Oberly, John, 135
Office of Strategic Services, 213
Office of War Information, 213
oil industry, 233
Oklahoma City bombing, 247
Olympius, 33
On the Origin of Species (Darwin), 130
one-world government, 143, 259
Operation Condor, 224–225
Operation Gladio, 225–226
Operation Unthinkable, 204
Orbán, Viktor, 273–274, 281, 296
O'Reilly, Tim, 263
Organisation armée secrète (OAS), 220, 221
original sin, 34–35, 72
Orwell, George, 205
Outlines of Political Economy (McVickar), 121
Overman Committee, 172

Paine, Thomas, 92
Palmer, A. Mitchell, 173
Palmerston, Viscount (Henry John Templeton), 123
panopticon, 95–96
papacy. *See also individual popes*
- distrust of, 51–52
- Philip IV and, 49–50
- power of, 45–46

Paris Commune, 127
Passing of the Great Race, The (Grant), 158
Patton, George, 184
"Peace of God" movement, 42–43
Peace of Westphalia, 77–78
Pearl Harbor, 188
Pearson, Charles H., 153–154
Pence, Mike, 272, 293, 295
Pennsylvania Gazette, The, 90
People's Will, 142–143
Pétain, Philippe, 197–198
Peters, Ken, 293
Petrarch, 69
Pettee, George S., 213
Philip IV (France), 49–51
Philip Morris, 233

Index

Philippines, 146
Philosophy of Manufactures, The (Ure), 119–120
Phoenix Program, 226, 252
Pinochet, Augusto, 224, 238–239, 268
Pipes, Richard, 242–243
Pitt, William, 101
Pius VII, Pope, 110
Pizarro, Francisco, 66
Pizarro, Gonzalo, 66
plague, 54–55, 80
"Plan Z" conspiracy, 224
planned obsolescence, 228–229
Plato, 70, 71, 73, 80, 88, 168, 299
Platonov, Oleg, 277
police force, coordinated, 100–101
Pollard, Edward, 138–139
polytheism, 16, 20–21, 30, 36, 59
Popish Plot, 80, 85
population change, paranoia over, 154–155, 296
population growth, 130
Porphyry, 24
Powell, Enoch, 239, 275
Powell, Lewis, 232–234, 257, 283
"Powell Memo," 233
Prague Spring, 227
Pratt, Richard Henry, 135
predictive policing, 251
press/media
- Hitler and, 193
- Metternich and, 117
- Napoleon and, 109–110
- opposition to Obama and, 257–258

Prester John, 72
Price, Richard, 98
Princip, Gavrilo, 159–160
printing press, 75
PRISM program, 251
prison ships, 95
Proofs of a Conspiracy Against All the Religions and Governments of Europe (Robison), 99
Protestant Ethic and the Spirit of Capitalism, The (Weber), 77
Protestantism, 75, 76–77, 80, 85, 94
Protocols of the Elders of Zion, The, 143–144, 172, 180, 196, 287
Putin, Vladimir, 277–278, 298
Putnam, Robert D., 259

QAnon, 5, 286–288, 289, 292, 295
Queipo de Llano, Gonzalo, 200

race riots, 175
racial hierarchy, 84
racism, Enlightenment and, 111–112. *See also* slavery; white supremacy/white nationalism
radicalization, 5, 266–267, 275
Rand, Ayn, 235, 255
Randolph, A. Philip, 230
rape, as weapon of terror, 200, 220
Raskob, John, 187
Ratzel, Friedrich, 150
Reagan, Ronald, 239–240, 257, 261
Reconstruction, 140
Red Summer, 174–175
reducciónes, 64
Reeves, John, 101
Reflections on the Revolution in France (Burke), 98
Reformation, 75
regicide, 78
Reign of Terror, 105–106, 115
religious freedom, 77–78
"religious freedom" bills, 272
religious revival, 234–235
religious syncretism, 16
Renaissance, 86
replacement theory, 158–159, 275–276, 285, 296
Report on the Subject of Manufactures (Hamilton), 120
Republic, The (Plato), 70, 73
Republican Party, 137, 139, 217, 236, 257–259, 261–262, 284, 292, 295
"Requirement, The," 64
Restoration, 80
Revelation, Book of, 1, 2, 3, 19–20, 287
revelatory knowledge, concept of, 106
Revolution of 1848, 125, 127
Rhodes, Cecil, 123–124, 146–147

Index

Ricardo, David, 119
Richard II, 57
Richards, Mary, 120–121
righteous persecution, concept of, 31
Rising Tide of Color Against White World-Supremacy, The (Stoddard), 176–177
Robertson, Pat, 242, 247, 272–273
Robespierre, Maximilien, 106–107
Robison, John, 99
Roe v. Wade, 297
Romantic movement, 129
Rome
  Christianity in, 8, 15–17, 22–35
  Constantine and, 25–29
  crises in, 23–24
  fall of, 36, 37
  Great Fire of, 13, 14–15
  Isis and, 17–18
  Nero and, 14–15, 17, 18–19
  patriarchy of, 22
  pilgrimages to, 48
  siege of, 34
  social stratification in, 22
Romme, Gilbert, 105
Roof, Dylann, 276
Roosevelt, Franklin D., 184–189, 201, 204–205
Roosevelt, Theodore, 154
Röpke, Wilhelm, 237
Roque, Frank, 248
Rosenberg, Alfred, 192
Rositzke, Harry, 214
Rougier, Louis, 237
Russia. *See also* Soviet Union
  American right wing and, 276–277
  World War I and, 164
Russian Revolution, 164–170
Ryan, Jenna, 294
Ryutin, Martemyan, 203

Saint-Domingue, 111, 112–113
same-sex marriage, 272–273
Sandy Hook Elementary School, 261
Sartre, Jean-Paul, 220–221
Savio, Mario, 227–228
Saxons, 36–37
Schall, Thomas, 186–187
Schmitt, Carl, 204–205, 206
scholarship, Christian opposition to, 32
scientific management, 157, 202
Scientific Revolution, 86, 88, 131, 265
secret police, 141
secret societies, 89, 92, 142
"Secret Speech" (Khrushchev), 209–210
segregation, 235
Seneca Falls Convention, 138
September 11, 2001, 245, 246–249
Sepúlveda, Juan Ginés de, 65
Serdica, Edict of, 25
serfdom, abolition of, 57
Seven Years' War, 91, 96
Shelley, Martha, 231
Shelley, Mary, 129
shock treatment/therapy, economic, 238, 243
Siler, Charles, 260
Simonini, Jean-Baptiste, 116
slavery, 67–70, 73, 84, 91, 92–93, 110–111, 137–140
Sloan, Alfred P., 228
Smith, Adam, 91, 121, 184, 266
Smith, Al, 186
Smyth, William Henry, 157
Social Democratic Party (SDP), 177–178
social media, 266–267, 287–288, 289
social stratification, 40
Sodhi, Balbir Singh, 248
Sol Invictus, 26, 29
Sons of Liberty, 92
Sophie (wife of Franz Ferdinand), 160
Soros, George, 274, 291
South African War, 124
Southern Conference on Race Relations, 230
Southern Democrats, 137, 139
Soviet All-Union Institute for Scientific Information, 212
Soviet Union. *See also* Bolshevik Party; Cold War; Russia; *individual leaders*
  collapse of, 242–243
  Czechoslovakia and, 226–227
  as kingdom of Antichrist, 1–2
  "Secret Speech" (Khrushchev) and, 209–210
  U.S. policy regarding, 214–215
Spain, colonization and, 59–60, 63–66

Index

Spanish Civil War, 199–200
Spanish Miracle, 201
Spartacus League, 178
Speer, Albert, 193
Spencer, Herbert, 131
Spengler, Oswald, 181
Spiritualism, 129, 279
Stalin, Joseph, 168–169, 202, 203–204, 205, 209–210, 212
Stamp Act (1765), 91–92
Starving Time, 84
sterilization, forced, 158
Stevens, Brooks, 228
Stilicho, General, 33
Stoddard, Lothrop, 176–177, 194
Stone, Roger, 294
Stonewall Inn, 231
Strauss, Leo, 236
Strong, Josiah, 146
student organizations, ban on, 117
Sturm und Drang movement, 129, 149–150
Suez Canal, 122
suffrage, 155–156
Sumner, Walter Taylor, 159
Supreme Court, 297
surveillance capitalism, 264
Sydnor, Eugene B., 233
System of Nature, The (Thiry), 88

Taft-Hartley Act, 207
Taíno people, 59, 61–62
Taliban, 249, 253
Talleyrand-Périgord, Charles Maurice de, 102–103
Tarrant, Brenton Harrison, 276
taxation, 48, 91–92, 97, 104, 131–132
Taylor, Frederick W., 157, 202
Tea Party, 257–258
technocracy, 157, 175–176
technology, 262–263
Temple, Henry John (Viscount Palmerston), 123
terrorism, 142–143, 245, 246–247, 252
Thatcher, Margaret, 236, 239, 275
Theodosius, Emperor, 32–33
Theosophical Society, 130
Théot, Catherine, 107
Thessalonica, Edict of, 30
Third Section, 141
Thirty Years' War, 77
Thiry, Paul-Henri, 87–88
Thomas Aquinas, 40
Thornwell, James Henley, 140
Thus Spoke Zarathustra (Nietzsche), 191
Thyssen, Fritz, 189
Tiananmen Square, 269
time, changes in measurement of, 104–105
tobacco industry, 233
Total Information Awareness, 251
Traditionalism, 279–281, 284, 296
Tree of Knowledge, 32
trenchocracy, 179
Trotha, Lothar von, 151
Trotsky, Leon, 166, 167, 168, 203
Truman, Harry, 205, 207, 213, 214–215
Truman Doctrine, 207
Trump, Donald, 5–6, 12, 253, 258, 263–264, 281–289, 291–297, 300
Twelve Articles, 75–76

Übermensch, 190–191, 279
Uighurs, 270
Ulyanov, Vladimir Ilyich. *See* Lenin, Vladimir (Vladimir Ilyich Ulyanov)
Unam sanctam, 49
Underground Railroad, 138
Unite the Right rally, 6, 285–286
United States. *See also* Cold War; *individual presidents*
  Cold War and, 214–216, 225
  conspiracy theories regarding, 241
  faith in, 2
  founding of, 10
  intelligence and, 213–214
  military planning in, 213–215
  mythology of exceptionalism of, 10–11
  9/11 attacks and, 245, 246–248
  Operation Gladio and, 225–226
universities, rise of, 50
Urban II, Pope, 41–42, 43–44, 58
Ure, Andrew, 119–120, 121
utilitarianism, 95
Utopia (More), 72

Index

utopianism, 71–73
Uvarov, Sergey, 141

Vallejo-Nájera, Antonio, 200
Vardaman, James K., 174
Vichy France, 197–198
Victoria, Queen, 144–145
Victorinus, St., 20
Vietcong, 226
Vietnam, 222, 225–226, 232
Villain, Raoul, 162
Vinson, Carl, 177
Virginia Company of London, 84
Virginia Slave Codes, 84
Visigoths, 34
Volk, 150
Voltaire, 111–112
voting rights, 85, 104, 155–156, 292

Waddell, Alfred Moore, 153
Walker, David, 138
Wallace, George, 218, 241
Waller, Littleton, 114
War of the Worlds, The (Wells), 161
War on Terror, 248, 251, 259, 263
Washington, George, 112–113, 132
Waters, Walter W., 184
wealth, concentration of, 9
Web 2.0, 263–264
Weber, Max, 77
Weber, Randy, 258
Webster, Nesta Helen, 196
Welch, Robert, Jr., 218
Wells, H. G., 147, 161
Whiskey Rebellion, 131–132
White, Paula, 292
"White Declaration of Independence, The," 153
White Lion, 84
"White Man's Burden, The" (Kipling), 146
white supremacy/white nationalism
  in American South, 140, 152–153, 230
  British imperialism and, 123–124
  Charlottesville, Virginia, and, 285
  Christianity and, 112
  conspiracy theories and, 6, 93
  Enlightenment and, 111
  entrenched power and, 11
  Germany and, 152
  mass incarceration and, 262
  Trump and, 5–6
  World War I and, 174–175
Whitefield, George, 89–90
Whitney, Richard, 183
Whore of Babylon, 19
wickedness, fascination with, 77
Wiener, Norbert, 210–211
Wilhelm II, Kaiser, 177
William of Orange, 81–82
Wilson, Woodrow, 114, 157–158, 170, 171–172, 174, 175–176
Winthrop, John, 85
witch trials, 86
Wittman, Carl, 231
Wolfram, Herwig, 39
Wollstonecraft, Mary, 98, 104
women
  abolitionism and, 138
  feminist movement and, 231–232, 235
  voting rights and, 104, 155–156
World Anti-Slavery Convention, 138
World Bank, 206
world policemen theory, 204
World Trade Center attacks, 245, 246–249
World Trade Organization, 270
World War I, 160–162, 163, 171, 173–176, 177–178, 184
World War II, 188–189, 220
Wretched of the Earth, The (Fanon), 221
Wycliffe, John, 52

Yeltsin, Boris, 243
Young, Arthur, 103
YouTube, 267

Zuboff, Shoshana, 264
Zuckerberg, Mark, 266, 267
Zurara, Gomes Eanes de, 67–68

- ABOUT THE AUTHOR -

Jared Yates Sexton is the author of *American Rule, The Man They Wanted Me to Be,* and *The People Are Going to Rise Like the Waters Upon Your Shore.* His political writing has appeared in publications including *The New York Times, The New Republic,* Politico, and *The Daily Beast.* Sexton is also the host of *The Muckrake Podcast,* the author of three collections of fiction, and covers current events at the website Dispatches From A Collapsing State. He can be found on Twitter at @jysexton.